Calvinism and Middle Knowledge

Calvinism and Middle Knowledge

A Conversation

EDITED BY
John D. Laing,
Kirk R. MacGregor,
AND Greg Welty

PICKWICK *Publications* · Eugene, Oregon

CALVINISM AND MIDDLE KNOWLEDGE
A Conversation

Copyright © 2019 Wipf and Stock Publishers. All rights reserved. Except for brief quotations in critical publications or reviews, no part of this book may be reproduced in any manner without prior written permission from the publisher. Write: Permissions, Wipf and Stock Publishers, 199 W. 8th Ave., Suite 3, Eugene, OR 97401.

Pickwick Publications
An Imprint of Wipf and Stock Publishers
199 W. 8th Ave., Suite 3
Eugene, OR 97401

www.wipfandstock.com

PAPERBACK ISBN: 978-1-5326-4573-0
HARDCOVER ISBN: 978-1-5326-4574-7
EBOOK ISBN: 978-1-5326-4575-4

Cataloguing-in-Publication data:

Names: Laing, John D., editor. | MacGregor, Kirk R., editor. | Welty, Greg, editor.

Title: Calvinism and middle knowledge : a conversation / edited by John D. Laing, Kirk R. MacGregor, and Greg Welty.

Description: Eugene, OR: Pickwick Publications, 2019 | Includes bibliographical references.

Identifiers: ISBN 978-1-5326-4573-0 (paperback) | ISBN 978-1-5326-4574-7 (hardcover) | ISBN 978-1-5326-4575-4 (ebook)

Subjects: LCSH: Molinism | Calvinism | God—Omniscience | Freedom (Theology) | Free will and determinism | Religion—Philosophy.

Classification: LCC BT135.2 L145 2019 (print) | LCC BT135.2 (ebook)

We would like to thank the publishers and editors of the following book, journals, and website for grating us permission to reproduce their copyrighted material.

Chapter 7 is reprinted from *Westminster Theological Journal* 71.2 (2009) 437–54. Copyright ©2009 Westminster Theological Seminary.

Chapter 14 is reprinted from https://www.reasonablefaith.org/videos/interviews-panels/calvinism-vs-molinism/. ©2014 Reasonable Faith. It also previously appeared in *Journal for Baptist Ministry and Theology* 11.1 (2014) 62–77. ©2014 The Baptist Center for Theology and Ministry, New Orleans Baptist Theological Seminary.

Manufactured in the U.S.A.   01/04/19

Contents

Contributors

Guillaume Bignon is a French analytical philosopher and computer scientist who works in the financial industry in New York. He is an executive committee member of Association Axiome, a society of French-speaking Christian scholars.

William Lane Craig is Research Professor of Philosophy at Talbot School of Theology, La Mirada, California and Professor of Philosophy at Houston Baptist University, Houston, Texas.

Paul Helm is a Teaching Fellow at Regent College, Vancouver. He was Professor of the History and Philosophy of Religion at King's College, London, from 1993 to 2000.

Kenneth D. Keathley is Senior Professor of Theology occupying the Jesse Hendley Chair of Theology and directs the L. Russ Bush Center for Faith and Culture at Southeastern Baptist Theological Seminary, Wake Forest, North Carolina.

John D. Laing is Professor of Systematic Theology and Philosophy at Southwestern Baptist Theological Seminary, Havard School for Theological Studies, Houston, Texas.

Kirk R. MacGregor is Assistant Professor and Chair of the Department of Philosophy and Religion at McPherson College, McPherson, Kansas.

Terrance L. Tiessen is Professor Emeritus of Systematic Theology and Ethics at Providence Theological Seminary, Otterburne, Manitoba.

Bruce A. Ware is the T. Rupert and Lucille Coleman Professor of Christian Theology at the Southern Baptist Theological Seminary, Louisville, Kentucky.

Greg Welty is Professor of Philosophy and Program Coordinator of the MA in Apologetics and Christian Philosophy at Southeastern Baptist Theological Seminary, Wake Forest, North Carolina.

Preface

JOHN D. LAING, KIRK R. MACGREGOR, AND GREG WELTY

CALVINISM AND MIDDLE KNOWLEDGE is an anthology of essays and dialogues presented in or directly related to the 2012–14 Molinism/Middle Knowledge Consultation of the Evangelical Theological Society. The major goals of the consultation were three in number. First, it sought to help move the discussion of Molinism/middle knowledge out of the philosophical arena, where it has almost exclusively remained, and into the broader theological community. The hope was that theologians, historians, biblical scholars, and others would join the conversation about the fruitfulness or deficiencies of this model of divine knowledge/providence. Second, the consultation aimed to spark an ongoing conversation between Calvinists and Molinists about Calvinist concerns with middle knowledge and Calvinist appropriation of middle knowledge without embracing libertarian human freedom. Third, the consultation endeavored to see what explanatory role middle knowledge may or may not play in Calvinist and Molinist accounts of providence and practical theology.

Ultimately, this book is meant to introduce laypersons, ministers, Bible college and seminary students, and theologians/biblical scholars to the discussion of Molinism and to spur further conversation between Molinists and Calvinists. We hope you find this volume stimulating and edifying!

Introduction

JOHN D. LAING, KIRK R. MACGREGOR, AND GREG WELTY

Molina, Middle Knowledge, and the Controversy over Efficacious Grace

THE DOCTRINE OF MIDDLE knowledge was first articulated by Jesuit Counter-Reformation theologian Luis de Molina (1535–1600) in his massive *Concordia*, a work originally meant to be a commentary on Aquinas' *Summa Theologiae* but which only addressed the relationship between human freedom and divine grace in salvation. Middle knowledge was Molina's attempt to reconcile God's specific providence with human freedom. The *Concordia* immediately drew criticism from the Dominicans, who feared it smacked of Pelagianism because it seemed to make the efficaciousness of God's grace dependent upon free human decisions. The initial criticism grew into a full-fledged controversy within the Roman Catholic Church, and it occupied the thoughts and minds of many leaders for twenty-five years, though it was never fully resolved.

The controversy over efficacious grace arose in a time of intense political upheaval and ecclesiastical reform in Europe. Just a quarter of a century prior to Molina's birth, the Catholic Church dominated Western Europe. But by the time of Molina's *Concordia*, Protestantism had gained a foothold in most of the major powers, with not only religious but also political consequences.[1] The only decidedly (major) Catholic country in Europe during

---

1. Germany had been in an uproar ever since Martin Luther nailed his Ninety-Five Theses to the church door at Wittenberg in 1517. His preaching had stirred the people of Germany and built upon a growing nationalism there. With the signing of the Peace of Augsburg in 1555, both Lutheranism and Catholicism were officially recognized in Germany. England was also affected by a growing nationalism and spirit of reform. Although Henry VIII had been a zealous supporter of the Catholic Church in

Molina's life was Spain. Charles V, Holy Roman Emperor, sat on the throne of Spain for much of Molina's childhood, but he abdicated when forced to sign the Peace of Augsburg in 1555. He was succeeded by Philip II, who encountered significant opposition in many quarters of the empire. He was, for a short time, titular king of England due to his marriage to Mary Tudor, but was not accepted by the English people and had to return to Spain after only a few years. He also faced opposition in France due to a conflict he had with Pope Paul IV. After reconciling with the Catholic Church under Pius IV, he increased the intensity of the Inquisition in Spain and Portugal, and joined the pope in a successful naval campaign at Lepanta.[2] But his Armada suffered a crippling defeat in 1588 when he tried to take England back "for the glory of God" from the Protestant Queen Elizabeth. It was during Philip II's reign that the controversy over efficacious grace emerged.

In addition to increasing the intensity of the Inquisition, the Church also instituted reforms in response to the Protestant challenge. In 1547, Pope Paul II convened the Council of Trent in an effort to define true

---

its battles with Protestants, he became embroiled in a bitter power struggle with Pope Clement VII over his desire to have his marriage to Catherine of Aragon—sister of Holy Roman Emperor Charles V—annulled. Henry eventually appointed a man favorable to his plight, Thomas Cranmer, as Archbishop and convinced Parliament to pass the Supremacy Act of the Crown (1534), which proclaimed the king and not the pope as the only supreme head in earth of the Church of England. After Henry's death in 1547, England took a stronger Protestant identity under Edward VI first, and then after a brief and unpopular reign by his half-sister Mary (an ardent Catholic and wife to Phillip II of Spain), under Elizabeth I. Elizabeth restored the *Book of Common Prayer* and was subsequently excommunicated by Pope Pius V. Her long reign ensured that England's break with Catholicism was complete. The situation for the Roman Church in France was no better. The country was plagued by civil war and theological unrest. Protestantism was gaining a foothold against strong Catholic opposition. In 1572, the St. Bartholomew's Day Massacre took place, leaving thousands of Huguenots (French Protestants) in Paris and surrounding cities dead. That same year, Henri, a Protestant, took the throne of Navarre and by 1589 he had united France and was crowned king (Henri IV), much to the dismay of both the pope and Philip II of Spain. Yet in 1593, after much discussion, thought, and prayer (and not a little political pressure), Henri IV converted to Catholicism. While this seems a defeat to the Protestant cause, it was not, for in 1598, Henri signed the *Edict of Nantes*, which allowed free exercise of religion for Huguenots in certain cities. Thus, in his own lifetime, Molina saw much of Europe move away from Catholicism and (at least) tolerate Protestantism.

2. Portugal was annexed by Spain in 1580. The political and ethnic tensions between Spaniards and Portuguese added to the controversy between Molina, a theology professor teaching in Portugal, and his chief antagonist in the Church, the Spanish theology professor Domingo Báñez. Even within the fledgling Jesuit Order, tensions existed between the two groups. Spaniards had held control of the order since its inception, but by 1581, when Claudius Acquaviva was named General of the Order, their power began to wane. They sought autonomy and appealed to both the Inquisition and Philip II, who wrote to the pope on their behalf.

Catholic doctrine against Lutheranism. Other reforms came, some in the form of new orders. The Society of Jesus was formed by Ignatius Loyola in 1534 out of a desire to send missionaries to Jerusalem, then controlled by the Turks. Although the Society began as a missionary enterprise, the Jesuits were concerned with theological questions from the beginning, particularly related to salvation and the Protestant problem. For example, Loyola's *Spiritual Exercises*, a work of devotional piety, included an appendix that warned against an overemphasis upon divine grace in salvation to the neglect of human free will.[3] This set the tone for later Jesuit theology of salvation as epitomized in the works of Molina and Francisco Suárez.

But the Jesuit emphasis upon free will was not well received by all in the Catholic Church and faced fierce opposition from the Dominicans (Order of Preachers), who saw theology as their exclusive purview virtually from their inception.[4] Amid growing tensions between Jesuits and Dominicans, a disputation was held at the University of Salamanca on January 20, 1582. Jesuit Prudencio di Montemayor was defending a series of propositions when he was attacked by senior professor of theology, Dominican Domingo

3. He wrote, "We should not lay so much stress on the doctrine of grace as thereby to encourage the holding of that noxious doctrine which denies the existence of free will [an obvious reference to Reformed Protestant ideas]. We should, therefore, only speak of faith and grace in such a manner that our teaching may, with the help of God, redound to His greater honour, and, above all in these dangerous times, certainly not in such a way that good works and free will are thought to be of lesser importance, or are even regarded as of no value at all" (quoted in Fülop-Miller, *Jesuits*, 85–86).

4. While it is true that the Dominicans and the Jesuits approached theology from very different perspectives, most scholars also believe that the rancor of the Dominicans was due in large part to their perception that the Jesuits were engaged in work for which they were neither authorized nor qualified. Pastor argues that the Dominicans saw the Jesuits as innovators and invaders: "In the apologetic works of the Jesuits there occurs again and again a complaint at the manifest injustice of such attacks [like that of Báñez upon Montemayor, discussed below]. The reason why they were being thus persecuted could not be found in the doctrines which they had taught, since others had taught the same things without their having provoked any attack. The historian certainly cannot describe this complaint as unfounded; the passion displayed by some of the Dominicans against the new Order is too manifest to allow of any such thing. On the other hand the bitterness is easy to explain. The young and rising Society of Jesus had in several cases entered the lists against the older Order, which was already covered with renown, and had won brilliant successes, especially in the field of pastoral work and teaching. How then could it have failed to seem unjust to certain Dominicans, who for centuries had borne the heat and burden of the day, that they should be left behind by these newcomers at the eleventh hour? The Order of Preachers had jealously looked upon theological science as its privileged field. But now that the work of Molina, which had made its appearance as the first book by a Jesuit on scholastic theology, had been followed by other important works by Molina himself and by Suárez, it seemed as though the younger Order was preparing to storm the last fortress of the older" (Pastor, *History*, 24:300–301).

Báñez, who accused him of heresy. An Augustinian theologian, Luis de León, came to Montemayor's defense because he believed the ferocity of the attack grounded in hatred of the Jesuits.[5] A widely publicized debate between Báñez and de León was held, with Báñez accusing de León of Pelagianism and de León calling Báñez a Lutheran. The Dominicans appealed to the Inquisition and used their considerable political power to secure a censure of Montemayor and a reprimand for de León in 1584. Thus, when Molina's *Concordia* was first published in 1588, he feared the Dominicans would attempt to block its publication.[6] It was granted an imprimatur and endorsement by the official censor, Bartolomeo Ferreira, but Cardinal Albert (the viceroy of Portugal), who was granted the first copy by Molina himself, forbade its sale. Molina requested that all objections to his work be made in writing and signed by the critic. While Albert was making his decision, the royal councils of both Aragon and Castile judged Molina's work favorably.

The tension between the Dominicans and Jesuits grew in intensity, and even included an attempt by Báñez to hold a public disputation on religious vows.[7] Although the disputation was prevented when the Jesuits appealed to

5. There is good reason to think this was the case. Broadrick notes that Báñez was trained by Melchor Cano, a man who "persisted down to the day of his death in 1560 in regarding the Spiritual Exercises of St Ignatius, solemnly approved by the pope in 1548, and many times since, as a little book loaded with heresies, and the Jesuits themselves as spawn of the devil, sent of the destruction, not only of all good theology, but of all good Christian living" (Brodrick, *Bellarmine*, 192).

6. Molina sought a *nihil obstat* without further censorship for the publication by having three Jesuits, Jorge Serrano, Antonio Carvalho, and Ferdinand Perez, endorse the *Concordia*. He believed this could be obtained on the strength of Serrano's recommendation because the Inquisition held him in high esteem. The Jesuits thought this move would appear subversive, so they convinced Molina to hand the *Concordia* over to Ferreira. The imprimatur was granted, despite considerable opposition by the Dominicans, who overwhelmed Ferreira with accusations against Molina. It was presumed that Molina's book defended the ideas condemned earlier at Salamanca, and some (e.g., Báñez) argued that the honor of St. Dominic was at stake. Ferreira informed Molina of the accusations and gave him the opportunity to respond. He denied the first accusation and reminded Ferreira that he was not appointed censor to protect the interests of the Dominican order, but of the Church. Further, Molina added that he would call for a ban of his own work if it were found to be in conflict with the Church. Apparently, Ferreira, after reading the *Concordia*, was convinced (Pastor, *History*, 24:294–95). Brodrick believes that the Portuguese Inquisitors gave Molina a pass because he was their compatriot and was being harassed unfairly by the Spaniards (*Bellarmine*, 193).

7. The Jesuits took very simple vows, and it was Báñez's contention that this was irreligious. Thus, the Society of Jesus should not be seen as a *bona fide* religious order. Báñez seems to have been unaware that only five years earlier Pope Gregory XII had issued a bull that explicitly affirmed the vows of the Jesuits as religious. Báñez was later ordered to issue a retraction and apology before the University of Salamanca

the apostolic nuncio in Madrid,[8] the controversy continued in the publication of pamphlets, disputations,[9] and anti-Jesuit sermons by local priests.[10] Some of the public debates even resulted in riots. Such a heated controversy proved unsettling to both ecclesiastical and secular authorities, who eventually appealed to Rome to intervene.[11]

---

community.

8. Brodrick explains that the Jesuits did not find out about the disputation until five days before it was scheduled, and the trip to Madrid took three days each way. Thus, in order to get word to the nuncio and return with a verdict in time to prevent the disputation, a courier was needed who could ride day and night. Such a rider (whose name has not been preserved) was found, and relays of horses were ready on the route so that no prolonged stops would be necessary. He writes, "The courier, by headlong riding day and night through the pelting rain, galloped up to their [the Jesuits] residence in Salamanca covered in mud [it had rained torrentially for the duration of the ride] from head to foot and utterly exhausted, but bearing triumphantly, the nuncio's ban on the disputation, just five hours before it was due to open" (Brodrick, *Bellarmine*, 193–94).

9. Apparently, Molina made the trip from Évora to Madrid (approximately 325 miles) on two separate occasions to defend his own position as well as that of Francisco Suárez, and to attack the views of Báñez and his close follower Mercedarian Zumel, before the Inquisition.

10. Pastor describes the state of affairs during this period, although he attributes the hatred of the Jesuits to a "single man" instead of the majority of the Dominicans, who he describes as "moderate." It will be helpful to quote him at length: "The ever increasing tension reached its climax at Valladolid. There, at the Gregorian College of the Dominicans, the declared adversary of the Jesuits was Diego Nuño; he set the doctrine of Molina before the students as being contrary to the faith, and Molina himself as an ignorant, presumptuous and blaspheming man, and often attributed to his adversary opinions which the latter had expressly rejected and refuted. The horror aroused against the supposed heretic was manifested in the lecture halls by a general stamping of feet every time the name of Molina was mentioned. A colleague of Nuño prayed for the conversion of Molina, since he might become a dragon like the one in the Apocalypse, who swept away a third part of the stars of heaven. To complete the confusion, the most bitter anti-Jesuit among the Dominicans Alonzo de Avendaño, went to Valladolid to preach the Lent, and inveighed from the pulpit against the new Order, though he did not mention it by name. Gradually, even the best friends of the Jesuits began to be afraid lest not all these accusations which were hurled from the pulpit and the lecturer's chair, should prove to be purely imaginary" (*History*, 24:302). Ironically, one of the professors of theology at Valladolid, Garcia Coronel, judged Molina's *Concordia* to be in agreement with both Augustine and Aquinas, although it was the first detailed treatment of how efficacious grace works. Coronel regarded the work to be of value to those theologians who were engaged in battle with the Protestants (ibid., 24:297).

11. In 1594, the apostolic nuncio wrote to Cardinal Aldobrandini, the nephew of Pope Clement VIII, asking for papal intervention. Similar petitions were sent by King Philip II, the Grand Inquisitor, and several bishops. Cardinal de Castro wrote directly to the pope. His letter lends insight into the ferocity with which the debate was conducted: "This, then, is how the Dominicans treat the teaching of the Jesuits. In their public discourses and lectures they qualify it as erroneous, and warn the people to avoid its defenders as men tainted with heresy . . . As their authority is very great in Spain,

The appeals to Rome were heard; the superiors of both orders were to prepare written treatises to present to the pope, and both groups were ordered, on pain of severe penalty, to cease further debate until a decision could be reached.[12] The task of reading and interpreting the treatises fell to Robert Bellarmine, the papal theologian. Although Bellarmine was a Jesuit, he was fair and criticized both Báñez's and Molina's views where he deemed them in error.[13] Báñez did not like his views being evaluated by a Jesuit,

---

the Jesuits have become suspects and reckoned as people of no account" (Brodrick, *Bellarmine*, 195). De Castro's concern lays more with how the dispute could prove destructive for the Catholic Church and subsequently strengthen the position of the "heretics" (i.e., Protestants). His argument is twofold. First, he appeals to the pope on behalf of Catholics who reside in *heretical countries* (most likely Germany and France, but England, Switzerland, and perhaps Austria could be included). If the faithful in these countries were to find out that there was a war waging within the Church, their morale would be shattered. However, de Castro's plea was not simply a call for peace for peace's sake; theological issues were at stake. He feared that the Dominican attack upon the Jesuit view of free will would be perceived as an endorsement of the Protestant view. Second, he appeals to the pope on behalf of the Church as a whole, arguing that the Jesuit Order, more than any other, had defended the Catholic doctrine against Protestantism. If Jesuit doctrine were condemned, then the Lutherans and Calvinists could claim victory: "The heretics . . . will triumph and be able to laugh at the Catholics, seeing that the doctrine of those whom they regard as their most redoubtable adversaries is condemned by their own co-religionists as opposed to the faith" (ibid.).

12. The order was difficult to enforce, as several theologians of both orders were preparing works on the subject. Soon, attacks were again underway, but this time, Philip II intervened. He conferred with his confessor, Diego de Yepes, as well as Jesuit Garcia de Alarcón and the Dominican provincial, Juan de Fillafranca, in order to determine the best way to maintain peace. It was concluded that those involved in the fighting would be dismissed from teaching. In addition, members of one order were prohibited from attending disputations of the other order, and they were warned against referring to the other's views as heretical. As a result, Dominican Nuño and Jesuit Padilla were both removed from their teaching posts, but peace was restored for a year (Pastor, *History*, 24:310).

13. For example, Bellarmine criticized both Molina and Báñez on efficacious grace, though he was harder on Molina. Molina seemed to agree with those Scholastics who maintained that grace is efficacious if an individual cooperates with the grace he receives, but this suggests that efficaciousness is dependent upon the creature's will. Bellarmine wrote, "This opinion seems to me to be false and therefore rightly reprehended in the censure of the Dominicans" (Brodrick, *Bellarmine*, 197). Báñez and his followers held that the efficacy of grace is what determines how an individual will choose and is thus determined prior to the act of creaturely will. Bellarmine believes this view to be destructive of human freedom and to border on the Protestant view of divine providence. He wrote, "It seems to me to be no less false and dangerous than the first opinion; for to begin with, it destroys sufficient grace as the other does efficacious grace . . . then it appears to contradict the Council of Trent . . . Thirdly, this opinion does not seem to save free will nor can it be distinguished from the formulae used by the modern heretics" (ibid.). Ultimately, Bellarmine suggested that the pope needs to make a personal judgment on the issue.

so he wrote directly to Pope Clement VIII, asking him to lift the ban on the Dominicans while retaining the ban on the Jesuits. He complained that the ban effectively placed innovations on a par with the Tradition. He also resorted to a polemical attack on the Jesuit order in general and on Bellarmine in particular. Ironically, Clement passed the document to Bellarmine for evaluation.[14] In an effort to preserve peace, Bellarmine suggested that Clement issue an edict exhorting the parties to focus on battling enemies of the Church; scholarly theological discussion should be allowed, but polemic should not (on threat of excommunication).

After receiving Bellarmine's report, Clement appointed a commission to examine Molina's *Concordia* and allowed discussion of efficacious grace to continue. The commission, composed of seven men (none supporters of Molina), was prepared to condemn Molina after little more than three months' time (the Inquisition had taken three years to render a decision). However, before its final decision could be codified, a huge box filled with the materials from the Inquisition arrived and had to be considered. After only eight months, the commission informed the pope that it was prepared to condemn Molina. Jesuits appealed to several high-ranking officials, and the cumulative effect of the commission's haste and the intercessions convinced Clement to seek an alternate resolution to the conflict.[15] On January 1, 1599, he ordered theologians from each party to present their arguments before the Prefect of the Inquisition, Cardinal Madruzzo. The two generals—General Acquaviva of the Jesuits and General Beccaria of the Dominicans—appeared before Madruzzo with theologians of their choosing, but the meeting accomplished little. Madruzzo asked both parties to prepare written expositions on the disputed point of grace, and enlisted Cardinal de Ascoli of the Dominican order and Cardinal Bellarmine of the Jesuit order to aide his evaluation. As the debates progressed, it became clear that some misunderstanding had prevailed in the dispute, but some genuine disagreement also remained.[16] Unfortunately, Cardinal Madruzzo died before a decision was reached.

14. Bellarmine condemned Báñez's work here as "derogatory to the Pope" because it claimed Clement was unjust and hurtful to the Church. Bellarmine went on to note that Báñez's writing assumed the Dominican position to be correct, even before a ruling by the Holy See; this was both arrogant and premature (Brodrick, *Bellarmine*, 201–4).

15. The Jesuits appealed to Empress Maria of Austria, King Philip III of Spain, and Archduke Albert of Austria, among others.

16. Pastor reports that General Beccaria said that "if Molina had admitted all that the Jesuits had conceded in the presence of Madruzzo, there would have been no reason to take action against him." The Jesuits believed they could prove just this point (*History*, 24:333).

Clement again turned to the seven-man commission, but this time only twenty propositions were condemned, whereas the previous two findings condemned sixty-one and forty-two propositions, respectively. The Jesuits immediately appealed the decision. News spread throughout the Spanish world that Molina was about to be condemned; it was even rumored as far as Chile and Peru that Molina had been burned at the stake as a heretic. Amid these rumors Molina was laid to rest; he died in October 1600 in Madrid. Although the rumors were false, there was widespread belief that Clement would rule against the Jesuits. Bellarmine urged the pope to tarry and investigate the issue, and Clement seemed to take this advice. He decided in 1602 to settle the matter himself—even though he was not known for his theological acumen—by presiding over debates later called the *Congregatio de Auxiliis*. Ironically, neither Molina (who died a year and a half earlier) nor Báñez was present for the debate.[17] On March 5, 1605, Pope Clement VIII died without ever rendering a decision on the *Congregatio*. He was succeeded by Pope Leo XI, who only lived three weeks longer.

Cardinal Borghese, who had attended the meetings up to this point, was elected pope on May 16, 1605 and took the name Paul V. He resumed the meetings but wanted to put an end to them. He had other, more pressing concerns. In a power struggle with the Venetian states, Paul V found his staunchest supporters among the Jesuits.[18] Fülöp-Miller claims that this probably saved the order, but this is doubtful.[19] After almost twenty years of dispute over Molina's book, Paul V called a special meeting of all the

17. Báñez died in 1604 while the dispute was still under investigation. A Jesuit provincial noted that just before he died, Báñez spoke of the Jesuits "in friendly terms, saying that he had always wished our fathers well, and that if he had waged war against them in the controversy de Auxiliis, it was only because he considered his own opinion to be the truth" (Brodrick, *Bellarmine*, 213).

18. The Venetian state had long been a thorn in the side of Pope Clement VIII. The rulers had regularly interceded in matters that were deemed proper to the Church. For instance, two priests had been arrested and examined by the secular authorities in defiance of the longstanding tradition of immunity of the clergy. When Paul V became pope, he demanded that certain laws of Venice be repealed, namely those which conflicted with the power of the Church. When his demands were ignored, he threatened excommunication of the Venetian Senate and interdict for the whole territory within twenty-four days. The state hired Paolo Sarpi, a Servite, as its lawyer. He advised the state to ignore the excommunication, and the Senate forbade all religious orders to publish the excommunication on pain of death. Almost all clergy of Venice obeyed the directive of the state. When Paul V heard of this, he was furious and almost deposed all the Venetian bishops. The Jesuits were the first to submit to the interdict of the pope. As a result, the Senate permanently banished the Jesuits from Venice. In addition, it passed measures seizing the order's revenues and properties, and even criminalizing association with Jesuits or their colleges (Pastor, *History*, 25:129–39; Harney, *Jesuits*, 166).

19. Fülöp-Miller, *Jesuits*, 99.

cardinals involved in the controversy to ask their opinions. Only one, Cardinal de Ascoli (a Dominican), voted to condemn Molina. The other seven did not believe Molina's views worthy of condemnation, although two favored Báñez's position. Du Perron and Bellarmine favored Molina, but urged the pope to abstain from any pronouncement. Seeing that even his most trusted confidants could not come to agreement and perhaps due to a sense of indebtedness to the Jesuits, Paul V chose to not condemn Molina (and the Jesuits).[20] Instead, he noted that he would postpone his decision until a more opportune time. In the meantime, the Dominicans were ordered, under threat of severe penalty, to refrain from calling the Jesuits Pelagians. Likewise, the Jesuits were ordered to stop calling the Dominicans "Calvinists," and the Inquisition placed a ban on the publication of books dealing with efficacious grace. Interestingly, no final decision has ever been made, and it is generally agreed that both positions are acceptable approaches to understanding salvation in the Catholic faith.[21]

Middle knowledge or *scientia media*

The doctrine of middle knowledge gets its name from the fact that it is thought to be in the middle of Aquinas' traditional categories of divine thought—natural and free knowledge—and by this, two things are meant: (1) it has characteristics of both kinds, and (2) it comes *in between* natural and free knowledge in the logical order of God's pre-creative deliberations.[22]

20. When the news reached the general populace, celebration broke out. In Salamanca, some friends of the Jesuits placed a poster on the university wall which read, "MOLINA VICTOR!" In Villagarcia, a bullfight was organized to celebrate the salvation of the Jesuits, and at several of the Jesuit colleges, fireworks displays were enjoyed. This, however, displeased Acquaviva, who believed strongly in the humility of the priesthood. He immediately sent letters of disapproval and even suspended some of the rectors who organized the activities. These celebrations, though, point to the importance of the outcome for the Jesuit order. The writings of one man had not been under investigation; rather the whole order had been in jeopardy.

21. This Introduction does not include a similarly detailed exposition about the origin and development of Calvinism, as that is more well-known to Protestants in general and evangelicals in particular. Some relevant sources include: McKim, *Cambridge Companion to Calvin*; Bagchi and Steinmetz, *Cambridge Companion to Reformation Theology*; George, *Theology of the Reformers*; Helm, *Calvin's Ideas*; Barrett, *Reformation Theology*; Bratt, *Rise and Development*.

22. Obviously, an omniscient being does not have thought processes per se; he knows all truths immediately and completely, but theologians have typically referred to divine knowledge this way to address the relationships between the truths God knows. Some truths are dependent upon other propositions being true (or false) and thus, we speak of a logical order existing between those truths, and so, a logical order in divine

Natural knowledge refers to the knowledge God has by means of his nature; since he is a necessary being, he knows all necessary truths (metaphysically necessary truths and statements of possibility) by knowledge of his own nature. In virtue of its being necessary, natural knowledge is independent of God's will, or prevolitional.[23] Free knowledge refers to the knowledge God has by means of his will; since God's free act of will establishes which possibilities will be realized, he knows these contingent truths—truths about what actually will be the case—by knowledge of his own will. Thus, free knowledge is postvolitional. By natural knowledge, God knows what could (and couldn't) be the case, and by free knowledge, He knows what will (and won't) be the case. So natural knowledge is necessary and independent of God's will, while free knowledge is contingent and dependent upon God's will.

Molina posited a third class of knowledge that informs God's decision about what sort of world to create, and this includes truths that are contingent and independent of God's will, which he called *scientia media* (middle knowledge). He suggested that propositions about what all possible free creatures would do in all possible situations are independent of God's will because the nature of free will requires no outside determinants, but contingent because the creatures can act or not-act if truly (i.e., libertarianly) free. It has become customary to refer to these propositions as *counterfactuals of creaturely freedom* (even though they are not all counter-to-fact, if they are actualized). For any given creature in any particular set of circumstances wherein he is faced with a choice to act, there is a true proposition about what s/he will or will not do (of the form "If person *P* were in circumstances *C*, *P* would freely perform action *A*"; of course, there is a corresponding false proposition of the form "If *P* were in *C*, *P* would not freely perform *A*"). Thus, Molinism is the belief that God's creative decisions are informed by his knowledge of all possibilities via natural knowledge and of how

knowledge.

23. This means that God has no control over the truth of propositions known by natural knowledge, but this suggests no deficiency in his omnipotence. To deny him the ability to perform the logically impossible is not to reduce his power, but rather to require that our theology conform to categories of truth and error and to rationality. It simply makes no sense to suppose any being—even God—could make a necessary truth false. A favorite example in the literature has been the statement, "All bachelors are unmarried." This statement is both obviously and necessarily true because of the meaning of the words used. A bachelor is, by definition, unmarried and could never be otherwise (without simply redefining terms). Thus, it is no deficiency in God's power for him to lack the ability to make the statement "All bachelors are unmarried" false. It simply makes no sense to suppose it could be made false, and in order to do so, one would need not only to deny the fundamental laws of logic but also, in so doing, affirm abject relativism.

all possible free creatures would act in all possible situations via middle knowledge. Since the truths known by both of these type of knowledge are independent of God's will, they limit the kinds of worlds (i.e., complete descriptions of the ways things could be) he can create/actualize. His act of will in creating then grants him foreknowledge via free knowledge, and also affords him extraordinary providential control without violating creaturely freedom. It does so by allowing him to actualize a world where the counterfactuals of freedom, along with other relevant factors, result in the outcome(s) he desires.[24]

Middle knowledge is not without its critics, even today, as evidenced by the vigorous debate in the later chapters of this book. While many have expressed concern over the issue of God's efficacious grace, the majority of challenges have come in the form of questioning the coherence of the

---

24. One of the most useful concepts in the modern philosophical discussion of middle knowledge has been that of possible worlds. In brief, a possible world is a way of conceiving a complete set of propositions describing the way things could be (what the creation is like, which creatures exist, what they do, etc.). In theory, God contemplated all possible worlds prior to creating, and actualized (i.e., brought into being) one of those that best meets his purposes/desires for creating. Two items are worth mentioning. First, not all possibilities are live options for God because the true counterfactuals of freedom limit the worlds that can be actualized. Only those possible worlds where the true counterfactuals obtain are actualizable. Those worlds are referred to in the literature as feasible worlds. Those worlds where the false counterfactuals obtain are infeasible. Perhaps a biblical example will help illustrate the concept. Suppose it is true that if Adam were offered the forbidden fruit, he would freely eat it, and suppose this is true no matter which circumstances obtain; whenever Adam is confronted with the choice to eat, he always accepts. In this case, the counterfactual of freedom, *If Adam were offered the forbidden fruit, he would freely eat it*, is true, and the counterfactual, *If Adam were offered the forbidden fruit, he would freely refrain from eating it*, is false. Since it is logically possible for Adam to refrain from eating, the corresponding counterfactual is true in some possible worlds, even though those worlds are not feasible for God to actualize because the counterfactual is not true (i.e., Adam would freely eat if offered). If this were the case (and it might have been), then, modern Molinists assert, a world where Adam is free and refrains from eating is not feasible for God, even though it is logically possible. God could actualize a world where Adam is free and eats or where Adam is not free and refrains, but he could not actualize a world where Adam is free and refrains. In this way, world-feasibility (and the true counterfactuals of freedom) limits God's choices with respect to creating. Second, the standard possible worlds semantics postulates that propositions are true in the actual world if they are true in the possible world closest to the actual world (Stalnaker, "Conditionals," 102–4; Lewis, *Counterfactuals*, 92; Plantinga, *Necessity*, 174–75). This similarity relation has played a significant role in some of the discussions surrounding the truth of counterfactuals of creaturely freedom, though not all Molinists accept the application of the semantics to these issues (Freddoso, "Introduction," 74–75; Freddoso, "Human Nature, Potency, and the Incarnation," 43–45; MacGregor, "Neo-Molinist Square Collapses," 197–208; Laing, *Middle Knowledge*, 63–64, 100).

system and/or the notion of counterfactuals of creaturely freedom.[25] At their most basic, most of the objections take issue with the Molinist claim that there can be (and are) truths about what creatures will (libertarianly) freely do before they act or if they do not act, and independent of God's determining will. Some claim that all that can truly be said is what creatures would *probably* or *might* do,[26] while others claim that propositions about what creatures will definitely do can be true, but they would abrogate libertarian freedom and result in some form of determinism.[27] The latter charge is strengthened in Molinism because of the way God uses counterfactuals of freedom to ensure that his purposes/intentions in creating are realized. Perhaps the most popular argument against counterfactuals of creaturely freedom is the grounding objection because it questions if their truth has proper grounds. Proponents of the objection argue that counterfactuals of freedom cannot be grounded in God's nature or will because that would make them either necessary or dependent upon God's free knowledge. The former results in fatalism while the latter results in compatibilism, both violations of essential Molinist principles. They further argue that counterfactuals cannot be grounded in the actions, personality, or psychological makeup of the individual to whom they refer because they are true prior to the individual's actions and existence, and grounding in personality appears to violate libertarian freedom. Thus, they argue, there seems to be nothing which makes counterfactuals of creaturely freedom true.[28]

A related class of objections charge that Molinism cannot live up to its claims because of the way priority operates in the system and its relationship to the truth of counterfactuals of freedom. For example, in one version both Adams and Kenny have complained that counterfactuals of creaturely freedom cannot be true soon enough to be of use to God (at least not in the way

25. For example, in a relatively recent publication Romanus Cessario has charged Molina with Pelagianism ("Molina and Aquinas," 312–15).

26. This charge is typically made in one of two ways: either as a challenge to the principle of conditional excluded middle (CEM, i.e., "If A, then either B or ~B") or as an assumption regarding the implications of libertarian freedom for true propositions about actions free persons will (or will not) perform. Some, for example Lewis, have claimed to offer counterexamples to CEM (*Counterfactuals*, 80–82). Molinists have responded that the former objection fails because middle knowledge only depends on the principle of bivalence, the supposed counterexamples to CEM can be answered, and that the typical arguments depend on unsubstantiated claims regarding proximity of possible worlds. They have rejected the latter argument because it simply begs the question of incompatibilism. See Wierenga, *God*, 132–35; Plantinga, *Necessity*, 180.

27. See, for example, Hasker, *God, Time, and Knowledge*, 21–23, 40–49; Hasker, "Providence and Evil," 95; Hasker, "New Anti-Molinist Argument," 293–97.

28. Adams, "Anti-Molinist Argument," 343–54; Hasker, *God, Time, and Knowledge*, 29–33; Hasker, "Refutation," 545–57; Hasker, "Middle Knowledge," 223–26.

that middle knowledge supposes). They point out that the truth of counter-factuals must be settled before God creates so that he can consider them in his creative decision, but that their truth must be open until God settles by his decree which possible world will be the actual world. Thus, they argue, Molinism fails. Similarly, Adams and Hasker have both offered variations of an argument that claims Molinism is circular because God's decision about which world to actualize is dependent upon which world is actual.[29] This is due to the fact that God's decision relies on his analysis of how the true counterfactuals in each possible world will play out, yet which counterfactuals are true in any given possible world depends upon how close that world is to the actual world, at least under the standard possible world semantics.

Of course, Molinists have responded to these objections in a variety of ways. Some have questioned the grounding requirement, and some have noted that other types of propositions (e.g., statements about the future, or more properly, about future free actions) are similarly ungrounded yet widely thought to have truth values (i.e., either true or false).[30] Some have noted that the grounding objection presupposes the incompatibility of lib-ertarian freedom and there being true propositions describing future free actions, and some have suggested that there may be ways to ground the truth of counterfactuals of freedom without removing their contingency.[31] Molinists have responded to the priority objections by challenging the way priority or dependency are used in the arguments and by rejecting the Stal-naker/Lewis approach to evaluating truth claims by appeal to proximity of possible-but-not-actual worlds to the actual world.[32]

Molina's Theology of Social Justice

Molina is best known for his contributions to philosophical theology, and so these are naturally the focus of the debates in this book. However, Molina

---

29. Kenny, *God*, 70; Adams, "Middle Knowledge," 109–17; Adams, "New Anti-Mo-linist Argument," 343–53; Hasker, *God, Time, and Knowledge*, 38. See also Zagzebski, *Dilemma*, 146–49; Hasker, "Anti-Molinism Undefeated!" 128; Hasker, "Explanatory Priority," 389–93.

30. Plantinga, "Replies," 374–5; Kvanvig, *All-Knowing God*, 135–36; Otte, "Defense," 161–69; Freddoso, "Introduction," 71–74.

31. Craig, *Foreknowledge*, 261–64; Gaskin, "Middle Knowledge," 189–203. Some ground their truth in the actions of the individual to whom they refer in the closest-but-not-actual world, in the individual to whom they refer, in the omniscience of God, etc. See Flint, *Divine Providence*, 133–34; Zagzebski, *Dilemma*, 143.

32. See Flint, *Divine Providence*, 164–76; Craig, "New Anti-Molinist Argument," 857–61; Craig, "Hasker's Defense," 236–40.

made equally significant contributions to moral theology which are typically unknown to Protestants in general and evangelicals in particular. These contributions must be briefly discussed here to gain a full appreciation of Molina's legacy. While his moral theology doesn't seem to apply distinctive *Molinist* theses as such, they are nevertheless suggestive: a "middle" view of private property as necessary prudential (neither absolute nor to be abolished), and a conviction that human maintenance of physical liberty for all persons (by ending the slave trade) should follow God's gift of spiritual liberty to all persons (by granting them libertarian free will). Philosophical theology is never done in a vacuum, and Molina's contributions here could serve as a new source of both constructive appraisal and criticism.

Molina dealt with issues of social justice in his 1596 *De justitia et jure.* For Molina social justice was total justice, namely, the virtue that directs all human actions to the common good. He likened his definition of social justice to Aristotle's concept of political prudence, which stipulated what each person ought to do as part of the total community. Molina argued that political prudence placed demands on both the subjects and the prince. The prince needed to show hierarchical prudence in determining the laws that fairly established the rights and duties of each person within the community. The subjects then needed to use their rights and carry out their duties in such a way as to positively contribute to the commonweal. Molina also compared his definition of social justice with the idea of justice bequeathed by the Roman legal tradition. The Roman jurist Ulpian (c. 170–223) had characterized justice as the unswerving and perpetual will of each person to give every other person his or her due, which represented a commutative notion of justice. According to Molina, this not only entailed the individual duty to pay others what was owed them and fairness in the distribution of social goods, but it also presupposed the prince's duty actively to cultivate the morality of his citizens.[33] Piecing together Greek and Roman influences, Molina contended that social justice required from the prince both the formulation of fair laws and the nurturing in subjects of the virtues that the common good demanded. Moreover, Molina contended that social justice meant that subjects should embrace the habit of a moderation that refused to seek more public or private goods for themselves than "was appropriate for geometrical proportion" (*Geometricam proportionem appropriandum*).[34] Molina proceeded to apply his conception of social justice to various economic issues, including private property and the African slave trade—two

---

33. Alonso-Lasheras, *Molina's De Iustitia*, 187–88.

34. Molina, *De justitia*, 1.12.5.

of the most significant governmental and ethical problems confronting the Iberian Peninsula.

Private property

Molina commenced by arguing on philosophical and theological grounds that private property did not exist at the beginning of creation; rather, there existed a community of goods. Philosophically, Molina followed Aristotle's assertion that nature offers indistinguishably to humans all that is necessary to domestic and political life.[35] Theologically, Molina grounded the community of goods in the doctrine of creation. God is the Creator and therefore the Lord (*dominus*) of created things. By virtue of their bearing the image and likeness of God, every human possesses dominion (*dominium*) over created things.

Unique to Molina among the theologians of his age was the way he conceived the original human community. The original community was not a negative community, in which no one owned anything, but things waited for people to take ownership of them. Nor was the original community a positive community, in which all humans collectively owned all material things in the fashion of a corporation owning property. Rather, the original community was a middle community, located between a negative and a positive community. Molina maintained that everything was once held by everyone in the sense that God gave all material things to humanity as a congregation without any distinctions (*congregationis indistincte*), not as separate groups or individuals.[36] Thus there exists a right to all things by every member of the human congregation. This distinctive way of imagining the original community enabled Molina to defend the shift toward the division of goods after the Fall.[37]

According to Molina, private property, like concentrated political power, proved a necessity in a post-Fall world. Molina deemed the institution of civil government indispensable for maintaining peace and tranquility after the Fall, though unnecessary before the Fall.[38] Likewise, although common property was proper in an age of human innocence, after the Fall private property became beneficial and indispensable. For Molina private property served as a prudentially necessary means to an end, namely, the end of all humans enjoying the goods of creation in a world after the Fall.

35. Ibid., 2.20.4–5.

36. Ibid., 2.20.6–7.

37. Caycedo, *Ideas jurídicas*, 20.

38. Molina, *De justitia*, 2.120.1.

Because the right to private property was a prudential necessity, Molina regarded the right as not absolute. He therefore exhorted his readers to adopt a modified form of evangelical poverty in which they lived on precisely what they needed—no more, no less—and made all remaining goods available to the poor and needy. He instructed his readers that property should be held privately but could never be absolutely private. This is because property represents a trust from God. Molina repeatedly insisted that excess property always must be available to brothers and sisters in need. It is highly significant that, for Molina, the refusal to live such a simple life and to share with those in extreme or nearly extreme necessity constituted mortal sin. Every person must have regard for the neighbor so that the hungry are fed, the thirsty refreshed, and the naked clothed.[39] Molina perceived that human lordship over created things included the responsibility of being good stewards and dispensers of these things. He maintained that no one could accuse him of teaching that the poor should steal from the rich and make it common property; rather, it was the responsibility of the rich to give their surplus to the needy.

African slave trade

Molina viewed the coming of Europeans to the New World as a missiological problem, wondering how the Christian faith could best be spread.[40] Through his discussions with Spanish and Portuguese merchants, Molina acquired a detailed knowledge of the African slave trade. Molina was also cognizant of non-European slave trading practices in India, China, Cambodia, and Japan through the writings of Jesuits who evangelized all these places. Molina decisively rejected the widespread proslavery argument that Christian ownership of slaves would likely bring about the conversion of those slaves.[41] Conversely, Molina held that such an arrangement would put undue pressure on slaves to ostensibly convert to Christianity while never making a personal commitment to follow Christ. In fact, such forced pseudo-conversion would incite slaves to harden their hearts against Christ, thus vastly heightening the probability of their eventual damnation. As entailed by his doctrine of free choice, Molina insisted that true conversion could never be coerced. The only way missionaries could effect the genuine conversion of unbelievers in pagan lands was to oppose their enslavement and to work for the emancipation of any unbeliever who was already enslaved.

39. Ibid., 2.20.14.
40. Vereecke, *Da Guglielmo*, 597–613.
41. Kaufmann, "Slavery," 214.

Furthermore, social justice itself demanded that the cause of freedom from slavery be championed by all Christians. Hence Molina wrote forcefully in favor of the liberation of slaves, as this would prove tremendously beneficial to the cause of evangelization and promote the just cause of liberty. For Molina the example set by God in giving spiritual liberty to all persons, regardless of God's middle knowledge of whether or not they would use it properly, must be followed by believers in extending physical liberty to all persons regardless of their religious persuasions. Molina thus pronounced that slave traders were guilty of mortal sin, as were all others involved in the African slave trade, including the king of Portugal, his heads of state, and the priests and bishops who readily absolved slave traders of their sins without restitution.[42]

On this score, Molina rejected all of the pseudo-religious racial justifications of slavery, which had been circulating on the Iberian Peninsula since the mid-fifteenth century. These racist justifications alleged that a non-European people were inherently guilty of some moral or spiritual defect that necessitated a just war against them; upon Christian victory in this war the members of the people could rightfully be captured as slaves.[43] Molina held, however, that by virtue of their creation in the *imago Dei*, all peoples were equally valuable. And by virtue of God's general revelation in nature and conscience, all peoples had access to salvation. Here Molina argued for what, in modern terms, is dubbed salvific accessibilism-inclusivism. Molina stressed that while the person and work of Christ were necessary for any person to receive salvation (John 14:6; Acts 4:12), explicit knowledge of the facts concerning Christ was not necessary for a person to obtain salvation. Based on Romans 2:7, Molina affirmed that persons with no conscious knowledge of Christ, living in any time and culture, would find salvation by placing faith in God and following to the best of their ability the natural law written on their hearts.[44] Upon hearing reports from Spanish and Portuguese traders about the faith of indigenous Africans and Indians, Molina thought that such persons had received salvation via their proper response to God's general revelation.[45] Since the second person of the Godhead to whom such persons had committed themselves was, in fact, Jesus, Molina reasoned that they had placed implicit faith in Jesus and so found salvation in precisely the same manner as did believers in the Old Testament, such as the patriarchs, the prophets, and the righteous Gentiles Melchizedek

---

42. Molina, *De justitia*, 2.35.16.

43. Kaufmann, "Slavery," 193.

44. Molina, *De justitia*, 5.46.13.

45. Alonso-Lasheras, *Molina's De Iustitia*, 71.

and Job.[46] Hence no argument could be validly made from the vulgarity or religious ignorance of any people to their enslavement. In this way, Molina proved a forerunner of the abolitionist cause of later centuries. We now turn to summarizing the contents of this book.

Overview of the Book's Contents

Part I deals with Molinism, evolution, and intelligent design. In chapter 1, John Laing argues that God could use his middle knowledge of the counterfactuals of genetic mutation to providentially ensure that random mutations lead to the development of new species. This would explain so-called vestigial organs and thereby provide an answer to the logical problem of creaturely flaws against the theory of intelligent design. In chapter 2, Kirk MacGregor argues that if macroevolution is true, its astronomical improbability would provide a modified teleological argument for the existence of a God with middle knowledge. Trans-group and simultaneous unrelated mutations could not occur by chance alone but must involve a designer who can make such events randomly and repeatedly occur in the course of nature. In chapter 3, Greg Welty responds that genetic mutations are not relevantly analogous to counterfactuals of creaturely freedom, and that Molinist interpretations of theistic evolution make God rely on luck. In addition, macroevolution + Calvinism has just as much explanatory power as MacGregor's macroevolution + Molinism, and Laing's Molinism is not needed to defuse the anti-ID argument from vestigial organs.

Part II deals with Calvinist concerns with Molinism. In chapter 4, Welty argues that the apophatic character of Reformed definitions of divine providence undermines the Molinist claim that Calvinism makes God the sufficient cause of sin. In addition, the Molinist model of divine causation is sufficiently analogous to sufficient causation, so that it inherits the alleged Calvinist liabilities with respect to divine authorship of sin. In chapter 5, Ken Keathley responds that on Molinism, the intent to sin originates in the sinner's free will, while Calvinists who hold to causal determinism seem committed to the belief that human intentions to sin did not originate in their compatibilist free wills, but in God's decree to create them so they would choose as they did. In chapter 6, Welty addresses Keathley's various points: whether Molinists understate the metaphysical side of their view of providence; the proper definitions of causal determinism, determinism, and libertarianism; the apophatic strategy; the category of "divine permission";

46. Molina, *De justitia*, 5.65.3.

Keathley's responses to the "Bullet Bill" argument; and what Molinists and Calvinists should say about "the important issue of intent."

Part III deals with the Calvinist appropriation of middle knowledge. Chapter 7 reprints a dialogue between Paul Helm and Terry Tiessen, originally published in the *Westminster Theological Journal*, that was the catalyst for Tiessen eventually abandoning "middle-knowledge Calvinism" in favor of traditional Edwardsian Calvinism. In dispute is whether Tiessen's *scientia hypothetica* modifies middle knowledge into compatibility with the orthodox Reformed theological tradition. In chapter 8, Bruce Ware defends "middle-knowledge Calvinism," which combines a compatibilist view of human freedom with biblical evidence for God's knowledge of counterfactuals. If God knows which circumstances tend to affect and influence what persons choose in accordance with their greatest desire, he can know their choices without being the direct cause of evil. In chapter 9, Laing argues that "middle-knowledge Calvinism" is a contradiction in terms, for whether God's knowledge of counterfactuals is placed in his natural knowledge or free knowledge, the knowledge is no longer "middle," and so the label is misleading. (In addition, placing it in natural knowledge leads to problematic anthropology, theology, and fatalism.) In chapter 10, Tiessen responds to Laing by arguing that "hypothetical-knowledge Calvinism" is not vulnerable to Molinism's grounding objection, does not feature odd notions of necessity, possibility, or personhood, and does not lead to fatalism. In addition, Tiessen's view is supposed to have a superior account of both gratuitous evil and human freedom.

Part IV deals with the ongoing conversation between Calvinism and Molinism. In chapter 11, Laing discusses how open theist and Calvinist theologies appropriate the concept of middle knowledge, and further interacts with the previous chapter by Tiessen. Most importantly, he illustrates the fundamental disagreement between Molinists and "middle-knowledge Calvinists" by showing how proponents of each group conceive of the logical steps in God's free knowledge differently. In chapter 12, Tiessen responds to Laing's chapter, agreeing that Calvinist attempts to place God's free knowledge within his natural knowledge are misguided. He argues that the heart of the Calvinist/Molinist disagreement is whether truths about compatibilist creaturely choice are tied to the nature of God rather than to the nature of the creature. In chapter 13, Guillaume Bignon argues that the determinist framework of Calvinism does not preclude applying "permission" language to God's providence over sin. First, indeterminism alone is insufficient to rescue the meaningfulness of divine permission of evil. Second, the truth of certain active/passive pairs of counterfactuals can provide a Calvinist-friendly criterion for "permission" language in theodicy. Chapter

14 transcribes a Calvinist-Molinist dialogue between William Lane Craig and Paul Helm that took place on the *Unbelievable?* radio program (later published in the *Journal of Baptist Theology and Ministry*). Whether or not libertarian human freedom compromises divine foreknowledge proves the crux of the exchange, although contrasting views of human sin and salvation are also discussed.

In the book's conclusion, Laing, MacGregor, and Welty offer prospects for further study and dialogue on issues of concern to Calvinists and Molinists within the evangelical community.

Bibliography

Adams, Robert Merrihew. "Middle Knowledge and the Problem of Evil." *American Philosophical Quarterly* 14.2 (1977) 109–17.

———. "A New Anti-Molinist Argument." In *Philosophical Perspectives 5: Philosophy of Religion*, edited by James E. Tomberlin, 343–54. Atascadero, CA: Ridgeview, 1991.

Alonso-Lasheras, Diego. *Luis de Molina's De Iustitia et Iure: Justice as Virtue in an Economic Context*. Studies in the History of Christian Traditions 152. Leiden: Brill, 2011.

Bagchi, David V. N. and David C. Steinmetz, ed. *The Cambridge Companion to Reformation Theology*. Cambridge: Cambridge University Press, 2004.

Barrett, Matthew, ed. *Reformation Theology: A Systematic Summary*. Wheaton, IL: Crossway, 2017.

Bratt, John H., ed. *The Rise and Development of Calvinism*. Grand Rapids: Eerdmans, 1959.

Brodrick, James. *Robert Bellarmine: Saint and Scholar*. London: Burns and Oates, 1961.

Caycedo, José. *Ideas jurídicas de Luis de Molina sobre la propiedad privada*. Excerpta Ex Disertatione in Pontificia Universitas Gregoriana. Rome: Pontificia Universitas Gregoriana, 1957.

Cessario, Romanus. "Molina and Aquinas." In *A Companion to Luis De Molina*, edited by Matthias Kaufmann and Alexander Aichele, 291–323. Leiden: Brill, 2014.

Craig, William Lane. *Divine Foreknowledge and Human Freedom*. Leiden: Brill, 1991.

———. "On Hasker's Defense of Anti-Molinism." *Faith and Philosophy* 15.2 (1998) 236–40.

———. "Robert Adams's New Anti-Molinist Argument." *Philosophy and Phenomenological Research* 54.4 (1994) 857–61.

Flint, Thomas P. *Divine Providence: The Molinist Account*. Ithaca, NY: Cornell University Press, 1998.

Freddoso, Alfred J. "Human Nature, Potency and the Incarnation." *Faith and Philosophy* 3.1 (1986) 27–53.

———. "Introduction." In *On Divine Foreknowledge (Part IV of the Concordia)*. Translated by and edited Alfred J. Freddoso, 1–81. Ithaca, NY: Cornell University Press, 1988.

Fülop-Miller, René. *The Jesuits: A History of the Society of Jesus*. Translated by F. S. Flint and D. F. Tait. New York: Capricorn, 1963.

Gaskin, Richard. "Middle Knowledge, Fatalism, and Comparative Similarity among Worlds." *Religious Studies* 34.2 (1998) 189–203.

George, Timothy. *Theology of the Reformers*. Nashville: Broadman, 1988.

Harney, Martin P. *The Jesuits in History: The Society of Jesus through Four Centuries*. New York: America Press, 1991.

Hasker, William. "Anti-Molinism Undefeated!" *Faith and Philosophy* 17.1 (2000) 126–31.

———. "Explanatory Priority: Transitive and Unequivocal, A Reply to William Craig." *Philosophy and Phenomenological Research* 57.2 (1997) 389–93.

———. *God, Time, and Knowledge*. Ithaca, NY: Cornell University Press, 1989.

———. "Middle Knowledge: A Refutation Revisited." *Faith and Philosophy* 12.2 (1995) 223–36.

———. "A New Anti-Molinist Argument." *Religious Studies* 35.3 (1995) 291–97.

———. "Providence and Evil: Three Theories." *Religious Studies* 28.2 (1992) 91–105.

———. "A Refutation of Middle Knowledge." *Noûs* 20.4 (1986) 545–57.

Helm, Paul. *John Calvin's Ideas*. Oxford: Oxford University Press, 2004.

Kaufmann, Matthias. "Slavery between Law, Morality, and Economy." In *A Companion to Luis de Molina*, edited by Matthias Kaufmann and Alexander Aichele, 183–226. Leiden: Brill, 2013.

Kenny, Anthony. *The God of the Philosophers*. Oxford: Clarendon, 1979.

Kvanvig, Jonathan. *The Possibility of an All-Knowing God*. New York: St. Martin's, 1986.

Laing, John D. *Middle Knowledge: Human Freedom in Divine Sovereignty*. Grand Rapids: Kregel, 2018.

Lewis, David K. *Counterfactuals*. Cambridge: Harvard University Press, 1973.

MacGregor, Kirk R. "The Neo-Molinist Square Collapses: A Molinist Response to Elijah Hess." *Philosophia Christi* 18.1 (2016) 197–208.

McKim, Donald K., ed. *The Cambridge Companion to John Calvin*. Cambridge: Cambridge University Press, 2004.

Molina, Ludovici. *De justitia et jure*. 5 vols. Cologne: Marci-Michaelis Bousquet, 1733.

Otte, Richard. "A Defense of Middle Knowledge." *International Journal for Philosophy of Religion* 21.3 (1987) 161–69.

Pastor, Ludwig. *The History of the Popes from the Close of the Middle Ages*. 24 vols. London: Routledge & Kegan Paul, 1950.

Plantinga, Alvin. *The Nature of Necessity*. Oxford: Clarendon, 1974.

———. "Replies." In *Philosophical Perspectives 5: Philosophy of Religion*, edited by James E. Tomberlin, 313–98. Atascadero, CA: Ridgeview, 1991.

Stalnaker, Robert C. "A Theory of Conditionals." In *Studies in Logical Theory, American Philosophical Quarterly Monograph No. 2*, 98–112. Pittsburgh: University of Pittsburgh Press, 1968.

Vereecke, Louis. *Da Guglielmo d'Ockham a sant'Alfonso de Liguori: Saggi di storia della teologia morale moderna, 1300–1787*. Milan: Edizioni Paoline, 1990.

Wierenga, Edward. *The Nature of God: An Inquiry into Divine Attributes*. Ithaca, NY: Cornell University Press, 1989.

Zagzebski, Linda Trinkaus. *The Dilemma of Freedom and Foreknowledge*. Oxford: Oxford University Press, 1991.

Part I

Molinism, Evolution, and Intelligent Design

Intelligent Design, Middle Knowledge, and the Problem of Creaturely Flaws[1]

John D. Laing

Introduction

THE THEORY OF EVOLUTION has almost always engendered controversy. Certainly from the time of Darwin, it has been plagued by a constant barrage of criticism. T. H. Huxley became one of its fiercest defenders (even though he was never convinced of the gradualism of Darwin's own idea), being dubbed "Darwin's bulldog." His debates with Samuel Wilberforce drew large crowds and created something of a scandal in the British Royal Society.

The most recent incarnation of criticism of evolution has come in the form of the modern Intelligent Design (ID) movement. The theory of Intelligent Design was thrust into the limelight in the past few years largely due to the now infamous Dover legal battle, *Kitzmiller v. Board of Education*, in which concerned parents sued the school board after it sought to require science teachers in the high schools to read a disclaimer regarding the scientific status of Neo-Darwinism and to offer an alternate book which proposed ID as an explanation for the origins and development of life (complex biological systems). The school board lost the legal battle and the teaching of ID in public schools was ruled unconstitutional. Judge John Jones III was particularly harsh on the school board members, largely due to the questionable tactics and nefarious activities of some.[2] Even though ID lost this battle, its merits continue to be debated and discussed in academic forums

---

1. While this chapter was originally read as a paper at the 2012 ETS Conference, much of the material also appears in chapter 8 of my book, *Middle Knowledge: Human Freedom in Divine Sovereignty* (Grand Rapids: Kregel, 2018), 263–275.

2. *Kitzmiller v. Dover,*, Supp. 2d 707.

and in the public square. In this chapter, I will examine a popular criticism of ID and offer an answer by drawing upon the theory of middle knowledge.

Problem of Creaturely Flaws

One objection to the theory of Intelligent Design draws upon the existence of certain undesirable features in creatures which were supposedly designed. The existence of so-called "vestigial organs"—organs that by definition, are *vestiges* of an earlier form of the creature which made use of the now defunct appendages, organs, or the like—is supposed to point to evolutionary development. As Michael Ruse points out, "Vestigial organs are another piece of evidence for the evolutionary case . . . Why do these exist? On any theory that makes adaptation totally ubiquitous, they would not have been created. But on a theory of evolution, they follow naturally as relics and evidence of the past—of past ancestors, that is, shared with organisms that still (as did the ancestors) use these features for their own adaptive ends."[3] In many cases, though, these apparently useless (or at least minimally functional) organs are not only seen as pointing to a distant past when they were adaptively useful before falling out of favor, but also as evidence against ID.[4] If there were an intelligent designer, so the argument goes, then there would be no unused organs, appendages, or other body parts. This argument has a wide appeal, as a cursory Google search of "vestigial organs" reveals. Consider the words of Sam Harris in his popular and influential *Letter to a Christian Nation*, a book written for the general audience in an effort to demonstrate the rationality of atheism over against the irrationality of theism:

> When we look at the natural world, we see extraordinary complexity, but we do not see optimal design. We see redundancy, regressions, and unnecessary complications; we see bewildering inefficiencies that result in suffering and death. We see flightless birds and snakes with pelvises. We see species of fish, salamanders, and crustaceans that have nonfunctional eyes, because they continued to evolve in darkness for millions of years. We see whales that produce teeth during fetal development, only to absorb them as adults. Such features of our world are utterly

---

3. Ruse, *Darwinism*, 42–43.

4. There is, in actuality, a rather spirited discussion about exactly what "vestigial" means. The common notion of useless or functionless organs is an oversimplification. One particularly helpful resource is the Talk Origins website: http://www.talkorigins.org/faqs/comdesc/section2.html.

mysterious if God created all species of life on earth "intelligently"; none of them are perplexing in light of evolution.[5]

Harris goes on to claim that the natural world has so many poor designs that it would take an entire book to catalog them all, the suggestion being that the weight of evidence speaks against ID [and God as Creator, for that matter!]. While we should expect Harris to know better, his use of the argument here demonstrates its persuasiveness to the person on the street.

However, it may be surprising to some to find it also propounded by top-notch scholars. For example, Ken Miller, noted biologist and distinguished professor of biology at Brown University, makes precisely the same argument against ID. In his discussion of the fossil record of proboscidean lineage, Miller claims that ID theorists cannot accept that *Elephas maximus* (Indian elephant) and *Loxodonta africana* (African elephant) evolved from a common ancestor, the comparatively smaller *Moeritherium*, which does not share their long trunks. He writes,

> Like it or not, intelligent design must face these data by arguing that each and every one of these species was designed from scratch . . . The hypothesis of design absolutely, positively requires the successive creation of increasingly elephant-like organisms over time. If some of the new "inventions" of structure and skeleton in *Paleomastodon* seem to be carried over in *Gomphotherium*, don't be misled. It's not because of ancestry. One organism has nothing to do with the other.[6]

This leads Miller to object to ID by calling into question the competence of the designer. He writes, "Almost by definition, an intelligent designer would have to be a pretty sharp fellow . . . biologists can have great fun with that notion . . . Our bodies do not display intelligent design so much as they reveal the evidence of evolutionary ancestry."[7] As evidence of this fact, Miller points to the unused yolk sac developed in human embryos, imper-

---

5. Harris, *Letter*, 75.

6. Miller, *Finding*, 95. Just in case the reader thinks this quote an anomaly: "This designer has been busy! And what a stickler for repetitive work! Although no fossil of the Indian elephant has been found that is older than 1 million years, in just the last 4 million years no fewer than nine members of its genus, *Elephas*, have come and gone. We are asked to believe that each one of these species bears no relation to the next, except in the mind of that unnamed designer whose motivation and imagination are beyond our ability to fathom" (97). Miller also writes, "This curious pattern of design that resembles succession is repeated countless times in the fossil record; and for each instance, Johnson, Berlinski, and their colleagues must claim that any impression of a sequence is just a figment of our imagination" (97, 99).

7. Miller, *Finding*, 100.

fections of the human backbone and feet for upright bipedal locomotion, the appendix, and even the functioning of the human eye. Here, then, Miller appeals to the existence of vestigial organs and creaturely flaws as evidence of evolutionary development and, more importantly, against the thesis of Intelligent Design: "Finally, whatever one's views of such a designer's motivation, there is one conclusion that drops cleanly out of the data. He was incompetent."[8]

It seems to me that this form of argument against ID is based on some assumptions about both ID and the intelligent designer that may not be true. First, it seems to make the misguided assumption that the theory of Intelligent Design is to be equated with the doctrine of special creation; and not just special creation, but a particularly conservative form. Clearly Miller has equated ID with the belief that each and every variation, even those within species, were specifically intended and created by direct action of God. This error has continually been addressed by the proponents of Intelligent Design. For example, Dembski has explicitly stated that ID is compatible with evolutionary processes: "intelligent design is compatible with the creationist idea of organisms being suddenly created from scratch. But it is also perfectly compatible with the evolutionist idea of new organisms arising from old by gradual accrual of change."[9] It is therefore a misrepresentation of the ID schema to suggest that it requires the immediate, sudden emergence of creatures or that it attributes every variation to the direct causative activity of an intelligent designer. This error could be an unintentional muddle caused by the large amount of support ID has received from the religious right, by creationists of all stripes, including young-earth creationists. This support, largely in the form of political pressure upon school boards to include ID in school science classrooms, has clouded the issues somewhat. Well-meaning creationists have often defended ID by means of creationist arguments, leading many critics (and reporters) to fail to distinguish the two movements. In fact, it has become a common tactic of the opponents of ID to lump it in with scientific creationism in an effort to discredit ID as science. Barbara Forrest and Paul Gross have argued that ID is just a subtle means by which creationists have sought to get their arguments equal hear-

8. Ibid., 102. It is interesting to note, at this point, that Miller refers to himself as a theistic evolutionist; he claims to hold a strong belief in God. While his words here may lead some to doubt the sincerity of this claim, it seems to me that such doubt is unwarranted. The better solution is that Miller has simply succumbed to the popular view which sees the spheres of science and religion as completely disparate. One's views on science have no impact on one's religion, and vice versa. This is a naïve position at best, but one which has been rather popular among scientists who wish to retain belief in God.

9. Dembski, *Design Revolution*, 178.

ing alongside Darwinism in the public school classroom; this same point has been made in the now famous remark that Intelligent Design is "just creationism in a cheap tuxedo."[10] A major problem with this line of argument is that it is almost always based either on comments about ID by non-specialists or on an impugning of ID because its proponents happen to have religious beliefs, but neither of these tactics is fair. Interestingly, many in the scientific community have accused proponents of ID of being dishonest or less than forthcoming, while they themselves argue by means of strawmen, red herrings, and the like. Whether this is deliberate falsehood or misguided criticism is for the reader to judge.

While ID theory makes no claims about the designer, it should be noted that many proponents are theists. Most of those publishing on the subject of ID are proponents of progressive creation, the thesis that God specially creates at least the beginning creature in a series (sometimes seen as genus, sometimes species) and that development of an evolutionary sort takes place at the micro-level. However, proponents of theistic evolution (the belief that God guides the process of Neo-Darwinian evolution) and of young-earth creationism have also been supporters of ID theory. Interestingly, even young-earth creationism does not discount the possibility of micro-evolution, while theistic evolutionists typically embrace both macro- and micro-evolution. This means that most proponents of ID allow for at least some evolutionary development within genus or even species, contrary to Miller's arguments.

Second, this form of argument is based on the assumption that if ID were true, the designer would have to make a flawless creature/creation. If the creature has flaws, then either the intelligence of the designer or the creature's being designed is called into question. Since the creature has flaws, then there must be no intelligent designer, and the theory of Intelligent Design fails. Here, of course, the opponents of ID have moved outside of the sphere of science and into the realms of religion, philosophy, and theology.[11] Therefore, a logico-theological answer is fitting. This objection

10. While both Barbara Forrest and Paul Gross have contributed numerous articles on the general topic of criticisms of Darwinism, their most substantive work is the book *Creationism's Trojan Horse: The Wedge of Intelligent Design* (Oxford: Oxford University Press, 2004; rev. ed., 2007). Although many people attribute the aforementioned quote to Richard Dawkins, it was actually made by paleontologist Leonard Krishtalka, professor at the University of Kansas and director of the University's Natural History Museum and Biodiversity Research Center.

11. This is the heart of the complaint against the *way* Darwinism is presented in many science texts. While it is clearly the best naturalistic explanation for the development of life forms, it is clearly lacking in its ability to address the more fundamental question of the origins of life. The proposed naturalistic answers to this question are

may be referred to as the logical problem of creaturely flaws for belief in Intelligent Design. The objection can be stated more formally as follows. A logical contradiction exists in simultaneously holding to the following propositions: (1) Creatures are designed; (2) The designer is intelligent; and (3) Creatures have flaws. If creatures have flaws, so the argument goes, then either creatures are not designed, or the designer cannot be intelligent (or both).[12]

One approach that many advocates of ID have taken to answering this objection is to argue that creatures in fact do not have flaws. Specifically, they have argued that there are no such things as vestigial and useless organs and/or structures, that they do not really exist. For example, one book by creationist authors Jerry Bergman and George Howe actually examines 100 supposed vestigial organs and offers explanations for their now-discovered use.[13] Similarly, Michael Behe has suggested that pseudogenes will eventually be shown to have a legitimate function, even if we do not now know what that may be.[14] It seems to me that this is the approach most proponents of a determinist framework for divine providence would be inclined towards, since on such a theory, God could presumably create whatever he wishes by whatever means he wishes; he is not constrained by circumstances save his own nature and, perhaps, logical possibility. This suggests, then, that every organ and/or structure was purposely included in the creature's physiology by the designer [for the theist, God]. Cornelius Hunter argues not only that many supposed vestigial organs may indeed have a yet-undiscovered function, but correctly points out that the labeling of organs as "vestigial" is question-begging: "If a penguin's wing is highly efficient for swimming, then why should we think it is vestigial, aside from presupposing it was formed by evolution? . . . Therefore, when evolutionists identify a structure as vestigial, it seems that it is the theory of evolution that is justifying the claim, rather than the claim justifying the theory of evolution."[15] Still, the complaint of Darwinists is not that the organs are vestigial, but rather that

necessarily speculative, yet they are not presented as tentative or mere possibilities. In this, then, the lines between science and metaphysics are blurred. But this is the very complaint most Darwinists have made against ID-theorists.

12. Some may object to my characterization of the claim because neither Miller nor Harris present a formal logical argument. However, given the tenor of their claims and the sarcasm in tone, it seems to be a fair representation. The either/or option posited by Miller—either creatures are not designed or the Designer is incompetent—suggests a logical argument.

13. Bergman and Howe, "Vestigial Organs."

14. Behe, Darwin's Black Box, 226.

15. Hunter, Darwin's Proof, 46.

they have no current use, so adjusting terminology from "vestigial" to "useless" does nothing to answer the substance of the objection to ID.

The strategy of denying useless organs has its problems; it is unproductive because it is purely reactionary in nature and requires proof of purpose for each and every example of useless organs or structures. Only one example of creaturely flaws is sufficient to make the argument against ID stand, and new supposed flaws are continuously discovered. Therefore, this approach is ill-equipped to ever dispose of the objection. Suppose, then, that there are flaws in creatures, that there are, indeed, genes (or organs or bone structures) which have no function. It is my intent to show that this in no way speaks against the belief that creatures are designed or that there is an intelligent designer, at least not if middle knowledge is correct.

The similarities of the argument against ID by appeal to vestigial organs to the atheistic objection to God's existence by appeal to evil is not incidental. I am going to argue that answers given for the logical problem of evil and its first-cousin, the emotive problem of evil, can give insight into answering this form of objection to intelligent design theory. Just as Christian philosophers have utilized the doctrine of middle knowledge and counterfactuals of creaturely freedom to demonstrate that the logical problem of evil has no force, so also I will employ the doctrine of middle knowledge and counterfactuals of genetic mutation to demonstrate that the logical problem of creaturely flaws has little to commend it. While it can be demonstrated that the emotive problem of evil reduces into the logical problem of evil and, in a similar way, that the emotive problem of creaturely flaws reduces into the logical problem of creaturely flaws, it is beyond the scope of this chapter to prove this connection. Nevertheless, if a satisfactory account of an intelligent designer's activity can be given which is consistent with the existence of creaturely flaws, then the objection to ID fails.

The Logical Problem of Evil

Consider the logical problem of evil. It is the suggestion that there is some form of logical contradiction in the claim that all of the following propositions are simultaneously true:

1. God is all-powerful (omnipotent)

2. God is all-good or all-loving (omnibenevolent)

3. Evil exists

Some have argued that God's being all-knowing (omniscient) is also required for the contradiction to stand. Thus stated, the argument is not very precise. As Alvin Plantinga has shown, the atheologian makes several assumptions regarding the implications of God's omnipotence, omniscience, and love. Specifically, the logical argument against God's existence assumes that an omnipotent and omniscient good being will always eliminate every evil it can, that there are no nonlogical limits to what an omnipotent being can do, and that an omniscient and omnipotent being can properly eliminate every evil state of affairs.[16]

Just as the logical problem of evil makes assumptions about what it means to say God is omnipotent and good, so also the logical problem of creaturely flaws makes assumptions about what it means to say that creatures are designed, that the designer is intelligent, and that creatures have flaws. For example, it seems beyond dispute that an intelligent designer will design items or creatures with as few flaws as he can, but this modest claim is insufficient to serve as a basis for the logical problem of creaturely flaws. A stronger statement must be made. Perhaps what the objector to ID has in mind is that an intelligent designer will design creatures with as few flaws as possible. Here, though, some assumptions about the level of intelligence of the designer have been made. After all, while human designers meet the qualifications of the first statement (they design items with as few flaws as they can), they surely do not meet the qualifications of the second, though nobody calls their intelligence into question. Consider the design of a car. The engineers who work for Toyota, for example, attempt to design their vehicles without any flaws, but just because a flaw exists in the design does not mean that the engineers are not intelligent. So when the requirement to design items with as few flaws as possible is laid on, something beyond mere intelligence is in use. It seems that, in order for the designer to design items with as few flaws as possible, he would have to be maximally intelligent. Thus, the objector to ID is really assuming that the intelligence of the designer is identical to that of the God of traditional theism, namely, infinite intelligence or omniscience. So his argument is really that a maximally intelligent designer will design creatures with as few flaws as possible. Whether this assumption is true or required by ID-theory is a matter to be discussed, but it seems fair to assume, at this point, that ID proponents would not object strongly to viewing the designer as being omniscient.

Interestingly, it also seems that assumptions have been made with regard to the power of the designer as well, for the logical objector to ID seems

---

16. Plantinga, *God, Freedom, and Evil*, 21–22. Plantinga's propositions have been renumbered to reflect the numbering of this paper.

committed to the belief that it is possible for creatures to have no flaws. On the surface, this belief seems reasonable enough, but this still does not get to a logical contradiction because developing a design and bringing it to fruition are two different things. The argument has to employ some concept of the power of the designer, about his ability to actualize creatures with no flaws. Note, though, that for the argument to work, the designer must have power such that he cannot be thought of as lacking the ability to actualize flawless creatures. That is, merely claiming the designer is intelligent is not enough. For the argument to work, the objector must claim that the designer is maximally intelligent (omniscient) and maximally powerful (omnipotent). All of the assumptions and arguments, if sound, can then lead the objector to conclude that if the designer is omniscient and omnipotent, then he can and must properly eliminate/prevent all creaturely flaws.

Finally, it seems that the logical objector to ID has also made assumptions about the kinds of creatures an intelligent designer will design and the purposes of those creatures. He has assumed that an intelligent designer will design creatures for optimal performance (for whatever purpose they are designed), and that creatures are designed with at least a primary purpose in mind. Behe has made these same points regarding the objection from imperfection.[17] Pennock has questioned the sincerity of these claims, though, pointing out that Paley's designer was conceived of as perfect and that he would [must!], therefore, create a perfect creation with all creatures perfectly suited to their habitats and purposes: "Does Behe really mean to deny that the perfect designer did a perfect job, or is he just making a virtue of vagueness?"[18]

While it may seem that this is enough for the objector to make his case, it is still lacking. The problem can be seen when we consider that there could be multiple purposes for creatures, and multiple purposes could lead to competition among the purposes. If two or more purposes were in conflict, then there could be reason to call into question the requirements that a maximally intelligent designer must design creatures with as few flaws as possible and that an omniscient and omnipotent designer can and must eliminate or prevent all creaturely flaws. Thus the logical problem of

17. Behe, *Darwin's Black Box*, 223.

18. Pennock, *Tower of Babel*, 248. While Pennock is always quick to point out instances in which *creationists* are unfair to modern Darwinians by mischaracterization, anachronism, or misrepresentation, he himself is guilty of the same here, for modern Intelligent Design theorists, even traditional theists, are under no obligation to hold that God must make a perfect Creation and that in so doing, he only had one option (i.e., "the best"). If postmodernism has done nothing else, it has caused many theists to recognize that there may be numerous ways to attain equally good ends, depending on what one's goal (or goals) is (or are).

creaturely flaws assumes that creatures are designed with only one purpose in mind, but this assumption is suspect at best. Why should we think that there is only one purpose for each creature? So already, we have good reasons for rejecting the logical problem of creaturely flaws. Flaws could exist as necessary fallout from more desirable outcomes. Nevertheless, suppose, for sake of argument, that it is true. We will see that there is still good reason for calling the logical problem of creaturely flaws into question. Even if creatures are designed with only one purpose in mind, and the designer is conceived as omniscient and omnipotent, the belief that the designer can and must eliminate or prevent all creaturely flaws is hardly indisputable and is in fact, doubtful.

The Free-Will Defense

The free-will defense is a strategy for answering the logical problem of evil by claiming that propositions (1) through (3) may all be held by the theist without contradiction or confusion by claiming that it is possible that at least some evil exists due to the free decisions of creatures. Put differently, it offers good reasons for doubting that even an omniscient and omnipotent being can and must properly eliminate every evil state of affairs, which is necessary for (1) through (3) to form a tight argument. Thus, all the theist has to show in order to answer the logical problem of evil is that it is possible that an all-powerful, all-loving God could not create a world where creatures are free but never commit evil (sin). If this possibility can be demonstrated, then it is not the case that an omniscient and omnipotent being must properly eliminate every evil state of affairs. The free will defender will readily admit that God *could* have created a world where there is no freedom and no sin; this is surely clear, but he will argue that true freedom means that there is no coercion, which means that truly free actions cannot be caused from without. This means that God cannot make creatures freely do anything, much less refrain from sinning, and it could have been the case that whenever creatures are free, they choose to sin at least once. Or, to put it in biblical terms, the free-will defense suggests it is possible that in every case (possible world) where Adam is free with respect to the forbidden fruit, he chooses to eat. (As previously noted, the defense does not require that this is the case or that it is even likely, but only that it is logically possible.) The free-will defense claims that there is no reason to think it impossible, and therefore it might be the case that God could not create a world where Adam is free and he doesn't sin, and the logical problem of evil fails.

Sometimes the question is raised of why an all-good being would choose to create free creatures, knowing that their freedom will lead to so much evil and suffering. Free will defenders have admitted that this is a legitimate concern and have suggested an underlying principle to the free-will defense, namely the following premise (or something very much like it). A world containing free creatures who sometimes commit evil actions is better than a world containing no freedom. The justification for this assertion is usually based in the concept of love as a non-coercive (free) response to others, and that a world with love (and evil) is still better than a world without love (and no evil, if that is even possible). While some may object to this language on grounds that it does not require libertarian freedom, the important point for purposes of this discussion is to note that there is an underlying principle in the free-will defense which lends it explanatory power. The proponent of the free-will defense has to show that an all-knowing, all-loving, and all-powerful being could be conceived of creating a world with evil without violating his essential goodness.

Middle Knowledge

The free-will defense makes certain assumptions about the nature of God which may not be readily apparent, namely that He knows truths such as that expressed by the proposition, "In every case where Adam is free with respect to the forbidden fruit, he would choose to eat," and that they inform His decision about what to create, which worlds to actualize, and which creatures to instantiate. This means that the doctrine of middle knowledge is essential to the free-will defense.[19] The doctrine of middle knowledge is the suggestion that there are three logical moments in the divine deliberative process regarding creation. At the two ends of the process are God's natural knowledge, which is composed of truths that are both necessary and independent of God's will (they are true not because God willed them to be that way) and His free knowledge, which is composed of truths that are both contingent and dependent upon His will (true because He willed them to be that way). According to the theory, there is a third category of divine knowledge called middle knowledge, which is composed of truths that are contingent and independent of God's will. Propositions known as

---

19. Due to time and space constraints, a full proof of the necessary connection between middle knowledge and the free-will defense will not be offered here. Such an argument will employ the requirement of the FWD that freedom be libertarian and that God would have to know that a greater good will come about as a result of freedom prior to his choice to actualize the given state of affairs.

counterfactuals of creaturely freedom, which state how possible creatures would freely act if in various circumstances, are thought to be the content of middle knowledge. For example, the proposition

4. If David were to remain in Keilah, the men of the city would freely hand him over to Saul

is thought to be a counterfactual of creaturely freedom which describes the actions the men of Keilah would have taken if David had remained there (or would take if David remains there). According to the theory of middle knowledge, God contemplated the virtually infinite number of propositions of this form which relate to all possible creatures and all possible situations they could find themselves in, and that this informed his decision about which possible world to actualize.

This allows the proponent of middle knowledge to hold to belief that humans have libertarian freedom and that God exercises meticulous providence. In terms of the free-will defense, it affords the theist the ability to believe that evil is the result of free creaturely decisions, that God knew a greater good would come about as a result of freedom, and that God is not directly responsible for evil or sin, while still maintaining his providence. Suppose it is true that in every case where Adam is free, he eats the forbidden fruit. According to middle knowledge, God has no power over the truth of this proposition and so cannot make it false. This means that the truths of how creatures would freely act constrain the kinds of worlds God can actualize. In this case, God can either actualize a world where Adam is free but there is sin, or God can actualize a world where Adam is not free and there is no sin, but God cannot actualize a world where Adam is free and there is no sin; such a world, while *logically* possible, is not *feasible* because of how Adam would act if free.[20] While the content of God's middle knowledge most often discussed in the literature has been counterfactuals of creaturely freedom, there may be other propositions God knows via middle knowledge. This will be the theme of the following section.

---

20. Of course, this is a bit imprecise. A counterfactual more broadly stated, though, could certainly do the trick: In every possible world where humans are free, they (or at least one) choose(s) to sin.

The Intelligent Mutation Defense

Just as the theist only need show that it is possible that an all-powerful, all-loving God could not create a world where creatures are free but never commit evil in order to answer the logical problem of evil, so also in order to answer the logical problem of creaturely flaws, the proponent of ID only need show that it is *possible* that the intelligent designer could not have developed creatures with the complexity they have without the flaws they have.[21] Note that this does not say that it has to be the case or that it is, in fact, the case that the designer could not have developed creatures with the complexity they have without the flaws they have. The ID theorist only need show that it is possible. If he can do this, then the logical problem of creaturely flaws fails.[22] So in some ways, both the Molinist and determinist could make use of the argument. However, if we wish to move beyond merely responding to the argument and to reflect upon *how* the intelligent designer [for Christians, God] actually did create, then we must admit that the argument offered here is not available to the determinist because he is

21. Or, to be more precise, it is possible that the Intelligent Designer could not have developed a world with creatures that are as complex as those which exist without some creatures also having flaws.

22. One other point is worth noting, and this is related to the limiting of the discussion to the realm of possibility. The critic of ID may suggest that, while it may be possible that the intelligent designer could not have developed creatures with the complexity they have without the flaws they have, the preponderance of the evidence of vestigial organs still speaks against ID. That is, he may argue that the great number of flaws which exist in the natural world point to a purely naturalistic process devoid of any intelligent guidance or direction. He may argue that the fact that so many species have gone extinct speaks against an intelligent (or benevolent, for that matter) designer. Let us call this objection the emotive problem of creaturely flaws, due to the fact that it makes a claim upon our emotional response to the evidence of flaws in the natural world. This would not be an unreasonable objection, especially since ID theorists such as Dembski have suggested that ID is really concerned with inference to the best explanation. However, we will see that this objection does have its problems. Most first-year philosophy students will immediately notice the similarity of this sort of argument to the so-called emotive problem of evil (to belief in the existence of God). This form of argument, while seemingly persuasive, is really just a veiled form of the logical arguments, for the attempt to quantify acceptable negative states of affairs always fails. When atheologians are asked to quantify how many instances of evil *would* be acceptable for belief in the existence of God to be rational, they invariably claim none. Consider, for example, the claim by Sam Harris: "An atheist is a person who believes that the murder on a single little girl—even once in a million years—casts doubt upon the idea of a benevolent God" (*Letter*, 52). This same strategy works with the a-ID theorist. If only one flaw speaks against the existence of an intelligent designer, then the emotive problem of creaturely flaws collapses into the logical problem of creaturely flaws. Therefore, if the logical problem is answered, then the objection from creaturely flaws is answered.

committed to the claim that the designer must have the ability to instantiate creatures with the complexity they have without the flaws.

How can the proponent of ID make his case? It seems to me that he can call upon the very mechanisms that the proponent of evolution does—random genetic mutation and natural selection—but he can claim that these mutations still fall within the purview of an intelligent designer, or in the case of my faith, God.[23] This may be accomplished by means of the doctrine of middle knowledge.

Counterfactuals of Random Genetic Mutation

Consider the following two propositions:

> If situation S prevails, then random genetic mutation M will occur

and

> If situation S does not prevail, then random genetic mutation M will not occur.

If these propositions are possibly true, then it is possible that the intelligent designer could not have developed creatures with the complexity they have without the flaws they have because S could involve undesirable mutations or the existence of useless organs, and in this way, the proponent of ID has answered the objection. Suppose it is true that S is necessary for M to occur. In that case, if God wants mutation M to occur (at least randomly), he would have to actualize situation S (either strongly or weakly). At this point, then, the beginnings of an explanation of how an intelligent designer (such as the traditional God of theism) could make use of random genetic mutation to guide evolutionary processes to the end he desires emerge. However, it is not at all clear that these propositions are true or even possibly true. Several items merit further comment.

First, some may complain that they cannot be true, that they are not possible. That is, the very wording of the counterfactuals represented by the propositions may seem contradictory or self-referentially incoherent

---

23. I understand that many of the opponents of Intelligent Design have made just this charge—that Intelligent Design is a veiled attempt to insert Christianity into science, and that my reference to the designer as "God" adds credence to this claim. However, it is somewhat dishonest for me to refuse to refer to the designer as God if I do, indeed, believe God to be such. In addition, in this paper, I am using arguments developed to defend belief in God, so it is just as legitimate to refer to the one defended by analogy as "God."

insofar as the random nature of the mutation requires that it could occur (or not occur) whether S prevails or not. This argument claims that there can be no truths regarding when random events would or would not—or will or will not—occur because truly random events must be indeterminate. The indeterminate nature of random events precludes there being truths about when and in which situations they will or will not occur. This form of argument against the truth of counterfactuals of random genetic mutation is similar in form to the grounding objection to the truth of counterfactuals of creaturely freedom, and I would expect the determinist to make use of it here. There is not time to answer it here, except to say that there is no causal relationship between the antecedent and the consequent in the counterfactuals. Rather, their relationship is merely explanatory.[24]

Second, even if the aforementioned objection can be overcome, the basis for the truth of propositions regarding when a random event will or will not occur cannot be found in God's will, for the random nature of the events preclude a deterministic cause behind their occurrence, even the will of God. This is not to say that God cannot cause genetic mutation, but it is to say that such mutations cannot properly be deemed random. This means that God's knowledge of such propositions must be part of his middle knowledge.

Third, it should be noted that situation S could include a whole host of events, prior mutations, and scenarios. This means that for mutation M to occur, there may be required some other mutations that are not desirable. It is hard to see how, following a random mutation process, we can require that the designer be able to bring about all desired mutations without any undesirable mutations as well. Suppose that mutation M is necessary for the complexity of creature C and that situation S includes flaws in C. Is such a supposition possible? It seems to not only be obviously so but also quite plausible. If C develops by means of evolution, we should expect it to do so by means of certain helpful mutations and there seems no reason to suppose that S could not include flaws in C. At any rate, while there may be no way to judge the truth of the supposition, it seems obvious that it *could* be true and that it is not necessarily impossible! The possibility that M is necessary for the complexity of C and that S includes flaws in C means that both of the aforementioned propositions ("If S occurs, then M will occur" and "If S does not occur, then M will not occur") are also possible and, therefore, it is at least plausible that the designer could not create such complex creatures without flaws if he wished to use a process with randomness.

24. It is also the case that epistemological uncertainty does not imply metaphysical uncertainty; just because we do not know whether (5) or (6) is true does not mean that they cannot be true.

In addition to these considerations, two objections need to be considered: First, an explanation for why an intelligent designer might choose to design a creation or creatures where adaptation is necessary must be given. It is not immediately clear that an intelligent designer would/should choose to include adaptability in his design. Note, again, that what needs to be shown is that an explanation is possible; it need not be the most plausible explanation (though such would be good to offer!). Second, an explanation of why an intelligent designer might choose to utilize a random, rather than determined, process for development must also be proffered. This seems to be the most difficult question to answer.

Problem of Intelligent Designer's Preference for Creaturely Adaptability

In the same way that the free-will defense needed a basis for saying why God would prefer a world with evil and freedom rather than a world with no freedom and no evil, a defense of Intelligent Design against the logical problem of creaturely flaws will need a similar premise explaining why an intelligent designer would prefer a world where creatures develop in a way which utilizes random genetic mutation and have flaws, rather than a world where creatures come to be by fiat creation and undergo minor, if any, developmental change and do not have flaws.

Just as there are many possibilities available to the theist for answering the question of why God, who is all-powerful and all-loving, would create a world with evil and suffering, there are also many possibilities available to the ID-theorist for answering the question of why an intelligent designer might use a process such as evolution. For example, he could argue that a world where creatures adapt to a changing environment is better (i.e., more reflective of intelligence) than a world where they do not so adapt. This suggestion seems to offer a plausible explanation as to why an intelligent designer might give creatures a capacity to adapt/evolve. After all, if the environment changes, it just makes sense to give creatures within that environment a chance at survival. So the argument works *given* an environment characterized by change. Yet some may wonder why an intelligent designer would not design a stable environment; they may claim that a stable—not changing—environment would be more reflective of the handiwork of an intelligent artificer. Here, though, several answers or explanations can be proffered.

For example, it could be argued that a dynamic environment is more beautiful, and that beauty reflects intelligence. Consider the following proposition:

> A world characterized by change is more beautiful than a world that does not change.

This proposition needs to be augmented in order to get to a justification of an intelligent designer. That is, the further claim that a beautiful world is more reflective of an intelligent designer than a world that is not beautiful, would need to be proven. While this line of argument may be sound (and I am inclined to think it is), it is beyond the scope of this piece to defend it. Such a defense would need to include an explanation of how change in the world is beautiful while stasis in the divine nature (as classically/traditionally conceived) is preferable. It suggests that an intelligent designer must create the most beautiful world, and so a defense may also require an argument for the supreme beauty of this world. Of course, this would only be required if the intelligent designer is thought to be perfectly intelligent (i.e., omniscient). While, as already noted, ID-theory makes no claims regarding the quality or quantity of the intelligence of the designer (except to say that the design exhibits signs of intelligence), it is generally thought to be greater than that of even the brightest humans, and traditional theistic proponents of ID do believe in the essential omniscience of the designer.

Fortunately, the aforementioned argument is not the only defense of the intelligibility of an environment characterized by change, and quite frankly, is neither the best nor the most straightforward. Consider the following argument:

5. An unchanging environment requires stasis

6. Stasis prevents relationality among finite beings

7. A world with relationality is more reflective of an intelligent designer than one with no relationality.

The argument here is admittedly basic, but seems sound. Some may wish to contest (7), but it is unclear what such an argument would look like. In fact, it is not at all clear how a world populated (in any meaningful sense of the term) with any sort of creatures could possibly not be characterized by relationality. (Here relationality is being used in a most basic sense—to refer to the fact that there is interaction, in the very least, at the most basic levels.) In fact, a static world may not even be a possibility. No matter how intelligent (or powerful for that matter!) the designer may be, it simply may not be within his ability to create a world without change because finitude seems to require movement, interaction, and change. That is, it seems that a world with living organisms requires at least *some* change because of the relationality of finite beings. Change is fundamental to any environment populated by finite beings and is therefore a constituent part of an intelligently designed cosmos. Thus, the claim that a world where creatures adapt is better than a world where they do not, can stand because the presuppositions behind it are sound (or at least, defensible).

Problem of the Intelligence of Random Mutation

One objection to the line of argumentation offered here is to question the intelligence of using random genetic mutation to spur evolutionary development. After all, so the argument might go, it is terribly inefficient. Why would an intelligent designer choose to create beings with an ability to adapt, but place that ability at the guidance of *random* events? Why would it not be more intelligent to use directed genetic mutations? If no good answer can be given, or the intellectual superiority of directed genetic mutations can be proven, then there may be good reason to doubt the possibility of the designer's inability to develop creatures with such complexity without having any flaws (that is, there may be good reason to suppose that the designer could, and indeed *must,* create complex creatures with no flaws), and the random genetic mutation defense fails.

Fortunately (or providentially), there are several avenues the proponent of ID might follow in attempting to answer this objection. One could be to simply agree that it actually would be *more* intelligent to use directed mutations. Admitting this does nothing to detract from Intelligent Design since it only requires that the process actually followed was/is intelligent, not that it was/is *most intelligent.* While this certainly answers the objection, properly speaking, most proponents of ID would find it unsatisfying. Thus, answers that actually address the issue at hand are in order. At least three such answers are available to the ID theorist who believes the designer to have attributes similar to those ascribed to God in traditional theism.

First, some cognitive psychologists have suggested that thoughts and actions are merely the expression of changes and movement at the atomic level in the brain. If all genetic mutations were controlled, then the development of brain states would also be determined, and human freedom would be illusory (at least libertarian freedom), but, as already noted (in the free-will defense), a good case can be made for preferring human freedom to determinism. Randomness and indeterminacy at the genetic and quantum level may, indeed, be necessary for (libertarian) human freedom. The problem with this approach is that it smacks of identity-theory physicalism, which is clearly antithetical to the idea of an intelligent designer.

While some proponents of ID and some theists have made cases similar to this based on nonreductive physicalism, it still seems to be at odds with a broad-based dualist view of reality, which ID seems to imply.[25] A better answer can be given.

Second, it could be argued that the use of random processes to produce an orderly system requires more intelligence than it does to use controlled processes for the same purpose. Random genetic mutation leading to the evolution of complex life, then, actually points to the glory of God. Van Till hints at this line of reasoning when he calls his own (theistic evolutionary) position the *"fully gifted creation perspective."*[26] According to Van Till, the capabilities for self-organization and transformation necessary for evolutionary development—something he describes as "humanly incomprehensible"—are granted by God's "unbounded generosity and unfathomable creativity."[27] This line of reasoning fits well with the doctrine of middle knowledge, for only an infinite mind could comprehend all of the virtually infinite possibilities regarding random genetic mutations and then bring about a world where the desired mutations occur. The fact that God is constrained by the counterfactuals of creaturely freedom and the counterfactuals of genetic mutation detracts nothing from his infinity, conceived either in terms of knowledge (omniscience) or in terms of power (omnipotence).

Third, the random character of mutations could be attributed to the Fall. That is, under a Christian interpretation, one could argue that as a result of the Fall and the emergence of sin into the created order, the cosmos has been characterized by chaos and randomness at the most basic level (e.g., quarks and gluons). Yet, until such time as God recreates or restores the heavens and the earth, he will preserve a measure of peace and order. His use of random mutation and survival of the fittest is due to his grace in extending the current age (2 Pet 3:8–10).

It seems that all three options provide a basis for answering the question of why an intelligent designer might use random genetic mutation to allow for creaturely adaptation. The second and the third may be combined to provide a powerful theological statement that is consistent with both theistic evolution and progressive creation.

Conclusion

The logical problem of creaturely flaws does not serve to unseat Intelligent Design theory, as it is a move into the realm of philosophy and religion. At

25. See, for example, Murphy and Ellis, *Moral Nature of the Universe*, 32–37; Murphy, *Beyond Liberalism and Fundamentalism*, 149–52.

26. Van Till, "Fully Gifted Creation," 173.

27. Ibid.

a minimum, it assumes the designer is both omniscient and omnipotent. A satisfactory explanation of why even a maximally intelligent and powerful being might produce flawed creatures is possible. While other answers can surely be given, the most satisfactory approach is to draw upon the doctrine of middle knowledge and argue that the designer could use his knowledge of how random genetic mutations *would* proceed in order to bring about the adaptations and changes in creatures he desires. However, his ability is constrained by the true counterfactuals of random genetic mutation and, therefore, it is possible that undesirable mutations may be required. Satisfactory reasons can be supplied for why an intelligent designer might wish to create creatures with the ability to adapt and to do so by means of random mutation. Ultimately the very process points to the intelligence of the designer, and the critique of ID-theory fails.

Bibliography

Behe, Michael. *Darwin's Black Box: The Biochemical Challenge to Evolution*. New York: Free, 1996.

Bergman, Jerry, and George Howe. *"Vestigial Organs" Are Fully Functional: A History and Evaluation of the Concept of Vestigial Organs*. Chino Valley, AZ: Creation Research Society Monograph, 1990.

Dembski, William. *The Design Revolution*. Downers Grove, IL: InterVarsity, 2004.

Forrest, Barbara, and Paul Gross. *Creationism's Trojan Horse: The Wedge of Intelligent Design*. Rev. ed. Oxford: Oxford University Press, 2007.

Harris, Sam. *Letter to a Christian Nation*. New York: Knopf, 2006.

Hunter, Cornelius G. *Darwin's Proof: The Triumph of Religion over Science*. Grand Rapids: Brazos, 2003.

Miller, Kenneth R. *Finding Darwin's God*. New York: Perennial, 1999.

Murphy, Nancey. *Beyond Liberalism and Fundamentalism*. Valley Forge, PA: Trinity, 1996.

Murphy, Nancey, and George F. R. Ellis. *On the Moral Nature of the Universe: Theology, Cosmology, and Ethics*. Minneapolis: Fortress, 1996.

Pennock, Robert T. *Tower of Babel: The Evidence against the New Creationism*. Cambridge: MIT Press, 1999.

Plantinga, Alvin. *God, Freedom, and Evil*. Grand Rapids: Eerdmans, 1974.

Ruse, Michael. *Darwinism and Its Discontents*. Cambridge: Cambridge University Press, 2006.

Tammy Kitzmiller, et al. v. Dover Area School District, et al., 400 F. Supp. 2d 707 (M.D. Pa. 2005).

Van Till, Howard J. "The Fully Gifted Creation." In *Three Views on Creation and Evolution*, edited by J. P. Moreland and John Mark Reynolds, 159–218. Grand Rapids: Zondervan, 1999.

2

The Impossibility of Evolution Apart from a God with Middle Knowledge

Kirk R. MacGregor

Popular culture and not a few prominent scientists (e.g., Richard Dawkins, Massimo Pigliucci)[1] regularly assert that biological evolution is the death knell to belief in God, a sentiment prevalent since the 1859 publication of Darwin's *Origin of Species*. While not nearly taken as the death knell to theism, ambivalence surrounds the theory of evolution among the community of Christian scholars. Although microevolution, or evolution within kinds, is taken by virtually all Christian thinkers as biblically unobjectionable, macroevolution, or evolution from one kind to another stemming from a common ancestor of all organisms, stands for many Christian thinkers in contradiction to the Genesis depiction of God's creating each kind of organism (Gen 1:11, 12, 21, 24, 25, 26). Affirming God's special creation of each kind, these thinkers argue that macroevolution is just as problematic on scientific grounds as it is on biblical ones. Here the most frequent strategy by special creationists is to call attention to the tremendous improbability of macroevolution in two fundamental respects. First is the enormous improbability of the myriad genetic mutations which would have had to materialize in order to facilitate the transition from one major taxonomic group (kingdom and phylum) to another.[2] Second is the enormous improbability of unrelated mutations occurring simultaneously to produce certain biological systems within organisms, an idea which lies at the heart of the ID concept of irreducible complexity.[3]

1. Dawkins, *God Delusion*, 85, 137–68; Pigliucci, *Tales of the Rational*, 53–64.

2. Dembski, "Reviving the Argument from Design," 101–45; Morris, *Scientific Case for Creation*, 61–62.

3. Denton, *Evolution*, 308–25; Behe, *Darwin's Black Box*, 39–48, 187–208. Note that Denton and Behe are not themselves special creationists but advocate what might

I quite agree that all such mutations are, mathematically speaking, extraordinarily improbable, and I believe that special creationists have done the Christian community a great service in drawing our attention to them. However, I disagree entirely with the way special creationists use these evidential data. Special creationists infer from the vanishingly small probability of trans-group genetic mutations and simultaneous unrelated genetic mutations that such mutations did not occur, such that God directly created either the new taxonomic group or the irreducibly complex biological system under investigation. But this is not the only explanation of the data. If it could be independently verified that trans-group and simultaneous unrelated mutations did occur, then their extreme improbability would show that, while occurring by chance, they did not occur by chance *alone*. In other words, they would constitute powerful evidence for the existence of a God who created a universe where all of these astronomically improbable events would naturally occur rather than a universe where they would not. But what kind of a God could create a universe in which astronomically improbable mutations would repeatedly occur in the course of nature, as opposed to the special creationist's universe where these mutations did not occur but where God repeatedly intervened to produce the same long-term effects as if they had occurred? I contend that only a God endowed with middle knowledge, or knowledge of all counterfactual truths, would be able to create such a "specially gifted" universe, to employ Howard Van Till's terminology.[4]

This piece will proceed in three steps, the third of which will constitute the bulk of my case. First, I will argue that macroevolution is not incompatible with an inerrantist position on the Genesis creation narrative. Second, I will explain why I believe macroevolution accurately explains the development of physical life on Earth, providing evidence for the occurrence of trans-group and simultaneous unrelated mutations. Third, I will delineate how macroevolution and all its concomitant improbabilities demonstrate the existence of not just any deity but a God with middle knowledge. Accordingly, one of the invisible divine attributes which the creation of the world evinces (Rom 1:19–20) is the most robust type of omniscience.

---

be called "progressive creation" or "guided evolution," where God intervenes at key junctures in the course of macroevolution to produce biological systems whose generation purportedly lies beyond the capacity of natural selection operating on random mutations.

4. Van Till, "Fully Gifted Creation," 161.

Inerrancy, Macroevolution, and the
Genesis Creation Narrative

Properly expressed, the doctrine of biblical inerrancy stipulates that, for each pericope within every document of the Scriptural canon, when we first take into consideration that pericope's original literary genre and the rules for what does and does not constitute an error in that genre, the pericope contains no errors.[5] Elsewhere I have defended the view,[6] in concert with such expositors as Henri Blocher, Derek Kidner, Meredith Kline, Gordon Wenham, and Bruce Waltke,[7] that Genesis 1–3 belongs to the ancient Near Eastern literary genre of poetic-structural narrative and is thus rightly explained by what has been termed the framework hypothesis. On this hypothesis, the days of the creation week were never intended to be taken literally but serve as literary markers (ABCABCD) linking the contents of Day 1 with Day 4, Day 2 with Day 5, and Day 3 with Day 6 and establishing via Day 7 that the entire domain of human history is the cosmic Sabbath during which God invites humanity to find ultimate rest in communion with and reliance upon him. Days 1 through 3 comprise "days of forming" where God forms the respective realms of light, water, and dry land, and Days 4 through 6 comprise "days of filling" where God lovingly actualizes all the potentialities of each realm by filling it with all the kinds of being it can accommodate. Since poetic-structural narrative, by definition, reports truths in highly figurative and poetic ways within a chiastic literary structure, it would defy the literary genre of the Genesis creation narrative to argue from its statements about God making various "kinds," forming various realms, and filling those realms to anything other than *that* God accomplished all these events. The text, correctly understood, gives no information about *how* God accomplished any of these events and so does not imply that God performed them through repeated acts of direct intervention. Beyond the act of creating the universe, the only element of the creation narrative that would require God's direct intervention is the creation of humanity in God's image (Gen 1:26–27), namely, humanity's becoming a living *nephesh* (Gen 2:7).[8] If one embraces, as I do, the position of the Protestant Reformers

5. This is both a recension and expansion of the definition provided by the 1978 Chicago Statement on Biblical Inerrancy, with which I am sympathetic; for the complete text of the statement see Geisler, *Inerrancy*, 493–502.

6. MacGregor, *Molinist-Anabaptist Systematic Theology*, 174–83.

7. Blocher, *In the Beginning*, 39–59; Kidner, *Genesis*, 54; Kline, "Because It Had Not Rained," 155–56; Kline, "Space and Time," 2–15; Wenham, *Genesis 1–15*, 1:69; Waltke, "Literary Genre," 2–10.

8. It is far from obvious that the other instances of *bārā'*, "to create," in the Genesis

(as well as many others throughout Christian history)[9] that, since God is an infinite soul or immaterial mind, the image of God designates the finite soul or immaterial mind distinct from the brain, then God's creating humanity by endowing hominid bodies with souls would leave no trace in the genetic record and no break in the fossil record.[10] In that case, God's use of macroevolution to make various "kinds" and the physical bodies of primal humans is perfectly compatible with the inerrancy of the opening chapters of Genesis.[11]

Reasons for My Acceptance of Macroevolution

In history and in science, explanatory power, or the ability to account for a large number of seemingly independent categories of evidence, constitutes one hallmark of a valid theory. Macroevolution displays precisely this ability in explaining various categories of evidence. The plethora of corresponding similarities among adults, embryos, and molecules of organisms are accounted for as traits shared through common descent. The nested hierarchy of form, or higher-level groupings of similar categories of organisms wherein the organisms themselves display lower-level grouping through similarities with each other, is accounted for through the successive branching pattern of evolutionary transformation. Suboptimal improvisations, or features that do not suit an organism ideally but still allow the organism to survive, are accounted for through the transformation of organisms through a natural process limited in resources and constrained by history. Vestigial structures,

---

creation narrative refer to material creation rather than functional creation. Although overstating his case that *bārā'* only refers to functional creation in Genesis 1, John H. Walton has in my judgment demonstrated that *bārā'* typically conveys this meaning in the creation narrative (*Lost World of Genesis One*, 36–45).

9. Luther, *Genesis 1–5*, 60; Zwingli, *Clarity and Certainty*, 60–61; Calvin, *Institutes*, 1.15.3; Arminius, *Works*, 3:102, 111–12, 118. For the place of this doctrine in the history of Christian thought see Pelikan, *Emergence of the Catholic Tradition*, 300–301. This is also the unofficial Roman Catholic position announced in Pope Pius XII's 1950 encyclical *Humani Generis* and bolstered by Pope John Paul II's 1996 address to the Pontifical Academy of Sciences.

10. This is just like God's performing all other spiritual events (i.e., regeneration, empowering the soul, communicating directly with the soul, and so forth), none of which by definition leave any physical residue.

11. Such a conclusion was foreshadowed, interestingly enough, by the fourth-century church father Augustine, who postulated on the basis of exegetical considerations alone that God did not perform special acts of creation to make each species but created a world endowed with certain potencies that unfolded on their own over the progress of time (*De Genesi ad litteram*, 1.42–43), a theory submitted 1,500 years prior to Darwin which sounds strikingly like macroevolution.

or structures with reduced or no function, are accounted for as structures that have fallen into disuse because of evolutionary change. The phenomenon of macrobiogeographical distribution, or concentration of major types of organisms near to each other (attested prominently, e.g., in the distribution of Australian marsupials), is explained by their descent from a common ancestor and their evolutionary diversification. The change in fossils through the fossil record is accounted for by the continuous change of organisms throughout time. The orders of first appearance of plant phyla, vertebrate classes, arthropod classes, and organisms in the phylogeny of humanity are accounted for by the preservation of major evolutionary transformations in the fossil record. Series of fossils (e.g., the horse series, the elephant series, the camel series, the mammal-like reptile series, the early birds, the early whales) and stratomorphic intermediates, or fossils that stand both in the fossil record and structurally between the group from which they descend and the group to which they are ancestral, are accounted for as distinctly preserved steps in the evolutionary process.[12]

In contrast to macroevolution, special creation finds difficulty in explaining some of these evidential categories. Regarding suboptimal improvisations and vestigial structures, I concur with Stephen Jay Gould that special creation of each kind precludes these less than ideal designs.[13] To illustrate, God's special creation of whales with useless leg bones appears inexplicable, for whales would no longer descend from land-living ancestors with legs.[14] No one could validly argue that such structures resulted from sin, as they emerged on anyone's reckoning before the Fall.[15] Regarding stratomorphic intermediates, these transitional forms from one major taxonomic group to another prove that tremendously improbable trans-group genetic mutations did in fact take place. In the fossil record, these intermediates include *Ichthyostega* standing between fish and amphibians, anthracosaurs standing between amphibians and reptiles, mammal-like reptiles standing between reptiles and mammals, *Pakicetus* standing between terrestrial mammals and whales, phenacodontids standing between hyraxes and horses, *Archaeopteryx* standing between dinosaurs and birds, *Purgatorius* standing between

12. In this section I have followed closely Wise, "Origin," 232, 221–23, 226. However, I disagree with Wise that these evidential categories, for which he admits "macroevolution is a powerful theory of explanation" (232), are better explained by special creationism and a global flood.

13. Gould, *Panda's Thumb*, 19–26.

14. Bejder and Hall, "Limbs and Limblessness," 445–58.

15. Unless one treads the path taken by Dembski (*End of Christianity*, 32–42) that the effects of the Fall were retroactive and so furnished God a ready world into which to drive Adam and Eve as punishment for their sin, which I find a recourse of desperation.

plesiadapiforms and primates, and *Proconsul* standing between monkeys and hominoids.[16] Related to this is the fact that these transitional forms did not have transitional organs but fully functional organs, which constitute examples of irreducible complexity and so demonstrate the occurrence of simultaneous unrelated mutations. Further evidence of the occurrence of such mutations was furnished in 2006 by a research team at the University of Oregon's Center for Ecology and Evolutionary Biology, which employed techniques for restoring ancient genes to reconstruct the evolution of an irreducibly complex molecular system, namely, the specific partnership of the hormone aldosterone with the receptor protein that allows the body's cells to respond to the hormone.[17] For these reasons, I believe that macroevolution exhibits superior explanatory power to special creationism in accounting for the various lines of evidence and so find it the most plausible theory of biological development. Hence the fossil and genetic evidence establishes, in my judgment, the historical incidence of highly unlikely transgroup mutations and simultaneous unrelated mutations.

To up the ante on this improbability, John Barrow and Frank Tipler (no friends to special creationism) have highlighted ten steps established by the fossil and genetic evidence to have transpired in the course of human evolution: the development of the DNA-based genetic code, the development of aerobic respiration, the development of glucose fermentation, the origin of photosynthesis, the origin of mitochondria in the cells, the formation of the centriole/kinetosome/undulipodia complex necessary to eukaryotic reproduction and nerve cells, the development of the eye, the development of the inner skeleton, the development of chordates, and the evolution of *Homo sapiens* in the chordate lineage. Each of these steps, they have calculated, is so improbable that before it could have occurred by chance alone, the sun would have ceased to be a main sequence star and would have incinerated the earth. Consequently, the odds for the evolution of the human genome are on the order of one chance out of 4 to the power of 360 times 110,000, a number which is incomprehensibly low.[18] Thus Barrow and Tipler tellingly remark that "there has developed a general consensus among evolutionists that the evolution of intelligent life . . . is so improbable that is unlikely to have occurred on any other planet in the entire visible universe."[19] Remarkably, then, the fossil record and genetic data provide hard evidence

16. Wise, "Origin," 227; MacFadden, *Fossil Horses*, 86–87.

17. Bridgham, Carroll, and Thornton, "Evolution of Hormone-Receptor Complexity," 97–101.

18. Barrow and Tipler, *Anthropic*, 561–65.

19. Barrow and Tipler, *Anthropic*, 133.

that many biological events occurred whose probability is virtually zero and thus could not have transpired in a naturalistic world. In other words, the evidence for macroevolution is evidence that an array of miracles transpired and thus evidence for the existence of God. But what kind of God? Can any divine attributes be recovered from God's creation of a world where biological life emerges through macroevolution?

Macroevolution as Evidence for a God with Middle Knowledge

To answer the aforementioned questions, we should note two features of macroevolution, namely, its teleological randomness and its nomic randomness. Teleological randomness means that macroevolution is comprised of events which are not determined by any future state, aim, or goal. Thus whether or not an absolutely essential variation occurs in an organism is completely independent of the needs, desires, or prospects of that organism. Nomic randomness stems from the governance of every macroevolutionary process by laws that are purely and ultimately stochastic, such that, in the words of Del Ratzsch, "every relevant process is driven fundamentally by utterly random, chance events."[20] Combining these two types of randomness, macroevolutionary events are random not merely in the sense that they occur irrespective of the good or harm of the respective organisms on which they operate but also in the sense that they are sparked by indeterminate and spontaneous quantum phenomena. We have already indicated that many life-permitting clusters of such events, including trans-group mutations, simultaneous unrelated mutations, and Barrow and Tipler's ten steps necessary to human evolution (individually and collectively), are exceptionally improbable, such that it is highly likely that, given teleological and nomic randomness, life-prohibiting clusters of events would materialize. Thus, if God chose to create simply any universe where a teleologically and nomically random evolutionary process would take place,[21] it is vastly more probable that life-prohibiting clusters of events rather than these life-permitting clusters of events would naturally ensue. The only way God could have created a universe where these life-permitting clusters of events would naturally ensue is for God to know the following five categories of counterfactuals:

20. Ratzsch, "Design, Chance and Theistic Evolution," 303.

21. This itself is no small feat but would require the fine-tuning of the initial conditions of the universe, a fact which forms the centerpiece of the fine-tuning argument for God's existence; for the details of this argument see Craig, *Reasonable Faith*, 157–72.

1. What spontaneous quantum phenomenon would indeterminately occur under any possible set of circumstances

2. For each quantum phenomenon, what macroevolutionary event (e.g., genetic mutation), if any, that phenomenon would cause

3. How each macroevolutionary event would affect the organism on which it operates

4. How each macroevolutionary event would randomly cluster with other quantumly generated macroevolutionary events

5. How each cluster of macroevolutionary events would affect the organism(s) on which it operates.

Through this knowledge, God would discern precisely what initial quantum phenomenon would, against all the odds, randomly inaugurate an extraordinarily lengthy chain of further random events producing life in all its complexity and culminating in the biological evolution of humans. By directly creating this initial quantum phenomenon, God would indirectly accomplish the desired ends of fashioning the various kinds of organisms up to and including human beings, incorporating the foreknown results of utterly random processes. This accomplishment would be deliberate and intentional and yet entail no supernatural intervention at any point throughout the evolutionary chain.

That such a chain exists for God to know is evident from two facts. First, this chain bears a probability which, though exceedingly remote, is nonzero; by definition, anything with a nonzero probability is physically possible. Notice that this is not to say that the chain could have taken place naturalistically, for on naturalism the initial quantum phenomenon would be randomly selected as well. If the initial quantum phenomenon were randomly selected, then it is certain, practically speaking, that any chain of events triggered by that phenomenon would be life-prohibiting rather than life-permitting. For the odds against its being life-prohibiting is greater than all the seconds (10^{18}) in the universe's history and even than all the subatomic particles (10^{80}) in the universe. To modify an analogy from William Lane Craig, suppose there was a lottery containing $4^{360(110,000)}$ black balls (one followed by over twenty three million zeroes black balls) and one white ball. Each black ball represents an initial quantum event that would not inaugurate a chain giving rise to hominid evolution, and the white ball represents the lone quantum event that would inaugurate a chain giving rise to hominid evolution. There is no doubt that, if a ball was randomly drawn, it would be black rather than white. The only way the white ball could be drawn is if the lottery was rigged such that the ball was chosen deliberately. Hence apart from the existence of a chooser who could tell the difference between a black and white ball, namely, a life-prohibiting and a life-permitting quantum event, hominid evolution could not have occurred. As for the second reason the chain giving rise to hominid evolution exists for God to know, we have seen that this chain actually unfolded in space and time, as shown by the fossil and genetic evidence. Each link in the chain ultimately tracks back to the initial quantum phenomenon. Hence the chain's pre-creation possibility is ensured by its post-creation actuality.

Let us step back and assess the significance of what God's knowledge of this chain would entail. Using our lottery analogy, it would entail that God could discern the difference between a black and white ball. Since no ball is intrinsically black or white but is only so because of its setting in motion a chain of indeterministically linked events either preventing or enabling the generation of hominids, God would need to know the outcomes of a plethora of smaller (yet extremely large) possible lotteries represented by counterfactual categories 1 and 4, namely, counterfactuals of quantum phenomena and counterfactuals of random clustering. Such counterfactuals are utterly stochastic, i.e., sporadic and unconstrained by any direct cause. It just is the case that, for any given set of possible circumstances C (where C includes the entire history of the world up to the relevant moment), in C a spontaneous quantum phenomenon Q would transpire and/or a group of macroevolutionary events G would cluster, and God would know all such truths. God would also need to know the biological effects of quantum phenomena and groups of macroevolutionary events on organisms, information expressed in counterfactual categories 2, 3, and 5. Only by combining these categories of knowledge could God discern which initial quantum phenomenon would give rise to a lengthy series comprised of further quantum events, groups of macroevolutionary events, and organismic changes leading to the biological evolution of humanity and so which proverbial ball out of the countless array of options is white. Thus in picking the white ball, God weakly actualizes the physical evolution of human beings through a chain essentially incorporating teleologically and nomically random events.

Since macroevolution entails that the God who exists must know counterfactuals involving teleologically and nomically random events (categories 1 and 4) and counterfactuals of discrimination as to how such random events would affect organisms (categories 2, 3, and 5), it is apparent that God has knowledge of two types of counterfactuals, those he would just "have to know" and those he could "figure out," respectively. To put it another way, God has knowledge of both counterfactuals involving causally undetermined possible events and counterfactuals involving causally determined possible events. Since causally undetermined possible events plus causally determined possible events logically exhaust all possible events, macroevolution therefore demands that God has counterfactual knowledge of all possible events, which is to say that God possesses middle knowledge. Thus anyone who accepts macroevolution and looks carefully into its implications possesses tangible disproof of the grounding objection to middle knowledge. For the objection's complaint that the lack of sufficient epistemic grounding of counterfactuals precludes God from knowing them becomes null and void in light of scientific evidence for a phenomenon (macroevolution) which could only occur if God knows counterfactuals. While the philosophically informed proponent of macroevolution may not understand how God can know counterfactuals, this lack of understanding is trumped for her/him by the evidence that God does, in fact, know them.

Let us drive these points home by showing the infeasibility of macroevolution on any other model of divine omniscience. If God possessed simple foreknowledge (knowledge of only what will actually happen in the future), then God had no way of knowing which of the virtually uncountably many possible initial quantum phenomena would ultimately issue in hominid evolution. Hence God would have no means of choosing which possible initial quantum phenomenon to actualize and would simply have to guess, knowing only after making the choice whether or not it will give rise to life. But since there is no way to even make an educated guess regarding a life-permitting initial quantum phenomenon, as its life-permittingness depends on myriad stochastic events free from any causal restraint, the odds are overwhelming (recall the lottery analogy) that God would choose a phenomenon prohibitive of hominid evolution. The situation is even worse on open theism (where God lacks foreknowledge of contingent future events and only has foreknowledge of non-contingent future events), since God, after creating the initial quantum phenomenon, still does not know whether or not he made a life-permitting choice and must then wait through potentially billions of years before seeing that his choice failed. The only way, it seems to me, that one could subscribe to either simple foreknowledge or open theism and still accept macroevolution is to posit God's creation of a virtually uncountable number of parallel universes (one followed by over twenty three million zeroes many universes), each of whose histories began with a different initial quantum phenomenon. Only one of these universes emanates in hominid evolution, and our universe just happens to be it. Such a proposition seems enormously *ad hoc* and is therefore one which few theologians of any stripe would want to make. Even fewer evangelical theologians would want to suggest parallel universes, as God's creation of more than one universe, although not explicitly ruled out by Genesis 1, is certainly rendered unlikely by the creation narrative (on any genre) and by the remainder of the biblical revelation. Noting that a valid argument from silence is one where, if the proposed entity did exist, one would expect to find evidence of its existence but finds none, the fact that scriptural depictions of the final redemption of all things (in, for example, Isaiah, the Olivet Discourse, Paul, and Revelation) contain no mention of other universes which God would also want to redeem constitutes a very powerful argument against the existence of parallel universes. Typically, the parallel universe suggestion represents a last-ditch effort of atheists to avoid the theistic implications of the astronomically low probability of a life-permitting universe.[22] In sum, the probability that our universe would preclude biological evolution on simple foreknowledge or divine openness is equal to the probability that God possesses middle knowledge, a probability which approaches one (i.e., certainty).

Strict Calvinism (by which I mean the theology expressed in Calvin's *Institutes of the Christian Religion*) can make no sense of the indeterministic, stochastic events which characterize macroevolutionary theory.[23] It seems that a strict Calvinist could at most believe in the "progressive creation" or "guided evolution" of Michael Behe and Michael Denton, where God intervenes to directly cause each trans-group and unrelated mutation event which has an astronomically low probability. Although the fossil and genetic evidence would look identical on this view to the evidence on macroevolution, for our purposes we may simply point out that progressive creation/guided evolution is quite different from the macroevolution of mainstream biology. It is not our intention here to argue against progressive creation/guided evolution, except to ask whether its theological motive is sound. For it seems that a God who is sovereign over even contingent stochastic events is superior to a God whose sovereignty seems threatened by such events and therefore must step in to control them, which latter rationale ultimately causes a thinker to choose progressive creation/guided evolution over macroevolution. (As I have contended elsewhere, it seems that the Calvinist, per the dictum *reformata et semper reformanda*, should add middle knowledge to her/his theological arsenal and so ensure that her/his conception

---

22. Even if successful, the suggestion ultimately does nothing to disprove God's existence, who is still required as the cause of the mechanism for generating these parallel universes (normally identified as the initial quantum vacuum), since any such mechanism is shown by the Borde-Guth-Vilenkin Theorem to have had a beginning. Per the *kalam* cosmological argument, then, the mechanism which formed the multiverse needs a transcendent cause. For discussion see Borde, Guth, and Vilenkin, "Inflation Is Not Past-Eternal," 1–4.

23. MacGregor, *Molinist-Anabaptist Systematic Theology*, 17–18.

of God is that of the greatest conceivable being.[24] This is precisely what has been done by Alvin Plantinga and Del Ratzsch, two prominent Reformed thinkers who are Molinists.) However, our discussion underscores the point that the only model of divine omniscience compatible with the findings of mainstream biology is Molinism.

Concluding Reflections

Far from constituting a threat to theism, the macroevolutionary account of life's origins and development actually demonstrates the existence of God and the supremacy of God's knowledge. Due to the astronomically low probabilities of countless trans-group and simultaneous unrelated mutations, which I believe the scientific evidence demonstrates to have occurred, the God who created the universe must be endowed with middle knowledge. Such knowledge of what would happen in every possible biological scenario, especially those which are causally unconstrained, is the only means whereby God could choose to create a world where this dizzying and interdependent array of biological improbabilities would naturally materialize to generate life in all its complexity. In other words, the evolutionary schema, with its extraordinarily lengthy chain of remote probabilities, could only unfold in time-space if the God who exists knew what would contingently happen in every possible set of circumstances and then proceeded to create an initial quantum phenomenon which naturally issued in precisely those innumerable contingencies necessary for the evolution of intelligent life. Accordingly, each new genetic breakthrough and fossil discovery confirmatory of macroevolution in fact constitutes physical evidence for the existence of a God with middle knowledge, since the probability that these genetic and fossil findings would even exist are virtually zero and yet, obviously given our possession of them, do exist!

The only objection against God's existence that might be raised at this juncture from macroevolution is the problem of animal suffering. (This objection equally pertains to all forms of old-earth creationism.) However, this problem was recently diffused by Michael Murray in his *Nature Red in Tooth and Claw*, which shows that animals do not experience pain in the same way as humans do. Here Murray distinguishes three levels in an ascending pain hierarchy: (1) avoidance behavior resulting from harmful stimuli; (2) mental states of pain; (3) the awareness that one is oneself in pain. Creatures lower than vertebrates (i.e., spiders, insects, worms) experience level 1, as such creatures are not sentient beings at all with any sort of subjective,

---

24. Ibid., 84–85.

interior life. Although animals like dogs, cats, horses, zebras, and giraffes experience level 2 and therefore thrash about and scream when in pain, the neurological evidence remarkably proves that they do not experience level 3, the awareness that they are in pain. Brain studies show that there are two independent neural pathways associated with the experience of pain. One pathway is involved in producing states of pain (level 2), while the second pathway is associated with being aware that one is oneself in a level 2 state. This second neural pathway is a very late evolutionary development which only emerges in the humanoid primates.[25] (I would here build off the thesis of Richard Swinburne by postulating that level 3 also depends on the possession of the soul or self, without which self-awareness of anything is impossible.[26] If one denies that animals possess souls or selves, then a theological confirmation of our neurological argument can be marshaled.) So while animals have experienced pain states throughout the evolutionary process, they were not aware of being in pain and so did not suffer as humans would when they are in pain.

To illustrate by means of analogy, let us consider the phenomenon of blind sight in human experience. The experience of sight is also associated with two independent neural pathways in the brain. One pathway conveys visual stimuli about the external objects presented to the viewer, while the other pathway is associated with self-awareness of the visual states. Persons with blind sight have a normally functioning first pathway but a severely impaired second pathway. While these persons do "see" in the sense that they register visual stimuli conveyed by the first pathway (if one throws a ball to such a person, s/he will instinctively catch it), they aren't aware that they see anything and so lack any phenomenological experience of sight.[27] In precisely the same way, no creature was ever self-aware of being in pain throughout the virtual entirety of the long history of evolutionary development.

Let me close by citing an irony surrounding the special creationist's handling of mathematical and scientific data. While the special creationists we have engaged in this piece employ legitimate data, they draw philosophically illegitimate conclusions therefrom through the fallacy of opposing one field of knowledge to another field of knowledge. Thus special creationists often correctly point out the extraordinarily low probability that evolution should occur given naturalism but then invalidly appeal to this fact as an excuse for bypassing the evidence from genetics and biology that it did

25. Murray, *Nature*, 55–59.

26. Swinburne, *Evolution*, 203–61.

27. Murray, *Nature*, 53–54.

occur. This is precisely the same fallacy made by the atheist in rejecting, for instance, the resurrection of Jesus: pointing out the extraordinarily low probability on naturalism that a dead man could return to life, the atheist invalidly appeals to this fact as an excuse for ignoring the historical evidence that the resurrection occurred. Paradoxically, both the special creationist (unexpectedly) and the atheist (expectedly) irrationally suppose, by showing that something could not happen on a naturalistic worldview, that they have demonstrated its impossibility on a theistic worldview.[28] As we have here exhibited, the proper stratagem is to consider the evidence that the naturalistically impossible did happen and, if the evidence for its occurrence is persuasive, to mine that event for its theistic implications.

Bibliography

Arminius, James. *The Works of James Arminius*. 3 vols. Translated by James Nichols and W. R. Bagnall. Auburn, NY: Derby and Miller, 1853.

Augustine. *De Genesi ad litteram*. 2 vols. Translated by John Hammond Taylor. New York: Newman, 1982.

Barrow, John D., and Frank J. Tipler. *The Anthropic Cosmological Principle*. Oxford: Clarendon, 1986.

Behe, Michael. *Darwin's Black Box: The Biochemical Challenge to Evolution*. New York: Free, 1996.

Bejder, Lars, and Brian K. Hall. "Limbs in Whales and Limblessness in Other Vertebrates: Mechanisms of Evolutionary and Developmental Transformation and Loss." *Evolution and Development* 4.6 (2002) 445–58.

Blocher, Henri. *In the Beginning: The Opening Chapters of Genesis*. Downers Grove, IL: InterVarsity, 1984.

Bridgham, Jamie T., Sean M. Carroll, and Joseph W. Thornton. "Evolution of Hormone-Receptor Complexity by Molecular Exploitation." *Science* 312 (2006) 97–101.

Calvin, John. *Institutes of the Christian Religion*. 2 vols. Edited by John T. McNeill and translated by Ford Lewis Battles. Philadelphia: Westminster, 1960.

Craig, William Lane. *Reasonable Faith: Christian Truth and Apologetics*. 3rd ed. Wheaton, IL: Crossway, 2008.

Dawkins, Richard. *The God Delusion*. New York: Houghton Mifflin, 2006.

Dembski, William A. *The End of Christianity: Finding a Good God in an Evil World*. Nashville: Broadman and Holman, 2009.

———. "Reviving the Argument from Design: Detecting Design through Small Probabilities." *Proceedings of the Biennial Conference of the Association of Christians in the Mathematical Sciences* 8 (1991) 101–45.

Denton, Michael. *Evolution: A Theory in Crisis*. Bethesda, MD: Adler and Adler, 1985.

Geisler, Norman L., ed. *Inerrancy*. Grand Rapids: Zondervan, 1980.

Gould, Stephen Jay. *The Panda's Thumb: More Reflections on Natural History*. New York: Norton, 1980.

---

28. MacGregor, *Molinist-Anabaptist Systematic Theology*, 184.

Kidner, Derek. *Genesis*. Tyndale Old Testament Commentary. Downers Grove, IL: InterVarsity, 1967.

Kline, Meredith G. "Because It Had Not Rained." *Westminster Theological Journal* 20 (1958) 146–57.

———. "Space and Time in the Genesis Cosmogony." *Perspectives on Science and the Christian Faith* 48 (1996) 2–15.

Luther, Martin. *Genesis 1–5*. *Luther's Works, American Edition*, Vol. 1. Edited by Jaroslav Pelikan and translated by George V. Schick. St. Louis, MO: Concordia, 1958.

MacFadden, Bruce J. *Fossil Horses: Systematics, Paleobiology, and Evolution of the Family Equidae*. Cambridge: Cambridge University Press, 1992.

MacGregor, Kirk R. *A Molinist-Anabaptist Systematic Theology*. Lanham, MD: University Press of America, 2007.

Morris, Henry M. *The Scientific Case for Creation*. San Diego: Creation-Life, 1977.

Murray, Michael. *Nature Red in Tooth and Claw: Theism and the Problem of Animal Suffering*. Oxford: Oxford University Press, 2008.

Pelikan, Jaroslav. *The Emergence of the Catholic Tradition (100–600)*. The Christian Tradition: A History of the Development of Doctrine, Vol. 1. Chicago: University of Chicago Press, 1971.

Pigliucci, Massimo. *Tales of the Rational: Skeptical Essays about Nature and Science*. Atlanta: Freethought, 2000.

Ratzsch, Del. "Design, Chance and Theistic Evolution." In *Mere Creation*, edited by William A. Dembski, 289–312. Downers Grove, IL: InterVarsity, 1998.

Swinburne, Richard. *The Evolution of the Soul*. Rev ed. Oxford: Clarendon, 1997.

Van Till, Howard J. "The Fully Gifted Creation." In *Three Views on Creation and Evolution*, edited by J. P. Moreland and John Mark Reynolds, 159–218. Grand Rapids: Zondervan, 1999.

Waltke, Bruce. "The Literary Genre of Genesis, Chapter One." *Crux* 27 (1991) 2–10.

Walton, John H. *The Lost World of Genesis One: Ancient Cosmology and the Origins Debate*. Downers Grove, IL: IVP Academic, 2009.

Wenham, Gordon J. *Genesis 1–15*. 2 vols. Word Biblical Commentary. Waco, TX: Word, 1987.

Wise, Kurt P. "The Origin of Life's Major Groups." In *The Creation Hypothesis*, edited by J. P. Moreland, 211–34. Downers Grove, IL: InterVarsity, 1994.

Zwingli, Huldrych. *Of the Clarity and Certainty or Power of the Word of God*. In *Zwingli and Bullinger*, translated by G. W. Bromiley, 59–95. Philadelphia: Westminster, 1953.

3

The Evolution of Molinism

GREG WELTY

Introduction

IN LIGHT OF THE preceding two chapters, I'm tempted to call my response "The Evolution of Molinism." Such a title would be intended both seriously and ironically. On the *serious* side, evolution involves the adaptation of pre-existing structures to new and fruitful contexts. Likewise, Molinists are wise to investigate whether the pre-existing theory of middle knowledge, potentially so illuminating in matters of providence and freedom, might fruitfully be applied and adapted to non-traditional contexts. In this our authors follow in the footsteps of Thomas Flint, who at the end of *Divine Providence: The Molinist Account* seeks to deploy middle knowledge as a paradigm that illuminates such disparate issues as papal infallibility, prophecy, unanswered prayers, and so forth. Likewise, MacGregor and Laing evolve Molinism as a means to vindicate theological claims in the realm of biology. And why not? Truth is truth, and is of potential relevance to any area of inquiry.

And yet there is an *ironic* sense to my title, "The Evolution of Molinism." Because at the end of the day I think our authors have evolved Molinism into a very different beast, one that would not be recognized by Molina himself. Notice that Flint's applications of Molinism—to papal infallibility, prophecy, unanswered prayers, past-directed prayers—all involve divine providence over *human free will*. Clearly God cannot *cause* libertarian free will choices, but with the help of middle knowledge about them, he can plan for very precise outcomes and have infallible foreknowledge of these free acts. Unfortunately, it at least *looks* like God can easily and directly cause genetic mutations, since these are not agent-caused choices but just physical changes in physical strands of DNA in a cell's genome. The analogy to libertarian free will (LFW) strikes me as specious, and so does the attempt to place counterfactuals of genetic mutation into some genuinely middle realm. Even as Bruce Ware's "compatibilistic Molinism" strikes me as a contradiction in terms, because on that view middle knowledge is no longer middle, the same observation applies here. Or so I will argue.

Summary of MacGregor and Laing Chapters

MacGregor: macroevolution of complex life is impossible apart from a God with middle knowledge

1. The scientific evidence shows, by way of inference to the best explanation, that macroevolution is true.

2. Macroevolution of complex life proceeds by way of genetic mutations.

3. Genetic mutations are caused by quantum phenomena.

4. Quantum phenomena are random, stochastic processes.

5. Therefore, to bring about (2), God must have requisite knowledge of (4).

6. This knowledge is middle knowledge of which quantum events would occur in which circumstances, and of which genetic mutation that quantum event would cause.

7. Aspects of (2) are so improbable that they couldn't have come about naturalistically.

8. Rather, God had to guide the process via his middle knowledge.

9. Thus, macroevolution proves that God exists, and that Molinism is true.

10. As a bonus, we have an indirect answer to the grounding objection to Molinism: because macroevolution is true, and because it could only have been brought about by Molinistic providence, it follows that God *has* knowledge of ungrounded counterfactuals, even if we don't know *how*.

Laing: middle knowledge provides a rebutting defeater for the claim that vestigial organs are logically inconsistent with an omniscient and omnipotent intelligent designer

1. An intelligent designer would create a world where creatures *adapt to their environment by way of evolution*, rather than a world where creatures do not adapt by way of evolution.

2. An intelligent designer would bring about creatures by way of *random* genetic mutation rather than "directed genetic mutations."

3. For all we know, "the intelligent designer could not have developed creatures with the complexity they have without the flaws they have."

   a. This is because for all we know, the "counterfactuals of genetic mutation" are such that the beneficial mutations required for complex biological creatures are counterfactually dependent on the existence of these flaws.

   b. It is possible that random genetic mutation *M* would occur just in case biologically flawed situation *S* occurs. Given these counterfactuals, not even an omnipotent God could get *M* without *S*.

4. Therefore, the reality of an omniscient and omnipotent "intelligent designer" is *logically consistent* with the reality of biological flaws (such as vestigial organs).

5. Thus, by adapting Plantinga's "free-will defense" into a "biological flaw defense," the resources of Molinism are relevant in rebutting a key anti-ID argument.

Points of Assessment Common to the MacGregor and Laing Chapters

The "counterfactuals of genetic mutation" are not relevantly analogous to counterfactuals of libertarian free will

There is an obvious and relevant difference between agent-caused acts of libertarian free will (the traditional object of middle knowledge) and genetic mutations (the additional object of middle knowledge on "evolved Molinism"). For our authors to evolve Molinism in this new direction, the middle knowledge posited needs to be genuinely middle, involving prevolitional contingent truths over which God has no control. Now, on traditional Molinism, *facts about how libertarian agents would choose* are quite plausibly seen as facts over which God has no control, since God can't cause such acts. But why would *facts about physical mutations* be facts over which God has no control? Are not any laws of nature, probabilistic or otherwise, up to God? After all, quite unlike libertarian choices, genetic mutations are just physical changes to a physical DNA strand in a cell's genome. Why confuse these two very different things?

Laing rightly notes that *free will defenders* like Plantinga "will argue that true freedom means that there is no coercion, which means that truly free actions cannot be caused from without." But is it really the case that, analogous to this, *genetic mutations* "cannot be caused from without"? That seems highly doubtful. In contemporary bioengineering, human bioengineers can *create* the equivalent of mutations through gene resequencing in molecular cloning to create recombinant DNA. If humans can directly cause genetic mutations, why can't God do this?

In defending against the grounding objection, Laing says that "there is no causal relationship between the antecedent and the consequent in the counterfactuals [of genetic mutation]. Rather, their relationship is merely explanatory." (I do not know how to reconcile this with some of MacGregor's counterfactuals [2, 3, 5], which *do* assert such a causal relationship.) But which geneticists say that genetic mutations lack causes, or that there is no causal relationship between a mutation and the situation in which it arises? Is gene resequencing by human bioengineers just an illusion? It certainly *looks* as if human bioengineers can change any gene sequence, causing point mutations by swapping out single nucleotides. The view that all mutations lack causes seems *straightforwardly falsifiable* by scientific investigation, while the view that all libertarian choices lack causes *is not and could not be falsified* by any scientific investigation.

And that's why there's no plausible parallel between counterfactuals of genetic mutation and counterfactuals of LFW. God can't cause libertarian choices. Not so for mutations, which even human beings can cause. Surely God has natural knowledge of which effects he can directly cause. Perhaps, though, MacGregor and Laing would point out that even as libertarian choices are *undetermined*, so genetic mutations are *random*. Isn't this enough for a relevant similarity, despite the differences I've noted? Aren't the counterfactuals they're talking about counterfactuals about *random* genetic mutation? Let's investigate this.

No matter how we define "random," random mutations don't need to be weakly actualized

Whether an event's being "random" must exclude direct, intentional, divine causation depends on how we understand "random." In my view, no plausible definition of "random" requires Molinism to account for the *actual* truth of counterfactuals of genetic mutation (MacGregor's claim), or for their *possible* truth (Laing's claim). When geneticists and evolutionary biologists say that a mutation is "random," is the claim that the mutation occurs:

1. Independently of its *utility* for the organism?

2. Independently of an agent's *purposes*?

3. Without a sufficient *physical* cause?

4. Without *any* cause (physical or nonphysical)?

These aren't equivalent concepts, so what we say here matters. In my view God can easily and directly cause random mutations in senses (1) and (3) (which are the only senses confirmed in the physical sciences), and there is no reason to think (and good reason for theists *not* to think) that there are or must be any "random" mutations in senses (2) and (4).

"Random" in sense (1) simply means there is "no correlation between the mutation and its utility for the organism."[1] This seems to be the view of "random" held by Ernst Mayr and Elliott Sober. On Mayr's view, there is "no correlation between the production of new genotypes and the adaptational needs of an organism in a given environment."[2] On Sober's view, "there is no *physical* mechanism (either inside organisms or outside of them) that detects which mutations would be beneficial and causes those mutations to occur."[3] Why would randomness in this sense exclude intentional and direct divine causation? God might bring about the mutation, but not because it has utility *for that organism*. Rather, he brings it about for *other* purposes, perhaps long-range ones. Clearly, God could bring about such a mutation directly, even if it were "random" in this sense.

"Random" in sense (2) simply means "*unguided by a personal agent.*" This seems to be the view of "random" held by Stephen J. Gould and George Gaylord Simpson (and assumed by Richard Dawkins and Daniel Dennett). A "random" process is just a "purposeless" process. Of course, God *couldn't* cause mutations in this sense. But such a sense of "random" isn't available to the middle knowledge advocate of the present argument anyway, because he is talking about a process that *is* guided by a personal agent. On the view of our authors, *no* mutation occurs independently of God's (the Supreme Agent's) purposes; he weakly actualizes them to get the biological result he wants. As Laing puts it, God "makes use of random genetic mutation to guide evolutionary processes to the end He desires." This is clearly a *directed* process of (weakly) actualizing mutations, not an undirected process unguided by a personal agent. (Note well: senses (1) and (2) are clearly *different* senses of "random." But MacGregor's definition of "teleological

---

1. Plantinga, *Conflict*, 11.

2. Mayr, *Towards a New Philosophy*, 98.

3. Sober, "Evolution without Naturalism," 192.

randomness" for some reason combines them. His definition of "nomic randomness" involves either sense (3) or (4), which I will now discuss.)

"Random" in sense (3) says, perhaps in conformity with some probabilistic laws about quantum phenomena, that *no mutation has a sufficient physical cause*. It's unclear to me whether all mutations do lack a sufficient cause. It is also unclear whether all mutations are brought about by quantum events. I have been unable to verify these claims. But let's concede both of them and ask: why should *that* preclude God's intentional and direct causation of the mutation? After all, God is a *nonphysical* cause, and a mutation's having a nonphysical cause is entirely compatible with its having no sufficient physical cause.

As Thomas Flint himself puts it in *Divine Providence*, "Many theists are inclined to say that natural laws, when correctly understood, contain an implicit 'boundary condition' to the effect that the law prescribes what will occur *absent interference by a supernatural being*."[4] Alvin Plantinga uses this point to great effect in chapter four of his recent book, *Where the Conflict Really Lies* (2011). He argues for the compatibility of quantum mechanics and God's direct, special, and causal action in the world, by highlighting the fact that laws of nature only apply to closed and physical systems. They do not preclude nonphysical causes. So God can easily nonphysically cause events which lack a sufficient physical cause.

Finally, *"random" in sense (4)* means that the mutation is *without any cause, whether physical or nonphysical*. Of course, God *couldn't* cause mutations in this sense either. *No one* can cause an uncaused event. But there is simply no reason whatsoever (certainly no scientific reason) to think that mutations come about without any cause whatsoever. That would turn genetics into a theological theory (no nonphysical causes allowed!). Would it not be bizarre to rebut a scientist's claim that vestigial organs undermine the concept of an intelligent designer, by positing that "for all we know" all mutations are and must be uncaused in any way?

To those who persist in thinking "random" must mean "without any cause whatsoever," surely this would be a *contingent* thesis about mutations. Unlike acts of libertarian choice, it isn't intrinsic to the nature of mutations that they occur without a cause. They are simply physical changes to a physical genome. And so Molinism isn't *required* for successful macroevolution, nor is it required to preclude biological flaws. As long as it is open to God to directly cause these physical changes (and why not?), a Molinism evolved for this context seems gratuitous.

4. Flint, *Divine Providence*, 147–48.

I conclude that the only senses of "random" to which a theist can appeal (senses 1 and 3) are senses which do not preclude God's direct and intentional causation of the "random" mutation. Such strong actualization doesn't require middle knowledge (and so MacGregor's thesis isn't needed). And with such meticulous control over mutations, what need for an indirect permission of biological flaws? (And so Laing's thesis isn't needed.) Consider the free-will defense: if God could just *directly cause* free choices, what need for the permission of evil?

In short, even if genetic mutations are "random," middle knowledge proponents should reject the idea that Molinist providence is even possibly needed for their occurrence. Here I follow Alvin Plantinga: "You might wonder whether random genetic mutations could be caused by God: if these mutations are random, aren't they just a matter of chance? But randomness, as construed by contemporary biologists, doesn't have this implication."[5] I agree.

Herein we have an answer to Laing's claim that "the basis for the truth of propositions regarding when a random event will or will not occur cannot be found in God's will, for the random nature of the events preclude a deterministic cause behind their occurrence, even the will of God." There is simply no reason to think this. As argued above, God can cause random mutations in sense (1) or (3). The only reason to think that mutations are "random" at all is because of scientific theory, and no well-confirmed scientific theory requires that God *not* cause mutations. At best, such theories say there is no sufficient *physical* cause behind their occurrence, not that there is no cause.

The "greatest conceivable being," or the maximally lucky designer?

MacGregor is confident that the middle knowledge required for macroevolution "is the most robust type of omniscience"; it ensures that our "conception of God is that of the greatest conceivable being." Likewise, Laing stresses that "the fact that God is constrained by the counterfactuals of creaturely freedom and the counterfactuals of genetic mutation detracts nothing from His infinity, conceived either in terms of knowledge (omniscience) or in terms of power (omnipotence)."

I respectfully disagree. This seems to be a huge constraint, and one that does chip away at our conception of God as the greatest conceivable being. If the conditions for "intelligence" (on the part of the designer) and

5. Plantinga, *Conflict*, 11.

for "beauty" or "relationality" (on the part of any environment created by him) *require* God to create (if he creates at all) by way of random mutation in a changing environment, but God can only bring about his desired results by relying upon "virtually infinite" numbers of "counterfactuals of genetic mutation" (counterfactuals over which he has no control), then *all* of God's creative options in biology are *constrained by luck*. What if God wants to bring about a particular mutation in the context of other mutations, but the relevant counterfactual is false? He's out of luck.

Assume the cogency of MacGregor's argument. What *are* the chances that just that set of counterfactuals, that would enable an evolutionary process that has a "1 out of 10 with 23 million zeroes after it" chance of happening, would be true instead of false? We don't even have to calculate the odds here. The fact that the outcome God needs is *independent* of God's nature, *independent* of God's will, and even *independent* of human choices, is pretty disturbing. If "chance" means "uncaused," then the truth-values of the counterfactuals are determined by chance. So God has good reason to be very, very, very thankful that innumerable counterfactuals went his way, and allowed his biological purposes to come to pass. Should we worship God *and* the counterfactuals that allowed God's creative purposes to come to pass? How is this a view that enhances God's perfection?

What if the brute facts were such that God couldn't weakly actualize the right quantum phenomena, even if he wanted to? Here we see that Mac-Gregor's bringing in *divine agency* doesn't solve the problem of how to account for "enormously improbable" events, *for divine agency cannot ground the truths that God needs to be true to get the macroevolutionary job done.* On his view, the prospects for efficacious divine providence supervene on the actual brute facts, independently of God's wishes or power. In creation, he's in for the roller coaster ride of his life.

In fact, combining the conclusions of the two papers seems to exacerbate the problem, because they place two kinds of constraint on the counterfactuals. To satisfy MacGregor's fine-tuning argument for Molinism from the evidence for macroevolution, *the counterfactuals of genetic mutation had to have just those values that would permit God to bring about complex life.* If God needs a very improbable mutation along the road to life, but the relevant counterfactual is false, he's out of luck. The cosmic lottery didn't go his way. But to satisfy Laing's defense of the intelligent designer in the face of vestigial organs, *the counterfactuals of genetic mutation also had to have just those values that would preclude flawless organisms.* (The whole point is that God's knowledge and power are not impugned in the face of biological flaws, because the counterfactuals were such that God *couldn't* avoid such flaws.)

The composite picture here is extraordinary. What happens if the coun-terfactuals permit complex life, but don't require biological flaws as a condi-tion for that life? *Laing's "biological flaw defense" is blocked.* What happens if the counterfactuals require biological flaws, but don't permit complex life? *MacGregor's macroevolutionary proof of Molinism is blocked.* Would there be anything God could do about this outcome? No, and not even free agents would be to blame. Perhaps God's choice to actualize circumstances is a fine-tuned choice that speaks of intelligent agency. But *who* fine-tunes these innumerable CFs, so that they both (i) enable God to accomplish the extraordinarily improbable feat of evolving complex life, but yet (ii) require God to permit biological flaws? *Not God!* One might wonder: if this *fine-tuning of the counterfactuals* is independent of God and needs no appeal to God, why can't the *fine-tuning of life* be independent of God and need no appeal to God? In the end, don't these Molinist arguments shift the extraor-dinarily improbable fine-tuning from God to the counterfactuals?

Further Points in Response to the MacGregor Chapter

Macroevolution + Calvinism has just as much explanatory power as macroevolution + Molinism

MacGregor says that "Strict Calvinism . . . can make no sense of the indeter-ministic, stochastic events which characterize macroevolutionary theory." But Calvinists can *easily* make sense of physically indeterministic events: these events have a sufficient nonphysical cause, despite having no sufficient physical cause. If God can nonphysically cause quantum phenomena, and he knows he can do this, he doesn't need middle knowledge to bring about life by way of macroevolution. So even the alleged truth of macroevolution would be no evidence for Molinism over Calvinism.

MacGregor says that "the Calvinist . . . should add middle knowledge to her/his theological arsenal and so ensure that her/his conception of God is that of the greatest conceivable being." But he earlier defines "middle knowledge" as "counterfactual knowledge of all possible events," and Cal-vinists have always affirmed this of God. It's just that they, along with most of the medievals, reduce this knowledge to either natural or free knowledge. As far as I can tell, on the Calvinist view there are no counterfactual truths that God fails to know. So there is little reason for Calvinists to think God is anything less than "the greatest conceivable being."

Progressive creation has just as much explanatory power as macroevolution

MacGregor concedes that on the alternative, progressive creationist view, "God intervenes to directly cause each trans-group and unrelated mutation event which has an astronomically low probability." He further concedes that "the fossil and genetic evidence would look identical on this view [i.e., progressive creationism] to the evidence on macroevolution." But this seems to give away the whole store. If on progressive creation God can in fact "directly cause each . . . mutation event," and if the evidence would look *identical* on either theory, then *why do we have to believe in macroevolution rather than progressive creation?* Surely not because we're deistically inclined to reject divine intervention in favor of a "fully-gifted creation" that unfolds naturalistically from an initial quantum event? Why would such a view be scientifically, philosophically, or theologically preferable? Why would macroevolution + Molinism have more explanatory power than just progressive creationism without Molinism?

MacGregor says that "a God who is sovereign over even contingent stochastic events is superior to a God whose sovereignty seems threatened by such events and therefore must step in to control them, which latter rationale ultimately causes a thinker to choose progressive creation/guided evolution over macroevolution." I'm confused by this point. On progressive creation God *is* "sovereign over even contingent stochastic events." Assume these events are "contingent stochastic events" because they have no sufficient physical cause. Nevertheless, *God* causes them. I hope that's enough for "sovereignty"!

MacGregor says the providential "situation is even worse on open theism." But it's hard to see how. Why couldn't the open God simply *purpose* to create human life by way of billions of years of macroevolution, then *purpose* to nonphysically and directly cause whatever quantum events and/or mutations are required to fulfill that prior purpose, and then on the basis of this twofold divine willing know there will be humans?

Further Points in Response to the Laing Chapter

The arguments that God *must* rely on random,
undirected genetic mutation seem flawed

Call the "biological flaw defender" someone who argues that, for all we know, the counterfactuals of random genetic mutation are such that it was not possible for God to bring about biological creatures by way of random mutation, unless he permitted flaws in those creatures. Even if we concede this, why exactly must God bring about creatures *by way of a process of random mutation*? For if God *could* create biological creatures apart from random mutation, then the counterfactuals of random mutation are irrelevant as constraints on his feasible creative options, even if they were true. So why would a "maximally powerful" or "omnipotent" Creator be confined to *random* mutation as a creational resource? Laing endorses two arguments for why an *intelligent* designer would use *random* genetic mutation to spur evolutionary development, rather than "directed genetic mutation," even if the latter were open to him.

According to *the "intelligence" argument*, Laing says, "it could be argued that the use of random processes to produce an orderly system requires *more* intelligence than it does to use controlled process for the same purpose" (my emphasis). But this isn't convincing. A Molinist view doesn't require any *more* "intelligence" than what would be required on a determinist view. In either case God relies on true counterfactuals he knows, in order to decide how to proceed. In the Molinist case God relies on counterfactuals of *middle* knowledge. In the determinist case God relies on counterfactuals of *natural* knowledge ("If I were to will that such-and-such be a law of nature and then change such-and-such DNA strand, such-and-such mutation would occur"). It's hard to see how one decision-process requires more "intelligence" than the other.

According to *the "because of the Fall" argument*, Laing says that "the random character of mutations could be attributed to the Fall. That is, under a Christian interpretation, one could argue that as a result of the Fall and the emergence of sin into the created order, the cosmos has been characterized by chaos and randomness at the most basic level (e.g., quarks and gluons)." But again, this isn't convincing. Surely whatever "the Fall" amounts to is under God's control. Are we to suppose God *couldn't* curse mankind and the earth *without* introducing "chaos and randomness at the most basic level (e.g., quarks and gluons)"? Are there actually true "counterfactuals of divine cursing," such that God couldn't curse the earth unless he did *this* rather than something that fell short of this? (Beyond this, if "his use of random mutation" is due to the Fall, why can't we cut out the Molinist middleman, and respond to the anti-ID proponent by saying that vestigial organs and other biological flaws are *directly* a result of the Fall? If the Fall has explanatory power for why the curse must involve randomness, certainly it has explanatory power for why the curse must involve biological flaws!)

The non-Molinist, undercutting defeaters supplied by Laing are
sufficient to defuse the anti-ID argument anyway

Laing surveys several undercutting defeaters of the original anti-ID argument, none of which require Molinism. These seem sufficient to address the anti-ID argument. A rebutting defeater would be nice, but is strictly unnecessary. Even as Plantinga criticized Mackie's "quasi-logical rules" for unpacking key terms in the logical problem of evil, Laing criticizes the following assumptions of the anti-ID argument as inadequately argued:

1. "Maximally intelligent design" requires as few flaws as possible.

2. A "maximally powerful designer" requires an ability to actualize creatures with no flaws.

3. "An intelligent designer will [always] design creatures for optimal performance."

4. Any creatures will be "designed with at least a primary purpose in mind."

5. "God must make a perfect Creation and . . . He only had one option (i.e., 'the best')."

6. (Notice that these undercutting defeaters, like Plantinga's, don't require an appeal to Molinism.)

Bibliography

Flint, Thomas P. *Divine Providence: The Molinist Account*. Ithaca, NY: Cornell University Press, 1998.

Mayr, Ernst. *Towards a New Philosophy of Biology: Observations of an Evolutionist*. Cambridge: Harvard University Press, 1988.

Plantinga, Alvin. *Where the Conflict Really Lies: Science, Religion, and Naturalism*. Oxford: Oxford University Press, 2011.

Sober, Elliott. "Evolution without Naturalism." In *Oxford Studies in Philosophy of Religion*, Volume 3, edited by Jonathan L. Kvanvig, 187–211. Oxford: Oxford University Press, 2013.

Part II

Calvinist Concerns
with Molinism

4

Molinist Gunslingers

God and the Authorship of Sin[1]

Greg Welty

Introduction

Calvinism and Molinism on God's authorship of sin

I INTEND TO PRESENT an argument about the Molinism/Calvinism controversy that I have not seen anywhere else. I'm keenly aware of the fact that there may be a very good reason why I have not seen this argument anywhere else! But those of us who are philosophers and theologians have to stick our neck out at times, so that we have a chance to learn from our friends where we may have gone wrong.

Molinists often claim that their view of divine providence is preferable to a classical Calvinist view, because Calvinism makes God the author of sin whereas Molinism does not. For instance, in his recent book *Salvation and Sovereignty: A Molinist Approach* (2010), Ken Keathley argues that Calvinism is subject to a dilemma to which Molinism is not subject, namely, "adhering to a deterministic view of sovereignty without blaming God for the fall of Adam."[2] On Molinism, God "is perfectly free from the sin and evil of this world,"[3] and "God is not the author of sin,"[4] but on Calvinism God is not perfectly free from sin and evil, and he is the author of sin.[5]

---

1. A revised version of this chapter and chapter 6 appears as chapter 2 of *Calvinism and the Problem of Evil*, ed. David E. Alexander and Daniel M. Johnson (Eugene, OR: Wipf and Stock, 2016).

2. Keathley, *Salvation and Sovereignty*, 4.

3. Ibid., 19.

4. Ibid., 25.

5. Ibid., 26–27; Little, "Evil and God's Sovereignty," 292–93.

To these charges, Calvinists have standard replies ready at hand. For instance, in part IV section IX of *The Freedom of the Will*, Jonathan Edwards distinguishes between two different senses of the phrase "author of sin," such that God is the author of sin in one sense, but not in the other.[6] According to Edwards, God *is not* the author of sin in the sense that God himself is—with respect to any specific sin—"the Sinner, the Agent, or Actor of Sin, or the Doer of a wicked thing." So if by "author of sin" we mean that God is the *doer* of evil, the agent who actually performs the sinful act and with wicked intentions, then no, God is not the author of sin. Edwards says that "it would be a reproach and blasphemy, to suppose God to be the Author of Sin" in that sense. It "is infinitely to be abhorred." But according to Edwards, God *is* the author of sin in the sense that he ordained the existence of sin. He is "the Disposer and Orderer of Sin." He is "a disposer of the state of events, in such a manner, for wise, holy, and most excellent ends and purposes, that Sin . . . will most certainly and infallibly follow." So if by "author of sin" we mean "one who ordains that moral evil shall in fact occur," then yes (says Edwards), that appears to be the repeated teaching of Scripture. But since God is not the author of sin in the first sense, he has no moral culpability or blame in the matter.

Unfortunately, this distinction is not going to do it for the Molinist critic of Calvinism. The Molinist already believes that God ordains whatsoever comes to pass, and this includes ordaining that acts of moral evil come to pass.[7] What bothers the Molinist is that, on Calvinism, God seems to be the *sufficient cause* for various acts of sin that occur in his universe, and this means that God is *responsible*—morally responsible—for every sin that occurs. In addition, it's hard to deny that given this sufficient causation in Calvinism, God is *culpable* for the sin that occurs; he is not only responsible but blameworthy. In short, the Molinist will insist that the *way* that God ordains sin on Calvinism is by way of causal determinism, which implies that God is the sufficient cause of sin, which implies that *God* is a sinner, with all the responsibility and culpability that that entails. Whereas on Molinism, all of this is avoided.

What I intend to argue is that *Molinists may be making two mistakes* when they adjudicate this particular dispute in favor of Molinism. *First*, by imputing to Calvinists the thesis that God governs his universe by way of strict causal determinism, Molinists may be overlooking the apophatic character of Reformed definitions of divine providence, as these are enshrined

---

6. Available at: http://www.ccel.org/ccel/edwards/works1.iii.v.ix.html.

7. Keathley, *Salvation and Sovereignty*, 139: "Of course, God is the ultimate cause of all that exists."

in historically Reformed confessions of faith. For Calvinists, these negative formulations are not a bug, but a feature; they are there by design. *Second*, even if Molinists are correct in thinking that Calvinism must make God the sufficient cause of sin, such that he is its author and blameworthy for it, *their own* model of divine causation is *sufficiently analogous* to sufficient causation, such that Molinism inherits all of the alleged Calvinist liabilities anyway, with respect to divine authorship of sin, responsibility, and blame. You might say that the first mistake is finding in Calvinism something that may not be there; the other mistake is failing to find in Molinism something that may in fact be there.

Calvinism and Causal Determinism: Apophatic Definitions of the Decree

Concerning this first point, Paul Helm provides extended commentary on the following definition of divine foreordination, found in the *Westminster Confession of Faith* III.1 (also found, near verbatim, in the Baptist parallel in the 1689 *London Baptist Confession of Faith*) "God from all eternity, did, by the most wise and holy counsel of His own will, freely, and unchangeably ordain whatsoever comes to pass; yet so, as thereby neither is God the author of sin, nor is violence offered to the will of the creatures; nor is the liberty or contingency of second causes taken away, but rather established."

Helm points out that this definition consists of a positive claim ("God from all eternity, did, by the most wise and holy counsel of His own will, freely, and unchangeably ordain whatsoever comes to pass") that is followed by a series of negative claims, "three significant denials," or what B. B. Warfield called "protecting clauses":[8]

1. "neither is God the author of sin,"

2. "nor is violence offered to the will of the creatures,"

3. "nor is the liberty or contingency of second causes taken away."

On Helm's view, "there is no attempt to explain why there is the decree, nor (in particular) to explain how it is that although God decrees all that comes to pass, yet no violence is done to the will of the creature, nor are liberty and contingency are taken away, but are rather established."[9] There is no explanation of how the positive claim can be true in light of the negative claims; no detailed model or mechanism is provided that would

8. Helm, "God's Eternal Decree," 147.

9. Ibid., 143–44.

illuminate for us their interrelations. This seems exactly right. The attempt to construct such a detailed model is not forbidden, but the authors, signers, and adopters of this confession do not grant such models the status of Reformed confessional consensus.

Helm continues: "In this sense, the structure of the wording of the decree is a piece of negative theology. The logical structure of this part of the Chapter, the prominence of 'yet so . . . neither . . . nor . . . nor' is similar to that of the Chalcedon definition's 'withouts.'"[10] Again, this seems exactly right. Chalcedon does not attempt to penetrate into the mystery of the hypostatic union, such that we can see *how it is* that Christ is one Person with two natures. It simply states this, and then protects the positive claim by a series of protecting clauses: "without division, without separation, without conversion, without confusion." So the Westminster definition of the decree is a cop-out, I suppose, only if the Chalcedonian definition is.

Given this apophatic definition of the decree, the authors leave it a mystery why (for instance) if God ordains everything that comes to pass, and if human sin comes to pass, why it is that God is not responsible or culpable for those sins. It doesn't explain how, in light of God's comprehensive decree, the liberty or contingency of second causes are not taken away. How does God as primary cause of what occurs relate to all of the created, responsible secondary causes? My only point here is that the thesis of universal causal determinism, or divine sufficient causality of sin, is not in play here; it is simply not to be found. (As Helm points out, "it is crude and misleading to assimilate the working of the divine decree to intramundane models of causation, and particularly to general physical determinism."[11]) But *without* the notion of causal determinism or divine sufficient causality, this definition of the decree does not make God the author of sin in the first, objectionable sense ("the Sinner, the Agent, or Actor of Sin, or the Doer of a wicked thing"), though it allows for God being the author of sin in the second, unobjectionable sense (God ordains that moral evil shall in fact occur).

It is important not to lump all Calvinists into the same category. There are the "mysterian" Calvinists who rest content with apophatic formulations, in the grand historical tradition of Chalcedon. It's not clear *they* make God the author of sin in any objectionable sense. And then there are the "creative" Calvinists (the "industrious" Calvinists?) who supplement or "fill out" the confession's teaching on the decree with the thesis of universal causal determinism, and perhaps even occasionalism. If they are subject to critique, so be it, but we need to be clear just who is saying what, rather

10. Ibid., 144.
11. Ibid., 154.

than claiming that Calvinists—as a group—eschew mystery and apophasis in favor of causal determinism, divine causal sufficiency, and so on.

Molinism Sufficiently Analogous to Sufficient Causation, for All Moral Intents and Purposes

Secondly—and here I embark on a much longer point—let's assume that everything I just said is wrong. Let's assume for the sake of argument that Molinists are right in their views of what Calvinists must believe if their characteristic claims about divine providence (both positive and negative) are to "make sense." Let's say that Calvinism *must* make God the sufficient cause of sin, and so its author in an objectionable sense. What I want to argue is a simple case of *modus ponens*:

1. If divine causation in Molinist providence is *sufficiently analogous* to sufficient causation, then Molinism inherits all of the Calvinist liabilities anyway, with respect to divine authorship of sin, responsibility, and blame.

2. Molinist providence *is* sufficiently analogous to sufficient causation. And so it follows that:

3. Molinism *does* inherit any Calvinist liabilities with respect to divine authorship of sin, responsibility, and blame.

Thus, given our ordinary intuitions about cases involving sufficient causation and moral responsibility, Molinism makes God the author of sin (in the objectionable sense) if Calvinism does. My strategy will be to elicit our ordinary moral intuitions in a range of relevant cases, such that my minor premise is adequately supported: Molinist providence is sufficiently analogous to sufficient causation for all moral intents and purposes. I start with the "ordinary gun" case.

Guns, Bullet Bills, and Molinism

The "ordinary gun" case

What I call the "ordinary gun" case is described as follows: I pull a gun out of my pocket, aim it at a person at point-blank range, and pull the trigger. I have in fact murdered him, and I bear moral responsibility for murdering him. I am the author of this sin, because it was "up to me" how I used my libertarian free will (LFW) in this case. I could have refrained from pulling the trigger. No one coerced me into pulling the trigger. I pulled the trigger knowing that this gun was in good working order, and knowing what ordinarily happens when you pull triggers on working guns at point-blank range. Knowing all this, I am responsible not just for the fact that I pulled the trigger, but that the man died as a result. And it doesn't matter if my intention in killing him was to bring about a further effect (such as my winning the New York Marathon). I'm still responsible for killing him.

Our metaphysical and moral intuitions here seem clear: I am the author of this sin, and I bear moral responsibility for bringing about the man's death. Let's review six aspects of the "ordinary gun" case.

First, I *actualize a set of circumstances* in which something else happens. That is, *I pull the trigger.* Pulling the trigger brings about a real effect in the world: it releases a spring-loaded hammer in the gun, which hits the explosive cap (the primer) at the rear of the bullet, which explodes, igniting the gunpowder (the propellant) in the bullet, which creates gas pressure that sends the bullet down the barrel of the gun at high speed towards its target.

Second, *my action* of actualizing a set of circumstances *is not (by itself) sufficient for the outcome*: the death of the person I'm aiming at. Imagine that I pull the trigger in an environment where laws of nature pertaining to momentum, or friction, or inertia, or explosions, or gas pressure, or conservation of mass-energy, or even gravity, do not obtain. It's pretty clear that in the absence of these laws of nature, not much of anything will occur beyond my actualizing the initial set of circumstances. You might say that my actualization of circumstances would be impotent, apart from the laws of nature. To give another illustration: if I release a pen in this room, it will fall to the ground, but if I release the same pen in zero-gravity, it will float. What makes the difference here is not what I do, but the environment in which I actualize the circumstances. Merely releasing the pen is not (by itself) sufficient for the intended outcome.

Third, in order to kill the man with my gun, *I am relying upon laws of nature which are only contingently the case.* None of our well-confirmed physical theories give us any indication that the laws of nature are logically necessary. We can certainly imagine the force of gravity being stronger or weaker than it actually is, either because the gravitational constant is different, or the exponent in the denominator of the law is different. (E.g., rather than $F = Gm_1m_2/r^2$, we have $F = G\,m_1m_2/r^3$ or $F = G\,m_1m_2/r^{1.5}$.) Additionally, as theists it seems quite plausible that *God* could have made different laws of nature obtain; they are contingent in virtue of being (quite literally) contingent on the will of God. Advocates of the argument for God from the fine-tuning of the laws of nature have produced excellent defenses of the contingency of these laws.

Of course, there are various philosophical accounts of laws of nature on offer. Perhaps the laws are separate from the objects they govern, being a contingent tie between universals that then get instantiated in particulars (i.e., David Armstrong or Michael Tooley). Or perhaps the laws are constitutive of objects, such that the law of gravity is understood in terms of substances having particular powers and having liabilities to exercise those powers, which is the view of laws of nature presupposed by Richard Swinburne throughout his book *The Existence of God*, a view which "was the way familiar to the ancient and medieval world, before talk of 'laws of nature' became common in the sixteenth century. It was revived by Rom Harré and E. H. Madden in *Causal Powers*. [fn. 8: (Blackwell, 1975).]"[12]

But neither view of the laws of nature—as separate from objects or constitutive of objects—requires us to regard these laws as anything other than *contingent* realities. In firing the gun, then, I am *relying* on further realities being the case, and these realities didn't *have* to be the case. Laws governing momentum, friction, inertia, explosions, gas pressure, conservation of mass-energy, and gravity only contingently hold. In other possible worlds, different laws of nature (or different specifications of these laws) hold. Nevertheless, knowing that various laws of nature are *in fact* the case, I fire the gun, and I am responsible for the outcome.

Fourth, the contingent *laws of nature* on which I rely to get the job done are useful to me precisely because they *ground the truth of counterfactuals about what would occur in various circumstances*. Laws of nature are not mere accidental generalizations which describe what in fact happens. They ground counterfactuals (CFs) about what *would* occur if such-and-such takes place, and these CFs are true even if the circumstances specified in their antecedents are never actualized. The law of gravity tells me that this pen would fall to the ground if I were to release it. Even if I don't release the pen (and put it back in my pocket), nevertheless there is a truth about what *would* have happened if I *had* released the pen.

Likewise, if I don't pull the trigger on the gun, all the laws of nature pertaining to momentum, friction, inertia, etc. still obtain, and tell me what *would* have happened if I had pulled the trigger. Indeed, this knowledge of true CFs vouchsafed to me by my knowledge of laws of nature is precisely why these laws are useful to me in intelligently and intentionally bringing about effects. In firing the gun, I act on this knowledge, and my expectation of the outcome is well-grounded. The CFs assure me ahead of time what to expect, and in this knowledge lies (at least in part) my responsibility for the

---

12. Swinburne, *God*, 32–33.

outcome. The act of pulling the trigger is not analogous to pulling the lever on a slot machine, or flipping a coin.

Fifth, the laws of nature are not up to me; they are (from my perspective) "prevolitional" truths on which I rely to get the job done. It is not up to me that laws pertaining to explosions, inertia, mass-energy conservation, and so on actually obtain. I can neither repeal nor establish the law of gravity; it is only open to me to act in accordance with it. Consequently, in killing the man by firing the gun, I am relying on truths over which I have no control. They are (again, from my perspective, as the agent who chooses to fire the gun) brute facts that help me bring about the outcome. Both my choice to pull the trigger and the obtaining of the laws of nature are contingent matters. But one is up to me (my choice to pull the trigger), and the other is not (the laws). (Notice how the consequence argument for incompatibilism stresses this truth: neither prior states of the universe nor the laws of nature are up to me.)

Sixth, I bear responsibility for killing the person in "the ordinary gun case." I bear responsibility because I actualize circumstances in which I rely on contingent prevolitional truths about what would occur if I were to actualize those circumstances. Knowing that that would occur, I pull the trigger. The contingency of these truths does not absolve me of responsibility. The fact that I don't control these truths does not absolve me of responsibility. The fact that my action of pulling the trigger, strictly speaking, is not sufficient for the outcome, does not absolve me of responsibility.

The "Bullet Bill gun"

PARALLELS TO THE "ORDINARY GUN" CASE

What I call the "Bullet Bill gun" case is described as follows: I pull a gun out of my pocket, aim it at a person at point-blank range, and pull the trigger, thus killing the person. However, this gun is different from an ordinary gun. When I pull the trigger, it creates *ex nihilo* a Bullet Bill in the chamber. "Bullet Bill" is a character in Nintendo video games (Super Mario Bros., Mario Kart, Super Mario Galaxy 1 & 2, etc.), typically represented as a black metal bullet with eyes and an evil grin, which chases Mario as soon as Bullet Bill is shot out of a cannon, gun, etc. For my purposes, I assume that Bullet Bill is sentient, a homunculus encased in steel, possessing LFW. I further assume that the one who fires the Bullet Bill gun knows the relevant counterfactuals of creaturely freedom (CCFs) about each Bullet Bill that gets created, and that he uses that knowledge to kill people with the gun. For instance, he may know that the next trigger pull would create Bullet Bill A, who (if created) would freely fly out of the barrel and kill Angie, that the next trigger pull would create Bullet Bill B, who (if created) would freely fly out of the barrel and kill Beth, that the next trigger pull would create Bullet Bill C and kill Caroline, and so on.

I maintain that if I had such a gun and used it in this way, then I would bear moral responsibility for every death I brought about through my use of it, the same as any murderer would. Analogously to the "ordinary gun" case, I am the author of this sin, because it was "up to me" how I used my LFW in this case. I could have refrained from pulling the trigger. No one coerced me into pulling the trigger. I pulled the trigger knowing that this Bullet Bill gun was in good working order, and knowing what ordinarily happens when you pull triggers on Bullet Bill guns at point-blank range. In fact, by knowing the relevant CCFs I know what would specifically happen after the next three trigger pulls on the gun. Knowing all this, I am responsible not just for the fact that I pulled the trigger, but that Angie, Beth, and Caroline died as a result. And it doesn't matter if my intention in killing them was to bring about a further effect (such as my winning the New York Marathon). I'm still responsible for killing them.

I submit that our metaphysical and moral intuitions in the Bullet Bill case are at least as clear as in the "ordinary gun" case, such that I am the author of this sin, and I bear moral responsibility for bringing about these deaths. Like the "ordinary gun" case, I actualize circumstances (pulling the trigger), circumstances that are not (strictly speaking) sufficient for the outcome. Rather, I rely on contingent CCFs about Bullet Bill, even as in the "ordinary gun" case I rely on contingent laws of nature. Like laws of nature, the CCFs are CFs about what would occur in various circumstances, and like laws of nature, what these CCFs are is not up to me. They are "prevolitional" truths in either case. By analogy to the "ordinary gun" case, then, I bear responsibility for killing the various persons by way of my "Bullet Bill gun."

There are of course *differences* between the "ordinary gun" case and the "Bullet Bill gun" case, chief of which is the existence of Bullet Bill. But the question is whether these differences are *relevant* for the purpose of assessing *my* moral responsibility in each case.

ORDINARY BULLET VS. BULLET BILL:
A RELEVANT DIFFERENCE?

For instance, in the "ordinary gun" case the bullet is not morally responsible for much of anything, being an ordinary bullet lacking mental states, consciousness, intentions, a will, and so on. Ordinary bullets are not agents, whereas in the "Bullet Bill gun" case, Bullet Bill is an agent, who is himself morally responsible for killing the people he kills. Despite the fact that there are true CFs that passively record what Bullet Bill would do in a particular set of circumstances, it is nevertheless up to Bullet Bill to fly out of the chamber and go this way or that. In another possible world Bullet Bill (in the same exact circumstances) flies beside Angie and strikes up a friendly conversation, rather than blowing her up.

So there *is* a clear difference here in the two cases because of a difference in the bullets. But does Bullet Bill's individual responsibility somehow lessen *my* responsibility, the one who aims and shoots the Bullet Bill gun and thereby kills three people in rapid succession? I don't see how. It just doesn't strike me as plausible that the man who wields the Bullet Bill gun is any less responsible simply because he didn't directly *cause* Bullet Bill to do what he did. Indeed, in the "ordinary gun" case I don't directly cause the killing; I do so indirectly by way of contingent, prevolitional realities pertaining to gun and bullet, realities over which I have no control. In each case the fact that I *capitalize on and exploit* such prevolitional contingent realities is what *grounds* my responsibility (far from lessening it).

To be clear, with the "ordinary gun" I do not make it the case that, given initial circumstances, the bullet *would* fly out of the chamber and kill someone. What the bullet would do, and subjunctive truths about what the bullet would do, is up to the laws of nature, the properties of the bullet, etc. None of that is up to me. But I do make it the case that the bullet *will in fact* fly out of the chamber and kill someone. What the ordinary bullet in fact does is up to me. Likewise, with the Bullet Bill gun I do not make it the case that, given initial circumstances, Bullet Bill *would* fly out of the chamber and kill someone. What Bullet Bill would do, and subjunctive truths about what Bullet Bill would do, is up to brute facts about Bullet Bill. None of that is up to me. But I do make it the case that Bullet Bill *will in fact* fly out of the chamber and kill someone. What Bullet Bill in fact does is up to me.

So the cases seem perfectly parallel precisely where they need to be parallel for the purposes of assessing the moral responsibility of the shooter. I am responsible for there being a bullet which does what it in fact does (kill a man), even as I am responsible for there being a Bullet Bill who does what he in fact does (kill a man).

Sufficient vs. insufficient cause:
a relevant difference?

What about the fact that, apparently, in the "ordinary gun" case I am the sufficient cause of the bullet's speeding down the chamber and killing the person, but in the "Bullet Bill gun" case I am, apparently, *not* the sufficient cause of Bullet Bill speeding down the chamber and killing the person? If Bullet Bill but not the ordinary bullet has LFW, than how can I be the sufficient cause in both cases? The problem (as I see it) is that any disambiguation of "sufficient cause" will be contextually dependent. Depending on which factors we hold fixed, I am (alternately) an insufficient cause in both cases and a sufficient cause in both cases. I think this continued parallel supports my overall case. Let's examine this further.

I certainly don't give the (ordinary) bullet the propensity it has to behave a certain way under particular circumstances. So in that respect I am not the sufficient cause of its traveling down the chamber. But my actualization of initial circumstances is sufficient for the outcome *given other things* (such as laws of nature), things which are not up to me but which I exploit to bring about the outcome. So (speaking *very* strictly), I am not the sufficient cause of the bullet's speeding down the chamber. Why then do we naturally say, in most conversational contexts, that I am? Because in assessing whether I am the sufficient cause, we do not ordinarily take into account those realities over which I have no control (such as the laws of nature); rather, we stipulate that those are in place and then ask whether, *given those realities*, my action is sufficient for the outcome. And, of course, it is.

The Bullet Bill case seems exactly parallel in the same respects. I certainly don't give Bullet Bill the propensity he has to behave a certain way under particular circumstances. So in that respect I am not the sufficient cause of Bullet Bill traveling down the chamber. Nevertheless, my actualization of initial circumstances is sufficient for the outcome *given other things* (such as the relevant CCFs), things which are not up to me but which I exploit to bring about the outcome. So (speaking *very* strictly), I am not the sufficient cause of Bullet Bill's speeding down the chamber. Why then is it natural—even here—to say that I am? Because in assessing whether I am the sufficient cause, we do not ordinarily take into account those realities over which I have no control (the CCFs); rather, we stipulate that those are in place and ask whether, *given those realities*, my action is sufficient for the outcome. And, of course, it is.

I conclude that I bear responsibility in the ordinary gun case, and cause the bullet to do what it does, even though I don't cause the laws of nature to be what they are. Likewise, I bear responsibility in the Bullet Bill case, and cause Bullet Bill to do what he does, even though I don't cause the CCFs to be what they are. In neither situation do I cause what *would* be the case. But in both situations I do cause what *will* be the case.

So we can take our pick. If we wish to speak very strictly, and say that the "Bullet Bill gun" is a case of insufficient causation at best, then we can say the same about the "ordinary gun" case. On the other hand, if the "ordinary gun" case is a case of sufficient causation (ignoring the relevant CFs which must also be in place), then so is the "Bullet Bill gun" case. At the very least, the parallels are such that my causal involvement when I wield the "Bullet Bill gun" seems *sufficiently analogous to cases of causal sufficiency*, that the ascription of moral responsibility goes through.

Molinism

Given the preceding, the application to a Molinist doctrine of providence can be brief. On Molinism *God actualizes circumstances* in which he knows (say) that an assassin will take out a number of targets. God's act of placing the assassin in those circumstances *is not (by itself) sufficient* for the murderous outcome. In addition to the actualization of circumstances, *there need to be true CCFs* about how the assassin would behave in those circumstances, and God is provident on Molinism because *he relies on these contingent truths about the assassin*, truths over which God has no control. These brute facts about the assassin are accurately described by *prevolitional truths that are not up to God in any way*. (For instance, they are not grounded in God's nature or his will.) As in the Bullet Bill case, on Molinism God is not responsible for what the assassin *would* do if placed in a particular set of circumstances. But if I've described the Bullet Bill case correctly, he is responsible for what the assassin *will in fact* do. After all, it is up to God to create an assassin with the liability to kill in a particular circumstance *and* it is up to God to actualize that circumstance. Since *this dual divine action ensures the outcome*, how can God not be said to have caused the outcome, and to be responsible for it?

In effect, I am assimilating the case of Molinist divine providence *over* an assassin shooting a gun, to the case of an assassin shooting a gun. From this perspective, created agents are God's gun (or at least his bullets). If the bullets are sentient, then sure, the bullets deserve blame. But that is a separate matter once we step back and look at the larger picture, and reflect on these analogies. God's firing of the gun is sufficient (given other things) to bring about the effect. Is that not also the case with the "ordinary gun" and the "Bullet Bill gun" cases? In each case the action is "sufficient (given other things)." So I conclude that on Molinism, God is the author of sin if, when I fire my ordinary gun, I am the author of sin. I don't directly put the bullet into the guy's heart; I do so by way of reliance on objects behaving according to the laws of nature. God doesn't directly put the assassin's bullet in the victim's heart. He does so indirectly by reliance on agents behaving according to CCFs.

In the end, I am looking for a relevant moral difference between these cases. What is the difference between someone who brings about an effect by way of actualizing a circumstance and relying on a law of nature, and someone who brings about an effect by way of actualizing a circumstance and relying on a CCF? Any moral difference? In fact, in the Molinist case things are even worse when it comes to responsibility, since the first agent has *infallible* knowledge of the outcome of his choice, something not had by the ordinary assassin (who has probabilistic knowledge only). The infallible knowledge on the part of God affords him a degree of exact control over the outcome not had by ordinary assassins.

In his "Introduction" to Luis de Molina, Alfred Freddoso states in a particularly explicit way the doctrine of divine providence that Molina wishes to uphold: "God, the divine artisan, freely and knowingly plans, orders, and provides for all the effects that constitute His artifact, the created universe with its entire history, and executes His chosen plan by playing an active causal role sufficient to ensure its exact realization."[13]

So on this view of providence, which Molina is said to share with his detractors (such as Báñez), God "plays an active causal role sufficient to ensure [the] exact realization" of "all the effects" in his creation. Molinists' giving God such a role has consequences that are often overlooked for the "author of sin" issue. It seems to me that Molinists have studiously focused on articulating a model in which the human agent remains responsible in a strong libertarian sense, but have not sufficiently attended to the fact that their model nevertheless makes God the author of sin and responsible for the fact that sin comes to pass. These latter questions do not go away simply in virtue of preserving human libertarian free will.

13. Freddoso, "Introduction," 3.

Answers to Objections

> "You fail to acknowledge relevant differences between the
> cases. It is simply not up to God what the assassin would
> do. He has LFW, and (ordinary) bullets don't."

But in the "ordinary gun" case, am I off the hook because it's not up to me that guns and bullets have the properties they do? Because it's not up to me that bullets have powers and the liability to exercise those powers in particular circumstances? Do I fail to be responsible for killing a man with a gun, simply because laws about momentum and mass-energy conservation and explosions aren't up to me? I think the answer to all these questions is "no." So why would appeal to the prevolitional status of contingent brute facts about the assassin be relevant in the Molinist case?

> "In the 'ordinary gun' case, given the circumstances and the
> laws of nature, the bullet could not do otherwise than what
> it does. But on Molinism, agents can do otherwise in the
> same exact circumstances."

Yes, but how does this help? After all, God creates the agents he actually creates, not other agents he could have created, and these agents that God creates are such that they would do what is described in the relevant CCF. The choice to go ahead and create these kinds of agents was up to him. In addition, strictly speaking, given the circumstances *and the truth of the relevant CCF*, the agent cannot do otherwise than what he in fact does in those circumstances. Yes, there is a possible world in which the agent does otherwise in the same circumstances, but *that* is a world in which the relevant CCF is *false*. Likewise, there is a world in which the bullet behaves differently despite the same trigger pull, but that is a world in which the laws of nature are different.

Here is where the facts stand, on Molinism: (1) God creates an agent who has the following property: he would do X if placed in circumstances C; (2) God didn't have to create an agent who has that property, but he did so anyway; (3) God actualizes circumstances C; (4) God didn't have to actualize circumstances C. In virtue of (1) and (3), God's twofold activity *ensures* that the agent's sin will come about. In virtue of (2) and (4), it is up to God to act as he does in these two respects. Therefore, God both makes it the case that the sinful events will come about, and he is responsible for making it the case. This is *in addition to* any responsibility we want to assign to the sinful agent.

> "Causation requires the laws of nature. These are appealed
> to in the first case, but not in the second or third. That's
> why the first is a case of causation, but not the others."

But causation does not require the laws of nature. If it did, then God didn't cause the world to exist, since *he* didn't make use of laws of nature in creating the world. But surely God caused the world to exist (including its laws). So causal relations can obtain even apart from laws of nature. In addition, given libertarian free will I cause my volitions, and that doesn't involve laws of nature. So both creation and LFW argue against the assumption that causation *per se* requires the laws of nature.

Any causation—in the absence of laws of nature—would need at least true counterfactuals stating what would happen if certain events came to pass. For instance, if it's not a fact that "If God were to will there to be an apple, there would be an apple," then God can't cause there to be an apple. God's creation of an apple *ex nihilo* is a case of causation precisely because the CF enshrines a fact about God.

> "You commit a fatal equivocation in your comparison
> between the CFs associated with laws of nature, and the
> CCFs associated with LFW. Yes, they both disclose to us
> prevolitional, contingent realities. But laws of nature are
> deterministic in their consequences; not so for CCFs."

It's not clear that this claim is true, or even relevant. It may not be true, because fundamental laws in quantum physics seem to be probabilistic and even indeterministic, but clearly I can be morally responsible if I construct and use a gun whose operation depends on the truth of these laws of quantum physics.

It's not relevant, because we can well imagine that only probabilistic laws of nature hold. Clearly, we would still regard someone as culpable for his use of a gun (whether an "ordinary gun" or a "Bullet Bill gun"), even if he only made use of prevolitional, contingent truths about what would be *highly likely* to occur. (And, in the ordinary case, no gun operates with 100% efficiency; this does not lessen culpability.) In fact, it looks as if Molinism would only increase the culpability, since God has infallible knowledge of how the agent *would* behave (not merely knowledge of how the agent would *likely* or *probably* behave), and then he creates agents who *would* so behave.

> "At best, all you've shown is that God is responsible for the *outcome* of the assassin's sin: the death the assassin brings about. You haven't shown that God is responsible for the assassin's sin itself. And it is this latter claim that is needed, to show that God is the author of sin in the objectionable sense."

Strictly speaking, this isn't the case. In the "ordinary gun" case, I not only bring about the end result (the death of the person); I bring about the intermediate state—the bullet speeding down the barrel of the gun. As far as I can tell, I can make the same argument with respect to the intermediate state that I made with respect to the end state: *both* states involve my actualizing circumstances in which a substance with powers, and liabilities to exercise those powers in those circumstances, would in fact exercise those powers. And again, as far as I can tell, the "Bullet Bill gun" case is parallel in these respects.

> "On Molinism, God's actualization of circumstances doesn't *cause* agents to do what they do. But pulling a trigger *does* cause the bullet to do what it does. You've missed an elementary feature of Molinism."

My point is that what happens in Molinist providence is *sufficiently analogous* to what happens in sufficient causation, such that claims about authorship, moral responsibility, and culpability go through. So even if the actualization of circumstances is not (strictly speaking) a sufficient cause, this won't affect the larger argument. Thus, we need to get some clarity on *why* Molinist providence isn't a sufficient cause of what occurs. If the factors cited are also present in the "ordinary gun" case, then—unless we wish to reject our clear intuitions about that ordinary case—it looks like those intuitions transfer to the "Bullet Bill gun" and Molinist cases.

For instance, one reason to think Molinist providence isn't a sufficient cause is that (strictly speaking) God's actualization of circumstances isn't sufficient for a particular outcome. But in the "ordinary gun" case, my actualization of circumstances isn't sufficient for a particular outcome. Or again, maybe Molinist providence isn't a sufficient cause because what agents would do in various circumstances isn't up to God. But in the "ordinary gun" case, what the bullet would do in various circumstances isn't up to me. So what, exactly, is the *relevant* difference between the two cases that makes a *moral* difference?

Conclusion

Authorship of sin, responsibility, and culpability

Molinism is often said to combine the best of both worlds: a meticulous doctrine of providence typically associated with the determinism of Calvinism, and a libertarian view of free will typically associated with the indeterminism of Arminianism. As I read it, Molinists want God to have all of the *benefits* of sufficient causality in providence, but none of the *responsibilities* (literally!), at least if that responsibility involves culpability. They want a providence in which it is *as if* God is the sufficient cause of events (for the purpose of meticulous control over the outcome), even though he isn't *really* the sufficient cause.

In the "authorship of sin" objection, what bothers Molinists is not so much the *sufficient causality* involved in Calvinism, but what that sufficient causality seems to *entail* for the Calvinist: God's authorship of sin, and his subsequent moral responsibility for it, and his culpability. My main point has been that these latter consequences seem to be involved in the Molinist view anyway, once we attend to requisite analogies that elicit clear moral intuitions.

Of course, there are various strategies available to the Molinist, in order to defend the claim that—in spite of the cases we've considered—God can be responsible for the fact that evil occurs without being *culpable* for that evil. They can *appeal to paradox*, by adapting the Plantinga-inspired epistemology advocated in James Anderson's recent *Paradox in Christian Theology: An Analysis of Its Presence, Character, and Epistemic Status* (2007). They can *appeal to inscrutability*, an approach inspired by either Austin Ferrer's agnosticism about the mode of the divine action, or some adaptation of Alston's/Wykstra's inscrutability thesis with respect to the problem of evil. They can *appeal to the Creator/creature distinction*, and *the consequent sui generis character of divine causation* (both pursued by Paul Helm in various venues). The relation between God and evil is defined apophatically (WCF III.1, V.4), even as the union of Christ's natures in one person is defined apophatically in Chalcedonian Christology.

Perhaps these and several other strategies are available to help Molinists avoid the "author of sin" problem, by grounding a distinction between responsibility and culpability. But clearly none of these strategies rely on any distinctive *Molinist* themes. They are strategies Calvinists have been using for centuries. They are available to Molinist and non-Molinist alike. But if there are no conceptual resources *distinctive to Molinism* to block the notion that God is the author of sin, if Molinists must fall back on typical Calvinist strategies in this regard, then is Molinism really preferable to Calvinism in avoiding the conclusion that God is the author of sin? Or should Molinists simply drop this claim from their repertoire of alleged advantages of Molinism over Calvinism?

In closing, I agree with Keathley when he says, "We are brethren, not adversaries, working in a mutual effort. Until we cross the veil, none of us has arrived on the journey of faith. So I look forward to this cooperative effort, convinced that the end result will be that we are better and more faithful witnesses of our common salvation. Calvinism and Molinism are much more similar than they are dissimilar, so I endeavor to avoid what might be called the narcissism of trivial differences."[14] I too want to avoid the narcissism of trivial differences. In fact, what I have argued is in that spirit: that when it comes to the 'author of sin' issue, "Calvinism and Molinism are much more similar" than Molinists let on.

Bibliography

Freddoso, Alfred J. "Introduction." In *On Divine Foreknowledge (Part IV of the Concordia)*, translated by and edited Alfred J. Freddoso, 1–81. Ithaca, NY: Cornell University Press, 1988.

Helm, Paul. "God's Eternal Decree." In *Reformed Theology in Contemporary Perspective: Westminster, Yesterday, Today, and Tomorrow?* edited by Lynn Quigley, 143–61. Edinburgh Dogmatics Conference Papers. Carlisle, UK: Rutherford House, 2006.

Little, Bruce A. "Evil and God's Sovereignty." In *Whosoever Will: A Biblical-Theological Critique of Five-Point Calvinism*, edited by David L. Allen and Steve W. Lemke, 275–98. Nashville: B & H Academic, 2010.

Swinburne, Richard. *The Existence of God*. 2nd ed. Oxford: Oxford University Press, 2004.

14. Keathley, *Salvation and Sovereignty*, 14.

5

Molinist Gunslingers Redux

A Friendly Response to Greg Welty[1]

KENNETH D. KEATHLEY

GREG WELTY AND I are friends and colleagues. In the times I've observed Welty in a disagreement or a debate, he has always demonstrated grace and patience. He is also one of the smartest fellows I know. Therefore, I take his objections seriously.

Welty presented a paper at a previous ETS annual meeting entitled "Molinist Gunslingers: God and the Authorship of Sin," which constitutes chapter 4 of this book. If I understand Welty correctly, his main thesis is thus: Molinism, with its belief that God perfectly accomplishes his will primarily by means of his exhaustive foreknowledge, has the same problems as Calvinism concerning God's relationship to sin, regardless of what view of human freedom that Molinism may affirm. The Molinist believes that God generally uses his knowledge of the possible choices of significantly free creatures in order to accomplish his will. (This knowledge is typically categorized as residing within God's middle knowledge.) But affirming libertarian freedom for humans does not help in dealing with the question of God's relationship to evil. Therefore Molinism is no better than Calvinism, at least concerning this issue.

In my response I argue that, on the matter of God's relationship to sin, (1) Molinism does not have a moral advantage over what Welty calls "mysterian," "apophatic" Calvinism, but Molinists don't claim that it does, and (2) Molinism indeed does have a moral advantage over the Calvinist versions that do employ causal determinism.

---

1. A revised version of this paper appears in *Perichoresis* 16.2 (2008) 31–44, which further addresses some of the points which Welty makes.

Summary of Molinist Gunslingers Chapter

Welty makes two arguments: (1) Molinists overgeneralize when they characterize Calvinism, and (2) even if they were correct in their characterization, their position does not enjoy the advantage they believe it does.

First argument: Molinists overgeneralize in their characterization of Calvinism

Proponents of Molinism (me, in particular) claim that Molinism has an advantage over Calvinism in that "Calvinism makes God the author of sin whereas Molinism does not." Welty provides what he calls "standard . . . Calvinist . . . replies." He cites Jonathan Edwards (*Freedom of the* Will, part IV section IX), who distinguishes between two senses of "cause." God is not the cause of sin in the sense of being "the Sinner, the Agent, or Actor of Sin, or the Doer of a wicked thing," but he is the cause of sin in the sense that God "ordains that moral evil shall in fact occur." So God is not the efficient cause of sin, but his plan and his purpose are the formal and final causes of evil. But these distinctions are acknowledged by all orthodox Christians, including Molinists, so Calvinists face no dilemmas in this regard that are not faced by other Christian traditions also.

Welty claims that "this distinction is not going to do it for the Molinist critic of Calvinism," though he does note that Molinists, just as Calvinists, affirm that "God ordains whatsoever comes to pass, and this includes ordaining that acts of moral evil come to pass," and he cites me to this effect.[2] He continues:

> What bothers the Molinist is that, on Calvinism, God seems to be the *sufficient cause* for various acts of sin that occur in his universe, and this means that God is *responsible*—morally responsible—for every sin that occurs . . . In short, the Molinist will insist that the *way* that God ordains sin on Calvinism is by way of causal determinism, which implies that God is the sufficient cause of sin, which implies that *God* is a sinner, with all the responsibility and culpability that that entails.

Welty suggests that, on this matter, Molinists may be making two mistakes: imputing to Calvinism an adherence to causal determinism, and failing to recognize that Molinism is "sufficiently analogous" to Calvinism with

---

2. Keathley, *Salvation and Sovereignty*, 139.

regard to imputing responsibility to God. Fleshing out responses to these two perceived mistakes constitutes the bulk of Welty's two arguments.

Welty responds to the question of Calvinism's relationship to causal determinism by noting what he calls the "apophatic definitions of the decree." He points to the *Westminster Confession of Faith* III.1 and the significant role it plays in the thinking of Reformed theologians such as B. B. Warfield and Paul Helm. In Westminster's words, "God from all eternity, did, by the most wise and holy counsel of His own will, freely, and unchangeably ordain whatsoever comes to pass; yet so, as thereby neither is God the author of sin, nor is violence offered to the will of the creatures; nor is the liberty or contingency of second causes taken away, but rather established." Welty argues that the wording is reminiscent to that of the Chalcedonian creed concerning the hypostatic union of Christ:

> There is no explanation of how the positive claim can be true in light of the negative claims; no detailed model or mechanism is provided that would illuminate for us their interrelations . . . Given this apophatic definition of the decree, the authors leave it a mystery why (for instance) if God ordains everything that comes to pass, and if human sin comes to pass, why it is that God is not responsible or culpable for those sins.

Welty acknowledges that some Calvinists do indeed embrace causal determinism, but he distances himself from them. He first describes apophatic, mysterian Calvinists: "It is important not to lump all Calvinists into the same category. There are the 'mysterian' Calvinists who rest content with apophatic formulations, in the grand historical tradition of Chalcedon. It's not clear *they* make God the author of sin in any objectionable sense." He then describes creative, industrious Calvinists: "And then there are the 'creative' Calvinists (the 'industrious' Calvinists?) who supplement or 'fill out' the confession's teaching on the decree with the thesis of universal causal determinism, and perhaps even occasionalism. If they are subject to critique, so be it." Welty admonishes Molinists to distinguish between the two: "but we need to be clear just who is saying what, rather than claiming that Calvinists—as a group—eschew mystery and apophasis in favor of causal determinism, divine causal sufficiency, and so on."

Welty does not say that an apophatic approach embraces or allows for a libertarian view of human agency. He seems to leave this as an open question. Perhaps he believes that such an approach does not have to commit to a model of human agency. However, many would argue that, in regard to human choice, determinism and libertarianism are the only two options. If the conceptual space is exhausted by these two options, and one wishes to reject determinism, isn't one left with libertarianism?

Second argument: Molinism possesses no superiority
over Calvinism concerning the problem of evil

Welty claims that, even if everything he wrote so far turned out to be incorrect, Molinism would still not be (morally) superior to Calvinism, because it is "sufficiently analogous" to Calvinism. "If divine causation in Molinist providence is *sufficiently analogous* to sufficient causation, then Molinism inherits all of the Calvinist liabilities anyway, with respect to divine authorship of sin, responsibility, and blame." To make his case, Welty presents a thought experiment. He compares a murder committed with an ordinary gun to a murder committed using a "Bullet Bill" gun in which the bullets possess libertarian free will. (One has to appreciate Welty's use of a classic video game to make an argument!) Using an ordinary gun, the killer actualizes the circumstances, but the act of pulling the trigger is not sufficient by itself. He is relying on the laws of nature to finish the job. Moreover, these laws are contingent (because they could have been different) and prevolitional (at least from the perspective of the shooter). Yet, the killer's responsibility would be universally recognized.

But regarding the Bullet Bill gun, the bullet in this case would be the Mario Brothers character—a black bullet with the evil grin. Welty supposes, for the sake of his argument, that Bullet Bill possesses libertarian free will. Even though Bullet Bill freely chooses to kill the targeted victim, the one wielding the gun also is culpable. This applies to Molinism because the person firing the gun has counterfactual knowledge of what Bullet Bill will do. And the person pulling the trigger is aiming at the victim. "On Molinism *God actualizes circumstances* in which he knows (say) that an assassin will take out a number of targets." Though the circumstances by themselves are not sufficient to cause the murder, though God is using truths that were prevolitional to him, and though the assassin possesses libertarian freedom, God "is responsible for what the assassin *will in fact* do." Thus Welty concludes:

> It seems to me that Molinists have studiously focused on articulating a model in which the human agent remains responsible in a strong libertarian sense, but have not sufficiently attended to the fact that their model nevertheless makes God the author of sin and responsible for the fact that sin comes to pass. These

latter questions do not go away simply in virtue of preserving human libertarian free will.

Response to Welty's Gunslingers

We should note that Welty addresses a significant claim of Molinism, but not Molinism's central or primary claim. Initially, in response to the historical challenge of fatalism as espoused by the Greek Stoics and later by Islam, the primary concern of Molinism was to establish the contingency of future conditionals in the light of God's exhaustive foreknowledge.[3] Later, determinism of the Hobbesian variety became a challenge when Jonathan Edwards incorporated Hobbes's views into his theology of providence.[4] As many Calvinists followed Edwards in embracing determinism (particularly in America), proponents of Molinism argued that their model enjoyed the advantages that Welty is challenging. So even if Welty's critique is correct, he has not addressed the central concern of Molinism. But I don't think his critique is correct, at least not in the main.

Response to first argument

Do Molinists overgeneralize in their depiction of Calvinism? And more to the point: does Molinism enjoy a moral advantage over "mysterian, "apophatic" Calvinism specifically concerning God's relationship to sin? Short answers: no and no, at least not compared to the type of "apophatic" Calvinism as Welty defines it. In fact, Welty's complaint seems to overgeneralize about Molinists. He states, "By imputing to Calvinists the thesis that God governs his universe by way of strict causal determinism, Molinists may be overlooking the apophatic character of Reformed definitions of divine providence, as these are enshrined in historically Reformed confessions of faith." Welty claims that Molinists overgeneralize in their characterization of Calvinism. But I don't think I made that mistake in *Salvation and Sovereignty* (my book is the only Molinist work cited). I make a point to quote Calvinists who are critics of causal determinism.[5] The book notes in a number of places that on this issue there are different streams of thought within Calvinism.

---

3. Craig, *Foreknowledge.*

4. Guelzo, *Edwards.* The debate continues as to how much Edwards depended on Hobbes.

5. Keathley, *Salvation and Sovereignty,* 97–99.

I also distinguished between those causal determinists who acknowledge its problems from those who don't. To illustrate the difference between the two, I compared and contrasted the approach of R. C. Sproul Sr. with that of his son, R. C. Sproul, Jr.[6] Both affirm determinism, but come to very different conclusions concerning how and why Adam and Eve chose to sin. Sproul Sr. takes the mysterian approach advocated by Welty: "In spite of this excruciating problem we still must affirm that God is not the author of sin . . . One thing is absolutely unthinkable, that God could be the author or doer of sin."[7] Sproul Jr., by contrast, rushes in where his father feared to tread. He contends that God directly changed Eve's inclinations from good to evil. In this way, God introduced evil into the world; he is "the culprit" (Sproul Jr.'s term). "Of course it's impossible for God to do evil. He can't sin," reasons Sproul Jr. "This objection, however, is off the mark. I am not accusing God of sinning; I am suggesting that he created sin."[8] I took pains to point out that most Calvinists have not followed the approach taken by Sproul Jr.[9] so Welty's objection on this point seems to be off the mark.

I also make a point of noting, that in regards to God's eternal decree, there is little difference between Molinism and infralapsarian Calvinism (see the section "The Similarities of Infralapsarian Calvinism and Molinism").[10] Molinism, with its more robust definition of "permission," may be simply a more consistent version of infralapsarianism. This is why many Arminians reject Molinism.[11] Note the titles to certain articles: "Is Molinism as Bad as Calvinism?"[12] and "Is Molinism as Depressing as Calvinism?"[13] Molinists have no real problem with what Welty calls the "standard" Calvinist "replies." We affirm, along with Edwards, the distinction between efficient causation and formal or final causation. Molinists also appeal to the *Westminster Confession of Faith* III.1. As William Lane Craig declares, "Now this is *precisely* what the Molinist believes! The Confession affirms God's preordination of everything that comes to pass as well as the liberty and contingency of the creaturely will, so that God is not the author of sin. It is a tragedy that in rejecting middle knowledge Reformed divines have cut

---

6. Ibid., 80–86.

7. Sproul Sr., *Chosen*, 31.

8. Sproul Jr., *Almighty*, 54.

9. Keathley, *Salvation and Sovereignty*, 85, 89, 96, 98.

10. Ibid., 140–42.

11. Olson, *Arminian Theology*, 194–99; Picirilli, *Grace*, 62–63.

12. Walls, "Is Molinism as Bad as Calvinism?"

13. Craig, "Q&A #236."

themselves off from the most perspicuous explanation of the coherence of this wonderful confession."[14]

Welty and I both have signed the *Abstract of Principles*, which most recognize to be a fairly Calvinistic document: "God from eternity decrees or permits all things that come to pass and perpetually upholds, directs and governs all creatures and all events; yet so as not in any wise to be author or approver of sin nor to destroy the free will and responsibility of intelligent creatures" (article 4). The Molinist affirms this wholeheartedly.

Response to second argument

Is Molinism, morally speaking, "sufficiently analogous" to the type of Calvinism that embraces causal determinism? Welty's main claim is this:

> Let's assume that everything I just said is wrong. Let's assume for the sake of argument that Molinists are right in their views of what Calvinists must believe if their characteristic claims about divine providence (both positive and negative) are to "make sense." Let's say that Calvinism *must* make God the sufficient cause of sin, and so its author in an objectionable sense . . . Thus, given our ordinary intuitions about cases involving sufficient causation and moral responsibility, Molinism makes God the author of sin (in the objectionable sense) if Calvinism does.

So what is my short answer to his second claim? Not so. On this point I don't think Welty has made his case.

Welty's argument, if successful, would seem to succeed too well. All theological systems that uphold the traditional view of God's omniscience would be open to this charge. (Welty may contend that that's exactly his point.) But what does this say about the efforts of apophatic Calvinists to distance themselves from the implications of causal determinism? Most Calvinists distinguish between primary and secondary causation, and embrace infralapsarianism over supralapsarianism. This is why Welty takes an apophatic approach while throwing the causal determinists under the bus ("If they are subject to critique, so be it"). Many of our Reformed brethren recognize the moral difficulties posed by an adherence to causal determinism.

But I'm not sure that claiming mystery on this point helps. For there are three options for locating mystery. The first location constitutes *why God created this particular world knowing that evil would occur*. As far as I

---

14. Craig, "Molinism vs. Calvinism."

know, both Molinists and Calvinists confess this type of mystery. No problem. The second location constitutes *how God accomplishes his will through other causal agents.* Molinists contend that God, with precision and success, perfectly accomplishes his will through genuinely free creatures primarily by means of his omniscience. If, concerning God's concurrent actions with other agents, apophatic Calvinists wish to appeal to mystery on this point, then this would not seem necessarily to be an item of conflict between Molinists and Calvinists. Molinists provide a possible model while apophatic Calvinists do not, but both affirm that God can and does perfectly accomplish his will. Again, no problem.

The third location constitutes *why God is not culpable for the evil actions he causally determined.* Here's a real difference. I'm not sure apophatic language works at this point. It's one thing to say that it is a mystery how God concurrently accomplishes his will through other agents. It's another thing to say that it is a mystery as to why God is not accountable for their sins. If this is what is meant when Calvinists appeal to mystery, then indeed Molinists and Calvinists are at odds at this point. R. K. McGregor Wright argues that God is not accountable simply because he has no one to whom he must give an account.[15] True, but beside the point.

As Welty notes, most Calvinists want to preserve the concept of permission. Consider the following from Bruce Ware:

> It seems to me, that the strain in Calvinism that has been reluctant to embrace the "permissive will of God" simply rejects one of the very conceptual tools necessary to account for God's moral innocence in regard to evil. Surely more is needed than just this manner of divine activity. But I don't see how we can proceed if God's sovereign dealings in matters of good and evil are, in fact, symmetrical.[16]

Welty has good reason to distance himself from causal determinism, but in so doing he is disagreeing with a significant portion of modern Calvinists. However, I don't think his argument is successful, and it does not address the important issue of intent.

The crucial issue is the origin of intentions. The origin of intent matters, and so do the differences in intent. Welty helpfully notes that his argument is based on "our ordinary intuitions" about moral culpability. Our intuitions about intent play a role in our understanding of responsibility. However, the ethical distinction between a sting operation and entrapment is the origin of the intent to commit the crime. As long as the intent to commit the crime

15. McGregor Wright, *No Place for Sovereignty,* 177–204.

16. Ware, *God's Greater Glory,* 26.

originated in the mind of the criminal, and the police merely facilitate the crime (or feign facilitating the crime), then no entrapment has occurred. In the libertarian model of Molinism, intent originates in the doer of evil. Like law enforcement officials that implant the intent, Sproul Jr. himself illustrates that adherents of causal determinism have difficulty not laying responsibility at the feet of God. In this regard, the differences between (soft) libertarianism and (soft) determinism (i.e., compatibilism) really do matter. The distinctive feature of libertarianism, as advocated by proponents such as J. P. Moreland, is agent causation ("the notion of an active power").[17] We are created beings, so whatever freedom we have is not autonomous. But we are created in the divine image, so we reflect his ability to make moral choices. This ability is limited, derived, but real. Robert Saucy says that this power constitutes what might be termed "a little citadel of creativity *ex nihilo*."[18]

But one does not see a difference in intent in Welty's thought experiment. In the example of the two shooters, are they "sufficiently analogous" so that the one using Bullet Bill is just as morally culpable as the first shooter? I think most would agree that the answer is yes. But I don't think his example applies to Molinism. For it is doubtful this one example could be extrapolated to apply to all relevant scenarios, and, more importantly, this example does not seem to apply to *any* scenario posited by Molinists. The question at hand concerns moral culpability. In Welty's example, the intent of both shooters (it appears) is to commit murder. The fact that the second shooter used a gun containing a bullet possessing libertarian freedom (Bullet Bill) absolves him of nothing. We all agree that the person who hires a hit man is also guilty of the hit man's crime. Moreover, all Christians affirm that God indeed works through the evil done by wicked agents (Gen 50; Isa 10; Acts 2). But it really does matter whether or not those agents were the origins of their respective choices, and that at significant points they possessed the genuine ability to make those choices. For the Molinist, God doesn't have the intention, "I am creating Smith merely in order that he commit the sin I know that he will freely commit." In moral arguments, intentions matter. Even a strongly Reformed voice such as Paul Helm emphasizes this: "In the case of evil, whatever the difficulties may be of accounting for the fact, God ordains evil but he does not intend evil as evil, as the human agent intends it . . . There are other ends or purposes which God has in view."[19] God's intentions and purposes are different from the evil intentions and purposes of the wicked through whom he works or of those he permits to do evil. Molinism

---

17. Moreland, "Miracles," 141.

18. Saucy, "Theology," 38.

19. Helm, *Providence*, 190.

understands these evil persons to be the causal agents of their deeds. Thus Molinism is not "sufficiently analogous" to those versions of Calvinism that affirm causal determinism.

For example, *God can permit or allow an evil for just reasons.* During World War II, the Allies broke the secret codes of the Germans. According to some historians, the British knew beforehand of German plans to carpet bomb the city of Coventry. It was determined that if special actions were taken to defend the city, then that would tip off the Nazis that the Allies were intercepting their messages. Churchill reportedly made the difficult decision to allow the bombing to occur. Most would agree that Churchill's responsibility is not "sufficiently analogous" to that of the Axis forces.

Further, *God can accomplish righteous purposes through agents that have evil intentions.* Consider the execution of a heinous criminal. Imagine that the executioner carrying out the death sentence secretly delights in killing other humans, and enjoys legally performing an act that otherwise would be considered murder. The executioner's evil intent does not impugn the state's just cause. The intent of both is not "sufficiently analogous."

The difficulty of assigning moral responsibility in a causally determined universe

Those of us opposed to determinism are not simply shadow boxing. The challenges posed by determinism to morality become very clear in the writings of Darwinists. In his *The Moral Animal: The New Science of Evolutionary Psychology*, Robert Wright (a former Southern Baptist) argues for genetic causal determinism. He does not hesitate to describe humans as "puppets" and "robots." He disposes of notions such as free will and moral responsibility. Evil does not exist. He laments that humans are "robots" held "responsible for their malfunctions."[20] The primary advocates of determinism are not Calvinists, but atheists and Muslims.

I rejoice that mysterian Calvinists such as Welty also reject causal determinism. It may have been helpful if Welty spelled out clearly what models of human agency he believes to be compatible with apophatic Calvinism. The mysterian Calvinist seems to be noncommittal on whether or not God causes sin. If God causally determines sins, then the Calvinist position is indeed more problematic than the Molinist position, regardless of a claim to mystery. And it seems that if one denies that God causally determines sinful actions, then one needs Molinism to get the robust sense of God's sovereign control of all things. For the Christian, the options are divine determinism

20. Wright, *Moral Animal*, 355.

(either of an occasionalist variety or of an Edwardsian strongest desire variety) or (some form of) libertarianism. What other option is there?

Conclusion

For the reasons given above, Molinists believe that preserving libertarian freedom makes a significant difference in distinguishing between the just and pure decisions by God either to permit or work through the wicked and impure actions of humans. According to determinism, humans are not agents but rather are mere instruments. The Molinist believes that persons are causes, and for this reason they can be and, in fact, are morally responsible creatures.

Bibliography

Craig, William Lane. *The Problem of Divine Foreknowledge and Future Contingents from Aristotle to Suarez.* Leiden: Brill, 1988.

———. "Q&A #326: Is Molinism as Depressing as Calvinism?" Posted July 15, 2013. Available at: https://www.reasonablefaith.org/writings/question-answer/is-molinism-as-depressing-as-calvinism/.

Edwards, Jonathan. *Freedom of the Will.* In *Works of Jonathan Edwards*, Vol. 1, edited by P. Ramsey. New Haven, CT: Yale University Press, 1957.

Guelzo, Allen C. *Edwards on the Will: A Century of American Theological Debate.* Middletown, CT: Wesleyan University Press, 1989.

Helm, Paul. *The Providence of God.* Downers Grove, IL: InterVarsity, 1994.

Keathley, Kenneth D. *Salvation and Sovereignty: A Molinist Approach.* Nashville: B & H Academic, 2010.

McGregor Wright, R. K. *No Place for Sovereignty: What's Wrong with Freewill Theism.* Downers Grove, IL: InterVarsity, 1996.

Moreland, J. P. "Miracles, Agency, and Theistic Science: A Reply to Steven B. Cowan." *Philosophia Christi* 4.1 (2002) 139–60.

Olson, Roger. *Arminian Theology: Myths and Realities.* Downers Grove, IL: InterVarsity, 2006.

Picirilli, Robert E. *Grace, Faith, and Free Will.* Nashville: Randall House, 2002.

Saucy, Robert. "Theology of Human Nature." In *Christian Perspectives on Being Human: A Multidisciplinary Approach to Integration*, edited by J. P. Moreland and D. M. Ciocchi, 17–52. Grand Rapids: Baker, 1993.

Sproul Jr., R. C. *Almighty over All: Understanding the Sovereignty of God.* Grand Rapids: Baker, 1999.

Sproul Sr., R. C. *Chosen by God.* Wheaton, IL: Tyndale House, 1986.

Walls, Jerry. "Is Molinism as Bad as Calvinism?" *Faith and Philosophy* 7.1 (1990) 85–98.

Ware, Bruce A. *God's Greater Glory: The Exalted God of Scripture and the Christian Faith.* Wheaton, IL: Crossway, 2004.

Wright, Robert. *The Moral Animal: The New Science of Evolutionary Psychology.* New York: Vintage, 1994.

$$6$$

Molinist Gun Control: A Flawed Proposal?

A Reply to Ken Keathley's "Friendly Response"

GREG WELTY

Introduction

MY PIECE, "MOLINIST GUNSLINGERS: God and the Authorship of Sin," sought to address a particular criticism that Molinists make of Calvinists: Calvinistic divine providence makes God the sufficient cause of sin, and therefore Calvinists make God the author of sin and blameworthy for sin. By way of contrast, Molinists escape this charge because (on their view) God actualizes circumstances but he doesn't cause sins. So this is an objection that (allegedly) applies to Calvinism but not to Molinism.

My little point: apophatic theology

In that paper, I had a little point and a big point. *The little point* was to draw attention to "the apophatic character of Reformed definitions of divine providence, as these are enshrined in historically Reformed confessions of faith." The Reformed do make a very sweeping positive claim: "God from all eternity, did, by the most wise and holy counsel of His own will, freely, and unchangeably ordain whatsoever comes to pass." But they have always been careful to add to this positive claim about divine ordination a series of negative claims ("protecting clauses") intended to ward off various inferences one would otherwise make from the positive claim: "neither is God the author of sin," "nor is violence offered to the will of the creatures," "nor is the liberty or contingency of second causes taken away." This apophaticism may not be intellectually satisfying, but it seems just as acceptable as Chalcedon's apophatic definition of the incarnation of Christ.

I then made an analogical argument from the theological orthodoxy of Chalcedon to the theological orthodoxy of decretal Calvinism. Each position (Chalcedon, Calvinism) *seems* to involve untoward implications. For Chalcedon, the oneness of the person of Christ seems to involve *conversion or confusion of natures*, and the twoness of the natures seems to involve *division of the person or separation of the natures*. In response, Chalcedon simply adds four protecting clauses that explicitly deny these implications. Something parallel is going on in Calvinism: the ordination of all that comes to pass seems to involve universal causal determinism, or divine sufficient causality of sin, or authorship of sin in an objectionable sense. In response, the Reformed confessions simply add protecting clauses that explicitly deny these implications. *Neither* move is entirely satisfactory, intellectually speaking, because apophatic or "mysterian" positions get around these charges by *subtraction* rather than addition, and subtraction is not ordinarily a source of intellectual insight. But it's not as if Calvinists are in bad company to make a move like this.

My big point: the relevance of an underlying causal metaphysic that is common to the scenarios

The big point of the paper was something else entirely: to develop and defend at length tight parallels in the *underlying causal metaphysic* at work in the ordinary gun, Bullet Bill gun, and Molinist scenarios. What these parallels show is that even if "Calvinism must make God the sufficient cause of sin, such that he is its author and blameworthy for it," Molinists' "*own* model of divine causation is *sufficiently analogous* to sufficient causation, such that Molinism inherits all of the alleged Calvinist liabilities anyway, with respect to divine authorship of sin, responsibility, and blame." So Molinists should just drop this objection "from their repertoire of alleged advantages of Molinism over Calvinism."

Three Reasons Why Someone Might Think that God Is "The Author of Sin"

Let's back up for a moment and consider at least *three reasons why someone might think that God is "the author of sin" and is culpable for Adam's sin*:

1. God *intends* Adam's sin

2. God *infallibly ensures* that Adam will sin

3. God *causes* Adam to sin

Re: intentions, Molinists can easily deflect this objection by denying the claim. It's not that God intended Adam's sin, but that God *intended to use* Adam's sin for praiseworthy ends (including the praiseworthy end of creating the most valuable kind of world that could be created). But, of course, Calvinists can say the same exact thing, and have been saying it for centuries. Indeed, Keathley cites Paul Helm's use of this strategy.

Re: infallible ensuring, Molinists will agree that, necessarily, if God ordains that something come to pass, it will come to pass. But, they will say, it is the *way* that God ordains the future that makes all the difference here. God, says the Molinist, infallibly ordains the future existence of sin without causing that sin. He at worst "weakly actualizes" the sin by strongly actualizing the circumstances within which it occurs. But he doesn't cause the sin itself, even though he ordained that it come to pass. Unfortunately, Calvinists cannot avail themselves of this strategy, because they have no place for a weak actualization of sin that falls short of the causation of sin.

And so we get to the real issue, the third option above, the one that is supposed to bring out a crucial difference between Molinism and Calvinism. God-the-Molinist doesn't cause Adam to sin but *God-the-Calvinist does cause Adam to sin*. There is a difference in the *underlying causal metaphysic* endorsed in each system. And because of this, Calvinism makes God the author of sin and culpable for Adam's sin, but Molinism does not.

Keathley's Description of Molinist Providence

I am concerned with how Keathley repeatedly seems to understate the metaphysical side of Molinist providence. He describes Molinism as the *"belief that God perfectly accomplishes his will primarily by means of his exhaustive foreknowledge."* But this isn't quite right. The reason my critique works is because it exploits, not the Molinist appeal to foreknowledge, but rather the Molinist commitment to *God's actualizing circumstances*, as a way of pressing causal analogies between the ordinary gun, Bullet Bill gun, and Molinist cases. At some point in the Molinist scheme *God does something*, and I think I'm correct in thinking that at the very least he actualizes circumstances. This is analogous to the trigger pull in the two gun cases. It is true that God actualizes circumstances in light of his knowledge of CCFs, but it is *the circumstance-actualization*, not the knowledge of CCFs, that provides the "causal oomph" here. We must be careful not to underdescribe Molinism in a way that makes reference to mere foreknowledge, and not to God's actualizing of circumstances.

Again, Keathley says, *"The Molinist believes that God generally uses his knowledge of the possible choices of significantly free creatures in order to accomplish his will."* If only it were true that we could construct a doctrine of divine providence via omniscience alone! But Molinists do not do that. It can't be *mere knowledge* that God uses, because mere knowledge of CCFs doesn't get us a world with moral agents in it. Rather, and most crucially for my evaluative purposes, God *creates and places moral agents in circumstances,* "in order to accomplish his will." It is only when one focuses on divine actualizing of circumstances that one is in a place to appreciate the tight parallels between the ordinary gun, Bullet Bill gun, and Molinist scenarios. The ordinary gun trigger pull is a culpable action that surely seems to bring about a death that I cause. Likewise, God's actualization of circumstances is a culpable divine action that surely seems to bring about subsequent sin. The intermediary Bullet Bill case makes this clear.

Keathley on My Relationship to Causal Determinism

Keathley says, *"Welty acknowledges that some Calvinists do indeed embrace causal determinism, but he distances himself from them."* But this isn't correct. I never explicitly *reject* the thesis of causal determinism in the paper, so the distancing is not rejection. Rather, "mysterian Calvinists" are simply those *"who rest content with apophatic formulations, in the grand historical tradition of Chalcedon."* They see no *need* to appeal to causal determinism, in any statement of their beliefs. But *withholding* belief in causal determinism is different from *rejecting* causal determinism.

One reason for my reluctance to commit one way or the other to causal determinism is that I haven't yet seen a clear statement of the doctrine which is such that it is obvious that Calvinists must sign on to it. For instance, here is the definition provided in the *Stanford Encyclopedia of Philosophy*: *"Causal determinism is, roughly speaking, the idea that every event is necessitated by antecedent events and conditions together with the laws of nature."*[1] But as long as miracles occur, causal determinism defined in this way is false. In addition, God's non-physical causation in the world (whether regular or miraculous) cannot be assimilated to laws of *nature*, and there are no laws of *supernature* to take their place. So I don't see any reason for a theist to accept the doctrine, defined this way.

---

1. Available at: http://plato.stanford.edu/entries/determinism-causal/.

On the other hand, many of the reasons often given for *rejecting* the doctrine also strike me as dubious. For instance, the idea that unless we reject causal determinism we make God culpable for sin. Thus the second section of my gunslingers paper.

Keathley says that I take *"an apophatic approach while throwing the causal determinists under the bus ('If they are subject to critique, so be it')."* But just to be clear: I'm *not* throwing them under the bus. I neither rejected nor endorsed causal determinism, choosing not to address that issue for the sake of having a fairly efficient and focused paper. I was happy to accept it *for the sake of argument*, in order to argue that one particular Molinist objection is misguided.

Keathley on "Determinism and Libertarianism [as] the Only Two Options"

Keathley seems favorable to the view that *"in regard to human choice, determinism and libertarianism are the only two options. If the conceptual space is exhausted by these two options, and one wishes to reject determinism, isn't one left with libertarianism?"* Not that I can see. Here I am highly influenced by the "semi-compatibilist" position articulated by John Martin Fischer and Mark Ravizza.[2] *First*, compatibilism is not an assertion that determinism *is* true and that humans *are* free. Rather, it is an assertion that these two realities (if they are realities) are *compatible*. *Second*, semi-compatibilism is the view that, while determinism may rule out freedom, it doesn't rule out moral responsibility. Fischer and Ravizza are searching for a theory of moral responsibility which is such that it would survive the discovery that determinism is true, *or* the discovery that indeterminism is true. In other words, whether or not human beings are morally responsible doesn't hang upon the thread of scientific discovery that causal determinism is true (or false). It could survive either discovery. *But the semi-compatibilist thesis doesn't involve the belief that determinism is true.* That's where I'm at, partly because I think that's a pretty robust theory of moral responsibility (if it works, of course).

Keathley on How I Overgeneralize about Molinists

Keathley says my "complaint seems to overgeneralize about Molinists," as if they think that all Calvinists are causal determinists. Well, in my original

---

2. Fischer and Ravizza, *Responsibility and Control*.

paper, I didn't say all Molinists! But I concede I could have been clearer, and so I should change my reference from "Molinists" to "many Molinists," and that would accommodate the distinctions in Keathley's book.

At the risk of committing the "no true Scotsman" fallacy, it does seem to me that in referring to Jewett, George, and Berkouwer as "Calvinists who are critics of causal determinism,"[3] Keathley may be referring to those who are one or the other, but not both. The quote from Jewett makes a distinction between the *way* God determines our wills and the way he determines inanimate, physical things (skin color, hair). That seems sensible, and it's not clear why an advocate of causal determinism would deny it. The quote from George eschews a "strict determinism" that doesn't make room for creaturely freedom. But why is that a rejection of causal determinism? Berkouwer is rejecting "mechanistic-deterministic causality," but so would any Calvinist who doesn't reduce the *imago Dei* to *mechanism*. Nobody thinks we're built up out of gears and switches. Unlike car transmissions, we have intentions, goals, desires, reasons, and we deliberate. Surely no Christian committed to causal determinism denies this. (In addition, I think the late Berkouwer left the Calvinism of the early Berkouwer in favor of Barthianism.[4])

Still, regardless of any disagreement over how to interpret sources, I should have acknowledged that Keathley's book has room for both kinds of Calvinists. So I should just say "many Molinists." It did seem to me that Keathley's *Salvation and Sovereignty* focused rather intensely on the thesis that Calvinism *just is* a form of causal determinism. For instance, he says that Calvinism's moral dilemma results from its *"adhering to a deterministic view of sovereignty."*[5] The phrase *"causal determinism"* is used twenty-seven times in the book, and it is clearly intended to be descriptive of the Calvinistic stance critiqued there. So my point in that first section of the paper was not to argue that Molinists claim an advantage over *more apophatic formulations* of Calvinism, but to bring to light that such apophatic formulations *actually exist!*

Keathley on the Apophatic Strategy

Keathley says he's *"not sure the apophatic language works"* to deflect the charge *"why God is not culpable for the evil actions he causally determined."*

---

3. Keathley, *Salvation and Sovereignty*, 97–99.

4. John Murray (*Collected Writings*, 4:323–30) wrote a negative review of Berkouwer's book on election; see also Henry Krabbendam, "Warfield Versus Berkouwer," 413–46 and Baker, *Berkouwer's Doctrine of Election*.

5. Keathley, *Salvation and Sovereignty*, 4.

But of course the whole point of the apophatic language is to *eschew* the language of "causal determinism": you don't give a deterministic theory, *or any other theory*, about *how* God brings about all the things he has ordained.

Keathley says, "*It's one thing to say that it is a mystery how God concurrently accomplishes his will through other agents. It's another thing to say that it is a mystery as to why he's not accountable for their sins. If this is what is meant when Calvinists appeal to mystery, then indeed Molinists and Calvinists are at odds at this point.*" But this distinction will not do, such that we can accept a mystery of concurrence but not a mystery of divine accountability. These issues are clearly linked. If we don't know *how* "*God concurrently accomplishes his will through other agents,*" then how can we settle the matter as to whether or not he is accountable for their sins? On *some* accounts of divine concurrence, perhaps he turns out culpable; on other accounts, he doesn't. If there's not even a possibility that these two issues are linked, I daresay hardly anyone in church history would have *cared* about carefully articulating the doctrine of concurrence. But many, many have!

Keathley on Divine Permission

One reason I constructed the analogies I did is that "divine permission" turns out to be useless in solving the *moral* difficulty. Keathley quotes Bruce Ware: "*It seems to me, that the strain in Calvinism that has been reluctant to embrace the 'permissive will of God' simply rejects one of the very conceptual tools necessary to account for God's moral innocence in regard to evil.*" But *if I'm right*, Ware is flat wrong, and quoting him doesn't fix this. Make Molinism as permissive as you please. My point is that you *still* don't have the "*conceptual tools necessary to account for God's moral innocence in regard to evil.*" As long as God is an actualizer of circumstances who relies on his knowledge of contingent, prevolitional, counterfactual truths in order to bring about an effect, we have all the features in place in the *Molinist* scenario that generates culpability in *the ordinary gun* scenario. So permission is a thin reed on which to lean in order to solve the problem of divine culpability. (The reason why the issues are so parallel here between Calvinism and Molinism is because of the *orthodoxy* that we have in common as brothers in Christ: creation, providence, the omni-attributes. You can only void this parallel by embracing a much more interesting but sadly heterodox position, like open theism, and even that is a big maybe.)

Keathley's Responses to the Bullet Bill Argument

"Welty's argument, if successful, would seem to succeed too well."

Keathley points out that *"All theological systems that uphold the traditional view of God's omniscience would be open to this charge."* Not at all! My critique doesn't apply to any *traditional Arminian account,* according to which God *lacks* middle knowledge, and thus *does not know*—in advance of his decision to create—what Adam would do if he were placed in different circumstances.

The reason my critique applies *to Molinism* is because it appeals to features *specific to Molinism*: the ordinary gun, Bullet Bill gun, and Molinist scenarios have the following *underlying causal metaphysic* in common: *in each case an actualizer of circumstances relies on his knowledge of contingent, prevolitional, counterfactual truths in order to bring about an effect.* If in virtue of this underlying causal metaphysic we would hold the actualizer culpable for the effect in the ordinary gun and Bullet Bill gun scenarios, why wouldn't we hold the actualizer culpable for the effect in the Molinist scenario? Now the ball is in Keathley's court: what is the difference in the *underlying causal metaphysic,* between the ordinary gun case and the Molinist case, such that God-the-Molinist isn't culpable for the outcome?

Keathley says that *"many of our Reformed brethren recognize the moral difficulties posed by an adherence to causal determinism."* Sure. The point is that you can't avoid *that* problem by embracing Molinism instead. And *that* is surely a challenge to one of the central points in Keathley's book. When it comes time to critique explicitly deterministic forms of Calvinism, Keathley clearly thinks they make God the author of sin *and Molinism does not.* I'm arguing against *that* claim. Pointing out that Reformed brethren recognize moral difficulties doesn't help to avoid my parity argument.

Keathley says that he's *"not sure that claiming mystery on this point helps."* But in the *second* section of the paper, appeal to mystery is explicitly *eschewed,* rather than "claimed." In the *second* section, what I claim "helps" on this point is *not* mystery, but close attention to analogies between uncontroversial cases of efficient causation and Molinism. So, to be clear, in this paper I'm not trying to *avoid* the charge that Calvinism makes God the author of sin. I'm trying to show that alleged Molinist differences from Calvinism don't absolve *Molinists* of the charge.

"The crucial issue is the origin of intentions."

Who caused the intentions of the shooter?

Keathley says that my argument is not successful because *"it does not address the important issue of intent."* But that's because the issue of intent is irrelevant. The intentions of an agent are brought about on Molinist providence just as much as anything else. God ordains *whatsoever* comes to pass. So one can simply reapply my argument all over again, this time to the intentions of the earthly agent, and you get the same result. Here's how.

Keathley says that "As long as the intent to commit the crime *originated in the mind of the criminal,* and the police merely facilitate the crime (or feign facilitating the crime), then no entrapment has occurred." But if by "originated in" Keathley means "is caused by," then he is simply begging the question against me. If, as I argued, Molinist providence *can* be assimilated to the ordinary gun scenario, then *God* causes the agent's intentions even as *I* cause the bullet to speed down the chamber. Or, alternatively, if God doesn't cause the agent's intentions then I don't cause the bullet to speed down the chamber. It is up to Keathley to argue for a morally-relevant difference here, because I gave an extended argument for a common underlying causal metaphysic in the two scenarios. So whether one understands "origination" or "causation" strictly or loosely, the parallel remains for all morally-relevant purposes. I cause Bullet Bill (the libertarian bullet) to come out of the chamber just in case I cause the ordinary bullet to come out of the chamber. In each case I am pulling triggers and relying on counterfactual truths over which I have no control.

Because this point is so important, we need to be crystal clear on the exact parallels (I pointed these out in my original paper, particularly in response to the sixth objection). In the ordinary gun case, *I do not cause the bullet to have its causal powers.* And *I do not cause the bullet to have the liability to exercise its causal powers in particular ways in particular circumstances.* In fact, I have nothing to do with the bullet's causal powers and liabilities. They are what they are quite *independently* of me. But surely as the shooter I am not off the hook simply because I don't cause the bullet's causal powers, or its liabilities to exercise those powers! Rather I am *on the hook* because I did something (pull the trigger) knowing that if I actualized that circumstance (the pulling of the trigger) the bullet *would* exercise its causal powers and do its thing.

How are things any different, *in these crucial respects*, when it comes to Molinism? God doesn't make it the case that the agent *would* do such-and-such, in particular circumstances. Like the law of nature in the ordinary gun scenario, what the agent *would* do is a brute fact over which God has no control and does not cause. It's up to the agent what he would agent-cause in particular circumstances. Notice that in the ordinary gun scenario *I don't cause* these features of the bullet, and in the Molinist scenario *God doesn't cause* these features of the agent. *In each case I (or God) rely on brute facts that we didn't cause and over which we have no control.* Keathley's pointing this out in the Molinist scenario doesn't deflect responsibility from God, even as pointing this out in the ordinary gun scenario doesn't deflect responsibility from the shooter. (In fact, things are *worse* on Molinism because God creates the agent and his causal powers and sustains the agent and his causal powers over time. The shooter doesn't create the bullet or its causal powers or sustain it in being. There is no relation of concurrence between the shooter and the bullet, as there is between God and the agent. So if I'm culpably involved in the ordinary gun scenario, *how much more* is God culpably involved in the Molinist scenario!)

What is the moral difference between the shooter and God, between someone who *brings about an effect by way of actualizing a circumstance and relying on a law of nature* (i.e., the shooter), and someone who *brings about an effect by way of actualizing a circumstance and relying on a counterfactual* (i.e., God)? This question remains, even if we make the "effect" the human agent's own intention. Again, the intentions of an agent are brought about on Molinist providence just as much as anything else. God ordains *whatsoever* comes to pass. In short, God is the sufficient cause of the agent's intentions if and only if the shooter is the sufficient cause of the bullet's movement. Due to the parallel, the causal claim is true in the one scenario just in case it's true in the other one, and then we assess culpability accordingly.

Keathley attempts to illustrate the alleged moral advantages of Molinist providence by referring to Winston Churchill's "difficult decision to allow the bombing to occur" (the Axis bombing of Coventry, that is). *But Churchill is not a plausible stand-in for Molinist providence*, because Churchill was not actualizing circumstances while relying on contingent, prevolitional, counterfactual truths in order to ensure the actualization of a meticulous outcome. In Molinism, this is exactly what God does! And in all *those* respects, it's exactly similar to my pulling a trigger on an ordinary gun. (Indeed, in Keathley's example Churchill doesn't have to *do* anything, but clearly God-the-Molinist *does* something: he actualizes circumstances.)

What are God's intentions with respect to the human agent's sin?

Keathley thinks there is a disanalogy between the ordinary gun scenario and the Molinist scenario in terms of *causation*: the shooter *causes* the bullet to move but God *doesn't cause* the agent's intentions. We've already seen how that begs the question.

But Keathley alleges a *second* disanalogy between the cases with respect to intentions, and it has to do with *God's intentions*. On the gun scenarios (ordinary and Bullet Bill),

> the intent of both shooters (it appears) is to commit murder. The fact that the second shooter used a gun containing a bullet possessing libertarian freedom (Bullet Bill) absolves him of nothing. We all agree that the person who hires a hit man is also guilty of the hit man's crime.

Thus, in the gun scenarios, the shooters *intended* to kill and so are culpable (given their intentions). By way of contrast, in the Molinist scenario, *"God's intentions and purposes are different from the evil intentions and purposes of the wicked through whom he works or of those he permits to do evil."* God *doesn't* intend the sinful deeds of human agents, and so he is off the hook as far as culpability. Keathley says, *"For the Molinist, God doesn't have the intention, 'I am creating Smith merely in order that he commit the sin I know that he will freely commit.'"* So my analogies allegedly fail: conditions for culpability are satisfied in the first two scenarios, but not in the third (the Molinist one).

Notice that this criticism doesn't dispute the underlying causal metaphysic that I argue is common to all three cases. Indeed, Keathley's criticism *accepts* that the Bullet Bill shooter *is* culpable, even though Bullet Bill caused his own intentions! "The fact that the second shooter used a gun containing a bullet possessing libertarian freedom (Bullet Bill) absolves him of nothing." Doesn't that concede my main argument?

In any event, rather than disputing the underlying causal metaphysic, Keathley deflects divine culpability by insisting that God doesn't *intend* the sins that he ordains. Human agents intend their sins for evil ends, whereas God intends to work such sins (or allow such sins) for very good purposes, and it is those good purposes which he intends, not the sins. I say, "Amen! This is a fine piece of reasoning." But it is equally available to Calvinists, and has in fact been employed by Calvinists for centuries. Indeed, Keathley cites the Calvinist Paul Helm as making this exact point: *"In the case of evil, whatever the difficulties may be of accounting for the fact, God ordains evil but he does not intend evil as evil, as the human agent intends it . . . There are other ends or purposes which God has in view.*[6]

The reason why this is a fine piece of reasoning has little to do with Molinism and everything to do with *the basic moral fact that intentions are not closed under known entailment.* If S intends that p, and S knows that p implies q, it does not follow that S thereby intends q. So let's say that God intends the world he creates in virtue of some property p that applies to the whole: its overall intrinsic value, or the fact that it tends to promote his glory, or manifests the full range of his attributes. God intends the world in virtue of this property p, even though he knows that his creation of the world implies sinful human intentions q. Since intentions are not closed under known entailment, it does not follow that God thereby intends q. As Aquinas puts it when talking about killing in self-defense, "Nothing hinders one act from having two effects, only one of which is intended, while the other is beside the intention . . . Accordingly the *act* of self-defense may have two effects, one is the saving of one's life, the other is the slaying of the aggressor."[7] *So if Molinists get the doctrine of double effect, so do Calvinists.*

It follows that since the strategy Keathley is employing to get God off the hook is already available to Calvinists, then once again the argument "sufficient cause therefore culpable author of sin" does nothing to distinguish Calvinism from Molinism. It should therefore be dropped from the Molinist repertoire of objections to Calvinism (just as I originally argued). Keathley's strategy here therefore *confirms* the overall conclusion of my previous paper: there are no resources *distinctive to Molinism* that can help deflect the "author of sin" charge.

I *thought* the charge was that Calvinism is committed to an *underlying causal metaphysics* that makes Calvinism *uniquely* susceptible to the charge of divine culpability for sin. If one wants to argue instead that it is divine *intention*, rather than divine causal efficacy, that is relevant to the charge of divine culpability, well OK, but Calvinists have handled that one for centuries by distinguishing between divine intent and human intent with respect to one and the same set of events.

(I can't pass over the fact that Keathley seems to think that Calvinists believe the divine intention is correctly captured by the following: "*I am creating Smith merely in order that he commit the sin I know that he will freely commit.*" But surely *no* Calvinist believes this, or believes anything that implies this! Which Calvinists say that God creates people *merely in order* that they commit sin? The very idea turns God into a short-range moral

---

6. Helm, *Providence*, 190.

7. Aquinas, *Summa Theologiae*, II.ii, q. 64, a. 7 *respondeo*.

idiot. If there's anything Calvinists have been clear about, it is that God has *long-range purposes* in his decree. "By the decree of God, *for the manifestation of His glory*" (WCF III.3). No one is created *merely in order* that they do the things they do.)

Keathley on the Causal Analogies

The ordinary gun, Bullet Bill gun, and Molinist scenarios have the following *underlying causal metaphysic* in common: *in each case an actualizer of circumstances relies on contingent, prevolitional, counterfactual truths in order to bring about an effect.* (That one claim applies to all three scenarios.) If in virtue of this underlying causal metaphysic we would hold the actualizer culpable for the effect, in the ordinary gun and Bullet Bill gun scenarios, why wouldn't we hold the circumstance-actualizer culpable in the Molinist scenario?

Bibliography

Aquinas, Thomas. *Summa Theologiae.* 5 vols. Westminster, MD: Christian Classics, 1981.

Baker, Alvin L. *Berkouwer's Doctrine of Election: Balance or Imbalance?* Phillipsburg, NJ: Presbyterian & Reformed, 1981.

Fischer, John Martin, and Mark Ravizza. *Responsibility and Control: A Theory of Moral Responsibility.* Cambridge: Cambridge University Press, 1998.

Krabbendam, Henry. "B. B. Warfield Versus G. C. Berkouwer on Scripture." In *Inerrancy*, edited by Norman L. Geisler, 413–46. Grand Rapids: Zondervan, 1980.

Murray, John. *Collected Writings of John Murray.* Carlisle, PA: Banner of Truth, 1982.

Part III

Calvinist Appropriation of Middle Knowledge

7

Does Calvinism Have Room for Middle Knowledge?

A Conversation

Paul Helm and
Terrance L. Tiessen

I. *Helm:* "No"

Terrance L. Tiessen has recently offered a detailed advocacy of why Calvinists should believe in divine middle knowledge while at the same time rejecting Molinism.[1] He believes that such a position has various advantages. In this rejoinder I first examine the cogency of the position that he defends, and then take a look at the supposed benefits of it, and finally consider an objection.

1. *Background*

It is a great merit of Professor Tiessen's presentation that as part of it he engages with the history of Reformed theology, notably with the Reformed Orthodox such as Francis Turretin. So it is appropriate that we should briefly remind ourselves of aspects of the position that they adopted, particularly the distinction that they drew (drawing in turn on medieval discussions) between God's *natural knowledge* and God's *free* knowledge. Turretin, for example, puts the distinction in the following way:

---

1. Tiessen, "Why Calvinists Should Believe," 345–66. Professor Tiessen advocated this position in his *Providence and Prayer*. For a similar view, see Ware, *God's Greater Glory*.

It [viz., God's knowledge] is commonly distinguished by theologians into the knowledge of single intelligence (or natural and indefinite) and the knowledge of vision (or free and definite). The former is the knowledge of things merely possible and is therefore called indefinite because nothing on either hand is determined concerning them by God. The latter is the knowledge of future things and is called definite because future things are determined by the sure will of God. Hence they mutually differ: (1) in object because the natural knowledge is occupied with possible things, but the free [knowledge is] about future things; (2) in foundation because the natural is founded on the omnipotence of God, but the free depends upon his will and decree by which things pass from a state of possibility to a state of futurition; (3) in order because the natural precedes the decree, but the free follows it because it beholds things future; now they are not future except by the decree.[2]

The object of God's natural knowledge

is both himself (who most perfectly knows himself in himself) and all things extrinsic to him whether possible or future (i.e., as to their various orders and states; as to quantity—great and small; as to quality—good and bad; as to predication—universals and singulars; as to time—past, present and future; as to state—necessary and free or contingent).[3]

On this way of thinking the two sorts of knowledge are exclusive and exhaustive. There is no room for a third category, middle knowledge. "There is nothing in the nature of things which is not possible or future; nor can future conditional things [viz., the contents of the supposed middle knowledge] constitute a third order."[4]

Though this distinction between natural and free knowledge is a mere distinction of reason (or order, as Turretin put it) and so does not represent a temporal distinction in the eternal mind of God, yet it might not be altogether inaccurate to think of God's natural knowledge as the knowledge of infinite possible worlds, each world a maximal possible state of affairs,[5] and his free knowledge as the knowledge of that world which through the

2. Turretin, *Institutes*, 1:212–13.

3. Ibid., 1:207.

4. Ibid., 1:214. For a brief modern account of the traditional view of God's natural and free knowledge in the context of a discussion of Molinism, see Flint, *Divine Providence*, 35–71.

5. For a standard modern account of possible worlds, see Plantinga, *Necessity*, 44–69.

divine decree is created, and so becomes actual.[6] It would not be inaccurate, that is, if we thought of the divine decree as an act of selection from among the infinite array of possible worlds known naturally by God in virtue of his omnipotence, even though the act of selection is nonetheless timelessly eternal, not an action in time.

2. Professor Tiessen's proposal

Besides the natural and the free knowledge of God, which he recognizes, Professor Tiessen proposes to insert a category of divine knowledge in between them, a form of conditional knowledge, and in that sense a form of middle knowledge. Yet he is emphatic that this is not the middle knowledge of Molina or of modern proponents of Molinism such as W. L. Graig or Alvin Plantinga, whose proposal is strongly motivated by the need to make provision for causally indifferent or indeterminately free human choices. Tiessen is resolutely opposed to such an account of freedom, and so the need to safeguard it and provide for it forms no part of his proposal. As Tiessen explains things, middle knowledge (as he understands it) is God's knowledge of what possible creatures *would* do, and this "is significantly or categorically different from his knowledge of what they *could* do (necessary knowledge) but is logically prior to God's knowledge of what actual creatures will do."[7] Both God's knowledge of what possible creatures *could do*, and what they *would do*, is prior to any decree that God makes as to what they *will* do.

As I understand it, Professor Tiessen's proposal amounts to the following: God has knowledge of what A would do in circumstances C.[8] What he would do, given who A is, depends upon A's dispositions, desires, plans, etc., at that time, what the circumstances are at that time, and how A appreciates these circumstances. This is what A *would* do. For Tiessen this is distinct, "significantly or categorically different," from what A in C *could* do. What A could do is more abstract. What A would do in C is or may come to be an element of an entire possible world, in fact of more than one possible world. In contemplating the possible world which is to become the actual world

---

6. Tiessen himself favors this way of representing the distinction: "He [God] knows everything that *could be*, he knows all possible worlds" ("Why Calvinists Should Believe," 347).

7. Tiessen, "Why Calvinists Should Believe," 347.

8. In what follows, each time I use "what A would (or could) do in C" as my central example, A represents a person, with an array of beliefs, desires, and objectives, and C stands for the circumstances A is in, some features of which at least A is aware of.

God may insert the segment, what A would naturally do in C, as part of that world, along with his own activity in intervening in the life of A in that world (if such activity is judged to be wise). Because of the compatibilistic character of A's free action, God would know how A would behave if his circumstances were to be affected by such divine activity. Tiessen is not very specific about the character of this intervention, but it presumably could include miracles, and other supernatural influences of various kinds. So what A *would* do in C is a relatively independent subset of a possible world, and in becoming part of the possible world that God decrees, it may or may not be modified, depending upon the wisdom of God and so forth.

> God is then able to decide whether he will simply permit people (or angels) to do what they would naturally do in those circumstances, or whether he needs to introduce activity of his own Spirit, either by way of dissuasion . . . or by promptings of his own. It is only in God's decree that he decides which of the huge number of counterfactuals will be actualized, and how they will come to be, whether they are actively permitted (as in the case of evil) or brought about through more specific divine activity (as in the case of all the good which redounds to God's glory).[9]

Segments such as what A would do in C have a purely naturalistic character, a state of affairs whose accurate description contains no reference to God's activity, a character which God is appraised of, and which may then, by the divine decree, form part of the actual world. Tiessen repeatedly distinguishes between such counterfactuals (understood as actualizable conditionals) and the possible worlds in which they occur.[10]

So the first feature of his account of Calvinist middle knowledge is that such knowledge is composed of logically prior elements, such as what A would do in C, together with how God would, if at all, modify this element in incorporating it into the world he will create, in the light of his wise purposes for A and for others.

The second feature of the status of this middle knowledge is that its "moment" or "moments" are temporal moments, as the following passage makes clear.

> Thus, in my middle knowledge Calvinist model, *before* God decides what he will do by way of creating a world and ordering its history, God knows how particular creatures would act if they found themselves in particular sets of circumstances. This knowledge enables God to choose a world whose history

---

9. Tiessen, "Why Calvinists Should Believe," 352.

10. Ibid., 363.

is exactly the history that he wisely purposes, but to bring about that history through a combination of the morally responsible actions of rationed creatures and God's own actions.[11]

So the components of divine middle knowledge are features of the divine mind involved in a temporal process of deciding which world to actualize. As Tiessen puts it, there is a further stage, beyond God's natural knowledge, in which God

> would not simply be intuiting, he would be deliberating, analyzing, calculating "what if" scenarios that include both the creatures' actions and his own . . . I judge that this deliberative process of assessment, and of playing out scenarios, moves beyond what God knows simply because he knows himself and all that he could do consistently with his own nature. This deliberative process makes use of his natural knowledge, but it moves beyond it, and yet is prior to his decision to choose a particular world.[12]

This is an avowedly temporal process, a "deliberative process," involving the activities of analyzing and calculating. Such deliberation *must* be a temporal event or stage in the divine mind, not just an intermediate logical moment which we may introduce for the purposes of clarifying our own thought about the order of elements in the divine mind, but a temporal moment. But if the divine life has temporal moments, then in the preparation of the possible world that he will decree God is in time, he is temporal.

So what are the benefits of such an innovative proposal? Those proposed by Tiessen may conveniently be distinguished between benefits for God himself, and benefits for our understanding of God's relation to evil. As regards God himself Tiessen says,

> God's knowledge of what particular creatures *would do* in all possible circumstances is immensely useful to God. It enables him to choose the world history best suited to his nature and purposes for the world without having to force his will upon his creatures. In knowing how a particular creature would act in a given set of circumstances, God is able to choose the world in which the combination of the actions of God and his creatures would eventuate in exactly what God desired, but this can be brought about with minimal direct intervention. Thus, God need not force or coerce his creatures in order to have things turn out as he wished.[13]

11. Ibid., 352; emphasis in original.

12. Ibid., 355.

13. Ibid., 347–48.

And the benefits for us?

> This has valuable implications for understanding how God is
> genuinely responsive to human prayers and how God meticu-
> lously governs human history in a manner that preserves his
> absolute sovereignty without taking away the moral responsibil-
> ity of the human beings who bring about that history It helps us
> to understand why God is not morally responsible for the evil
> acts of his creatures, even though these are all part of his eternal
> purpose and are, therefore, done according to God's will.[14]

The idea is that in decreeing what A in C would do, in rendering it actual, God utilizes the choices and actions that A in C would naturally make,
make in an unforced or uncoerced way, what he would do. God does this
by (in a sense) "finding" A in C. A in C is already "there," already "present,"
present as a possibility, what God would do, part of his middle knowledge.

3. *Comments*

There is a lot here. I shall confine my response to an attempt to show the
unsatisfactoriness of this proposal by making three distinct points, and then
by answering a possible objection.

First, I shall probe the distinction (which Tiessen emphasizes, and
which is central to his account) between what A in circumstances C *could*
do, and what A in circumstances C *would* do. Second, I shall query the intelligibility of these purely naturalistic segments. Third, I shall say something
about what motivates Professor Tiessen in offering this account.

Could and Would. Tiessen thinks that God's knowledge of what A in
C *would* do is "significantly or categorically different" from what A in C
could do.[15] However he nowhere explains, as far as I can see, why there is
this significant difference, but simply asserts it. But he most certainly needs
to provide an argument for this claim if he is ever going to have a chance
of convincing the sceptic. Because it seems obvious that if there is some
particular thing that A *would* do in C, some particular choice that he would
make, for example, then it is also the case that A *could make* that choice. If
he would do it, then he could do it, and if he can't do it then he wouldn't
do it by willing it or wanting it or by bringing it about in some other way.
Generally, what a person *would do* is a subset of what that person *could* do.

14. Ibid., 348.
15. Ibid., 347.

Given Tiessen's failure to provide a reason to treat *would* as significantly different from *could*, the divine knowledge of what A *would* do in C, however we may suppose that this knowledge is gained, cannot contribute to anything that is significantly different from what the divine knowledge of what A in C *could* do, however this knowledge is obtained. And the knowledge of what A *could* do in C is part of God's natural knowledge.

For on the classic view of God's knowledge, God by his natural knowledge knows what A in all possible states of his mind could do in all possible sets of circumstances. The contents of all possible worlds containing A include propositions about what A would do if C were to be the case, of if D were to be the case, and so on. These are not so much counterfactual, as pre-factual. In the divine mind the states of mind and sets of circumstances of a possible agent A form elements in innumerable possible worlds, all of the possible worlds in which A exists. But given that he provides us with no argument it is not at all clear on what basis Tiessen claims that there is a significant difference between God knowing what A *could* do in C and knowing what A *would* do in C. It is obviously not sufficient for him simply to assert that Calvinist middle knowledge requires this distinction between could and would, for the prior question must be, is there this distinction in the first place?

It is striking that despite the significance of the distinction for his case, Tiessen does not say much about its basis. But perhaps he provides a clue to his thinking in the contrast that he draws between "the knowledge God has of things which are possible by virtue of their consistency with God's own nature (his natural or necessary knowledge) and his knowledge of what creatures *would* do in particular circumstances."[16] Here Tiessen appears to be thinking on the one hand of what A in C could do considered only in the light of God's own nature, as being somewhat abstract or unspecific, and on the other hand what it is concretely possible for A to do in sets of circumstances such as C, what A would do. This is borne out by the later claim that by his natural knowledge God has the knowledge of logical relations, causal relationships, and so on, that ground "his more *particular knowledge* in the middle stage."[17]

But there are two things problematic about such a suggestion. One is the problem of what an account of this more abstract relation of A to God's nature would look like, and the other is whether Tiessen is giving an accurate account of the natural knowledge of God as this has been understood in the tradition. Tiessen also appears to think that his view of God's

---

16. Ibid.

17. Ibid., 365; emphasis added.

natural knowledge is prefigured by something Richard A. Muller says about the orthodox Reformed view, which he quotes. Muller refers to this account of natural knowledge as indefinite, "inasmuch as its objects are possibilities, not actualities."[18] But this does not mean that all the objects of natural knowledge are abstract or that they in any respect lack the specificity of the objects of his free knowledge, actualities.[19] Some of them certainly are abstract, including the hosts of necessary truths that God knows. For in addition to knowing all possibilities, God by his natural knowledge knows all necessities, propositions that are true across every different possible world he knows. In this sense the necessary truths God knows may be said to be more abstract than the possibilities God knows. But Professor Tiessen does not seem to have these in mind here.

It is characteristic of the account of God's natural knowledge, not that it concerns (merely) all possible beings, such as A, but that God by his natural knowledge knows with full specificity what A (in all possible states of his mind and body) would (or could) do in all possible circumstances. The schedule of the immense range of A's states of mind and body placed in the immense range of circumstances in which he could be situated would be doubly immense, but still relatively small in comparison to the remaining sets of possibilities in which these immensities could (or would) in turn be placed as they form the elements of possible worlds.

It is in such terms that it is plausible to understand the traditional account of the natural knowledge of God. Turretin, for example, says, "Natural and free knowledge embrace all knowable things and entities."[20] God by his natural knowledge knows all knowable possibilities, not merely sets of individuals and sets of circumstances in abstraction. And at one point Tiessen himself says that God "knows everything that *could* be, he knows all possible worlds."[21] But if God's natural knowledge includes all possible worlds, then he knows (in complete detail) all the possible worlds in which A exists, with all their differing circumstances from world to world. So it remains doubtful whether there is any distinct category of what *would* be as against what *could* be that could (or would) form the basis of a category of divine middle knowledge of a Calvinist kind.

---

18. Ibid., 346 n. 8.

19. We noted earlier that Turretin contrasts the indefiniteness (*indefinitam*) of God's natural knowledge with the definiteness (*definitam*) of his free knowledge. But this contrast is not made in terms of the specificity of the knowledge but of its temporal fixedness.

20. Turretin, *Institutes*, 1:214.

21. Tiessen, "Why Calvinists Should Believe," 347.

Secondly, as I understand what he says, Tiessen believes that what God knows about what A *would* do in C, where what A would do in C is considered "naturalistically," precedes his knowledge of what A would do in C*, where the circumstances are altered by some specific divine intervention(s). As he says, there is first what such as A would do "*apart from any intervention on his [viz., God's] part*," and then there is "what they would do if God changed the situation in some way by actions of his own."[22] But the value of discriminating in this way between A in "natural" circumstances, C, and then as A and his circumstances are immediately affected by the possible intervention of God, in circumstances C*, is once again not at all clear. For on the traditional account of creation, God brings to pass all creatures and their actions, willingly permitting whatever is evil. These causal influences include, in the case of some, the enlightening and regenerating activity of his Spirit.

The Temporalist Implication. It is important to note that divine temporalism is essential to Tiessen's Calvinist middle knowledge. Often when reflecting on the components of the divine decree theologians distinguish a first and a second aspect, a before and an after, recognizing all the while that these are distinctions of reason that are made in order for us to understand things a little more clearly than otherwise. But as far as Tiessen is concerned the temporalist language must be an essential part of the description of the process by which God analyzes and deliberates, an essential part of the character of his middle knowledge. It is hard to see how any attempt to eliminate such tensed terminology could succeed without resulting in the "middle knowledge" becoming part either of God's natural knowledge or of his free knowledge.

Tiessen is sensitive to the issue of divine timelessness and temporality but it is not sufficient to parry the objection to say, as he does, "The Reformed tradition already allows for a process or function or activity involved in God choosing, from the immense array of possibilities, what he will bring about (directly and indirectly)."[23] But there is a significant difference between a logical distinction and a temporal process. Further, it is not a question of moving from middle knowledge to free knowledge, but of what goes on within middle knowledge. God's deliberating and calculating as he draws conclusions as to his middle knowledge entails that his acquisition of middle knowledge entails a temporal process, and hence God must be in time.

---

22. Ibid., 352.
23. Ibid., 364.

As far as I can see there is nothing incoherent in the supposition that God is in time, nevertheless it is a proposal that runs flatly against the orthodox Reformed theological tradition and ought not to be abandoned without very good reason.

But the introduction of a temporalist understanding of the divine life is not the only novelty. Tiessen's proposal also carries implications for the character of divine natural knowledge, as we have seen, and for the traditional account of divine omniscience. On the traditional account of divine omniscience, God eternally knows all creatures and their actions, and he does this by being immediately and intuitively aware of the contents of his own mind (natural knowledge) and what he has freely decreed to come to pass, his free knowledge. But Tiessen's proposal requires significant changes in the way in which God knows, and these changes imperil divine omniscience. They represent God's knowledge of his own mind regarding what world he decrees to create as a result of a process, and as a process that involves deliberation. The process involves coming to certain conclusions on the basis of that deliberation. So there are periods in the deliberative process, during the deliberation, when God does not know what to do for the best until he has concluded the deliberation. This is clearly inconsistent with the traditional account of omniscience.[24] Professor Tiessen says that the outcome of the deliberation adds nothing to God's knowledge in any way that could be identified as an improvement.[25] But improvement or not, it does involve God in learning, in gaining knowledge that he earlier lacked.

Tiessen's second novelty is based upon the previously noticed misunderstanding of the idea of God's natural knowledge which, because it contains the knowledge of all possible worlds, involves all those possible worlds in which God would intervene in one way or another. Given such orthodox accounts of the natural knowledge of God, he does not have to contemplate, at some intermediate, middle stage, how his interventions might work out; he immediately and intuitively knows how they would work out, as part of his natural knowledge of all possibilities, which include possible worlds in which he does not intervene in any way and possible worlds in which he intervenes in some way or another, I shall return to this shortly.

We here witness a familiar phenomenon. The traditional "grammar" of God, largely bequeathed to the Western church by St, Augustine, is a package deal, a highly integrated conceptual scheme. Proposing a modification to an aspect of this scheme inevitably has knock-on effects. We see that the

---

24. It is ironic that in its original form Molinist middle knowledge, from which Tiessen distances his own account, whatever else it may be burdened with, is not burdened with a temporalist account of God.

25. Tiessen, "Why Calvinists Should Believe," 365.

temporalist character of Professor Tiessen's proposal regarding the character of Calvinist middle knowledge has at least the following domino consequences: it changes the character of God's natural knowledge, it creates a category of divine knowledge in which God learns, so imperiling divine omniscience, and it places divine immutability in jeopardy.

So we must now ask, given the considerable costs that Professor Tiessen's proposal would impose upon the Reformed theological tradition, is it worth the benefits that he claims for it?[26]

In trying to answer this question I shall not dwell on the way in which the tradition safeguards the character of God against the charge that being sovereign God is the author of evil, by arguing that evil is a privation, or by invoking divine willing permission, or by utilizing the distinction between primary or secondary causation. Instead I shall focus simply on the alleged benefits of Professor Tiessen's proposal. These accrue because on this scheme "God need not force or coerce his creatures in order to have things turn out as he wished."[27]

Tiessen writes of God knowing how a particular creature would act in a given set of circumstances, by becoming acquainted with what A *would* do in C. But in the suggestion that God "finds" this possibility, there is a certain kind of imaginative self-deception, if this is indeed what Tiessen means. God is not first offered a blueprint of what A in C would do, and then adapts it in order to make possible his wise purposes for A.[28] But suppose that he was offered such a blueprint. What would the source of the blueprint be? Where would it originate? One possibility is that its source, whatever exactly it is, is independent of the divine mind. But this suggestion does not look to hold much promise, as it would undermine God's sovereignty in a big way. The only alternative possibility (as far as I can see) is that the source is A himself. But how could it be that A is the source of what A in C would do? For A does not yet exist, he is only a possible person. How could a possible person be the source of such information? Because, on Tiessen's assumptions, the freedom of all God's possible human beings is compatibilist in character, God's knowledge of how such freedom could or would be exercised is straightforward and uncontroversial. He would know,

26. Ibid., 348.

27. Ibid.

28. According to the evidence provided by n. 12 on p. 348, Bruce Ware also suffers a very similar deception. Ware asserts, "Because God knows the natures of each person perfectly, he knows how those natures will respond to particular sets of factors presented to them. But in no case does he cause the evil to be done." But God does not know by learning from these possible beings. No, they are a necessary part of the contents of an omniscient mind. (As Tiessen himself recognizes; see p. 361.)

intuitively and immediately, what A in C would do. Thus God would not need to resort to middle knowledge.

For as part of his natural knowledge God has the idea of A in C as a possibility, along with his knowledge of A possessing innumerable different beliefs and desires in innumerable different sets of circumstances, and (given such knowledge), in his wisdom God creates A in C, creates him down to the last atom and molecule, evil apart, and immediately sustains his life nanosecond by nanosecond, even as, while being sustained by his Creator, A in C perpetrates evil. Such a state of affairs does not necessarily involve divine coercion or compulsion, not in the usual senses of these words, though it will if God in his wisdom decrees to create A as being in some circumstances not responsible for his actions. It is not that God in his wisdom permits possible persons such as A to exist, rather he brings it about that they exist by decreeing that they do, and (in his wisdom) he permits their perpetration of evil.

The absence of coercion is part of what it means for the divine decree and human responsibility to be consistent or compatible. How this happens, how it happens that what someone is decreed to do he may nonetheless be responsible for doing, is somewhat mysterious, as are all points where the divine nature intersects with the creaturely. As we have noted, Professor Tiessen is partly motivated in his account of Calvinist middle knowledge by the thought that it will help us to see further than the tradition has so far taken us in understanding how God is genuinely responsive to petitionary prayer, and how he meticulously governs history in a manner that preserves his absolute sovereignty without taking moral responsibility away.[29] It is a natural human instinct to want to have that mystery lessened or alleviated. But we are seeing that the hope of shining more light on these opaque areas by positing Calvinist middle knowledge is illusory.

4. An objection

The implication of the line of argument that I have been deploying against Tiessen is that the proposed "Calvinist middle knowledge" is in fact a part of divine natural knowledge, and that it is both problematic, and theologically costly, to posit a separate category of middle knowledge. In his article Tiessen considers an argument against this line, one provided by David Werther, and so before ending this discussion I must say something about this objection, and the confusion that it contains.

29. Tiessen, "Why Calvinists Should Believe," 348.

As we have noted, various points in Tiessen's article reveal a possible misunderstanding of divine natural knowledge as understood in classical Calvinism. To add to those already noted, in discussing David Werther's claim that Calvinist middle knowledge is in effect a part of God's natural knowledge,[30] Tiessen asks whether all the worlds that God could possibly create include the proposition that it's necessarily the case that A in C will do X; is such a proposition necessarily part of God's natural knowledge? Tiessen's answer is that he thinks that God's natural/necessary knowledge of himself includes the principles of causation that underlie such a statement, but that other than this "I propose that God's contemplation of worlds containing moral agents which he could self-consistently create, and of how the history of each of such worlds would unfold if left to itself, and how it would unfold if he acted personally within the world, indicate that a further stage, beyond God's necessary knowledge, has been reached,"[31] the further stage being the "moment" of Calvinist middle knowledge. The grounds for making such a proposal, other than (once again) the desire to safeguard the Calvinist middle knowledge thesis, are not made clear. The "proposal" looks to be purely stipulative, without any independent merit or rationale. It's hardly a strength of a proposal that the only reason for holding to it is that without it the position being advocated would be undermined!

Further, Tiessen asserts that to suppose that "necessarily, A in C will do X" as part of God's natural knowledge, would be to treat what has traditionally been deemed God's free knowledge as necessary "and so *all* of God's knowledge, including his knowledge of the *actual future,* would be necessary knowledge."[32] So if Werther is correct about middle knowledge then God's free knowledge is also called into question.

But there is a serious confusion here, the confusion between

(i) Necessarily (God knows that A in C will do X)

and

(ii) Necessarily, A in C does X.

God's necessary knowledge is the idea that God necessarily has knowledge of all possibilities and of all necessities. But it does not follow from this that all that God knows has the status of necessary truths. The propositions in the mind of God of the form "A in C does X" are not necessary truths, but sets of possibilities which God necessarily knows. Put another way, when

30. Ibid., 354–55.

31. Ibid., 355.

32. Ibid., 356.

one of the possibilities that form God's natural knowledge is freely decreed, then what is decreed is logically contingent; it might not have been decreed. Of course among the possibilities that God necessarily knows, and may decree, are *causally* necessary propositions of the form, "If A were to be in circumstances C he would (as a matter of causal necessity) do X." So it is important to bear in mind the distinction between logical or metaphysical necessity on the one hand, and causal necessity on the other, as well as the distinction between "God necessarily knows all possibilities" and "All possibilities known by God are necessary."

5. Conclusion

So I judge that Professor Tiessen's proposal regarding middle knowledge suffers serious defects. As a proposal it is unclear, and the distinction between what A in C could do, and what A in C would do, looks to be a distinction without a difference. The account of the character of God's middle knowledge commits a Calvinist to divine temporalism of a sort that both imperils God's natural knowledge as this is classically understood, and surrenders divine omniscience. Finally, the idea that the proposal casts new light on how divine sovereignty meshes with human responsibility is based upon an account of how God learns possible truths that in turn rests upon an illusion.[33]

II. Tiessen: "No, but . . ."

I am grateful to Paul Helm for his very helpful comments on my article in *Westminster Theological Journal*.[34] He has identified some places where I did not state myself clearly as well as some matters concerning which I now believe it wise to revise my earlier position. At other places, I welcome further discussion because I remain convinced that my proposal has something useful to offer a Reformed theological understanding of God's providential work.

1. God's knowledge of "could" and "would": necessary or middle?

I had posited that the distinction between God's necessary knowledge and his middle knowledge is a distinction between his knowledge of "everything

---

33. Thanks to Oliver Crisp for his comments on a previous draft.
34. Tiessen, "Why Calvinists Should Believe."

that *could* be," that is, of "all possible worlds" and his knowledge of "what creatures *would* do in particular circumstances, which may or may not ever occur, depending on which of the many possible worlds God decides to actualize."[35] Helm complains that I have not explained why the difference between these is significant and he doubts "whether there is any distinct category of what *would* be as against what *could* be that could (or would) form the basis of a category of divine middle knowledge of a Calvinist kind."

I have defended divine middle knowledge for a few years now, but since at least 2005 I have been pondering the possibility that God knows counterfactuals of soft-determinist freedom as an aspect of his necessary knowledge.[36] When I wrote my article for *WTJ* in 2007, I still saw value in distinguishing a "middle" knowledge, but even then I stated that "it is more important to me to reach agreement among Calvinists that God makes significant use of his knowledge of counterfactual (or true hypothetical events) than it is to reach agreement about *when,* logically, God has this knowledge."[37] Reflection on Professor Helm's recent comments has finally brought me to the conclusion that he is correct on this point. God's knowledge of counterfactuals is not different from his knowledge of possibilities; it is therefore part of his necessary knowledge.[38] My *WTJ* article would better have been entitled: "Why Calvinists Should Affirm God's Deliberate Use of His Knowledge of Counterfactuals in His Wise Decree, Although They Reject Molinism."

As I change my mind, I have naturally wondered why I took what I now view as an unhelpful turn. As I reflect upon my earlier error, two contributing factors come to mind. First, it is possible that I blurred the difference between divine and human knowledge. If we wish to predict and to influence another person's behavior, it is much more useful to know with certainty what that person would do in a particular set of circumstances than to know what they could (or might) do. But one of the great differences

35. Ibid., 347.

36. In an email message to John Frame on January 12, 2005, after we had discussed this issue in a brief exchange, I wrote: "I have come to see that the concept of MK, as such, is not as essential to my model as it is to the Molinist model because of my rejection of libertarian freedom . . . I still see God's knowledge of counterfactuals as important in this construct. But, I am now less sure that it matters whether he knows this as part of his essential knowledge or, distinctively, as part of a logically (and perhaps not completely non-chronologically) separate 'moment' or act of knowing."

37. Tiessen, "Why Calvinists Should Believe," 346.

38. Of course, this means that I was wrong to reject David Werther's case for including counterfactuals of compatibilist freedom in God's necessary knowledge (ibid., 354–56) and that I now agree with the perspective I quoted from John Frame (*Doctrine of God,* 502–3; cited in ibid., 354 n. 32).

between God and us human beings is that, however well we know another person, we never know them well enough to predict with certainty exactly how they will act. They are capable of surprising us. Such is not the case for our omniscient God. He knows people completely, understands circumstances exhaustively and, because God has given moral creatures the freedom of spontaneity (rather than libertarian freedom), he knows exactly what a particular sort of person would do in each hypothetical set of circumstances. Thus, the difference that exists in our human experience, between what we deem it possible for a person to do and what they will do, is a problem caused by imperfect knowledge not a matter of different kinds of knowledge.

Given the difference between God's knowledge and ours, it is clear that there is an important difference between *our* knowing what a person could (that is, might) do and God's knowing what that person *would* do. I erred seriously, therefore, in proposing that there is a difference between *God's* knowledge of what people could and what they would do. This is because God has not made moral creatures libertarianly free; they do not have the power of contrary choice.[39]

I consider God's knowledge of counterfactuals to be very helpful in our understanding of the compatibility between God's meticulous sovereignty and morally responsible creaturely freedom. Assuming the validity of the grounding objection to Molinism, if creatures were libertarianly free, the most that even God could know is the probability that a creature would act in a particular way; he could not know with certainty how they would act. Having that certain knowledge of how any moral creature would act in a set of circumstances is what enables God to decree a world history in which his will is always done, even though his creatures act as they choose.

---

39. I am aware that Helm believes the nature of human freedom to be a matter not revealed to us by Scripture (in Ware, ed,. *Perspectives*, 50), and that he thinks theologians who endorse without qualification a philosophical position on this issue make their theology "hostages to fortune" *(Perspectives,* 126). This is a serious concern and I do not take it lightly. At this point, however, I am greatly impressed by the explanatory usefulness of the concept of soft-determinist freedom in understanding Scripture's teaching. It is very clear to me that God is meticulously sovereign and equally clear that certain of God's creatures (angels and humans) are morally responsible, I find the compatibilist account offered by Jonathan Edwards, and widely appropriated by later Calvinists, very persuasive. If I am wrong about this, however, the effect of the error would be much more far reaching in its effects upon my theology than the concession that God does not have middle knowledge. Indeed, I would be left with much less to say of an explanatory nature and more appeal to mystery My doctrine of divine providence would become apophatic. Furthermore, much of the construction in the other models of providence described in my book *Providence and Prayer* would have to be dismissed as unjustified speculation.

The second factor that probably contributed to my error was the fact that it was from Molinists that I learned to appreciate the usefulness to God of his knowledge of counterfactuals. For some time, I have been acting on the belief that these advantages went with middle knowledge but that the Molinist construction needed to be revised to remove their error concerning the nature of creaturely freedom. I believed that compatibilist middle knowledge was the way to preserve what they had. What I had failed to see, during that time, was that the sole rationale for positing middle knowledge is to give room for libertarian creaturely freedom as a fact of the world God chooses to actualize. I now believe that rejection of the Molinist construction because of its faulty understanding of freedom also entails rejection of the concept of divine middle knowledge. If (as I believe) creatures are not libertarianly free, there can be no difference between *God's* knowledge of what creatures could do and what they would do, that is, what "A would do in C," as Helm puts it, and God knows this important truth necessarily.

Despite the claim in the title of my article, that Calvinists should reject Molinism, it is now obvious to me that I described the situation as Molinists would see it. For them a distinction *does* exist between what people could and what they would do. This is because they believe that, for creatures to act with genuine (morally responsible) freedom, they must have the power of contrary choice. From their perspective, A *could* act in more than one way, in circumstances C. What A *would* do is therefore the product of an act of will on A's part which is not determined by who A is. It would not suffice for God to know the nature of all possible creatures, he would also have to know their free choices in all possible worlds.

As Helm has rightly discerned, no distinction exists between what A *could* do and what A *would* do, in circumstances C, if soft-determinism pertains so that A has the freedom of spontaneity but not of contrary choice. Helm is also correct in his observation that my attempt to differentiate between God's (necessary) knowledge of possibilities as abstract and God's (middle) knowledge of counterfactuals as specific is invalid and fails to take into account adequately the traditional Reformed understanding of what God knows necessarily.

2. Effects of the rejection of middle knowledge upon my model of providence

Thankfully, conceding that God knows counterfactuals as part of his necessary knowledge (rather than as a middle knowledge) has virtually no effect on my account of divine providence. What has always been most important to me is that Reformed accounts of God's providential work in the world take into full account the usefulness to God, in his establishment of the decree, of his knowledge of counterfactuals.

One reason for deeming "middle knowledge" a helpful name for the knowledge of counterfactuals that I suggest God used, in wisely deciding which particular world history he would create, was that this term had already been used by Molinism in arguing this point. I discern that the primary cause of resistance to the Molinist proposal on the part of seventeenth-century Reformed theologians was that it was developed as part of a synergistic soteriology,[40] but I have stated clearly that I consider Molinism incoherent and that I affirm a classically Reformed monergistic soteriology.

Some of the other classic Reformed objections to the concept of divine middle knowledge depend on its Molinist, synergist, formulation. But some of those objections cut more deeply; they express a concern that God's use of his knowledge of counterfactuals makes him dependent upon the creature.[41] Consequently, if I concede that God's knowledge of counterfactuals is an aspect of his necessary knowledge but continue to argue that this knowledge is used by God when he decides upon which world he will create, much of my apologetic for what I have previously dubbed "middle-knowledge Calvinism" is still necessary. Nevertheless, that apologetic should be easier when the position being defended is disassociated from "middle knowledge" with its Molinist and synergistic association.

Bruce Ware is another Calvinist theologian who has frequently expounded a "compatibilist middle knowledge" understanding. He may continue to affirm divine middle knowledge but he need not do so. This is apparent if one reads his presentation of "compatibilist middle knowledge and divine providence" in his chapter for the four views book that he recently edited.[42] In my opinion, Ware succeeds in identifying biblical evidence that God knows counterfactuals *and* that he uses them in planning his work in the world. Nevertheless, if one were to replace Ware's references to "middle knowledge" with "God's knowledge of counterfactuals," and to grant that God has this knowledge necessarily, Ware's fundamental argument would be unaffected.

Richard Muller makes this pertinent remark in his discussion of middle knowledge: "If the issue were simply the divine knowledge of future possibility—even of possibilities arising out of the contingent interaction of finite creatures—it could be easily understood under the rubric of the divine

---

40. Tiessen, "Why Calvinists Should Believe," 356.

41. Ibid., 356–58.

42. Ware, *Perspectives*, 109–20.

scientia necessaria or necessary knowledge of all possibility."[43] If the necessary knowledge of God as understood in the Reformed tradition suffices for his wise decision to actualize a particular world, then the traditional Reformed view that God has only two kinds of knowledge is correct. I granted this possibility in my *WTJ* article,[44] but I now believe it to be the reality.

My response to the traditional Calvinist objections to divine middle knowledge, when their point of concern is God's deliberative use of the knowledge of "what A would do in C," is unaffected by a change in my terminology regarding God's knowledge. I now find myself in the line of theologians (like Gomarus, Walaeus, and Richard Baxter) who (as reported by Muller),

> though repelled by the Pelagianizing impact of this [i.e., Molina's] view, adapted the argument of Molina to refer, not to a *scientia media* between knowledge of the possible and knowledge of the actual, hut to a *scientia hypothetica* prior to all of the divine determinations. In this view, God rests his *decretum* upon his knowledge of how the world order is to be constructed in its most minute hypothetical workings. The decree, therefore, establishes the freedom of secondary causes and allows for or permits the eventuality of sin and evil, though only in a hypothetical sense, namely, as events that will occur, given the actuality of the circumstances preceding. The point, in other words, is not that God learns from or reacts to a future possibility, hut that God actualizes a particular concatenation of possibilities in which, given the particular set of circumstances directly willed, certain events will occur by reason of secondary causes, including the exercise of human free choice. The free choices belong, therefore, to the particular world order that God wills to actualize. As for God's "foreknowledge" of all such actual events, it is necessary, certain, and determinate as it follows the decree and rests on the certainty of the divine causality.[45]

This sounds significantly similar to the intentions of my own proposal. What I have spoken about when I conceive of God's choosing a world to actualize is essentially what Muller describes as the "particular concatenation of possibilities in which, given the particular set of circumstances directly willed, certain events will occur by reason of secondary causes, including the exercise of human free choice." Similarly, the point most important in

---

43. Muller, *Divine Essence and Attributes*, 418.

44. Tiessen, "Why Calvinists Should Believe," 356.

45. Muller, *Divine Essence and Attributes*, 420.

my previous construction is well described in Muller's description of the views of Walaeus, Gomarus, and Baxter: "God rests his *decretum* upon his knowledge of how the world order is to be constructed in its most minute hypothetical workings."

Given this strong similarity of intent, it may be that a more appropriate name for my model would be "hypothetical-knowledge Calvinism." That would have the advantage of not immediately attracting the negative response characteristically triggered in the Reformed tradition by reference to divine middle knowledge; it simply draws attention to a truth already affirmed by the tradition, the significance of which had not been sufficiently recognized.

Since the purpose of Molina's affirmation of divine middle knowledge was to include in God's deliberation leading up to his decree his knowledge of future counterfactuals (i.e., subjunctive conditionals) of libertarianly free acts, use of that term within a monergistic construction is counterproductive. A term such as "hypothetical knowledge" (or counterfactual knowledge) has the advantage that it focuses on the kind of knowledge God uses in formulating his decree rather than its place in the logical order. If that kind of knowledge is understood to be an aspect of God's necessary knowledge, then we need only unpack its usefulness to God; we need not postulate that his deliberative *use* of the knowledge is itself a new kind of knowledge.

3. God's relationship to time

Helm writes: "But as far as Tiessen is concerned the temporalist language must be an essential part of the description of the process by which God analyzes and deliberates, an essential part of the character of his middle knowledge. It is hard to see how any attempt to eliminate such tensed terminology could succeed without resulting in the 'middle knowledge' becoming part either of God's natural knowledge or of his free knowledge." He is troubled because "the status of this middle knowledge is that its 'moment' or 'moments' are temporal moments."

Perhaps my acknowledgment that God knows counterfactuals necessarily and does not, therefore, need middle knowledge, will alleviate Helm's concern. I am continuing to assert that God analyzes and deliberates, that he considers possible worlds and chooses to actualize one of them, but this is not a new form of knowledge (as middle knowledge would be), it is the wise use of what God knows necessarily. God needs nothing beyond that necessary knowledge to make his decision to create this particular universe, something which God does freely, not out of necessity.

Despite my use of temporal language in speaking about God's knowledge and decision, I would argue that my understanding of God's use of his necessary knowledge of counterfactuals in forming his decree does *not* depend upon essential divine temporality. After all, when we consider God's decree, we are speaking of God without a world. Even theologians who have argued for God's temporal immanence in the universe have posited that God was timeless without the universe.[46] I admit that it is very difficult for me to conceive of the dynamic relations between the persons of the Trinity and of a logical order of God's decrees in completely atemporal ways, or to think that God has no experience of a time before he created the world, or that the Son has no experience of *pre*-incarnate existence. Nevertheless, I acknowledge Millard Erickson's wisdom when he pleads agnosticism about whether God experiences succession and sequence within himself, because any assumption that God does would derive from an assumption that God's existence and experience are of just the same nature as ours and this would be folly.[47]

Professor Helm finds it "ironic that Molinist middle knowledge . . . whatever else it may be burdened with, is not burdened with a temporalist account of God." This is a very important observation because it demonstrates that even those who originally speculated that God has middle knowledge, a logical moment in which he contemplates what libertarianly free creatures would do in possible worlds, did not consider that deliberation to require divine temporality. Consequently, now that I have rejected middle knowledge, I see no reason why my description of God's deliberation upon his necessary knowledge of counterfactuals should pose any problems for complete atemporalists.

Francis Turretin writes: "The decree is ascribed to God not inasmuch as it is the effect of previous deliberation and consultation with reasoning passing from one thing to another (of which he has no need 'to whose eyes all things are naked and most open,' Heb, 4:13), but by reason of the certain

---

46. William Lane Craig, for instance, puts together three factors, that God exists in time, that time had a beginning, and that God did not have a beginning, and Craig concludes that "God must be causally, but not temporally, prior to the Big Bang. With the creation of the universe, time began, and God entered into time at the moment of creation in virtue of His real relations with the created order. It follows that God must therefore be timeless without the universe and temporal with the universe" (*Time and Eternity*, 233). John Frame posits that "God's experience of time, as Scripture presents it, is more like the atemporalist model than like the temporalist one" (*Doctrine of God*, 557). Yet, in light of God's temporal omnipresence, Frame concludes: "So God is temporal after all, but not merely temporal. He really exists in time, but he also transcends time in such a way as to exist outside it" (559).

47. Erickson, *God the Father Almighty*, 276–77.

determination concerning the futurition of things (according to which he does nothing rashly, but designedly, i,e,, knowingly and willingly)."[48] I do not know how God's determining the future "designedly" rather than "rashly" differs essentially from his determining it with "deliberation," but I do not perceive my proposal to be different in essence from that which Turretin affirms.

Furthermore, the temporality of my language concerning God's contemplation of possible worlds, when he wisely decides which one he will actualize, could function metaphorically within Turretin's own thoroughly atemporal concept of God's eternal decree. He wrote: "Although some decrees may be said to be prior or posterior to others, it does not follow that they are not eternal in themselves because this is not said on the part of God (for so they are one only and a most simple act in God), but with respect to our manner of conception (who, on account of the distinct objects, cannot conceive of the decrees except distinctly by priority and posteriority)."[49]

4. Conclusion

Clearly, Professor Helm's critique has been helpful to me. It has led me finally to abandon the attempt to incorporate divine middle knowledge into my Calvinist understanding of God's eternal purposing of the history of the universe, in all its detail. Since I do not share the Molinist desire to make libertarianly free human decisions a matter of God's knowledge distinct from his knowledge of himself, I have no need to affirm divine middle knowledge. Nevertheless, I continue to believe that God's knowledge of counterfactuals is useful to him in his wise decree concerning the futurition of everything that happens in the universe God creates and governs for his own glory.

---

48. Turretin, *Institutes*, 1:311 (4.1.3).
49. Ibid., 1:315 (4.2.6).

Bibliography

Craig, William Lane. *Time and Eternity: Exploring God's Relationship to Time*. Wheaton, IL: Crossway, 2001.

Erickson, Millard. *God the Father Almighty: A Contemporary Exploration of the Divine Attributes*. Grand Rapids: Baker, 1998.

Flint, Thomas P. *Divine Providence: The Molinist Account*. Ithaca, NY: Cornell University Press, 1998.

Frame, John. *Doctrine of God*. Phillipsburg, NJ: Presbyterian & Reformed, 2002.

Muller, Richard. *The Divine Essence and Attributes*. Vol. 3 of *Post-Reformation Reformed Dogmatics: The Rise and Development of Reformed Orthodoxy, ca. 1520 to ca. 1725*. Grand Rapids: Baker Academic, 2003.

Plantinga, Alvin. *The Nature of Necessity*. Oxford: Clarendon, 1974.

Tiessen, Terrance L. *Providence and Prayer: How Does God Work in the World?* Downers Grove, IL: InterVarsity, 2000.

———. "Why Calvinists Should Believe in Divine Middle Knowledge, Although They Reject Molinism." *Westminster Theological Journal* 69.2 (2007) 345–66.

Turretin, Francis. *Institutes of Elenctic Theology*. 3 vols. Edited by James T. Dennison Jr. Translated by George Musgrave Giger. Phillipsburg, NJ: Presbyterian & Reformed, 1992.

Ware, Bruce. *God's Greater Glory: The Exalted God of Scripture and the Christian Faith*. Wheaton, IL: Crossway, 2004.

———, ed. *Perspectives on the Doctrine of God: Four Views*. Nashville: Broadman and Holman, 2008.

8

Middle-Knowledge Calvinism

BRUCE A. WARE

"The history of this controversy on *scientia media* presents another instance of the rule; that usually mischievous errors have in them a certain *modicum* of valuable truth."

—ROBERT L. DABNEY, *Lectures in Systematic Theology*[1]

Introduction

CALVINISTS HAVE WANTED, HISTORICALLY, to affirm three tenets, each of which is essential to the overarching Reformed model of divine providence, yet they constitute three convictions that are difficult to hold together. 1) As fully and meticulously sovereign, God is the ultimate cause or determiner of all that takes place in the history of the universe, including all of the choices and actions of free creatures. 2) Although God's sovereignty is such that he determines all things, moral creatures nonetheless choose and act in ways that are both genuinely free and morally responsible. And 3) although God's sovereignty is such that he determines all things, God does not, in so doing, either originate evil out of himself nor does he give moral approval to the evil choices and actions he determines to take place. Hear, for example, the wording of the *Westminster Confession of Faith*, Chapter 3, "Of God's Eternal Decree," Section 1.1:

> God, from all eternity, did, by the most wise and holy counsel of his own will, freely, and unchangeably ordain whatsoever comes to pass: yet so, as thereby neither is God the author of sin, nor is violence offered to the will of the creatures; nor is the liberty or contingency of second causes taken away, but rather established.

---

1. Dabney, *Lectures*, 159.

Or again, the 4th article on "Providence" of the *Abstract of Principles*, written for the founding of The Southern Baptist Theological Seminary, and to this day the confessional statement both of SBTS and SEBTS, reads:

> God from eternity, decrees or permits all things that come to pass, and perpetually upholds, directs and governs all creatures and all events; yet so as not in any wise to be author or approver of sin nor to destroy the free will and responsibility of intelligent creatures.[2]

Calvinists, then, have wanted to understand God's activity in the world in which he ordains all things evil just as much as all things good, and yet they deny two sometimes assumed but false implications that might be thought unavoidable. First, although God ordains all things, including all of the choices and actions of moral creatures, they deny that genuine freedom and moral responsibility are removed. They argue instead that God's exhaustive determination and genuine human freedom and moral responsibility are compatible. Second, although God ordains all things, including all good and evil, God is never the author of evil, whereas, presumably, he is the author of each and every good thing that takes place (e.g., Jas 1:17). In other words, while God "ordains whatsoever comes to pass," the manner of divine agency by which he brings about the good that he has ordained must be different than the manner of divine agency by which he brings about the evil that he has ordained. There is, in short, an asymmetry in divine agency toward good and evil respectively. While God brings about good directly, as it were, from out of his own being since he alone is infinitely and perfectly good, by the very same token—i.e., that he is perfectly but only good, not evil—evil cannot come forth from out of himself (e.g., Ps 5:4; 1 John 1:5). The manner, then, by which he brings about the evil that he has ordained must be different than the manner by which he brings about good, which comes out of his own being. We might think of this as the "asymmetry problematic" for Calvinism. How can we understand the manner of divine agency by which God brings about evil that he has ordained in a way that is different from, and asymmetrical with, the manner of divine agency by which God brings about good that he has ordained? It is exactly here, on these twin convictions, where middle knowledge contributes something helpful to the Reformed model of divine providence.

To develop this briefly, allow me to ask and answer four questions: 1) What kind of divine knowledge is middle knowledge? 2) What does middle knowledge include? 3) Why does middle knowledge require compatibilist

---

2. See my explanation and analysis of Article 4 on divine providence in Mohler, *Confessing*, 24–30.

freedom? And 4) How does middle knowledge help Reformed Theology with its asymmetry problematic?

What Kind of Divine Knowledge Is Middle Knowledge?

Middle knowledge is God's prevolitional knowledge of what free creatures would do in various circumstances that God imagines. Luis de Molina's category of middle knowledge, as I understand it, is middle between God's natural knowledge—knowledge of all genuine possibilities and logical necessities, i.e., knowledge of what "could be" as well as of what "must be" (2+2=4) and of what "cannot be" (2+2=5)—and free knowledge—knowledge of all actualities, i.e., knowledge of what "will be" from the vantage point of God's will to create this, the actual world. So, for our purposes here, middle knowledge is middle between knowledge of what merely "could be" and what in fact "will be." What is middle between these? Knowledge of what "would be" under different circumstances and states of affairs. And for Molina, and for our purposes here, the "would be" knowledge that is especially important is knowledge of what free creatures would do in various circumstances and states of affairs that God imagines. This knowledge, remember though, is prevolitional, in that it is knowledge God possesses of free creatures he imagines in his own mind, apart from whether these free creatures turn out to exist in the actual world or not, and knowledge God possesses of what these free creatures would decide and do depending on varying circumstances in which God imagines them to be living.

It is important also to notice that God's middle knowledge, though a meaningful and important category of God's comprehensive knowledge, is itself simply part of the natural knowledge God possesses of all possibilities. Middle knowledge, then, is a subset, or subcategory, of natural knowledge, just as free knowledge, likewise, is a subset, or subcategory, of natural knowledge. That is, anything God knows that Fred "would do" or "will do" in one particular setting is obviously something that God, prevolitionally, knew that Fred "could do." But to say that middle knowledge (or free knowledge) is a subset of natural knowledge does not diminish the significance of considering what distinguishes it within the broader pool of God's natural knowledge. By analogy, just because the categories of "elders" and "deacons" are subsets of the broader category of "church members" does not render focused attention on what distinguishes these particular members along with what distinctive qualifications and responsibilities these particular members must have either illegitimate or trivial. So too here. Middle knowledge is a very significant subset of natural knowledge in which God knows not only the wide range of what Fred could do in the life God envisions him having, but God knows quite specifically, exactly, and definitely what Fred would do in any number of various circumstances in which God envisions Fred living. One important implication of understanding middle knowledge as a subset of natural knowledge, then, is that God's middle knowledge is in no way contingent upon the free choices and actions of the free creatures whom God imagines. Rather, as with all aspects of his natural knowledge, this is his knowledge by nature and not dependent upon some kind of "foresight" of what free creatures would decide or do—as we'll see, they do what they do with compatibilist, not libertarian, freedom. So, all items of middle knowledge, then, are items of God's natural knowledge, yet these items make up an important subcategory relating to God's prevolitional knowledge of what free creatures would do in various circumstances that God imagines.

What Does Middle Knowledge Include?

Middle knowledge includes four categories of knowledge, which might be referred to, respectively, as follows: 1) all middle knowledge might be thought of as God's "prevolitional counter-hypothetical knowledge," 2) a portion of middle knowledge is "pre-factual middle knowledge," 3) a portion of middle knowledge is "pre-counter-factual middle knowledge," and 4) a portion of middle knowledge is "pre-non-factual middle knowledge." Allow me to explain.

First, middle knowledge is not, strictly speaking, a subset of what are sometimes called counterfactuals of creaturely freedom. A counter-factual can only be a counter-*factual* when there is a fact established against which this hypothetical possibility is seen to be counter. For example, upon hearing on the radio news of an accident holding up traffic on the interstate, Fred might comment to Sally, "It's good we took surface streets instead of the interstate, or we would be caught in that huge traffic jam." Here, the actual facticity of the traffic jam on the interstate constitutes the fact against which Fred supposes, instead, that a contrary fact would have been true had he acted differently. If they had taken the interstate, they too would be caught in traffic. But with middle knowledge, because this divine knowledge is prevolitional (i.e., middle knowledge precedes the logical moment God chooses to create this, the actual world), there are, as yet, no facts established against which God envisions something contrary. Nonetheless, God is able to envision different scenarios as contrary to each other such that one scenario might constitute the hypothetical (yet not real) "fact" against which another scenario is considered. So, take Fred and Sally again. Yes, a true counterfactual obtains in the actual situation I described above, but now consider this same situation in the mind of God, prevolitionally. God can envision in his mind Fred and Sally leaving the house contemplating which route to take. God can know that if certain considerations are given prominence, Fred will choose to take surface streets. Yet God knows also that if other considerations are given prominence, Fred would instead choose to take the interstate. This sounds very much like the counterfactual situation described above, but it has this important difference: in God's mind, prevolitionally, no fact has yet been established as to the route Fred and Sally will take. Yet, God considers one as against the other, while both are hypothetical and neither is real. So, instead of calling middle knowledge instances of counterfactuals (which strictly they are not), perhaps we could conceive of them as counter-hypotheticals which, in the mind of God are known with certainty, and yet known only as hypothetical until God chooses (if he does) to select one of the set of hypothetical scenarios and render it actual in his choice to create the world that is. Hence, all of God's middle knowledge is God's prevolitional counter-hypothetical knowledge. Within this totality of middle knowledge, we can see three categories or types of middle knowledge, described in the following three points.

Second, God's pre-factual middle knowledge is God's prevolitional knowledge of what a particular person would do in a particular circumstance, which person and circumstance God subsequently wills to actualize in creating the real world. That is, every item of factual knowledge of what free creatures will do in the actual world God creates is known by God, prevolitionally, as pre-factual middle knowledge. In other words, all of God's free knowledge of what free creatures will choose and do in all the situations that obtain in the real world, also constitute a body of God's prevolitional middle knowledge of what those very free creatures would do in the very situations that will obtain in the world God creates. That is, if God has known, post-volitionally, that you and I *will choose* to be in this particular location on this day and at this time, he likewise knew, prevolitionally, that you and I *would choose* to be in this location on this day and at this time, given the persons and circumstances that he subsequently actualized.

Third, God's pre-counterfactual middle knowledge is God's prevolitional knowledge of all free choices and actions that free creatures would have done that stand counter to choices and actions that they actually carry out in the real world that God created. That is, every item of counterfactual knowledge is known by God, prevolitionally, as pre-counterfactual middle knowledge. This category of middle knowledge is one with the most biblical support. Passages like Exodus 13:17; 1 Samuel 23:8–14; Jeremiah 23:21–22; Matthew 11:21–24; and 1 Corinthians 2:8 give strong evidence that God has counterfactual knowledge in regard to choices and actions that free creatures make. But the question is, just when does God know that these people, in alternate circumstances, would have chosen differently? Does he know this only post-volitionally? This seems to be what some Reformed spokesmen have concluded. For example, in his article critiquing middle knowledge, Travis Campbell writes that

> these biblical passages [the ones cited above] only show us that God knows the nature of the free agent so well that, were that agent placed in another circumstance, God knows exactly what he would do. And this does not reconcile middle knowledge with libertarianism, but with compatibilism. More importantly, it is certainly possible that God knows this information only logically posterior to the divine decree.[3]

I must admit being a bit incredulous at this conclusion. If God indeed possesses accurate counterfactual knowledge, and since all of God's knowledge is eternal, does it not follow that God knows prevolitionally what these free creatures would do in alternate circumstances via middle knowledge, which knowledge he then possesses, post-volitionally, as counterfactual knowledge? Granted, he can only have counterfactual knowledge, *per se*, after the "facts" of what takes place in the history of free creatures is set by God's will to create the actual world. But all of that counterfactual knowledge is possessed by God, prevolitionally, as pre-counterfactual middle knowledge which then matches the counterfactual knowledge he possesses at the point he wills to create the actual world.

Fourth, God's pre-non-factual middle knowledge is God's prevolitional knowledge of all the free choices and actions which free creatures would do, which persons, actions, and choices never obtain in the real world. In other words, God may imagine many possible persons who make possible choices and actions, none of whom and which he chooses to actualize. Nonetheless, he still knows, via middle knowledge, both the natures of these imagined free creatures and the choices they would make in various circumstances, though this knowledge is neither pre-factual nor pre-counterfactual but rather pre-non-factual middle knowledge.

---

3. Campbell, "Middle Knowledge," 15.

Why Does Middle Knowledge Require
Compatibilist Freedom?

According to the notion of middle knowledge, God can envision a free agent in various sets of circumstances or states of affairs, such that God knows what the agent would do in each differing state of affairs. The problem here for traditional Molinism, with its commitment to libertarian freedom, is that since there is no necessary connection between knowledge of each state of affairs and knowledge of what the agent would in fact choose in each different setting, God could not know the agent's choice by knowing the circumstances. But, what if there were a necessary connection between knowledge of a given state of affairs and knowledge of what the agent would choose in that particular setting? If this were the case, then God could know what the agent would choose by knowing fully both the agent's nature and the circumstances in which the agent would make his choice. That is, because in any one given set of circumstances envisioned by God, the agent in that particular setting, with exactly that particular set of factors present, would make one and only one choice—a choice that would be called for by just those circumstances in that setting—therefore, God could know with certainty the choice the agent would make by knowing precisely and exhaustively both the nature of the agent comprehensively along with the setting in which the agent would make his choice.

Consider more specifically how middle knowledge might work if we assumed that human beings possessed compatibilist freedom—the freedom of inclination—rather than libertarian freedom. Recall that the freedom of inclination proposes that we are free when we choose according to our strongest inclination or deepest desire. In short, we are free when we do what we most want to do. This means that the circumstances and factors that influence our decisions result eventually in our having, at the moment of choice, *one* desire or inclination that stands above all others. The fact that we have *one* desire that is our *highest desire* explains why we make the *one choice* that we do, in that particular setting. Put differently, the set of factors in which the agent makes his choice, along with the nature of the free agent, constitute a set of individually necessary and *jointly sufficient* conditions[4]

---

4. "Necessary" conditions are those which must be present for the effect to occur; "sufficient" conditions are those which, whether necessary or not, when present require that the effect occurs. As an example, consider the individually necessary and jointly sufficient conditions of combustion. Each of the following is necessary for combustion to occur: oxygen, fuel, friction/heat. But, the presence of either merely one or two of these necessary conditions will not produce combustion. Rather, all three have to be present for combustion to occur, and when all three are present combustion will occur. Therefore, we can say that oxygen, fuel, and friction/heat are the *individually necessary*

for forming within the agent a strongest inclination or highest desire by which he then makes the one choice that is in accordance with that highest desire. And, his freedom is then expressed when he chooses according to that highest desire.

What is different about this understanding of middle knowledge is that since freedom means that we always do what we most want, and since what we "most want" is shaped by the agent's nature along with the set of factors and circumstances that eventually give rise to one desire that stands above all others, therefore God can know the circumstances giving rise to our highest desires, and by knowing these, he can know the choice that we would make, given that particular nature and those particular circumstances. What the Molinist version of middle knowledge lacked—viz., a necessary connection between knowledge of the circumstances within which an agent makes his choice and knowledge of just what choice the agent would make—is here remedied by replacing libertarian freedom with compatibilist freedom. So, as a result, middle knowledge is explicable and it "works" when compatibilist freedom is employed in a way it does not with libertarian freedom.

How Does Middle Knowledge Help Reformed Theology with Its Asymmetry Problematic?

While God ordains whatsoever comes to pass, he must bring to pass those aspects of moral evil in ways that guard his infinite and perfect righteousness while holding free agents fully culpable for the evil they do, which evil actions fulfill his decree. Given middle knowledge, God possesses the requisite means for bringing this about. Before God had created the world, indeed before he had "settled" on the exact plan by which the history of that world would unfold in exacting detail, God was able to envision, by middle knowledge, an array of situations in which his moral creatures (angelic and human) would choose and act as they would. More specifically, God was capable of knowing just what a moral agent would do in one situation, with its particular complex set of factors, as opposed to what that agent would do in a slightly different situation, with a slightly different complex set of factors.

This information was knowable to God due to five considerations: 1) God could envision exhaustively and exactly the natures of each and every moral agent he envisioned choosing and acting in morally responsible ways; 2) God could envision exhaustively and exactly the complete

---

(i.e., each must be present) and *jointly sufficient* (i.e., when all three are present the effect occurs) conditions for combustion.

sets of factors that would be true of each and every situation in which moral agents would make choices and perform actions; 3) because the moral creatures he envisioned had a freedom of inclination or compatibilist freedom, he could know the one strongest inclination or highest desire an agent would have in any particular situation he considered, since the agent's own nature would respond to the particular set of factors comprising a specific situation such that those factors would necessarily give rise to that one strongest inclination in the moral agent's mind and heart; 4) because the moral creatures he envisioned had a freedom of inclination or compatibilist freedom, God could know the particular choice an agent would make in each and every situation envisioned, since agents with the freedom of inclination always choose in accordance with their strongest inclinations or highest desires; and 5) God knows all that is knowable, and items 1) through 4) are knowable to God.

Among the situations God envisioned were situations in which sinful human beings would act according to their strongest desires and carry out the sinful and evil actions they freely wanted to do. But since these sinful humans all possessed the freedom of inclination, God could also envision slightly changed situations, in which an alteration of factors resulted in those sinful creatures having different highest desires and so carrying out different actions in those particular altered situations. In other words, by knowing their natures perfectly and by controlling the complex set of factors prompting the natures of moral agents to develop a strongest inclination within a given situation, God could effectively redirect the choice and action that the agent would carry out. And, because there was a necessary correlation between 1) the set of individually necessary and jointly sufficient factors of a given situation and 2) the strongest inclination elicited from those factors in the nature of a moral agent and by which he then would make his choice, God could know with exacting precision just what choices would be made in each and every situation he considered in his mind's eye.

Notice, then, that given his possession of middle knowledge, God would be able to know whether in certain situations he would permit an agent to carry out what he was most inclined to do, or whether God would alter the factors of that situation sufficient to alter the agent's strongest inclination, thus altering also the choice he would make. But in either case, the agent would respond to those factors according to his own nature and hence do what he most wanted to do. As such, he would be free and morally responsible in the choices he makes. And in either case, God has absolute and complete regulation of what the agent does, albeit through either permitting the choice that he could prevent, or by preventing the choice by redirecting the situation such that the agent would freely choose differently.

So then, this manner of divine agency, utilizing middle knowledge as part of the basis for determining actions and events free creatures bring to pass, has a special importance for God's regulation of evil. By controlling human sinful choices and actions in this manner, it never is the case that God either does evil directly (as he often does good directly), nor is it the case that he causes a person to do evil. Some may consider the description above as constituting God's causing the person to do evil, but I believe that this would be a misinterpretation of what actually is taking place. When God envisions various sets of factors within which an agent will develop a strongest inclination to do one thing or another, the strongest inclination that emerges from these factors is not caused by the factors, nor is it caused by God. Rather, in light of the *nature of the person*, when certain factors are present, his nature will respond to those factors and seek to do what he, by nature, wants most to do. In short, the cause of the strongest inclination and the resultant choice is the nature of the person in response to factors presented to it. So indeed, sinful men intend their evil as evil, but God intends his work through their evil acts for good (Gen 50:20).

Other Calvinists have seen the benefit of this way of thinking, even if they have not used the label "middle knowledge" to describe what is taking place. Consider, for example, this explanation from John Feinberg:

> God can decree all things and yet we can still act freely in the compatibilist's sense of freedom. God can guarantee that his goals will be accomplished freely even when someone does not want to do the act, because the decree includes not only God's chosen ends but also the means to such ends. Such means include whatever circumstances and factors are necessary to convince an individual (without constraint) that the act God has decreed is the act she or he wants to do. And, given the sufficient conditions, the person will do the act.[5]

Obviously, for God to know what circumstances and factors are necessary to convince an individual to act as God has decreed means that God also knows that the same person, in other circumstances in which a set of different factors would be present, would not act as God has decreed. In Feinberg's account, that the person would do this one thing as opposed to another under this specific set of circumstances implies God's knowledge that the person would act differently given an alternate set of circumstances. Middle knowledge, then, is here implied. I recall, as Dr. Feinberg's MDiv student, seeing the wisdom of this way of thinking for the Reformed model of divine providence. Since he did not mention "middle knowledge" within

5. Feinberg, "God Ordains All Things," 26.

this discussion, when I came to adopt essentially the same notion, I did not know that this was employing, implicitly, an appeal to divine middle knowledge to make sense of it. That middle knowledge was involved, though, came clear to me some years later when serving as a Teaching Assistant for Alvin Plantinga. While on sabbatical from Calvin College, Plantinga taught at Fuller Seminary while I was a PhD student. Since I had a freshly minted MA in philosophy, they assigned me to assist him. Sitting in on his class on "God, Freedom and Evil," I was introduced to middle knowledge, and the pieces began to fall together. I saw the utility of middle knowledge for God and evil, yet I also began to see that this can only work with compatibilist freedom.

Another statement showing an implicit appeal to middle knowledge comes from Loraine Boettner: "Perhaps the relationship between divine sovereignty and human freedom can best be summed up in these words: God so presents the outside inducements that man acts in accordance with his own nature, yet does exactly what God has planned for him to do."[6] Again here, while middle knowledge is not mentioned, the concept is embedded in the claim. For God to know what inducements would lead a man to act in accord with his own nature implies that God knows how other inducements would fail to bring about the desired action. Middle knowledge, then, is present.

Or again, when discussing divine permission, particularly as seen in the writings of Augustine and Edwards, Paul Helm describes God's specific (as opposed to general) permission, particularly of evil that humans carry out, in a way that invokes the concept of middle knowledge, though he never uses this label in his description. Consider his explanation of God's specific permission of some human evil action:

> God ordains all those circumstances which are necessary for the performance by a person of a particular morally evil action (say, an action of cruelty at a particular time and place). God himself does not perform that action, nor could he, for reasons already given [i.e., God is good and cannot do evil]. Nevertheless, he permits that action to take place. He does not prevent it to stop it. So in the circumstances ordained by God someone does an evil action; the circumstances are ordained, but the evil is permitted.[7]

6. Boettner, *Reformed Doctrine of Predestination*, 38.

7. Helm, *Providence*, 172. It may be noted that Helm, earlier in this volume, affirms the legitimacy of divine middle knowledge, yet he sees it as unusable for divine providence due to the Molinist commitment to libertarian freedom (57–61). I would agree with him on this, as I've argued earlier in this paper. Yet, when true moral freedom is

When Helm writes that God ordains "those circumstances which are necessary" for an evil action to be taken, this implies that God also knows other different sets of circumstances in which the human agent would carry out different actions and, in any case, the agent would not carry out this particular action. The agent would only carry out this particular action when "those circumstances which are necessary" obtain. Change the circumstances, change the precise action done. Hence, it follows that God knows what the agent would do in one set of circumstances, and he also knows the different action the agent would perform under different circumstances. Middle knowledge, then, is in view in this explanation, though not explicitly.

Last, an even stronger comes a statement from Robert Dabney, this one with explicit dependence on the concept of compatibilist middle knowledge. Dabney writes:

> This, then, is my picture of the providential evolution of God's purpose as to sinful acts; so to arrange and group events and objects around free agents by His manifold wisdom and power, as to place each soul, at every step, in the presence of those circumstances, which, He knows, will be a sufficient objective inducement to it to do, of its own native, free activity, just the thing called for by God's plan. Thus the act is man's alone, though its occurrence is efficaciously secured by God. And the sin is man's only. God's concern in it is holy, first, because all His personal agency in arranging to secure its occurrence was holy; and second, His ends or purposes are holy. God does not will the sin of the act, for the sake of its sinfulness; but only wills the result to which the act is the means, and that result is always worthy of His holiness.[8]

It is worth noting that Louis Berkhof quotes this passage from Dabney favorably in defense of essentially the same position in his own *Systematic Theology*.[9]

---

conceived as freedom of inclination as opposed to libertarian freedom (we're free when we do what we most want, as opposed to possessing a supposed power of contrary choice), then divine middle knowledge provides a helpful explanation for God's ordination of evil that moral creatures carry out both freely and culpably.

8. Dabney, *Lectures*, 288–9.

9. Berkhof, *Systematic Theology*, 174–75.

Conclusion

As I conclude, let me make sure that the reader understands the limitations of this study. First, I do not believe that the Reformed model must appeal to middle knowledge to deal with the so-called asymmetrical problematic outlined here. Many Reformed people have been content simply to say that while the Bible teaches that God ordains all things, including the evil acts of free creatures, we're not told how this happens. While this is adequate, I simply believe that it is better to make use of a biblical category (i.e., middle knowledge) and through meditation on passages consider how this "tool" can provide some small explanation on such a very large issue. Second, I also wish to be clear that I see absolutely no validity in an appeal to middle knowledge when it comes to how God works in the lives of sinners to save them. No consideration of various circumstances would ever succeed in taking a spiritually dead and depraved sinner and inclining him to trust in Christ. No, the Spirit must do a work in that sinner's heart, opening spiritual eyes and awakening spiritual vision to see Christ, believe, and be saved. And the same can be said of innumerable ways in which God works in the lives of believers to incline their hearts to want to do what he has called and ordained they do. Though God can and does control the circumstances of our choices, he also controls when and how our natures are affected by his grace enabling us toward goodness, holiness, and good works that no change of circumstances alone could ever elicit from us (e.g., Phil 2:12–3; 1 Cor 15:10).

Middle-Knowledge Calvinism, then, is a big name for a modest part of the larger Calvinist model of divine providence. But it does serve to help in an area notoriously difficult, and it serves in a way that upholds the integrity of God's holy character while also securing the real and genuine free and moral responsibility of sinful creatures. To the end that it helps vindicate God and show our just responsibility for all evil done, it surely is worth exploring and perhaps worth adopting.

Bibliography

Berkhof, Louis. *Systematic Theology*. London: Banner of Truth Trust, 1939.

Boettner, Loraine. *The Reformed Doctrine of Predestination*. Grand Rapids: Eerdmans, 1951.

Campbell, Travis James. "Middle Knowledge: A Reformed Critique." *Westminster Theological Journal* 68.1 (2006) 1–22.

Dabney, Robert L. *Lectures in Systematic Theology*. 1878. Reprint, Grand Rapids: Zondervan, 1972.

Feinberg, John S. "God Ordains All Things." In *Predestination and Free Will: Four Views of Divine Sovereignty and Human Freedom*, edited by David Basinger and Randall Basinger, 17–44. Downers Grove, IL: InterVarsity, 1986.

Helm, Paul. *The Providence of God*. Downers Grove, IL: InterVarsity, 1994.

Mohler, R. Albert, Jr., ed. *Confessing the Faith: The Living Legacy of Southern Seminary's Abstract of Principles*. Louisville: SBTS Press, 2016.

9

Middle Knowledge and the Assumption
of Libertarian Freedom

A Response to Ware

JOHN D. LAING

Introduction

BRUCE WARE AND I agree on a number of theological points beyond inerrancy and [Southern] Baptist principles. We both affirm meticulous divine providence, comprehensive divine foreknowledge, divine freedom and aseity, and divine use of counterfactuals of creaturely freedom in the exercise of His sovereignty. Of course, there are many other points upon which we agree, but these are the most pertinent for the present discussion. We do, however, disagree on the possibility of Calvinist Middle Knowledge, though not as strongly as I once thought (though it may not be quite so clear from my presentation here).

It was approximately fifteen years ago that I first began thinking about how one might reconcile a Calvinist view of providence with middle knowledge, and about twelve years ago that I first wrote a critique of the attempt by evangelical theologians such as Bruce Ware and Terrance Tiessen to do so.[1] This paper is an attempt to respond to some clarifications of the Calvinist middle knowledge position that have been offered since that time, with particular attention to the work of Ware and, to a lesser extent, Tiessen. In this paper, I will argue that the Calvinist middle knowledge proposal fails on several counts. Specifically, I will argue that it encounters many of the same supposed problems as Molinism, from the grounding objection to the divine weakness objection, and that it has some problems of its own, from unusual notions of ontology and necessity, to the potential for flirt-

---

1. Laing, "Compatibility," 455–67.

ing with fatalism. In the end, I suggest that proponents of Calvinist middle knowledge reevaluate their criticisms of libertarian freedom, and adopt full-blown Molinism or (probably more realistically) move to the Thomistic position of seeing God's knowledge of counterfactuals of creaturely freedom as part of his free knowledge.

One more comment before I move to the body of my paper: near the beginning of his response to Paul Helm's article in his edited volume on the doctrine of God, Ware complains that Helm drew from other writings of the authors to write a pre-emptive critique of their positions. He writes, "Rather than waiting for his opportunity to respond to what his dialogue partners presented in their own chapters, he took from previously published materials what he understood to be the substance of their views and spent nearly half of his allotted space to critique these alternative models of the doctrine of God."[2] I must admit that I have committed this same sin—while the paper was slotted to be a response to Ware's paper given here, I did draw from previously published materials as well. I hope that grace may abound here, and I should note that some of my concerns may not be applicable to Bruce's position, but to others who may hope to take up the mantle of Calvinist Middle Knowledge.

Calvinist Middle Knowledge

The doctrine of middle knowledge is based in the idea that God makes use of counterfactuals of creaturely freedom—statements about what possible free creatures would do (freely) in potential situations—in his deliberations (if we may speak anthropomorphically) about his creative activity, or in the philosophical terminology, in his determining which possible world he will actualize. While the doctrine has traditionally assumed libertarian freedom, the Calvinist middle knowledge proposal has suggested the wedding of the model with a compatibilist view of creaturely freedom, understood as freedom of inclination, or the ability to choose according to one's desires and the refusal that freedom requires the ability to choose to act or not-act. Suppose God wants me to freely eat a piece of chocolate cheesecake tonight. I don't know that this is the case, though I must admit that I'm inclined to think it is (or I am at least hopeful). How could God bring it about that I do so—that is, freely eat the cheesecake? Presumably, he has a whole host of options on how to do so; presumably there are a number of scenarios that result in my compatibilistically freely choosing to eat a piece of chocolate cheesecake tonight, but of course, there really only need be

2. Ware, "Responses to Helm," 70–71.

one such scenario for God to meet his ends in this regard. If this is the case, there is at least one proposition/subjunctive conditional (or counterfactual of creaturely freedom) of the form,

> If John were in situation S, he would freely eat a piece of choco-late cheesecake tonight;

and all God need do is ensure that S obtains in order to have the desired result. To be more precise, God could weakly actualize my eating the cheesecake by ensuring that S obtains (and I were in it). God could even weakly actualize S's obtaining through similar means, though that is not particularly relevant to our concerns here. So far so good—what I have de-scribed up to this point can be agreed upon by all—traditional Molinist and Calvinist middle knowledge proponent alike.

However, it is here where I am puzzled, not only by the Calvinist middle knowledge proposals like that of Ware and Tiessen, but also by the Reformed tradition's insistence that God's knowledge of subjunctive con-ditionals is part of his natural knowledge rather than his free knowledge. I must admit that, when I originally wrote my critique of middle-knowledge Calvinism, I had an erroneous view of what I took the position to be, for I assumed it would ground the truth of subjunctive conditionals such as that being discussed here in the will of God somehow, and thus, be known by his free knowledge. That is, I assumed that the grounding of the truth of the proposition that if I were in S, I would (compatibilistically) freely eat a piece of chocolate cheesecake would have to be located in the way God created me, or something similar. Part of the problem is that I assumed the proponent of Calvinist middle knowledge would agree that both

> If John were in S, he would freely eat a piece of chocolate cheese-cake tonight

and

> If John were in S, he would freely refrain from eating a piece of chocolate cheesecake tonight

are *possible*. Apparently, my assumption was in error, and it is this that I find troubling, not so much that I was in error, though I certainly do not relish being wrong, but because of what seems to follow.[3] According to the

---

3. I was also wrong to claim that the Calvinist middle knowledge position is not in the middle of anything because it must reduce to only two types of knowledge: natu-ral and free. I was correct that it reduces to those two, but Ware has correctly pointed out that he may coherently divide God's natural knowledge into subsets, as it were, and place God's knowledge of counterfactuals of compatibilistic freedom in the subset

position advocated by Ware and Tiessen, following Paul Helm and a host of Reformed luminaries (e.g., Turretin, etc.), if the first is possible, the second is not. Since we have been working on the assumption that it is true that if I were in S, I would eat the cheesecake, we will assume that the counterfactual,

> If John were in S, he would freely refrain from eating a piece of chocolate cheesecake tonight

is not only false, but *necessarily* false; it is not possibly true. Similarly, the counterfactual,

> If John were in S, he would freely eat a piece of chocolate cheesecake tonight

is not only true, but *necessarily* true; it is not possibly false. It is this assertion that I find perplexing and disturbing for reasons outlined below.

The Grounding Objection

It seems that the version of compatibilist middle knowledge Ware and Tiessen want to defend, where God knows counterfactuals as part of his natural knowledge, suffers from many of the same problems that libertarian middle knowledge does, especially with respect to the grounding of counterfactuals of creaturely freedom. What grounds the truth of the counterfactual of compatibilist freedom noted above? Calvinist critics of Molinism have typically employed the grounding objection against middle knowledge to argue that it is incoherent, and concluded that one is left with a choice between Calvinism and open theism, and in that case, the traditional Christian should accept Calvinism. Both Ware and Tiessen have made arguments of this sort in favor of their Calvinist middle knowledge proposal.[4] Unfortunately,

---

just (logically) prior to God's free knowledge, thus preserving its status as "middle" knowledge. Ware, "Responses to Helm," 74. Still, using the term "middle knowledge," given its direct ties to Molina's theory and the implication in the term that it is distinct from the other two forms of knowledge (natural and free), is misleading at best and ought to be abandoned due to its tendency to create more confusion than provide illumination. Helm is surely correct when he points out that the attempt to distinguish middle knowledge from Molinism is wrongheaded and historically inaccurate. He writes, "Strictly speaking, there is no 'Molinist version' of middle knowledge. Molinism *is* the doctrine of middle knowledge (though of course one can imagine minor variants of it), and intrinsic to middle knowledge/Molinism is the preservation of libertarian freedom" (Helm, "Classic Calvinist Doctrine," 45).

4 For example, Ware, *God's Greater Glory*, 112–13. Similarly, Tiessen has continued to maintain that the grounding objection is an insurmountable problem for Molinism because of libertarian freedom.

neither has really offered a clear explanation for how counterfactuals of compatibilistic freedom may be grounded [I will speak to Bruce's proposal in just a moment]. As already noted, I assumed they would want to ground them ultimately in the will of God—first, in the characters, dispositions, and/or souls of the free creatures to whom the counterfactuals refer—but secondarily, in the free choice of God to create those free creatures with those characters, dispositions, and/or souls, assuming God could create them so that their characters lead to different action (which is not at all clear on the model). In this way, the proponent of Calvinist middle knowledge would preserve the creative freedom and omnipotence of God, as well as the principle, "all truth is God's truth," admittedly not a biblical principle *per se*. This was the approach of Molina's Dominican opponents, and it is the assumption that most philosophers have taken when discussing the options for grounding.[5]

Consider the grounding objection: At heart, it asks what makes counterfactuals of freedom true. Since counterfactuals refer to non-actual persons and/or non-actual states of affairs, their truth presumably cannot be grounded in the activity of the agent spoken of in the counterfactual (never mind questions of backward causation). They cannot be grounded in God or God's will because that would make then either necessarily true or at least not independent of his will. Proponents of the grounding objection thus maintain that counterfactuals of (libertarian) creaturely freedom cannot be true and Molinism fails.

In an attempt to tie the truth of counterfactuals to the actions of the agent named, some Molinists have attempted to answer the objection by suggesting that the grounding of the truth of counterfactuals may be located in the agent's performance of the action in the closest-but-not-actual world where he finds himself in the situation noted. This solution has met with mixed reviews, even among Molinists; Calvinists have typically found it less than persuasive. Perhaps the most common response to the grounding objection by Molinists has been to question the need for grounding, suggest counterfactuals are something like brute facts about the agents, and compare counterfactuals with other, similar propositions which we know to be true (or to have truth-value) because they refer to the free actions of beings in the actual future. Apart from backward causation where the future occurrence grounds the past truth of the proposition, such statements also suffer from a lack of grounding, yet are far less controversial regarding their truth/falsity; they are often thought to have truth-value, even by those who

---

5 See, for example, Perszyk, "Molinism and Compatibilism," 26.

doubt that counterfactuals of freedom have truth value. It is hard to see how proponents of counterfactuals of compatibilist freedom can do any better.

Ware has attempted to offer a response to my critique. He argues that God's knowledge of counterfactuals of compatibilist creaturely freedom is grounded in the following: 1) the character of the creature, 2) all contingencies, 3) God's knowledge of how factors will influence the individual's desires, and 4) God's knowledge of how the person will choose in accordance with his desires.[6] Unfortunately, Ware has actually side-stepped the issue of grounding and instead answered the question of *how* God knows counterfactuals. I will say more about this in just a moment, but as an answer to the grounding objection, Ware has, at best, grounded the truth of counterfactuals in the character of the individual of whom the counterfactual speaks, but this does not really get at the question of grounding, at least not if libertarian freedom is not true; it only pushes it back one step. The question now arises: what grounds the truth of counterfactuals regarding the development of individual desires? We can assume that Calvinists such as Ware believe that there are truths about how an individual's desires will arise and or develop, e.g., If person P were in S, a desire D would develop in him. What makes it such that D would develop in P, given S, rather than a different desire, say D'? Ware has failed to address this issue, and herein lies the problem. His options, it seems to me, are three: he can either claim that such counterfactuals are not grounded or do not need grounding, or he can argue that they are grounded in God's will or his creative work. If he chooses the former, he is advocating nothing different from the traditional Molinist who subscribes to libertarian freedom. If he chooses the latter, then, as demonstrated in my earlier piece, he has grounded the truth of counterfactuals in the divine will and hence has really endorsed the position of Molina's primary critic, Domingo Báñez. The third option is to maintain they are grounded in the character of the individual and that the individual develops his own character through his actions/choices, but this leads to an infinite regress or a tacit endorsement of agent-causal libertarianism ("not that there's anything wrong with that," to, in a hermeneutically irresponsible way, borrow a phrase from *Seinfeld*). A fourth option is available and is suggested by Helm: they may be grounded in the divine mind. I believe this to be most promising, but it is no different from my own libertarian position.

One thing I should point out is that the Ware/Tiessen model has the unsavory consequence, often complained against the doctrine of middle knowledge, of limiting God's creative choices. The truth of counterfactuals

---

6. Ware, *God's Greater Glory*, 115 n. 10.

of freedom constrain the kinds of worlds God can actualize.[7] Of course, there is an advantage to this constraint, in that the proponent of Calvinist middle knowledge of this sort may make use of the free-will defense and actually believe it may be an accurate description of how things are (whereas a proponent who places the truths of counterfactuals of creaturely freedom in God's free knowledge, or dependent upon his will, can use the free-will defense, but must admit that he does not think it is an accurate description of reality).[8] So I see this as a strength of the position, as does Tiessen. However, it seems that Ware does not, as will be shown in my comments on Ware and libertarianism.

Odd Notion of Necessity/Possibility

While the idea of the constraints is helpful for theodicy, the particular manifestation of it in this Calvinist system leads to some perplexing metaphysical positions. Under this interpretation, even God cannot make it the case that

> If John were in S, he would freely eat a piece of chocolate cheesecake tonight

is false. He can alter circumstances in a variety of ways so that I do not find myself in S, or he can override my freedom, or he can make me different, but he cannot make it the case that

> If John were in situation, S, he would freely refrain from eating chocolate cheesecake tonight

is true.

Not only, though, does this mean that God cannot make it the case, but the upshot of placing the truth of counterfactuals in God's natural knowledge is that it is necessary that if I am in S, I eat chocolate cheesecake tonight. What needs to be explained, though, is the locus and nature of that necessity. It certainly cannot be logical necessity; there appears to be no violation

---

7. While they may defend their model by appeal to logical possibility, that is, they may claim that it is not unusual to see God restrained by logical possibility, as has already been pointed out, it is hard to see the constraints spoken of here as really instances of logical possibility/impossibility.

8. I have long maintained that Calvinists may legitimately make use of the free-will defense because it deals with logical possibility. So even if a Calvinist is uncomfortable with the suggestion that it may have been the case that God could not have created a world where, for example, Adam is free and does not sin, he may nevertheless use the argument because it *could* have been the case. In other words, as long as he can say that it is *possible*, he can use the argument.

of the fundamental laws of logic in my refraining from eating cheesecake; such action would not violate the laws of identity, non-contradiction, or excluded middle. But it does not seem to be a case of metaphysical necessity either; it does not seem intelligible to claim that my eating cheesecake is a fundamental function of the way things are. Yet these appear to be the only options that make sense of a necessity that constrains God's creative options. It seems to me that the difference really has to do with how we think about possibility. The problem is that the view of possibility is not at all clear or obvious, and even seems to contradict our normal notions of possibility.[9] Typically, when one speaks of possibility in the strict sense (as opposed to colloquial usage), he normally sees a close connection to conceivability. This is not to say that conceivability exhausts possibility; there are surely things possible of which we cannot even begin to imagine. However, there is a rich tradition that claims anything of which we can conceive is possible (this is the logic which undergirds the ontological argument). Surely both "in S, I eat chocolate cheesecake" and "in S, I refrain from eating chocolate cheesecake" are conceivable!

The content of God's natural knowledge has typically been understood to be all logically and metaphysically necessary truths. These are truths over which God has no control because they are both necessary and explanatorily/logically prior to his will, or are true independent of his will. For the compatibilist to place the truths of counterfactuals of creaturely freedom here seems odd, for it places these propositions alongside truths such as "1+1=2" and "All bachelors are unmarried" and "God exists," as well as "If an object is blue, then it has extension," and the like. It is hard for me to see how a proposition like, "If John were in S, he would compatibilistically freely eat a piece of chocolate cheesecake tonight" has the same status with regard to certainty and necessity as those just noted. All of the others seem not only intuitively true, but incoherently falsified. Helm claims that the type of necessity involved here is "causal necessity," and distinguishes it from logical and metaphysical necessity. One may think that the problem with this notion is that the sort of necessity due to causal chains, at least in the physical realm, is (at least in some ways) dependent upon the way God creates or the sort of universe and natural laws he actualizes, and may conclude that truths of this sort are dependent upon God's will and would be known by his free knowledge, but this would be a mistake. For consider the following counterfactual:

> If God were to create a world such as α and John were in S, he would freely eat a piece of chocolate cheesecake.

9. It also seems tautological in nature.

It does not appear that the counterfactual is dependent upon God's will and does not need to be known by free knowledge. It does seem to endorse world-indexed properties, which will be discussed below.

So we are back to the questions undergirding the grounding objection: what makes the counterfactual regarding my compatibilistically eating cheesecake true? It seems that those who locate the truth of counterfactuals of compatibilistic freedom in God's natural knowledge have no more options than their libertarian friends: they have to either claim ignorance about the grounding requirement, suggest that counterfactuals are akin to brute facts about the agent in question (facts over which even God has no control), or draw some kind of analogy to similarly-constructed propositions about free actions in the actual future, and argue that since they can be true, so also may counterfactuals. Of course, I have no problem with these strategies, but I think they are intuitively clearer when applied to contingent propositions referencing libertarian freedom than to metaphysically necessary propositions referencing compatibilistic freedom.

Flirting with Fatalism?

I ought to note that, when I first realized that this view sees counterfactuals of creaturely freedom as known by God's natural knowledge, my initial response was to see it as fatalistic because of the necessity attached to human action and the lack of options for God, but upon further reflection, I have come to see that this is not necessarily the case. The lack of options for God in this scheme could be seen as no different from the Molinist concept of world-feasibility, as noted below. However, the position does have the potential of slipping into a form of theological fatalism due to the combination of the necessity of the truth of counterfactuals of compatibilist freedom, along with the argument against libertarian freedom on the basis of logic/coherence and rationality of choice. I will say more about this in a moment, but if the argument against libertarian freedom is applied to God, such that he only has one option with regard to his activities and cannot choose between competing options, then I do not see how the position can evade charges of fatalism.

If I were a Calvinist, I would ground the truth of counterfactuals of compatibilistic freedom in God's will (free knowledge).[10] Actually, I wouldn't,

---

10. One question worth raising in this regard has to do with the heritage of non-Molinist approaches to the truth of counterfactuals of creaturely freedom. It is worth asking how those groups opposed to Molinism dealt with the issue and why they did so in the way they did. It is well known that Molina's own views were not well received

according to the theory, because I could not, for if I were a Calvinist, I would be a different person and would ground the truth of counterfactuals exactly where a Calvinist would ground the truth of counterfactuals—in God's natural knowledge! Joking aside, though, Tiessen considers this route and rejects it, noting that he agrees with the Molinists that the Dominican position obliterates human freedom.[11] However, just a few pages later, Tiessen argues against Werther's thesis that the truth of counterfactuals is part of God's necessary (natural) knowledge, claiming that it leads to fatalism. Tiessen writes, "Werther assumes that God's knowledge that Packer would join the band, if invited to do so, indicates a necessary property in Packer [the property of responding affirmatively if "his being asked to join a band" obtains], which would make this knowledge part of God's necessary knowledge . . . in that case, what has traditionally been deemed God's free knowledge would also be necessary and so all of God's knowledge, including his knowledge of the actual future, would be necessary knowledge . . . This indicates that it is very important to identify how and 'when' properties become essential."[12] Of course, Tiessen has come to reject his conclusion regarding Werther, as he now accepts that God knows counterfactuals of compatibilist freedom by his natural knowledge.

I have several points and/or questions related to this exchange. First, if freedom is obliterated if counterfactuals of freedom are dependent on divine will, how is freedom preserved when counterfactuals of freedom are necessary/necessarily true (part of God's natural knowledge)? Second, if counterfactuals of creaturely freedom are known by God's natural knowledge, how can this position avoid Werther's claim that an individual's action is tied to an essential property? In the example I have been using throughout, it seems that the Ware/Tiessen position requires that I have the essential property of eating chocolate cheesecake when in S. Third, what does Tiessen mean when he says it is important to identify when properties become essential?

---

by all in the Catholic Church when he first published his commentary on Aquinas' *Summa*, the *Concordia*. Leaving aside political posturings and jealousies amongst the various orders for the moment, it is worth noting that the Jesuits and Augustinians were largely supportive of Molina and his views, while the Dominicans (Thomists) saw his views as dangerous. The controversy over Molina's views—and it was quite violent— was primarily concerned with the efficaciousness of grace in his soteriology; so much of the writings of his opponents address issues related to salvation. They were concerned to preserve the absolute sovereignty of God over salvation, and so saw truths related to creaturely belief as dependent upon the divine willing. I wonder if Ware would place the truths similarly, as he insists that he does not use middle knowledge for soteriological concerns.

11. Tiessen, "Why Calvinists Should Believe," 351.

12. Ibid., 356.

Aren't essential properties those that a being, if it exists (even as an idea in the divine mind), possesses (by definition)? Essential properties are, like all other necessary truths, eternal, are they not? It simply makes no sense to speak of properties *becoming* essential. Perhaps I am being unfair in this question, since Tiessen has rejected his own argument here, and I certainly do not mean to saddle Ware with the erroneous views/arguments of others. Fourth, is Tiessen correct that Werther's position leads to fatalism? I am inclined to think that it does not (and, as already noted, Tiessen and Ware would agree). I cannot see how making counterfactuals of freedom part of God's natural knowledge necessarily collapses into God's free knowledge, unless one assumes that counterfactuals of freedom must be contingent in some sense. But then they would just be part of God's free knowledge and not part of his natural knowledge. Now, it should be noted at this point, that although most of these questions have been posed of Tiessen and have been directed at Tiessen's paper, they are applicable to any Calvinist middle knowledge position that places divine knowledge of counterfactuals of creaturely freedom in God's natural knowledge.

If Helm is correct and the distinction between would and could breaks down in a compatibilist framework, then it seems that only one option exists, at least for the creature. Does it mean the same thing for God? Helm is unclear on this issue, as he has suggested that even God does not possess libertarian freedom, and instead has something akin to compatibilist freedom.[13] If it is true for God, then all possibilities must be actualities—whatever God could do (create), he would do (create). In fact, Helm (consistently) denies that God has the freedom to choose between competing alternatives regarding his creative activity; he had to create this world. Helm sees that as not fatalistic because the constraint upon which worlds God can actualize is not logical or external to him, but is his own perfect nature.[14]

---

13 See Helm, *Eternal God*, 171–94. In his criticism of the thesis that God's freedom requires that he have options regarding world-actualization, Helm writes, "The problem with such a position is that, as before, when discussing Aquinas, it is hard to see how divine caprice can be avoided. For God is portrayed as actualizing one of a number of co-optimific goals. If we suppose this makes sense, on what grounds could God decide in favour of one rather than another? Clearly, not by reference to their character. There seem to be two alternatives; either he chooses on the basis of some accidental feature of one alternative lacked by all the others, a feature not related to optimificity, or he chooses as a result of pure whimsy. Neither of these alternatives is very appealing" (180). Helm does not explain why the first option is not appealing and does not seem to seriously consider it as an option.

14. Helm writes, "The argument does not depend on the idea of God choosing between equally optimific outcomes, which would appear to make God's instantiation of any universe an act of pure reasonless will. Rather the argument is that God's freedom consists in the rationality of his choice, in his having a good reason for what he

This, however, is doubtful for several reasons. In his chapter on fatalism as it relates to foreknowledge, Helm argues that his position is not fatalistic because what God foreknows is not logically necessary. The question that must be asked is, "Is this really the case?" If God's nature requires that he perform exactly the actions he perform and there are no other options, then it seems that there is a necessity to his activity. God necessarily creates, and this means that the future he decrees is necessary. I imagine Helm would argue that the necessity involved here is not logical necessity, but something else, perhaps metaphysical necessity or the like. However, if it is a matter of logical consistency that God's perfection requires the one and only perfect world, then it is hard to see how the transfer of necessity would not make the future also logically necessary, which results in fatalism. At any rate, a theological fatalism that is not logically necessary but where God has no other options is exceedingly problematic, for it suggests that we (and everything else) are necessary, even if not logically speaking.

Helm attempts to save the proposal from these fatalistic senses by appeal to God's free decree: "When one of the possibilities that form God's natural knowledge is freely decreed, then what is decreed is logically contingent; it might not have been decreed." But it seems to me, given Helm's comments regarding God's freedom, incorrect to say that it might not have been decreed. If God's necessary perfection requires that he decree exactly what he decrees and that, necessarily, he could not do otherwise, it is hard to see how any given decree *might not have been decreed*, no matter how much God's actions flowed from his perfect desires (and, thereby, freely). In addition, Helm claims that fatalism, properly understood, has to do with logical consistency, that all happens by means of logical necessity. While this is true of some forms of fatalism, it is inaccurate to claim that this is the heart of fatalism, classically understood. Fatalism was rather the claim that all happens as a result of a force called "fate"; fatalism claimed that all happens by necessity (but not only necessity of a logical sort), and even the gods were subject to fate. But there was never an argument presented to suggest that fate was tied to logical necessity. In fact, there were common notions that one could try to thwart his fate, though he always failed in the end. This was the basis of so many of the Greek Tragedies. The point to be made here is that it was not seen as *irrational* to try to avoid one's fate, though it was *futile*. So Helm's view does not escape the charge of fatalism by claiming that it does not appeal to logical necessity to explain God's actions. If I were Helm, I would instead argue that fatalism historically saw fate as some sort of force at work external to the gods to which they were subject. In Helm's

---

instantiates, not in his having no reason" (*Eternal God*, 178).

argument, God is not subject (if that is even a correct characterization) to something external to himself but rather is subject to his own nature, or put differently, his actions and will are simply consistent with, and reflective of, his nature. However, Helm's position, even so stated, still seems problematic because it retains many of the problems of classic fatalism.

The disconcerting aspects of fatalism have less to do with the *nature* of the constraints upon all, even God (or the gods), but rather with the *fact* of constraints upon all, even God. As Eusebius put it in his critique of Porphyry, "For if anything either good or the reverse is destined for men, it will of necessity occur, and, whether the gods will or not, it will come to pass. We ought therefore to worship Necessity only, and care little, or rather nothing, for the gods, as being able neither to annoy nor to benefit us."[15] It is difficult to see how the criticism does not also apply to Helm's presentation, where God acts of necessity and can do no other. Eusebius goes on to argue that the proper conception of God sees him as Lord over the fates and not subject to necessity.

It is for this reason that many Calvinists have rejected the idea that God only has one option. Both Ware and Tiessen maintain the aseity of God and the freedom of God in creating, which seems to be a more robust view of freedom than Helm proposes (though Helm uses the same language). As Ware puts it, "Although God exists eternally independent of all else in the infinite fullness of every perfection, and although he possesses no deficiency or lack which any finite reality could supply, nevertheless, he has freely willed to bring into being a contingent order to which he has voluntarily pledged his intimate and most personal involvement."[16]

Odd Ontology

In his debates with Tiessen and Ware over the possibility of Calvinist Middle Knowledge, Paul Helm has argued against the distinction of would/could in creaturely actions if one is to remain true to Calvinist principles. The would/could equation also suggests that, for any given possible set of creaturely actions, there exists a distinct creature. This has the unusual consequence of maintaining that the John who would eat chocolate cheesecake in *S* is a different John from he who would not eat the cheesecake in *S* (presumably

---

15. Eusebius, *Preparation*, 257.

16. Ware, "Modified Calvinist Doctrine of God," 84. Ware also writes, "God is supremely independent of the world, and hence he simply does not need the world he has made" (80). Also, he writes, "By his free word, all that is receives its existence (Ps 33:6; Heb 11:3)" (82).

due to some difference in character, desires, disposition, etc.). For any given set of decisions I might make, there is a distinct me (or should I say, John that is not-me). Thus, different possible worlds are populated by completely different beings. I am not aware of anyone explicitly arguing for this position, though some of Tiessen's comments are suggestive of it.[17] If this is a fair characterization, then it seems that the Calvinist is committed to an odd notion of ontology and perhaps modality.

In his magisterial work *The Nature of Necessity*, Plantinga asks about essential properties and distinguishes between several types.[18] What is of greatest concern to us here is his postulation of world-indexed properties that are essential to objects and beings (he uses the example of *being snub-nosed in α* for Socrates).[19] Is the Ware/Tiessen model, following Plantinga, appealing to world-indexed essential properties, such that I have the property of *eating chocolate cheesecake when in S in α*?

The upshot of Plantinga's rather detailed discussion of this issue is that, while it is proper to speak of certain essential properties of individuals being world-indexed (e.g., my *being in S and eating chocolate cheesecake in α*), such properties are only necessary *insofar as they are world-indexed*, but the property is not necessary *in itself*, apart from its world-indexed identification. As Plantinga puts it, "Hence Socrates has *being snubnosed in α* in every world in which he exists—i.e., essentially. And of course the same

---

17. See Tiessen's discussion of how God could bring about a different result than that spoken of in the counterfactual. Referring to a counterfactual about my free actions, he writes, "As a counterfactual, this is not dependent upon God's will; it is the way things would be if God chose to actualize the world in which Laing, being exactly who he is now, got into that particular situation. If God had reasons for wanting things to turn out differently, he would not allow the particular circumstances to obtain, or he would have brought into Laing's personal formation influences that would make him a person who would choose differently than this particular John Laing would do" ("Why Calvinists Should Believe," 353).

18. Some he calls *trivially essential properties* because they are properties that all things possess if they exist. *Self identity, being colored if red*, and *being something or other* are examples. He goes on to point out that there are properties that some things have essentially that others have only accidentally; for example, *being non-green* is essential to the numeral 7, but accidental to the Taj Mahal. Then there are accidental properties which persons and things may or may not possess; properties such as *being a philosopher, an Athenian, a teacher of Plato, having been born in 470 BC*, and *having been executed by the Athenians on a charge of corrupting the youth* are all properties accidental to Socrates (Plantinga, *Necessity*, 60–61). See also Plantinga, "World and Essence," 466–73.

19. Plantinga defines world-indexed properties as follows: A property *P* is *world-indexed* if and only if either (1) there is a property *Q* and a world *W* such that for any object *x* and world *W**, *x* has *P* in *W** if and only if x exists in *W** and *W* includes *x*'s having *Q*, or (2) *P* is the complement of a world-indexed property (*Necessity*, 63).

goes for every other world-indexed property he has. But for any world W and property P, either Socrates has P in W or else he does not—in which case he has the complement of the world-indexed property *having P in W*."[20] He continues by noting that "*Socrates is snubnosed* is true in W (for specific W)" and "Possibly Socrates is snubnosed" are not the same thing: "There are worlds W in which it is false that Socrates is snubnosed . . . [the property of] *Being true in W* (for specific W) entails but is not entailed by *being possibly true.*" In other words, Plantinga notes that even if I have the essential property of *being in S and eating chocolate cheesecake in α*, I also may have the property of *being in S and refraining from eating chocolate cheesecake in β* (or some other possible world). But the placement of counterfactuals in God's natural knowledge along with the denial of libertarian freedom suggests that I have the essential property of *eating chocolate cheesecake in S*, no matter which possible world we consider. If what I have presented up to this point is an accurate description of Helm's, Tiessen's, and, more importantly, Ware's position(s), then it seems that what they are really suggesting is that all beings' properties are not only not-accidental (or essential), but that they are equal to those beings' essences. This theory is not without its proponents and has come to be known as the Theory of Worldbound Individuals.[21] However, Plantinga has rightly shown that the principle of the Indiscernability of Identicals does not require that differences in the world-indexed properties one possesses in different possible worlds means he is a different being in each possible world, and this precisely because the properties are world-indexed.[22]

This leads Plantinga to consider the so-called problem of Transworld Identity.[23] What is most interesting here is Plantinga's characterization of

20. Plantinga, *Necessity*, 63.

21. See Kaplan, "Transworld Heir Lines," 88–109; Chisholm, "Identity," 1–8; Lewis, "Counterpart Theory," 113.

22. Plantinga, *Necessity*, 92.

23. This problem notes that an individual could be so different in two possible worlds, at least with respect to the normal characteristics by which we identify persons, as to make his identification as the same person (in the two worlds) virtually impossible. Thus, there seems to be no answer to the question of what makes an individual who he is, or put differently, it is impossible to identify the essential properties that define an individual. Plantinga responds by first drawing an analogy to the intelligibility of transtemporal identity even though we may not be able to identify those properties which prove/show that the individual at time t1 is the same individual at later time t2. Plantinga next questions the intelligibility of the argument for the problem, suggesting that it is based on the faulty conception of possible worlds as all actual (e.g., different dimensions or the like) such that their inhabitants may be examined: "The claim that I must somehow be able to identify Socrates in W—pick him out—is either trivial or confused" (*Necessity*, 97). Third, Plantinga notes that even proponents of the Theory

the Theory of Worldbound Individuals' answer to the problem—that all properties are essential—as "unsatisfactory."[24] Plantinga goes on to note that the Theory of Worldbound Individuals "implies the outrageous view that— taking 'property' in as wide a sense as you like—no object could have lacked any property that in fact it has."[25] Plantinga takes this as self-evidently and obviously false, for it suggests that here are no contingencies. He writes, "Further, consider any proposition p that is false but contingent; since *Socrates exists* is true only in α, where p is false, there is no world in which p and *Socrates exists* are both true; the latter, therefore, entails the denial of the former. Accordingly, *Socrates exists* entails every true proposition. And surely all of this is clearly false. If we know anything at all about modality, we know that some of Socrates' properties are accidental to him, that *Socrates is foolish* is not necessarily false, and that *Socrates exists* does not entail every true proposition."[26] Plantinga goes on to argue that counterpart theory offers no remedy for these problems and is therefore false.

If each of my properties are specific to the instantiation of me in α, such that instantiations in other possible worlds—for example, β or γ—are not me, then every property is necessary for me. No being in another possible world could have the property of being John Laing (though some may have that name), and this means that if God wanted to actualize a world with me (or a world with any other specific being), He would have only one choice of world—the actual world. This has the nasty consequence of suggesting, quite apart from the question of how God knows counterfactuals of divine freedom, that God really only had one feasible world, that God had to create exactly what he did create, which sounds awfully close to fatalism. Can the Calvinist maintain world-indexed properties while denying the Theory of Worldbound Individuals within a system that sees counterfactuals of freedom as part of God's natural knowledge? To be quite honest, I am not sure, but I am inclined to think not.

Ware on God and Evil

Ware highlights what he takes to be the advantages of the Reformed view over the Arminian view (somewhat surprisingly and admittedly courageously!) with respect to God's sovereignty over evil. He suggests that the

---

of Worldbound Individuals give an answer to the question of which properties are essential to any given being (Socrates) all of them.

24. Plantinga, *Necessity*, 98.

25. Ibid., 102.

26. Ibid.

Arminian view must accept "gratuitous and pointless evil" because of some misguided pledge on (the Arminian) God's part to not intervene because of his granting of libertarian freedom. By contrast, he argues, the Reformed view sees all evil—each and every instance of evil—as advancing and not hindering God's plans/purposes for the world.[27]

I have a couple of points to make here. First, Ware's description of Arminianism is somewhat misleading, or at least his description of the difference between the Arminian and Reformed conceptions on this issue are a bit overstated. Consider his summary statement of the Reformed view: "God regulates exactly the evil that occurs, since for any and every instance of evil, he specifically permits according to his wisdom and ultimate purposes what he could otherwise have prevented."[28] Contrary to Ware's claims, most Arminians could agree with this description. The language of permission and the prerogative of God to intervene and prevent any given instance of evil are hallmarks of orthodox Arminian theology. In fact, if God's regulation of evil only entails his permission and failure to intervene, then even heterodox Arminian theology (e.g., open theism) could agree.[29] I think what Ware was trying to get at is the idea that Calvinist theology distinguishes itself from Arminian theology on the issue of God's providence over evil by its more causative view of God's activity, and its claim that each and every instance of evil leads *directly* to a *specific* greater good for which that evil was *necessary*. By contrast, Arminians agree that there could, at least conceptually, be instances of gratuitous evil, though as already noted, they are under no obligation to affirm that there are indeed such instances. When they do affirm that seemingly gratuitous evil has occurred, they tie it to world-feasibility and God's choice to actualize a world that includes gratuitous evil but also meets his wise ends. The argument proceeds in much the same way as the free-will defense. The gratuitous evil contributes *indirectly* to the greater good of meeting the world's *telos*/accomplishing God's purposes in creating, and for reasons known only to him, God chose not to intervene. The gratuitous evil is thus seen as part of the world-history of the possible world God chose to instantiate. None of this should bother Ware, though, for if his Calvinist middle knowledge proposal works, it appears he could make the very same claim, and this leads to my next point.

Second, it is far from clear that Ware's middle knowledge view has this feature of necessarily escaping the notion that gratuitous evil may occur,

27. Ware, "Modified Calvinist Doctrine of God," 108.

28. Ibid.

29. I realize that some Arminians do not like having open theism associated with their position, but it is reasonable to suggest that open theism grew out of Arminian theology.

for recall that the truths of counterfactuals of creaturely freedom are not dependent upon God's will or the free decisions of the creature to whom they refer, but are simply just necessarily true. Since God has no control over the truth of counterfactuals of creaturely freedom, it means that his creative options are constrained by those that are true. One consequence of this concept is the notion that there may be instances of gratuitous evil because of the chance that the feasible worlds which meet God's ultimate ends all contain instances of evil that may not directly contribute to a specific greater good, but are nevertheless a part of that world which is one of the set of worlds that best meet God's purposes (and hence indirectly contribute to the greater good of God's ends being attained/met).[30]

Herein lies my question: If Ware's God cannot make the counterfactuals of creaturely freedom true, how does he avoid the same constraints? How is it not the case that the God of Calvinist middle knowledge may have some instances of gratuitous evil? If he has no control over the true counterfactuals, then the notion of feasible worlds must come into play (though, I believe the Ware/Tiessen model would equate feasibility with their notion of possibility due to the equation of would/could). It seems to me that the only way this conclusion can be avoided is to assume that for any given creature in any given instance, there is a corresponding counterfactual which states the agent will act, and another corresponding counterfactual which states the agent will not act, but this has the consequence of effectively making the truth of counterfactuals of creaturely freedom dependent upon God's will (they would hold not truth-value in God's natural knowledge, but merely express possibility, and be made true by God's act of will), or of plunging Calvinist middle knowledge into incoherence (by affirming that both are true in God's natural knowledge, and hence both are simultaneously necessarily true, a clear violation of the law of non-contradiction), or of affirming libertarian freedom (by claiming that it is possible an agent acts or not-acts in the same situation).

Consider our counterfactual again:

> If John were in S, he would freely eat a piece of chocolate cheesecake tonight.

---

30. These constraints seem to be no different from the Molinist/Arminian view. On the Molinist view, it is claimed that, as God considers which possible world to actualize, his options are limited by the true counterfactuals of creaturely freedom, and the combinations of true counterfactuals which give rise to whole sets of persons, scenarios, and ways-things-could-be. This is referred to as world-feasibility. Some logically possible worlds are not feasible for God to actualize due to the true counterfactuals.

According to the Calvinist middle knowledge model, God has no power over the truth of this statement, and so worlds in which I am in S and refrain from eating the cheesecake are not feasible for God (or even possible!). Suppose God does not want me to eat the cheesecake. How could the model account for it? If that were the case, then he could actualize a world where I do not find myself in S. Fair enough; this is precisely the same thing a Molinist would say. However, the lack of ability to control the truth of counterfactuals coupled with his desire to instantiate creatures with freedom (compatibilistic or libertarian) means that God's options are limited. It could be the case that all of the worlds that meet God's ultimate ends also find me in S. There seems no way, in Ware's model, for God to ensure that he have a world that meets his ends that does not also have me in S, and so it may be that God cannot meet his ends without my eating the chocolate cheesecake or without violating my freedom in this regard. If the proponent of Calvinist middle knowledge wishes to dispute this, then he must argue that God could make me a little different so that I would have different desires and would instead refrain from eating, but it would not then be me refraining. There is another problem with this suggestion, even if the Theory of Worldbound Individuals does not hold for Calvinism. In his response to my argument to this effect where I referred to Adam's eating or refraining from eating the forbidden fruit, Tiessen suggests that God could simply give Adam efficient grace to make him compatibilistically freely refrain from eating the forbidden fruit.[31] Fair enough, assuming there is a prescribed amount that can be given while still maintaining the freedom of Adam with respect to eating or not eating, but why should we assume that there is such an amount for any given situation? Is there not a point at which the grace overrides the individual's freedom in order to prevent his sinning? It seems that there would be, at least in *some* cases, and if I am correct in this, then the Calvinist may argue that instances of gratuitous evil could sometimes occur.

So now we are back to my original complaint with the system. It has all the supposed weaknesses of Molinism, with the additional problems of somewhat strange notions of necessity and ontology, as well as its flirtation with fatalism.

Ware's Criticism of Libertarian Freedom

I would like to make just a couple of other points with regard to Ware's comments on the failure of Molinism. On more than one occasion, he has noted that his own criticisms of Molinism are at root, really criticisms of

---

31. Tiessen, "Why Calvinists Should Believe," 354.

libertarian freedom.[32] I am inclined to agree with him; in fact, I think if he could be convinced of the possibility of libertarianism, he would accept it as true, and move to the traditional conception of middle knowledge as a separate notion from natural and free knowledge. Whether I am correct in this supposition or not, perhaps only God can know (if counterfactuals of creaturely belief may be true), but it is likely that it is correct with regard to at least some moderate Calvinists who are intrigued by middle knowledge. So, in an effort to offer clarification and, admittedly, in the hope of convincing some of the truth of middle knowledge, I would like to offer a few brief comments in response to Ware's criticisms of libertarianism, as I believe they represent common notions held by many Calvinists.

First, Ware argues that libertarianism undercuts the rationality of decision-making (my words, not his), for he sees it as requiring one follow the same reasons for choosing contrary courses of action. Since all factors involved in one's decision are present at the moment he chooses, if he can choose either A or not-A, then the same reasons would serve to explain the choice for A and the choice for not-A, and this renders the choice arbitrary. As Ware put it, "According to libertarian freedom . . . every reason or set of reasons must be equally explanatory for why the agent might choose A or B, or not-A. As a result, our choosing reduces, strictly speaking, to arbitrariness. We can give no reason or set of reasons for why we make the choices we make that wouldn't be the identical reason or set of reasons we would invoke had we made the opposite choice! Hence, our choosing A over its opposite is arbitrary."[33]

What is one to make of this argument? If it were an accurate description of libertarianism, I should think all would agree; indeed, I would go a step further and simply say that such a conception is incoherent! However, there are good reasons to doubt that it is accurate. First, I know of no proponent of libertarian freedom who conceives of libertarian decision-making in this way. Of course, an appeal to the lack of proponents of an erroneous theory admitting the errors within it does not prove it valid, but a number of libertarians have offered explanations of how libertarian decision-making can proceed in a way that is vastly different from Ware's description. For example, van Inwagen has demonstrated that "undetermined" and "uncaused" are not the same thing, and that "uncaused" is not the same as random.[34] Similarly, Kane and others have distinguished between reasons and mo-

---

32. Ware, *God's Greater Glory*, 112–13; Ware, "Modified Calvinist Doctrine of God," 111.

33. Ware, *God's Greater Glory*, 86.

34. van Inwagen, *Free Will*, 129; see also 134–42.

tives, even on an internalist understanding of decision-making; one may have reasons to act that do not move one to act and therefore cannot explain actual choices, but actual choices are made on the different reasons and motives one has for acting.[35] O'Connor argues that agent-causal theories of free action allow for reasons and intentions to influence, but not cause, actions, since it is the agent who exercises active power in decision-making. He expressly considers and rejects the argument against rationality in libertarian decision-making.[36] In addition, even opponents of libertarian free will

35. Kane writes, "While reasons 'explain' and motives 'move,' reasons cannot explain actual choices or actions unless they in fact move or motivate the agent toward the choice made or action performed; and, conversely, if motives actually move toward choice or action, they should play a role in explanation of why choices or actions occurred" (*Significance*, 30). See also McCall, *Model of the Universe*, 270–79.

36. O'Connor, *Persons and Causes*, 85–107. O'Connor specifically raises the objection that an action would be irrational or arbitrary if the agent did not act based on the belief that one action is better than the other. He offers several points of rebuttal. First, he argues that this does not undercut the agency theory, for it is an explanation of what drives individual decision (the individual himself). Second, he points out that persons sometimes make irrational decisions, which suggests that an appeal to agent-causation is the best explanation for human decisions. He admits, though, that this answer is not particularly satisfying, and that the critic may reply, "if that is all we can say, the power the agency theory confers on free agents is worthless. It is merely the power to make irrational decisions, and who wants that?" (89). He denies the criticism, pointing out that there is value in agents' freely choosing to be [act?] rational. Third, he disputes the central claim that there must be one best or most rational choice in every circumstance in which one is faced with a decision. By way of example, he posits one's being confronted with a cooler full of gallon jugs of milk at the grocer. If there is no difference in terms of expiration dates or damage to the jugs, it is difficult to see how one is to be favored over the others and how one is irrational when he takes one out and puts it into his shopping cart, even if he thinks choosing a different jug would have been just as rational and would have met his needs/desires just as well. O'Connor admits that, in choosing, the agent has reasons, but he denies that this necessarily means that those reasons favor the selection made over the other "equally possible choice of the one just next to it" (90). He goes beyond examples of virtually indistinguishable options, as he recognizes that they are both rare and uninteresting. He suggests that instances when one has competing desires—say to work on a book chapter or spend time with his young children—may also provide examples where either option is (at least possibly) equally rational or equally consistent with the agent's character and desires (90–91). O'Connor acknowledges that on many libertarian accounts, some form of chance winds up in the equation, often right at the moment of decision. He denies this, and instead notes that causes raise the likelihood that a certain kind of event will occur by their working on the "underlying structures of objects or systems" (97). The agent, as *cause*, carries a propensity to generate a specific intention. He concludes, "We may suppose, that is, that recognizing a reason to act induces or elevates an objective propensity of the agent to initiate the behavior. One large independent advantage of thinking of tendencies as being carried in this way on the cause, not the effect, side of the equation, is that we needn't mysteriously invoke chance when asked to explain why a particular tendency is realized. Instead, the agent himself brings about the intention's obtaining" (97).

have rejected this all-too-common line of argumentation. See, for example, Clarke, especially his discussion of the argument from luck, and Pereboom, who admits that coherence objections to agent-causal libertarianism do not stand up to scrutiny (he rejects it based on empirical evidence, which suggests that human behavior is determined by naturalistic factors, e.g., genetic make-up).[37]

Second, it is hard to see how the same argument could not be applied to God's activity. As already noted, Ware (and many Calvinists) attribute to God a freedom whereby he has the ability to choose to act or not-act, or act differently from how he has acted. Take, for example, God's freedom in deciding to create. Presumably God did not have to create a world like this one; he could have created differently. In fact, he could have chosen to not create at all![38] He is not needful of the creation and it contributes nothing to his glory, if he possesses infinite glory in himself. While God is naturally creative, that creativity can be expressed within the triune relations, so that his nature does not dictate that he must create a contingent order. Nevertheless, God, by his good pleasure, chose to create. This choice, which was not necessary, was still both wise and rational. In fact, Solomon wonders at the wisdom of God's creative act (Prov 8:22–31). It seems to me that there are only two ways Ware can avoid this conclusion: 1) Claim his argument is not indeed a matter of logic and is instead applied to the specific case of creatures, or 2) Claim it is a matter of logic but that the laws of logic do not apply to God. Neither is successful in withstanding scrutiny while still maintaining divine freedom and aseity, and calling God's freedom something other than libertarian freedom does nothing to remove the force of the problem's being applied to his choosing.

The second major problem with Ware's criticism of libertarianism has to do with how he conceives of God's knowledge of counterfactuals of

37. Clarke, *Libertarian Accounts*, 77–82; Pereboom, *Living without Free Will*, 55–88.

38. I take Ware's comments about God's freedom to imply this position regarding God's creative activity. For example, he writes, "God's transcendence can only be rightly understood, as Scripture makes abundantly clear, in light of the fact that God exists eternally independent of the world, as the One who is fully self-sufficient in his own infinitely perfect self-existence" (*God's Greater Glory*, 46). Similarly, "nothing can exist independent of him that could contribute in some way to enrich his very being or enlarge his possessions. God is supremely independent of the world, and hence, he simply does not need the world he has made . . . Our finite existence bears testimony not to any human capacity to be anything in itself, much less to some supposed ability to add anything to God, but only to God's gracious will in creating out of nothing all that is and in granting to all his creation each and every quality it possesses" (49). Amen. Whatever God's purpose in creating, this seems to imply, was not intrinsically necessary and/or could have been achieved some other way.

creaturely freedom. Ware suggests that God can know the truth of counterfactuals of compatibilist freedom because he knows the contributing
causal factors (specifically, the characters, desires, and dispositions of the
individuals), along with all the details of the particular situation noted in
the counterfactual. He argues that if creatures have libertarian freedom,
God cannot know the truth of counterfactuals of freedom because libertarianly free choices have no causes (or libertarian freedom is contra-causal).
Ware writes, "First, it is not at all clear how God can know by middle
knowledge just what choices free creatures would make in various sets of
possible circumstances. The problem here is that since freedom in the libertarian sense is defined as the ability, all things being just what they are,
to choose differently, it is impossible to know what decision will be made
simply by controlling the circumstances within which it is made. Because,
all conditions being just what they are, one can choose otherwise, control
of the conditions exerts no regulative power . . . in any and all possible sets
of circumstances."[39] Also, "The problem for traditional Molinism, with its
commitment to libertarian freedom, is that since there is no necessary
connection between knowledge of each state of affairs and knowledge of
what the agent would in fact choose in each different setting, God could
not know the agent's choice by knowing the circumstances."[40] Ware contrasts
this supposed weakness with a compatibilist view of freedom, where God
knows what the agent would do by knowing the causal chain: "But what if
there were a necessary connection between knowledge of a given state of
affairs and knowledge of what the agent would choose in that particular
setting? If this were the case, then God could know what the agent would
choose by knowing fully the circumstances in which the agent would make
his choice."[41] As already noted, this is really a caricature of libertarianism
(or at least all libertarians I know of see it as such), but that aside, the supposition regarding divine knowledge which undergirds the criticism seems
flawed. Why should God have to deduce the truths of what persons would
do? Why can he not just know, by his omniscience, all true propositions, so
that if there are true propositions about what creatures would freely do in
all possible situations, he would just know them? We need not think of God
as arguing or deducing the truths of counterfactuals of creaturely freedom.
How God knows what he knows is something of a mystery, for his knowledge is transcendent, complete, and immediate. Ware's complaint seems to
be based on the notion that the grounding objection has to do with how
God may know counterfactuals, and although I agree that it seems related, it
is not the substance of the objection, which has to do with how such propo-

---

39. Ware, *God's Greater Glory*, 112.

40. Ibid., 113.

41. Ibid., 113–14.

sitions may be true. It is probably better to just argue that counterfactuals of libertarian creaturely freedom cannot be true and that, therefore, there is simply nothing for God to know, rather than to argue that God cannot know them because they do not have an adequate causal chain that he may trace out to deduce their truth (or falsity).

Conclusion

I must admit that I am much more sympathetic to what Ware and Tiessen are trying to do than may initially be thought, given my criticisms here. Indeed, my own struggles with the grounding objection led me to make a very similar claim to what I believe Ware to be claiming—that the truth of counterfactuals of creaturely freedom are grounded in the individuals as they exist in the pre-creative mind of God as *ideas*.[42] In order to see just how close my own thinking is to Ware's on this issue, one need only consider Hasker's response to my suggestion: he accused me of holding to compatibilism![43] Some others have also tried to combine compatibilism with middle knowledge, but the result, even if successful (I don't think it is), has not been to reconcile Calvinism with Molinism.[44] So my raising the objection for the Ware/Tiessen proposal is less a challenge to the coherence of their view due to a lack of grounding for the truth of counterfactuals of compatibilist freedom or what I take to be the somewhat strange metaphysics I think they imply, and more a challenge to their charges against the coherence of Molinism due to a supposed lack of grounding for the truth of counterfactuals of libertarian creaturely freedom. The same problems and solutions appear available to both parties, and the real disagreement has to do with the nature of freedom. I would simply invite Ware and Tiessen to re-evaluate their arguments against the libertarian notion of freedom and

---

42. See my "Molinism and Supercomprehension."

43. Hasker served as the external reviewer for the dissertation; his comments were much appreciated and helpful (even though I disagree with this particular claim).

44 As best I can tell, it merely reconciles middle knowledge with what might be referred to as "philosophical compatibilism," the idea that determinism and libertarian freedom are compatible. Perszyk ("Molinism and Compatibilism," 26) has argued for the compatibility of compatibilism and middle knowledge, but it seems to me he merely endorses Hasker's arguments that middle knowledge leads to determinism and Molina's argument that libertarian freedom is preserved by middle knowledge. His argument does not reconcile middle knowledge with what theologians have come to refer to as "compatibilist freedom" (or freedom of inclination or freedom to follow one's desires without having freedom of choice). More recently, Van Horn ("Incorporating Middle Knowledge," 807–27) has attempted to reconcile middle knowledge with Calvinism. Unfortunately, what emerges from his discussion has little in common with the Calvinist tradition and, for my money, effectively endorses libertarian freedom.

accept traditional Molinism, or else move to the Thomistic view of counter-factuals as contingent, but dependent upon the free will of God.

Bibliography

Chisholm, Roderick. "Identity through Possible Worlds: Some Questions." *Noûs* 1.1 (1967) 1–8.

Clarke, Randolph. *Libertarian Accounts of Free Will.* Oxford: Oxford University Press, 2003.

Eusebius of Caesarea. *Preparation for the Gospel.* Translated by Edwin Hamilton Gifford. 1903. Reprint, Grand Rapids: Baker, 1981.

Helm, Paul. "Classical Calvinist Doctrine of God." In *Perspectives on the Doctrine of God,* edited by Bruce A. Ware, 5–52. Nashville: Broadman & Holman, 2008.

———. *Eternal God.* Oxford: Oxford University Press, 1988.

Kaplan, David. "Transworld Heir Lines." In *The Possible and the Actual: Readings in the Metaphysics of Modality,* edited by Michael J. Loux, 88–109. Ithaca, NY: Cornell University Press, 1979.

Kane, Robert. *The Significance of Free Will.* Oxford: Oxford University Press, 1998.

Laing, John D. "The Compatibility of Calvinism and Middle Knowledge." *Journal of the Evangelical Theological Society* 47.3 (2004) 455–67.

———. "Molinism and Supercomprehension: Grounding Counterfactual Truth." Ph.D. diss.: Southern Baptist Theological Seminary, 2000.

Lewis, David. "Counterpart Theory and Quantified Modal Logic." *Journal of Philosophy* 65.5 (1968) 113–26.

McCall, Storrs. *A Model of the Universe.* Oxford: Clarendon, 1994.

O'Connor, Timothy. *Persons and Causes.* Oxford: Oxford University Press, 2000.

Pereboom, Derek. *Living without Free Will.* Cambridge: Cambridge University Press, 2001.

Perszyk, Kenneth J. "Molinism and Compatibilism." *International Journal for Philosophy of Religion* 48.1 (2000) 11–33.

Plantinga, Alvin. *The Nature of Necessity.* Oxford: Clarendon, 1974.

———. "World and Essence." *Philosophical Review* 79.4 (1970) 461–92.

Tiessen, Terrance L. "Why Calvinists Should Believe in Divine Middle Knowledge, Although They Reject Molinism." *Westminster Theological Journal* 69.2 (2007) 345–66.

Van Horn, Luke. "On Incorporating Middle Knowledge into Calvinism: A Theological/Metaphysical Muddle?" *Journal of the Evangelical Theological Society* 55.4 (2012) 807–27.

van Inwagen, Peter. *An Essay on Free Will.* Oxford: Oxford University Press, 1983.

Ware, Bruce A. *God's Greater Glory: The Exalted God of Scripture and the Christian Faith.* Wheaton, IL: Crossway, 2004.

———. "A Modified Calvinist Doctrine of God." In *Perspectives on the Doctrine of God,* edited by Bruce A. Ware, 76–120. Nashville: Broadman & Holman, 2008.

———. "Responses to Paul Helm." In *Perspectives on the Doctrine of God,* edited by Bruce A. Ware, 53–75. Nashville: Broadman & Holman, 2008.

10

A Response to John Laing's Criticisms of Hypothetical-Knowledge Calvinism

Terrance L. Tiessen

Though Bruce Ware and I have never collaborated, we have reached similar conclusions about the usefulness of God's knowledge of counterfactuals in his deciding what world he would create, and I appreciate the work Ware has done. In *Providence and Prayer,* I had called my model of providence "middle-knowledge Calvinistm," and I explained further in a later article[1] why I believed Calvinists should affirm that God knows counterfactuals in a middle "moment" (logically), even though they reject Molinism. That prompted a letter from Paul Helm, which led to a very profitable discussion, at the end of which I came to agreement with him that there is no need to postulate that God knows counterfactuals in a middle "moment," if creatures are not libertarianly free. Within a soft-compatibilist understanding of creaturely freedom, God knows counterfactuals as part of his natural/necessary knowledge. Our conversation was published in another article, reprinted as chapter 7 of the present volume. This change has had no substantive impact on my model of divine providence, but I now speak of it as "hypothetical-knowledge Calvinism," in order to continue my emphasis on the usefulness of God's knowledge of counterfactuals to his plan or decree.

Laing's Objective

In his piece, Laing states:

> [T]he Calvinist middle knowledge proposal fails on several counts. Specifically, I will argue that it encounters many of the

---

1. Tiessen, "Why Calvinists Should Believe," 345–66.

same supposed problems as Molinism, from the grounding objection to the divine weakness objection, and that it has some problems of its own, from unusual notions of ontology and necessity, to the potential for flirting with fatalism. In the end, I suggest that proponents of Calvinist middle knowledge reevaluate their criticisms of libertarian freedom, and adopt full-blown Molinism or (probably more realistically) move to the Thomistic position of seeing God's knowledge of counterfactuals of creaturely freedom as part of his free knowledge.

I am always grateful for the opportunity to revisit my theological understandings through conversation with others who are interested in the subjects about which I have written, and so I am responding in detail to points at which Laing critiqued the understanding for which Ware and I have argued.

Is "Hypothetical-Knowledge Calvinism" Vulnerable to the Same Grounding Objection That Makes Molinism Problematic?

I'll start with Laing's proposal that the grounding objection, which both Calvinists and open theists level against Molinism, also applies to hypothetical-knowledge Calvinism. The "grounding objection" against Molinism is that, if creatures are libertarianly free, it is impossible for anyone (including God) to predict accurately what they would do in situations that never occur. Hence knowledge of the counterfactuals of future libertarianly free acts is impossible, and Molinism is incoherent. Since the incoherence lies in creatures having the power of contrary choice, why would Laing think that Calvinists, who generally reject that understanding of freedom in favor of the freedom of spontaneity, would be vulnerable to the same grounding objection?

Laing admits to being puzzled "by the Reformed tradition's insistence [with which I now concur] that God's knowledge of subjunctive conditionals is part of his natural knowledge rather than his free knowledge."

What grounds God's knowledge of counterfactuals in hypothetical-knowledge Calvinism?

First, let me say that I am happy that Laing understands my position correctly. Having grasped it accurately, however, he argues that neither Ware nor I "has really offered a clear explanation for how counterfactuals of compatibilist freedom may be grounded." I will not attempt to respond for Ware, but I will try to explain for the benefit of Laing and others who share his puzzlement what grounds God's knowledge of counterfactuals.

On Laing's original assumption that I believed God's knowledge of counterfactuals to be grounded in his free will, he assumed that God "could create [people] so that their characters lead to different action," though he does not find that stated clearly in the model. That assumption was seriously wrong, because the situation is completely otherwise when God knows counterfactuals naturally or necessarily. In that case, God's will has nothing to do with this hypothetical knowledge, rather, it rests on the nature of things, on the fact that creatures of a particular sort (including the complex of their inheritance, their nurture, their culture, their habits, their values, their motives, their "affections" [as Jonathan Edwards termed them], and their inclinations, etc.) would act in a particular way in a particular set of circumstances. God knows this truth about personal causation as he knows the laws of mathematics, and so he can predict exactly how a particular person would act in hypothetical situations, most of which will never occur.

To use Laing's own example, God knows Laing so completely that he knows whether or not he would voluntarily eat a piece of cheesecake offered to him in a given set of circumstances. God's knowledge of a truth about that hypothetical instance is not grounded in his knowledge of Laing's will (as per Molinism) but of his nature. God simply knows what any person *exactly* like Laing would choose in that specific situation. This is enormously useful to God when he decides which of many possible worlds he will actualize. It leaves creatures voluntarily free much of the time in those worlds, while giving God the ability to know what they would do. Hypothetical-knowledge Calvinism thus provides grounds for God's knowledge (soft-compatibilistically free agents and the principles of agent causation) which Molinism does not provide when it posits that Laing could eat or not eat the cheesecake in exactly the same circumstances.

I grant that God can know the probabilities (as open theist Greg Boyd emphasizes) but he cannot know the certainties and, given the immense number of decisions made by moral creatures in a world populated by as many people as ours, over so long a time, even if the probability that Laing would eat (or refrain from eating) were extremely small, the sum total of those uncertainties would make God's choice of any world very risky. This would put God in precisely the position of having to act responsively in the moment which open theists have so well described.

Molinism, hypothetical-knowledge Calvinism, and the role of the human will

I concur with Laing's statement of the grounding objection *as it is leveled against Molinism, but these objections do not apply to hypothetical-knowledge Calvinism.*

First, Laing observes that "since counterfactuals refer to non-actual persons and/or non-actual states of affairs, their truths cannot be grounded in the activity of the agent spoken of in the counterfactual (never mind questions of backward causation)." This is true in regard to Molinism, because it ascribes libertarian freedom to persons. If, in exactly the same circumstances, Laing (being who he is in the hypothetical situation) could eat the cheesecake or refrain from eating it, since God does not know which choice he makes in an instance that is still only hypothetical, God cannot predict what Laing would do in that hypothetical situation. Without an act of will on Laing's part, God could at best only say how probable it is that Laing would or would not eat the proffered cheesecake.

But this problem does not exist for the soft-compatibilist (i.e., the person who affirms that God's meticulous sovereignty is compatible with the moral responsibility of creatures who act voluntarily) because people's choice would be predictable with certainty if one knew both them and their circumstances completely, and knew the causative principles governing the choices that such people would make in such circumstances. So, on this point Molinism fails the grounding objection but hypothetical-knowledge Calvinism does not.

Molinism, hypothetical-knowledge Calvinism, and the role of God's will

Laing then presents the second key feature of the grounding objection to Molinism: counterfactuals "cannot be grounded in God or God's will because that would make them either necessarily true or at least not independent of his will."

I take this to be a very important concern, because it expresses an issue that also creates nervousness about hypothetical-knowledge Calvinism among many other Calvinists. They fear that if God makes use of his knowledge of counterfactuals concerning moral creatures, in a deliberative manner, when choosing a world (that is, determining his decree), he is making himself dependent upon the creature. There is no validity to this concern, however, precisely because no critical divine dependence occurs, given the situation I have outlined. It *would* be a problem if God were dependent on the *actual choices* of libertarianly free creatures, as in Molinism, but it is not a problem when the choices of voluntarily free creatures are predictable provided one knows the principles of causation which apply when particular creatures are in particular circumstances. What God knows counterfactually is not dependent on real creatures; it is dependent on principles which God knows naturally, like he knows that 1+1=2. These hypothetical facts are necessary truths, but their necessity, the principles of causation, is somehow *grounded in God's own being rather than his will*. They are like rules of logic. God did not have to create this or any world, but if he were to create a world it would have to be coherent with the being of God himself. God is not dependent upon the will of creatures in this world because it was he who chose this world, with all its peculiarities. He chose this particular world, *not* on the basis of his knowing what the creatures in it would libertarianly freely choose to do (as Molinism asserts), but because he knows the causative principles about the action of soft-compatibilistically free agents. This is a very important plank in my understanding of compatibilism.[2]

Hypothetical-knowledge Calvinism with respect to Molinist responses to the grounding objection

Laing describes some of the ways in which Molinists have attempted to answer the grounding objection and he explains why these fail. I concur with his analysis, but I definitely do not concur with his statement that "It is hard to see how proponents of counterfactuals of compatibilistic freedom can do any better with grounding." I think that I have done a great deal better, but I must leave it to my readers to judge how well I have succeeded.

Laing goes on to restate Bruce Ware's explanation of how the truth-value of counterfactuals concerning the future acts of morally responsible creatures is grounded, but he objects that Ware has only explained how God knows counterfactuals, not what grounds their truth. Laing thinks this to be the case because Ware asserts that God knows how the person will choose in accordance with his desires.[3] But Laing wants to know "what grounds the truth of counterfactuals regarding the development of individual desires?" He speculates about ways in which Ware could address this question, and he deems "most promising" a suggestion made by Paul Helm in his dialogue with me, namely, that they may be grounded in the divine mind. Of this most promising option, however, Laing asserts that it is "no different" from

2. See http://thoughtstheological.com/my-compatibilist-proposal/.

3. Ware, *God's Greater Glory*, 115 n. 10.

his own libertarian position, so "Calvinist middle knowledge" has the same grounding problem as Molinism.

Once again, I think that Laing is incorrect. To say that the principles of causation relative to persons with compatibilistic freedom are known by God naturally is to assert that God knows them because he knows himself perfectly. Here I refer back to my earlier comment about the necessary coherence of any world God were to create with God's own being. I speculate that Laing's assertion that Helm and he are asserting the same thing derives from Laing's assuming that what Helm means by "God's mind" is the same thing as Laing means by God's will. That cannot be the case since Helm believes God to know the truth of counterfactuals necessarily. I can't promise, however, that Helm would accept my own words concerning the necessary coherence of any world he would create with God's own being as synonymous with his own statement. What I can say is that I agree with Helm's assertion that God "would know, intuitively and immediately, what A in C would do." Helm unpacks that further:

> For as part of his natural knowledge God has the idea of A in C as a possibility, along with his knowledge of A possessing innumerable different beliefs and desires in innumerable different sets of circumstances, and (given such knowledge), in his wisdom God creates A in C, creates him down to the last atom and molecule, evil apart, and immediately sustains his life nanosecond by nanosecond, even as, while being sustained by his Creator, A in C perpetrates evil. Such a state of affairs does not necessarily involve divine coercion or compulsion, not in the usual senses of these words, though it will if God in his wisdom decrees to create A as being in some circumstances not responsible for his actions. It is not that God in his wisdom permits possible persons such as A to exist, rather he brings it about that they exist by decreeing that they do, and (in his wisdom) he permits their perpetration of evil.

I completely agree with Helm at this point, and I propose that what he and I are asserting with regard to God's natural knowledge of how a person A would act in circumstances C, where A is soft-compatibilistically free, is definitely not vulnerable to the grounding objection that is so frequently brought against Molinism. It is the soft-compatibilistic nature of human freedom (rather than an incompatibilist construction of libertarian freedom), which grounds the truth-value of the counterfactuals which God knows necessarily. By contrast, Molinists assert humans to be libertarianly free and they are unable to explain what grounds the truth value of the counterfactuals concerning the acts of those free creatures which they propose God knows in his middle knowledge.

In short, Laing's first objection to hypothetical-knowledge Calvinism fails. The grounding objection to Molinism does not apply to hypothetical-knowledge Calvinism.

Does hypothetical-knowledge Calvinism have an odd notion of necessity or possibility?

The second criticism Laing made of hypothetical-knowledge Calvinism was that it has an "odd notion of necessity/possibility." Laing agrees with me that hypothetical-knowledge Calvinism's idea of constraints upon God in his choice of a good world is "helpful for theodicy," but he thinks that "the particular manifestation of it in this Calvinist system leads to some perplexing metaphysical positions."

Laing observes that, in hypothetical-knowledge Calvinism, if it is false that if John were in situation S, he would freely eat a piece of chocolate cheesecake tonight, God "can alter circumstances in a variety of ways so that [John does not find himself] in S, or he can override freedom, or he can make [John] different, but God cannot make it the case that it is true that 'if John were in S, he would freely refrain from eating chocolate cheesecake tonight.'" It is good that Laing understands my proposal correctly at this point. Since God's knowing what John (being exactly who he is) would do in S is part of his natural knowledge, it is necessarily the case; it is not something God can will to be different. As I pointed out above regarding the grounding objection, what God knows naturally is the principles of causation by which particular kinds of creatures act in a particular way in particular circumstances.

What Laing wants explained "is the locus and nature of that necessity." He posits that: "It certainly cannot be logical necessity; there appears to be no violation of the fundamental laws of logic in my refraining from eating cheesecake in S; such action would not violate the laws of identity, non-contradiction or excluded middle." Fair enough. I concur. But I suggest that God's knowledge of the principles of causation, which God knows naturally, are analogous to the laws of logic. Just as God knows naturally that he could not create a world in which something both is and is *not* large and green, so he could not create a world in which a particular creature could both eat and refrain from eating cheesecake in exactly the same situation. This is fundamental to the compatibility of creaturely free agency of a morally responsible kind with God's meticulous providential sovereignty.

Laing then posits that: "It does not seem to be a case of metaphysical necessity either; it does not seem intelligible to claim that my eating cheesecake is a fundamental function of the way things are." Here, all I can say right now is that what does not seem intelligible to Laing does seem highly intelligible to me. I grant that whether or not John eats cheesecake seems to be too trivial to be deemed "a fundamental function of the way things are," but again we must consider what makes this the case. This is *not about John individually, nor is it about the circumstances*, particularly not about the eating of cheesecake. It is, rather, the *simple fact that a creature exactly like John would or would not eat a particular cheesecake in a particular set of circumstances*. There are causative principles, like mathematical truths or laws of logic, which are known naturally to God and which enable him to predict whether or not John would freely eat cheesecake were he to find himself in a particular set of circumstances. John himself would not even be able to predict such counterfactuals about himself with certainty, but this is a limitation of John's knowledge of himself and of the causative principles at work when moral creatures make free decisions. That is what makes us poor judges of what situations we can trust ourselves to get into without falling into sin, whereas God knows precisely when circumstances are such that temptation would be too strong for us.

Laing thinks that "the view of possibility in play here is not at all clear or obvious, and even seems to contradict our normal notions of possibility." In fact, it "seems tautological in nature." He finds it hard "to see how a proposition like, 'If John were in S, he would compatibilistically freely eat a piece of chocolate cheesecake tonight'" has the same status as truths such as "1+1=2," "all bachelors are unmarried," and "if an object is blue, then it has extension."

Perhaps the second of those three truths is where the difference between these two facts God knows necessarily is most clear. The truth that "all bachelors are unmarried" is, indeed, tautological. By *definition*, a bachelor is an unmarried man, but such cannot be said about the fact that a creature who is A would do X in S. What makes this necessarily true, and hence known certainly by God independently of his will, is not the definition of a person of type A or of a situation S; rather, as Paul Helm asserts, it is a "*causally* necessary proposition." "It is important to bear in mind," says Helm, "the distinction between logical or metaphysical necessity on the one hand, and causal necessity on the other, as well as the distinction between 'God necessarily knows all possibilities' and 'All possibilities known by God are necessary.'"

It was the difference between truths which are true by virtue of *metaphysical* necessity and those which are true by *causal* necessity which first led me to postulate that God's knowledge of counterfactuals was of a distinct sort, and that we might therefore speak of it in terms of a distinct ("middle") logical moment in God's knowing. In my conversation with Helm, however, I came to realize that this was a bad move on my part, particularly because the "middleness" of God's knowledge of counterfactuals, in Molinism, is brought about by the libertarianly free agency of the creature. In that construct, God's knowledge of what A would do in S is grounded in A's decision. As I pointed out in the previous section, if A is free to do X or not-X in situation S, then it is impossible to know what A would do, unless A decides which (X or not-X) he will do. So the situation S must actually occur, and A must actually find himself in that situation, and A must actually decide what to do, or no one can know with certainty what he *would* do. There lies the grounding objection to Molinism. That objection does not challenge hypothetical-knowledge Calvinism, however, because God's knowing what A would do in S is not dependent upon A's making a decision; it is dependent on God's knowledge of the causative principles operating when a particular sort of creature, A, is in a particular set of circumstances, S.

What Laing considers an "odd notion of possibility" is, in fact, not odd at all, provided one understands the concept of principles of causation which ground knowledge of counterfactuals. These principles are of the order of mathematical truths, so that they are known naturally to God, not because of his knowledge of particular creatures but of the principles of causation which make it possible for God to choose one of the possible worlds, knowing that everything will happen precisely as he intended when he chose it, not because he determined that it would be so, instance by instance, but because of principles in operation in all possible worlds. As Helm rightly discerned, in the soft-compatibilist model which I affirm, the distinction between what A *could* do in S, and what A *would* do in S, is "a distinction without a difference." It was my failure to see this that led me to speak of God's knowledge of what A would do in S as distinct from what A could do in S, hence leading to the suggestion that even Calvinists would do well to affirm middle knowledge. I now grasp much more clearly how soft-compatibilism works. It is precisely because creatures are *not* libertarianly free that God can know what hypothetical creatures would do in hypothetical situations. That has nothing to do with either the creatures or the situations as particulars; it derives from a knowledge of the causative principles which are necessarily at work in any world which God, being who he is, could choose to create and govern. This is, therefore, not at all an "odd notion"; it is highly comprehensible.

Does hypothetical-knowledge Calvinism have an odd ontology of personhood?

Laing's third concern is that hypothetical-knowledge Calvinism includes an "odd ontology of personhood," and I want to deal with that complaint now. In my conversation with Paul Helm, he pointed out an entailment of my hypothetical-knowledge Calvinism that I had not previously discerned. He observed that in my earlier work arguing for Calvinist middle knowledge, in order to remain true to Calvinist principles, the distinction which Molinists make between "would" and "could" should not be retained. Reflecting on that point, which I have now conceded, Laing writes:

> The would/could equation also suggests that, for any given possible set of creaturely actions, there exists a distinct creature. This has the unusual consequence of maintaining that the John who would eat chocolate cheesecake in S is a different John from he who would not eat the cheesecake in S (presumably due to some difference in character, desires, disposition, etc.). For any given set of decisions I might make (since all are necessary), there is a distinct me (or should I say, John that is not-me). Thus different possible worlds are populated by completely different beings.

Although Laing notes that Ware "certainly does not" affirm this, and although he is "not aware of anyone explicitly arguing for this position," he posits that "some of Tiessen's comments are suggestive of it." Laing's perception of what is entailed in my comments, as unpacked in the statement above, is what leads him to conclude "that the Calvinist is committed to an odd notion of ontology and perhaps modality." Since I reject the way in which Laing has conceptualized the situation in hypothetical-knowledge Calvinism, *I deny that the oddness about which he is concerned need trouble us.* Here is how the situation *should* be described. For starters, I grant that there is a truth embedded in Laing's statement that "different possible worlds are populated by completely different beings," since what he has in view is the essence of what makes them *different* worlds. The *problem* lies in Laing's speaking in terms of "different beings." The critical factor that brings about different outcomes in different worlds (e.g., Laing's eating or not eating cheesecake) is not in the being who acts in S, but in that the long series of circumstances lying behind Laing's decision at that moment has been different, and that is what brings about a different action on Laing's part, as anyone who knew all the details of the situation and the principles of causation could discern. Granted, there is a sense in which the Laing confronted with the opportunity to eat cheesecake in world A is "different" from the one in world B, but this is because, in world B, different circumstances have brought Laing to that point, so he has the different desires, dispositions, etc. which make him a being who would not eat the cheesecake in world B, though he would have eaten it in world A. The difference is explicable by comparing the complex of events prior to Laing's choice in each of the worlds which are similar enough that the person in those worlds could be deemed the "same person," in spite of the personal differences brought about by different prior histories.

What Laing is observing, therefore, is nothing other than what we can all see with regard to ourselves over time. Think of the common statement: "In ten years you will be the same person you are today, except for two things, the books you read and the people you meet." No one finds that an odd thing to say, and nothing different from this is being asserted in my own construction. So, no "odd notion of the ontology of personhood" is operative here.

The statement Laing quotes from my first piece in the *Westminster Theological Journal* still seems correct to me, so it is worth quoting here. On that occasion, I was responding to comments previously made by Laing about my model in *Providence and Prayer*, where I talked about how God could have brought about counterfactuals different from those that pertain in this world. Then, as now, Laing was arguing that God's knowledge of counterfactuals, in a Calvinist framework, should be viewed as part of his free knowledge, not, as I now believe (following the main line of Reformed tradition), as part of his natural knowledge. I had written:

> As a counterfactual, this is not dependent upon God's will; it is the way things would be if God chose to actualize the world in which Laing, being exactly who he is now, got into that particular situation. If God had reasons for wanting things to turn out differently, he would not allow the particular circumstances to obtain, or he would have brought into Laing's personal formation influences that would make him a person who would choose differently than this particular John Laing would do.[4]

This remains my perspective, and I hope I have been able to show why nothing odd, nor the least bit unusual, is being asserted about the "person who would choose differently" in world A than in world B.

Laing wonders if "the Ware/Tiessen model" might be following Alvin Plantinga's "postulation of world-indexed properties that are essential to objects and beings (he uses the example of *being snubnosed in a* for

4. Tiessen, "Why Calvinists Should Believe," 353.

Socrates)."[5] Might I be suggesting that Laing has the "property of *eating chocolate cheesecake when in S in a*"? Though I have not read this work by Plantinga, I can say with reasonable confidence that this concept of "world-indexed essential properties" is not where I am headed. As I understand the concept from the description Laing provides, and from his example, I conclude that it works only within synergism, which is where Plantinga lands. Although Reformed by affiliation, he has, like many Reformed philosophers, wandered into synergism, and he has thus been able to make good use of concepts enunciated by Molina, who proposed middle knowledge in order to explain how it is that God knows counterfactuals concerning free creatures, when such creatures are libertarianly free.

To speak of Laing as having the "property of *eating chocolate cheesecake when in S in a*," in the framework offered by Plantinga's synergistic understanding of possible worlds, is to assume that the critical factor bringing it about that Laing eats cheesecake in S, is Laing's decision to do so. I am assuming that Plantinga is trying to account for what grounds God's knowledge that Laing would eat cheesecake in S in world A, but not in world B, even though there is no difference between those two worlds in regard to either Laing or the situation. One possibility might be, I hear him suggesting, that what accounts for the difference in Laing's choices, where neither Laing nor the circumstances are different, lies in the world in which Laing makes his choice. Thus in world A, Laing would have the property of eating cheesecake in S, but in world B, he would have the property of *not* eating cheesecake in S. The only reason I can see for making such a suggestion would be if Laing has the power of contrary choice. Since I deny that, I have no use for the concept of world-indexed properties. As I elucidated in my first main point above, the principles of causation which God knows naturally, and which enable him to know what Laing would do in S, are true in all possible worlds. God only needs to know thoroughly both Laing and the situation S, to know what Laing would choose to do. The difference between worlds would not derive from properties Laing possesses by virtue of the worlds themselves, in any way additional to the differences in the complex personhood of the one making the choices and the complex of circumstances.

In the proposal described by Plantinga, certain essential properties of individuals are "only necessary *insofar as they are world-indexed*, but the property is not necessary *in itself*, apart from its world-indexed identification." Obviously, that is quite different from my own proposal. In that scenario, one would have to know what Laing decides in different worlds

---

5. Plantinga, *Necessity*, 60–61.

where both Laing and the circumstances are identical. Despite that same-ness, Laing decides differently in world A than he does in world B, and he can do so because of his libertarian freedom. The world-indexed proposal is a form of Molinism and is consequently vulnerable to the grounding objec-tion. My own proposal, as I demonstrated in my first main point, does not share that problem, because Laing is not libertarianly free. In my model, what Laing would do in each possible world can be known by God because of his knowledge of the principles of agent causation which enable God to know how a creature like Laing would act in situation S, precisely because Laing could not do otherwise, though he does it voluntarily.

Laing observes correctly that "the placement of counterfactuals in God's natural knowledge along with the denial of libertarian freedom sug-gests that I have the essential property of *eating chocolate cheesecake in S*, no matter which possible world we consider." It seems to Laing, therefore, that what Helm and Ware and I are suggesting "is that all beings' properties are not only not-accidental (or essential), but that they are equal to those beings' essences." In that conclusion, however, Laing makes a critical error, I think. He speaks as though there were something personal to an individual like Laing about the necessity that he eats or does not eat cheesecake in S. But there is nothing personal about it in my construct. When it comes to understanding God's knowledge of counterfactuals, as an individual person, "Laing" is irrelevant within a soft-compatibilist framework. What matters is the *kind* of person Laing is in each of the possible worlds, and the circum-stances in each of those worlds in which that kind of person finds himself. There is nothing "worldbound" about this. The principles of causation which are at work, and which inform God's knowledge of the counterfactuals of Laing's action in different worlds, are true in *all* worlds; they are not distinc-tive features of the particular world in which Laing might possibly live. I suggest, therefore, that there is *no issue of identity or ontology* at stake here. Synergists find the soft-compatibilist model odd, but its perceived oddness lies in the suggestion that if Laing were a particular kind of person, and if he were in particular circumstances, he would act in a particular way, and yet he would act with morally responsible freedom. It is compatibilism that generates a sense of oddness for synergists. But it is wrong to identify that perceived oddness as an oddness regarding the concept of personhood or ontology that is at work in the soft-compatibilist, soft-determinist, model.

Plantinga considers the theory of worldbound individuals to be "out-rageous" and, consequently, self-evidently and obviously false. "If we know anything at all about modality, we know that some of Socrates' properties are accidental to him, that *Socrates is foolish* is not necessarily false, and that

Socrates exists does not entail every proposition."[6] I think that Plantinga is right about this, because what makes it possible for God to know counterfactuals about the future acts of free agents is not about *essential* properties of the individual, and Laing can safely disassociate my understanding from the problems which are entailed in the concept of both worldbound individuals and world-indexed essential properties. Just as John Laing changes over time without ceasing to be John Laing, there could be worlds in which Laing would eat cheesecake in S and worlds in which he would not. A difference as slight as his having eaten a piece of cheesecake which made him sick in one world prior to his getting into situation S but not having had any bad experiences with cheesecake in other worlds could account for his eating in S in world A but not eating in S in world B. To suggest that this difference in his tastes constitutes him ontologically as a different person is both counterintuitive and completely unhelpful.

What particularly concerns Laing about the theory of worldbound individuals is that God would have had only "one feasible world, that God had to create exactly what he did create, which sounds awfully close to fatalism." That is an important concern, and it is, in large measure, why I reject the concept of there being a best possible world. It seems to me that, if there were such a thing, God would have been obligated to choose it, so that he did not libertarianly freely choose this one. (I have spelled out my position in this regard in a blog post entitled "Must God maximize his own glory?"[7] so I will not repeat it here.)

Laing's concluding comparison between hypothetical-knowledge Calvinism (where God knows counterfactuals necessarily) and Thomism (where God knows counterfactuals as part of his free knowledge) does not apply to my own construct. Laing posits that his analysis of the scenarios he had discussed

> shows that the compatibilist view of freedom and its coherence argument against libertarian freedom, coupled with the claim that counterfactuals of creaturely freedom are part of God's natural knowledge and, therefore, both necessary and independent of his will, results in the Theory of Worldbound Individuals. The result is that the "John" in [world A] is also different from the "John" in [world B], the result being that we really cannot know what John in B would do, at least not from our knowledge of the relevant counterfactual in [world A].

---

6. Ibid., 102.

7. See http://thoughtstheological.com/must-god-maximize-his-own-glory/.

I hope I have explained adequately why my model entails neither world-indexed essential properties nor worldbound individuals. What pertains in every possible world is the principles of agent causation, which God knows necessarily, not essential properties of either the persons who would make decisions in those worlds, nor essential properties of the circumstances in which those decisions would be made. There is no reason to believe that the complex of conditions pertaining in situation S in this particular world did not exist in any other possible world. Similarly, there is no reason to believe that a person just like Laing in this world did not exist in any other possible world, nor that such a person might have been called "John" by parents who were "Laings" in any other world. What we do know is that in any world where a person exactly like the John Laing in this world existed, if such a person was in exactly the situation S which exists at a moment in time in this world, that person would do exactly what John Laing does in this world. God did not have to choose this world, or other worlds which are only possible, in minute detail, to know what a person of that type would do in S. God only needed to know the principles of agent causation which operate in every possible world, which the omniscient God knows naturally or necessarily.

Laing thinks that the Thomist is in a better position than the hypothetical-knowledge Calvinist because what makes the counterfactuals true is God's having determined that they would be. In that scenario, the many possible worlds are all what they are because they are worlds God could have made. God could therefore have created a world in which a person exactly like John Laing in this world, when in circumstances exactly like the situation S in this world, eats cheesecake, but another world in which he does not eat cheesecake. The difference would lie in the libertarianly free will of John Laing, but it would only actually occur because God freely chose the particular world in which Laing freely chose either to eat or not to eat cheesecake. Like hypothetical-knowledge Calvinism, that is a form of monergism, but it is *hard*-compatibilism, holding together meticulous divine control and libertarian creaturely freedom. I do not share with Thomists the assumptions necessary for this compatibilism to be coherent (absolute divine timelessness, and divine action that is concurrent with creaturely action), though I think it would be splendid if the proposal were coherent. By contrast, Molinism affirms human libertarian freedom but denies meticulous divine control (hence the middleness of God's knowledge of counterfactuals). In Molinism, the determinative factor in most decisions made in this world is the will of creatures who could have decided otherwise than they do, rather than the will of God. Unfortunately, the grounding objection makes this proposal incoherent.

Particularly pertinent to this section of his paper, Laing thinks the Thomist position with regard to counterfactuals is superior to that of the hypothetical-knowledge Calvinist because the Thomist "may maintain that the 'John' spoken of in each possible world is the same person and does not have to resort to claims that the scenarios are different or the definitions equivocal." I can understand why Laing thinks that the hard-compatibilist model of the Thomist makes the persons *less* different between worlds than the soft-compatibilism of hypothetical-knowledge Calvinism does. For the Thomist, exactly the same person could choose differently in exactly the same circumstances, so that the difference in that choice need not be explained by different inclinations, habits, experiences, etc. in the person's life. But I suggest that the difference between the soft-compatibilistically free person who chooses to eat cheesecake in S in one world and the one who chooses *not* to eat cheesecake in S in another world is not significant. As I said earlier, what is at work are the factors which lead people to say very frequently that they or someone else is a "different person" from what they were ten years ago. I hope to be more like Christ five years from now than I am today, but I will still be "me" when I am more (or, God forbid, less) sanctified.

In short, *hypothetical-knowledge Calvinism's notion of personhood or ontology is not odd.* But it is coherent in ways that neither Molinism nor Thomism is. I would love to be able to assert that humans are libertarianly free. I understand how intuitively people in our culture assume that authentic freedom is libertarian. I think that Thomism's hard-compatibilism has a more biblical understanding of the minuteness of God's providential control than the incompatibilism of Molinism does, but I do not hold the tenets which are essential for Thomism's compatibilism. Molinism would be an easier sell than hypothetical-knowledge Calvinism precisely because it affirms libertarian freedom, but the grounding objection prevents me from affirming it as the best answer to the deficiencies of Thomism. I feel keenly the reasons why synergists object to compatibilism, but my reading of Scripture convinces me of the truth of soft-determinist monergism, and I think that hypothetical-knowledge Calvinism offers the best explanation for what makes divine sovereignty and human responsibility compatible.

Does hypothetical-knowledge Calvinism flirt with fatalism?

I now come to a fourth concern expressed by Laing about hypothetical-knowledge Calvinism, namely, that this perspective flirts with fatalism. Laing observes that, initially, he considered it fatalistic because it left God with no options. He came to see, however, that this is not necessarily true, since it could be seen as no more than an appropriation of Molinism's concept of world-feasibility. But Laing continues to believe that "the position does have the potential of slipping into a form of theological fatalism due to the combination of the necessity of the truth of counterfactuals of compatibilist freedom, along with the argument against libertarian freedom on the basis of logic/coherence and rationality of choice." In particular, if the argument against libertarian freedom is applied to God, so that he only has one option in regard to his actions, then the charge of fatalism is unavoidable. On this point, perhaps surprisingly, I agree.

It has been common for Calvinists to deny that even God is libertarianly free because they charge that libertarianly free choices are arbitrary and hence irrational and amoral. But I have come to believe that God has libertarian freedom, and I have therefore stopped using that particular objection to creaturely libertarian freedom. Laing discusses the manner in which Paul Helm defends something like compatibilist freedom on God's part but denies that this leads to fatalism, "because the constraint upon which world God can actualize is not logical or external to Him, but is His own perfect nature." Helm says that "the argument does not depend on the idea of God choosing between equally optimific outcomes, which would appear to make God's instantiation of any universe an act of pure reasonless will. Rather the argument is that God's freedom consists in the rationality of his choice, in his having a good reason for what he instantiates, not in his having no reason."[8]

Like Helm, I have rejected the idea that there was a best possible world which God necessarily chose, but I did this in order to protect God's libertarian freedom, which is not Helm's intention. To a large extent, I concur with Laing that if God is compatibilistically free in the same way as moral creatures are, not having the power of contrary choice, then it is hard to see how fatalism is avoided.

Thus, I believe that I have avoided the risk of fatalism concerning God's decision to create this particular world rather than some other possible world. God could have chosen a different world, but he had good reasons for choosing this one. Whether or not we will ever be capable of understanding God's reasons in that regard, we can be confident that God's choice was good as well as reasonable. God knew the counterfactuals of creaturely freedom, and he was able to do this because creatures are not libertarianly free, and because our choices are predictable in every possible set of circumstances if one knows with certainty what a particular kind of creature would

---

8. Helm, *Eternal God*, 178.

do in precisely those circumstances. This God knows naturally, through his knowledge of what I have referred to as the "principles of agent causation."

Laing notes that the Dominicans saw Molina's views as dangerous because they were concerned to protect the efficaciousness of grace in Aquinas's soteriology. "They were concerned to preserve the absolute sovereignty of God over salvation, and so saw truths related to creaturely belief as dependent upon the divine willing." I too want to preserve God's sovereignty in salvation, as in the governance of his creation in every aspect. But it seems to me both unnecessary and unhelpful to make counterfactuals of human choice and action dependent upon God's decree. To do so increases the risk of fatalism. Thomists avoided that danger by positing a hard compatibilism in which God is meticulously sovereign, even while moral creatures are libertarianly free. Molinism endangered that sovereignty, because it made God's knowledge of counterfactuals dependent upon the creature's will, positing a form of incompatibilism, albeit one in which God's determination is as strong as it could possibly be in an indeterminist framework. Soft-compatibilism maintains God's control of each and every incident in creation, including the repentance and faith of sinners. But its essence, I suggest, is integrally related to the tenets of hypothetical-knowledge Calvinism. God chose this particular world, including the beliefs and unbeliefs of all the spiritual beings in it, not because it was the world in which an optimal number of libertarianly free people would choose to believe God, but for good and wise reasons which we do not fully comprehend. Unlike the Molinist model, however, hypothetical-knowledge Calvinism posits that saving faith is effected by God's grace in the lives of the elect, so the possible world which God chose to actualize was a world in which God effectually calls and graciously preserves in faith all who are saved in this world. He was able to do this without making acts of human belief meaningless because they were genuinely of a free nature, since they were voluntary and uncoerced. Thus fatalism is avoided, and so is deism.

The contribution of hypothetical-knowledge Calvinism to our understanding of evil in the world chosen by the almighty and perfectly good God

I now address Laing's fifth concern, that what I call "hypothetical-knowledge Calvinism" does not effectively address the problem of gratuitous evil in the world chosen by God. Once again Laing's primary focus is on the work of Bruce Ware, but he draws me into it. Because Ware's view and mine are not exactly the same, I need to respond to Laing's critique, identifying my differences from Ware's view along the way. Laing begins by interacting with a statement by Ware:

> Ware highlights what he takes to be the advantages of the Reformed view over the Arminian view (somewhat surprisingly and admittedly courageously!) with respect to God's sovereignty over evil. He suggests that the Arminian view must accept "gratuitous and pointless evil" because of some misguided pledge on (the Arminian) God's part to not intervene because of His granting of libertarian freedom. By contrast, he argues, the Reformed view sees all evil—each and every instance of evil—as advancing and not hindering God's plans/purposes for the world.

Divine permission

Regarding Ware's position, Laing then makes two points. First, he posits that Ware has overstated the differences between the Arminian and Reformed conceptions on this issue, because Laing believes that "most Arminians could agree with this description": "God regulates exactly the evil that occurs, since for any and every instance of evil, he specifically permits according to his wisdom and ultimate purposes what he could otherwise have prevented."[9] Laing believes that Arminians could agree because:

> The language of permission and the prerogative of God to intervene and prevent any given instance of evil are hallmarks of orthodox Arminian theology. In fact, if God's regulation of evil only entails his permission and failure to intervene, then even heterodox Arminian theology (e.g., Open Theism) could agree.

I think, however, that Laing himself has grasped the point that Ware was making, namely that, in the Calvinist perspective, "each and every instance of evil leads *directly* to a *specific* greater good for which that evil was *necessary.*" In my view, Laing's understanding this point should have kept him from asserting that Arminians could agree with Ware's language. I grant that Arminians use the language of divine permission and speak of God's prerogative "to intervene and prevent any given instance of evil." But clearly there is a significant difference between God's decree to permit specific evil events for specific greater goods (as per Calvinism) and Arminianism's concept of a very *general* permission. In their framework, God permitted specific evils only in that he had given moral creatures libertarian freedom,

---

9. Ware, "Modified Calvinist Doctrine," 108.

and thereby voluntarily limited his ability to ensure that every detail of the world's history turns out as God wishes it would. God does his best to bring about his will, but he had tied his own hands (speaking anthropomorphically, of course) by making moral creatures the determiners of much of what transpires. Furthermore, however, I have frequently stated elsewhere that I think synergists, including both classic Arminians and open theists, put themselves right where they don't want to be when they complain against Calvinism, by asserting that God has not given up his right to intervene and to constrain a creature's libertarian freedom on occasion.

I think that that there is a frequently unacknowledged tension between the doctrines of general permission and the doctrine of reserved prerogative to intervene. Characteristically, synergists assert that the meticulous divine providence of God in Calvinist theology makes God responsible for evil. They remove themselves from that problem by asserting that God does not permit specific evils for specific good purposes, but that he has allowed authentically free creatures to do evil in spite of his doing all in his power to prevent that evil, through means short of overriding a creature's libertarian freedom. But to grant that God does that on some, admittedly rare, occasions, greatly weakens the synergists' complaint against monergists. To take an example like the Holocaust as a case in point, God could have given Hitler a fatal heart attack without even constraining any moral creature's freedom. An Arminian must account for God's choosing not to do that, just as a Calvinist must. Thus, though I might have spoken a bit differently than Ware did (assuming Laing's interpretation of his point to be correct), I agree substantially with him, and I don't think that Laing has helped the case of Arminians significantly.

Gratuitous evil

Laing doubts that Ware's middle knowledge view necessarily escapes "the notion that gratuitous evil may occur" because "the truths of counterfactuals of creaturely freedom are not dependent upon God's will or the free decisions of the creature to whom they refer, but are simply just necessarily true. Since God has no control over the truth of counterfactuals of creaturely freedom, it means that His creative options are constrained by those that are true." So far, I agree, and I think that this is one of the positive contributions made to Calvinist theology by the proposal that God utilizes his knowledge of possible worlds in deciding what world to actualize.

Laing goes on:

> One consequence of this concept is the notion that there may
> be instances of gratuitous evil because of the chance that the
> feasible worlds which meet God's ultimate ends all contain
> instances of evil that may not directly contribute to a specific
> greater good, but are nevertheless a part of that world which
> is one of the set of worlds that best meets God's purposes (and
> hence, indirectly contribute to the greater good of God's ends
> being attained/met).

Again, properly understood, I take this to be a valid restatement of my own position, though I don't speak for Ware. God chose an entire world. He did so with an intention for every event in that world, but his intention is only comprehensible in terms of the whole history of which these events are a part. In other words, each event was not necessarily chosen to occur because of its intrinsic and direct goodness, but because it was a necessary part of the whole history which God decreed should occur. This allows us to say of every incident, as Joseph did about the evil done to him by his brothers, that God intended it for good. But it does not allow us to say with certainty that God could have brought that good about *without* the inclusion of the brothers' evil act, in which their own intent was evil, and for which evil they (and not God) are morally accountable. If the brothers' act, which God determined to include in the history which was all of his choice, was a *gratuitous* evil (in the sense of not being warranted *directly* by an immediate good), God must have chosen it because of the greater good of the whole. What we can say is that, if there are some incidents which, taken alone and with a view to the immediate situation, could be deemed gratuitous, none is gratuitous when viewed in the light of the entire complex of events which God decrees will be the history of the world he created and governs.

I grant that this may seem less satisfying to people who prefer to believe that every evil that God permits to occur to them is because of a specific good for *them* personally, to which that evil contributes. Hypothetical-knowledge Calvinism calls upon us to be somewhat less individualistic than that perspective asserts, while still taking comfort from Romans 8:28–29 that God uses in the process of transforming us into Christ's image, even those events whose greatest good is realized on a larger scale. Joseph's case is a good illustration of this. The good intention which God had in decreeing to permit his brothers to sell him into slavery was not focused on Joseph himself, but on the good of the people who were heirs of the promise to Abraham (Gen 45:7–8; 50:20). This is not to deny that God had personal intentions for Joseph too; he was not simply instrumental in a plan focused only on the large scale. But Joseph himself understood that what really mattered in his own experience was its place within God's plan for the nation. Joseph died long before that was realized.

Of my own perspective, Laing writes in a way that needs correction:

> Tiessen suggests that God could simply give Adam efficient grace to make him compatibilistically freely refrain from eating the forbidden fruit. Fair enough, assuming there is a prescribed amount that can be given while still maintaining the freedom of Adam with respect to eating or not eating, but why should we assume that there is such an amount for any given situation?

Clearly, Laing speaks of the freedom which must be maintained for Adam in libertarian terms. Adam must have been able to eat or not to eat, given God's efficient grace. But that is not the freedom affirmed by hypothetical-knowledge Calvinism. Had Adam been libertarianly free (as in Molinism), God could not have known how Adam would decide in possible situations, and could not know what sort of divine assistance would be necessary to prevent Adam from disobedience. Laing's personal conviction that only libertarian freedom is authentic is evident in his next question:

> Is there not a point at which the grace overrides the individual's freedom in order to prevent his sinning? It seems that there would be, at least in *some* cases, and if I am correct in this, then the Calvinist may argue that instances of gratuitous evil could sometimes occur. I see this as a strength, despite Ware's argument to the contrary. Of course, if the Calvinist wishes to dispute my point regarding the overriding of freedom, then it seems that he is just endorsing the Thomistic position again—God's will is what makes the counterfactual true. It is God willing Adam to freely eat (by giving him an appropriate amount of grace) which makes the counterfactual true.

I do dispute Laing's "point regarding the overriding of freedom," if "freedom" entails the power of contrary choice, but I would not deny that there may be some occasions on which God can only get his will done by taking away even the compatibilistic freedom of an individual. If such occasions included an evil act by a creature, the creature would not be morally culpable, but offhand I can think of no example in which such occurred.

Most importantly, *I deny that my perspective collapses into Thomism, making the counterfactual true because God willed it to be so.* God's decision to give Adam sufficient grace not to fall, but not to give him efficient grace, was a decision to make true the statement "Adam, when tempted to eat of the tree of life, fell," but it does not make true the *counter*factuals which God took into account in making his decree. Rather, God's natural/necessary knowledge of those counterfactuals made it possible for him to choose a world in which Adam culpably disobeys God. God's eternal plan (decree) determined the facts of history, but it was his knowledge of possible worlds (i.e., of counterfactuals) which enabled God to choose a world in which Adam freely disobeyed. Very conceivably, there were worlds in which God could have given Adam grace which efficiently preserved him in obedience, as he later did by his Spirit in preserving the second Adam from disobedience, and as he will do for all the redeemed who inhabit the new earth. But God had reasons for wanting to create and to govern this particular world, which includes both the sin of Adam as representative of the human race, and also the redemption of much (possibly most) of that race by the life, death and resurrection of the second Adam.

Hypothetical-knowledge Calvinism and libertarian freedom

Thus far, I have responded to five criticisms leveled against hypothetical-knowledge Calvinism in Laing's work. My final main point in response to Laing's critique addresses his proposal that incompatibilist, libertarian freedom is superior to the compatibilism put forward by hypothetical-knowledge Calvinism.

Laing agrees with Bruce Ware's perception that his own criticisms of Molinism are, at root, really criticisms of libertarian freedom.[10] So Laing suggests that if Ware "could be convinced of the possibility of libertarianism, he would accept it as true, and move to the traditional conception of middle knowledge as a separate notion from natural and free knowledge." *In my own case*, this is not true, because accepting that God knows counterfactuals as middle knowledge (if that were possible) would entail divine indeterminism at the micro level. It would result in affirming Molinism, which is, I grant, the type of synergism or incompatibilism or indeterminism in which God has the most control of what happens in the actual world, but a large part of that history would be determined by creatures, at the most important, micro level, not by God. My reading of God's involvement with the world leads me to a strong conviction that God is meticulously in control of all that he created. Consequently, if I came to believe that libertarian freedom is compatible with God's meticulous governing of the world, I would have to affirm something like Thomism, where God knows counterfactuals as part of his free knowledge, providing a hard compatibilism rather than the soft compatibilism of Calvinism. If that were coherent, it strikes

10. Ware, *God's Greater Glory*, 112–13.

me as a wonderful situation, but I have not found a way to construct a hard compatibilism that looks viable.

I abandoned use of the term "middle knowledge" because Paul Helm convinced me that God's knowledge need only be middle if the truth of counterfactuals were contingent upon the decision of the actors involved. It is clear to me from Scripture that God knows counterfactuals concerning the future possible acts of morally responsible creatures, but he could not know what a libertarianly free creature would do in situations that are purely hypothetical, if those creaturely decisions were determinative of the history of creation, because only their *actually* deciding and acting in those situations would give truth-value to propositions concerning their action. So long as people have the power of contrary choice, if creatures determine most of the history of the world, there are no true counterfactual propositions concerning actions which are by definition purely hypothetical. God could, at best, assess the likelihood of a particular choice being made. In other words, God could know "might" counterfactuals, but not "would" counterfactuals. Therefore, since God knows counterfactuals of responsible creaturely action, those creatures must not be libertarianly free.

Laing offers "a few brief comments in response to Ware's criticisms of libertarianism," in "an effort to offer clarification and admittedly, in the hope of convincing some of the truth of middle knowledge." Since I am presumably included among those whom Laing would like to convince, I attended carefully to his comments.

The compatibilist charge that libertarianly free choices are arbitrary and hence not rational

Ware argues that libertarianism undercuts the rationality of decision-making (Laing's words, not Ware's), for he sees it as requiring one follow the same reasons for choosing contrary courses of action. Since all factors involved in one's decision are present at the moment he chooses, he can choose either A or *not-A*, then the same reasons would serve to explain the choice for A and the choice for *not-A*, and this renders the choice arbitrary. As Ware put it, "according to libertarian freedom, that every reason or set of reasons must be equally explanatory for why the agent might choose A *or* B, *or* not-A. As a result, our choosing reduces, strictly speaking, to arbitrariness. We can give no reason or set of reasons for why we make the choices we make that wouldn't be the identical reason or set of reasons we would invoke had we made the opposite choice! Hence, our choosing A over its opposite is arbitrary."[11]

Laing would agree with Ware if this "were an accurate description of libertarianism," but he doubts that it is accurate, first, because he knows "of no proponent of libertarian freedom who conceives of libertarian decision-making in this way." For quite a long time, I accepted as valid the charge that libertarian freedom was irrational, and hence amoral, because of its arbitrariness. I wrestled with this idea, however, whenever I was challenged by Arminians in regard to the nature of God's freedom. If God does not have libertarian freedom but has the sort of soft-determinist freedom that I believe God gave to moral creatures, then creation and everything else God does is necessitated by his nature. That would give us fatalism, not biblical determinism. But if God does have libertarian freedom, then it cannot be intrinsically arbitrary and irrational, for all of God's decisions are unnecessitated (though they are constrained) by his moral nature, and they are all-wise and good. Here Laing is correct in his response to this particular objection against creaturely libertarian freedom.

Though I admit that this particular objection to libertarian freedom is incorrect, I still have various reasons for believing that creatures are not libertarianly free. Among these is my belief that God knows counterfactuals of future free creaturely choices but that this would be impossible if those creatures were libertarianly free. That grounding objection to middle knowledge is not removed by the concept of agent causation, though I am attracted to that way of understanding the action of moral creatures, particularly within a soft-determinist framework. I remain unable to conceive of how God could know what an agent would choose if that choice is not predictable on the basis of the agent's reasons for the choice (together with his values, inclinations, etc.). I note that people who claim to have libertarian freedom, are frequently able to explain after a choice *why* they made it. Granting that those reasons did not *cause* their choice, they still have important explanatory value in the way that soft-determinists propose. Nevertheless, since God is libertarianly free, libertarianly free decisions cannot be intrinsically irrational. In God's case, however, God does not know counterfactuals concerning his own actions. His knowledge of possible worlds entails a knowledge of how those worlds would develop if creatures were soft-deterministically free, and if he were to choose to act personally in various ways and times to bring about situations that would not exist without his active intervention.

---

11. Ibid., 86.

Might God be able simply to know true counterfactual
propositions because he is omniscient, rather than deducing
them from his knowledge of how hypothetical persons would
act in hypothetical situations?

Laing's suggestion that this is the case reminds me of Alvin Plantinga's proposal that God's knowledge of counterfactuals of creaturely action is "properly basic," not contingent or deduced.[12] Laing is content to assert that "how [God] knows what he knows is something of a mystery." If we could be content to rest in mystery, together with Laing, the grounding objection could be left unanswered, but I am not satisfied to leave the matter there, since I think we have a better way to understand how it is that God knows counterfactuals of creaturely action. As Laing rightly discerns, however, the question of *how* God knows counterfactuals is really a question of "how such propositions may be true." Unfortunately, granting this slight difference does not take us any further, because the question of what grounds the truth-value of propositions regarding counterfactuals remains.

Concluding Comments

This brings me to the end of my reflections concerning John Laing's objections to hypothetical-knowledge Calvinism. I appreciate his willingness to engage with my ideas and Bruce Ware's, because it gives me an opportunity to note where my own position differs from Ware's, to clarify it for Laing's benefit. It also pushes me to revisit my own understanding of what God knows and how he uses it to govern his creation in a way that maintains creaturely moral responsibility and genuine agency, while retaining his meticulous control. This revisiting sometimes results in slightly different understandings or ways of stating my position, and all of this is very beneficial to me. So I thank John for his contribution to my own ongoing theological formation and formulation. I hope that my response will have some benefit to him as well.

---

12. Tomberlin and van Inwagen, ed., *Plantinga*, 375–79.

Bibliography

Helm, Paul. *Eternal God*. Oxford: Oxford University Press, 1988.

Plantinga, Alvin. *The Nature of Necessity*. Oxford: Clarendon, 1974.

Tiessen, Terrance L. *Providence and Prayer: How Does God Work in the World?* Downers Grove, IL: InterVarsity, 2000.

————. "Why Calvinists Should Believe in Divine Middle Knowledge, Although They Reject Molinism." *Westminster Theological Journal* 69.2 (2007) 345–66.

Tomberlin, James E., and Peter van Inwagen, eds. *Alvin Plantinga (Profiles)*. Boston: Reidel, 1985.

Ware, Bruce A. *God's Greater Glory: The Exalted God of Scripture and the Christian Faith*. Wheaton, IL: Crossway, 2004.

————. "A Modified Calvinist Doctrine of God." In *Perspectives on the Doctrine of God*, edited by Bruce A. Ware, 76–120. Nashville: Broadman & Holman, 2008.

Part IV

Calvinism and Molinism
The Ongoing Conversation

11

On Parsing the Knowledge and Will of God, or Calvinism and Middle Knowledge in Conversation

JOHN D. LAING

Introduction

IT SEEMS THAT EVERYONE wants to either attack Molinism or appropriate its basic principles into their system (or at least its terminology). (I was going to include a clever quip here, but could never quite come up with the right saying . . . "The enemy of my enemy is my ally" . . . not quite right; oh well.) I was recently at a philosophy conference where almost every paper included some sort of jab at middle knowledge, and it was routinely dismissed with no argument developed or presented; I suppose it was just assumed that all the attendees were aware of the criticisms of Molinism, and were fully convinced of their strength and veracity so that no proof or discussion was necessary, warranted, or needed. Most of the presenters were friendly to open theism. Molinism has long been the target of attack for those Christians with a more deterministic view of divine providence, from Dominicans Báñez and Alvarez in Molina's own day, to Turretin in the seventeenth century, to numerous others in more recent years.

Still, as has often been noted, Molinism touches upon such foundational concepts for many theists, that a number of theologians from differing parties/stances have attempted to use it in their own system for understanding divine providence. On one end of the spectrum, some Calvinists have sought to integrate some kind of (what they have called) middle knowledge into their theology with Terry Tiessen and Bruce Ware being two examples, though to be fair, Tiessen no longer calls his position "Calvinist middle knowledge" due to the confusion it engenders. On the other end of the spectrum, some open theists have referred to their position as "neo-Molinism"; in point of fact, I'm only aware of one published theologian who argues for this model—Greg

Boyd—and by his own admission, it has not garnered the kind of support he had hoped. However, anecdotal evidence suggests that his arguments have proven convincing to some; comments sections on websites often find at least a few persons extolling the virtues of Boyd's position, and I recently heard a professional philosophy paper advocating the strength of Boyd's model over traditional (if such a term is valid here) open theism.[1]

Middle Knowledge

While it may very well be a fair assumption to think that everyone present is familiar with the doctrine of middle knowledge and understands the distinctions it makes in divine knowledge, it may still prove helpful to set forth the basic premise in order to discuss the nuances of the various positions to be examined here. The doctrine of middle knowledge was first clearly articulated by sixteenth-century theologian/philosopher (and Catholic apologist) Luis de Molina in a commentary he prepared on Thomas' *Summa Theologiae* in order to refute (what he saw as) the deterministic Protestant view of divine providence and soteriology. Molina speculated about the divine deliberative process (if we may use such terminology of an infinite and eternal being's thoughts) regarding creation and suggested three logical moments, rather than the traditional two. It was generally accepted that a logical dependency relationship existed between God's choice of what sort of world to create and the possibilities from which he could choose, and up to the time of Molina, this relationship was expressed in terms of two logical moments and two ways God knows. Natural knowledge was the first logical moment, was known by God's knowledge of his own nature, and included knowledge of all necessary truths and all possibilities (which are necessarily true). Free knowledge logically follows, was known by God's knowledge of his own will, and included knowledge of what will take place as a result of divine intentions, decree(s), and creative work. Knowledge of how free creatures would act in any of a variety of possible circumstances was seen as part of God's free knowledge, since God makes creatures the way they are and with the desires they have, such that, through secondary causation, God can be said to bring about all creaturely actions. It may be diagrammed as follows:

---

1. Hess, "'Neo-Molinist' Account."

Traditional Thomistic scheme

1 Natural knowledge	2 Free knowledge
Necessary	Contingent
Independent of God's will	Dependent upon God's will
Logically and metaphysically necessary truths, as well as possibilities	Conditionals of divine and creaturely freedom
"All bachelors are unmarried"; "1+1=2"; "It is possible that grass is green"	"If John were in C, he would freely eat cheesecake"; "I will make a world where John is in C (and freely eats cheesecake)"

To these two categories, Molina added a third, which stood in between the other two, or *middle knowledge*. Like natural knowledge, the propositions known by middle knowledge were true independent of God's will; God did not cause them to be true by an act of his will. Like free knowledge, its propositional content was contingent and could have been otherwise. Molina thought of middle knowledge as composed of propositions that describe what all possible creatures would freely do in all possible circumstances. It is contingent because it depends on the will of a free being and could have been other, and it is independent of God's will because if it were dependent upon his will, it would be deterministic (and the creatures would not be free). This was thought to preserve libertarian freedom and creaturely responsibility, and to protect divine goodness in spite of the evil in the world.

Molina's middle knowledge proposal

1 Natural Knowledge	2 Middle Knowledge	3 Free Knowledge
Necessary	Contingent	Contingent
Independent of God's will	Independent of God's will	Dependent upon God's will
Logically and metaphysically necessary truths, as well as possibilities	Counterfactuals of libertarian creaturely freedom	Conditionals of divine freedom

1 Natural Knowledge	2 Middle Knowledge	3 Free Knowledge
"All bachelors are unmarried"; "1+1=2"; "It is possible that grass is green"	"If John were in C, he would (libertarianly) freely eat cheesecake"	"I will make a world where John is in C and eats cheesecake"

Boyd's "Neo-Molinism" and the Parsing of Natural Knowledge

I was really tempted to talk about Boyd's so-called "neo-Molinism," where he attempts to distinguish divine knowledge of "might-conditionals" from divine knowledge of possibilities. There is much that can be said with regard to Boyd's work, and it probably deserves a little more attention than it has been given. As noted in my introduction, there are some who have begun to adopt his schematic in an effort to add clarity to their own open theist positions. Drawing upon the work of Peter van Inwagen and others, who have insisted that true might-conditionals stand in contradiction to true would-conditionals, Boyd has argued that traditional Molinism cannot work, but that parsing divine natural knowledge into further logical moments may be fruitful for understanding the God of open theism and the providential options he holds.[2] Boyd argues that open theism on his understanding provides God with more providential control than a God with so-called simple foreknowledge.[3] I am inclined to agree with Boyd, largely because I am convinced that simple foreknowledge affords God no providential value at all, but that is no endorsement of his model. On the contrary, Boyd's proposal is fraught with numerous difficulties, as has been shown, and the Molinist is under no obligation to accept the base principle that might-conditionals negate the truth of would-conditionals.[4]

2. van Inwagen, "Against Middle Knowledge," 225–36; see also van Inwagen, *Essay on Free Will*.

3. See Boyd, "Neo-Molinism," 187–204; Boyd, "Open Theism View," 13–47.

4. For a critique of Boyd's proposal, see Werther, "Open Theism and Middle Knowledge," 205–15. For a critique of the opposition of might- and would-conditionals, see Wierenga, "Tilting at Molinism," 135–38 and Gaskin, "Conditionals," 421.

Calvinist Middle Knowledge and the Parsing of Natural Knowledge

Calvinists of the Edwardsian stripe typically accept the two-part division of God's knowledge into natural knowledge and free knowledge, and have historically rejected middle knowledge due to its libertarian commitments. However, this is not to say they reject divine knowledge of counterfactuals of creaturely freedom or that such propositions can be true. They have just rejected the notion of counterfactuals of libertarian creaturely freedom in favor of counterfactuals of compatibilist creaturely freedom, and placed divine knowledge of them in God's natural knowledge. As I noted in my previous work, most Molinists have rightly understood their Calvinist friends to deny the truth of counterfactuals of libertarian freedom in favor of counterfactuals of compatibilist freedom, but have wrongly assumed they must place God's knowledge of them in his free knowledge (as Molina's Dominican opponents seemed to do) and thereby make them postvolitional and dependent upon his will. This incorrect understanding led me to deny that Calvinist "middle knowledge" is in the middle of anything and to claim it an impossible position to hold. While I still maintain that it has problems, and I still think Ware's use of the term "middle knowledge" is more confusing than helpful (primarily because, as noted, the phrase "middle" is meant to set that knowledge in opposition to "natural" and "free" knowledge), I believe that further clarification of how we understand the details of our positions can aid understanding, and hopefully further the theological discussion and perhaps gain knowledge of God himself.

For Ware, all of God's knowledge comes via his knowledge of himself. Thus, Ware sees both middle knowledge and free knowledge as part of God's natural knowledge. He writes, "Middle knowledge, then, is a subset, or subcategory, of natural knowledge, just as free knowledge, likewise, is a subset, or subcategory, of natural knowledge." The value of placing God's knowledge of counterfactuals of creaturely freedom into God's natural knowledge, according to Ware, is that it prevents God's knowledge from being dependent upon creatures and avoids the logical difficulties of libertarian freedom.[5] I suspect that another driving influence for Ware and others is a concern to ground all truth in the nature of God as True (with a capital "T"). So, it seems to me, under a model such as Ware's, we may diagram the logical moments in God's knowledge as follows:

---

5. Ware, *God's Greater Glory*, 110–30.

Ware's Calvinist middle knowledge

God's natural knowledge (known by God
by knowing his own nature)

1 Natural Knowledge Proper	2 Middle Knowledge	3 Free Knowledge
Necessary	Necessary	Necessary
Independent of God's will	Independent of God's will	Independent of God's will
Logically and metaphysically necessary truths, as well as possibilities	Counterfactuals of compatibilist creaturely freedom	Conditionals of divine freedom
"All bachelors are unmarried"; "1+1=2"; "It is possible that grass is green"	"If John were in *C*, he would (compatibilistically) freely eat cheesecake"	"I will make a world where John is in *C* and eats cheesecake"

It should be immediately apparent why Ware has insisted that his use of the terminology borrowed from Molinism is valid, and why he claims that his Calvinist version of middle knowledge really is *in the middle* of natural and free knowledge, but it should be equally apparent why so many Molinists have found the model to be confusing. There are two items that Molinists like myself have found perplexing here: 1) that God's free knowledge may be necessary but dependent upon God's will, which is normally thought to be free, but in this model, freedom does not entail (or seemingly even include) contingency; contingency is illusory (at least if seen in opposition to necessity), and 2) that free knowledge may be said to be dependent upon God's will, for it seems that it, like natural and middle knowledge in this model, would be dependent upon God's nature and therefore, independent of his will. The answer to these concerns/questions (I think) is found in the simplicity of God (though I am not sure that such an appeal gets us any closer to a rational explanation).

I am extremely sympathetic to Ware's concerns and desires; some of my own work on the grounding objection sought to find a way to ground counterfactuals of libertarian creaturely freedom in God somehow. Still, as noted last year (chapter 9), I think there are several problems for this position. First, I argued that this move does nothing to assuage the force of the grounding objection. Such a claim may seem odd, since the grounding objection is usually couched in terms of a problem for libertarian freedom, to wit, there is nothing that may be pointed to as making or guaranteeing truths about future libertarianly free actions because the actions are not caused by God and the agent does not exist as an actor at the time the propositions are said to be true and used by God (in middle knowledge). Still, underlying the original complaint in the grounding objection was an assumption that if one were to reject libertarian freedom, truths about counterfactuals of creaturely freedom would thereby be grounded in God's will; he is the cause of their being true. For the Thomist, this is exactly the case. William Hasker, who was among the first to articulate the grounding objection in the modern discussion, assumed that counterfactuals of freedom cannot be true because of the problem they pose for libertarian freedom, and because (in his view) compatibilist freedom is no freedom at all.[6]

Before I move to the parsing of free knowledge in Molinism, I would like to offer a word of clarification on the problem of compatibilist freedom and grounding. I have argued that Calvinists cannot escape the force of the grounding objection because they cannot provide an answer to the question of what grounds the truth of counterfactuals of compatibilist creaturely freedom known by natural knowledge. Tiessen has attempted to answer the question by appeal to the chain of causation, but he has only provided an answer to how God can know the true counterfactuals (the same problem with Ware's answer to the grounding objection), not to how they can be true or what makes them true. He writes,

> But this problem does not exist for the soft-compatibilist (i.e., the person who affirms that God's meticulous sovereignty is compatible with the moral responsibility of creatures who act voluntarily) because people's choice would be predictable with certainty if one knew both them and their circumstances completely, and knew the causative principles governing the choices that such people would make in such circumstances. So, on this point, Molinism fails the grounding objection but hypothetical-knowledge Calvinism does not.

So Tiessen concludes that counterfactuals of compatibilist freedom are grounded in God's being, and draws an analogy between the operative principles of causation here and mathematical truths and the laws of logic. All are known by God's knowledge of his own being or nature, which serves as the ground for all Truth. Again, this makes sense to me (though I still think tying these to the divine mind or divine ideas makes more sense). What Ware, Tiessen, Helm and others have not explained, though, is what

---

6. See Hasker, *God, Time and Knowledge*; Hasker, "Middle Knowledge," 223–36; Hasker, "Must God Do His Best?" 213–23; Hasker, "New Anti-Molinist Argument," 291–97.

makes a particular person to develop the way he does, necessarily, such that even God could not will to make him develop differently. Clearly, Ware, Tiessen, et al. want to argue that if it is true that in circumstances *C* I freely eat cheesecake, then I am such that I could not freely refrain from eating cheesecake in *C*, but more than that, they claim that God could not create me so that in *C*, I freely refrain from eating cheesecake. What limits God's power here? According to Ware and Tiessen, it is just the way things are, presumably analogous to the way God's power is limited in his own actions; he must always do that which is best (if there is such a thing) and cannot do evil. Such restrictions on his power and/or ability are not deficiencies. To be sure, we would all agree that God's inability to perform evil presents no lack in him. However, the more perplexing claim is that my eating cheesecake and inability to refrain is of the same order/same type as God's doing best and inability to do evil. I can understand how it is the case that God's nature (as Purely Good) can be seen as restricting his activity in this way; I cannot makes sense of how his nature so defines creaturely actions like cheesecake-eating. Why could it not be just as consistent with his nature that in *C*, I freely refrain from eating cheesecake? The fact that both

> In *C*, John eats cheesecake

and

> In *C*, John refrains from eating cheesecake

seem to equally accord with God's nature is the heart of the grounding objection for counterfactuals of compatibilist freedom. For Ware and Helm, the problem has to do with the logic of libertarian freedom, but for Tiessen, it does not.

To be fair, Tiessen attempts to answer these concerns in his response to my criticisms. At heart, I fear it is more personal inclination than raw logical argumentation that will determine one's position on these issues. While it seems clear to me that either statement about my cheesecake eating could fit with God's nature, it is equally clear to Tiessen that only one can—the true one (whichever that is). But this seems to equate truth and necessity.[7]

---

7. Consider the following proposition: "If God makes John eat cheesecake in *S*, or if God makes John such that he eats cheesecake in *S*, then 'if John is in *S*, he will eat cheesecake' is necessarily true." If this is what the Calvinist is suggesting, then this seems no different from the following: "If it is true that 'if John is in *S*, he will eat cheesecake,' then 'if John is in *S*, he will eat cheesecake' is necessarily true." This amounts to an equation of truth and necessity, and that is not at all clear. Why should all truths be necessary? If all truths are necessary, does this not imply, again, fatalism?

In response to my query into the nature of necessity governing the truth of counterfactuals of compatibilistic freedom, Tiessen quotes me as saying, "it does not seem to be a case of metaphysical necessity either [in contrast to logical necessity]; it does not seem intelligible to claim that my eating cheesecake is a fundamental function of the way things are," and he responds, "Here, all I can say right now is that what does not seem intelligible to Laing does seem highly intelligible to me," and he goes on to try to discuss the difference between metaphysical necessity and causal necessity. What Tiessen et al. want to say is that all that happens and all that is, is necessary, but the necessity is of a different sort for different items. God's necessity is tied to his eternity and his ontology; he couldn't not-be, by definition. The creation's necessity is tied to God's work; it couldn't not-come to be. In this way, proponents argue, they are able to retain the contingency of the creation due to its dependency upon God for its origination and its sustenance, even while maintaining its necessity.

Second, and more pressing, I expressed fear that viewing God's freedom as compatibilist (and not libertarian) and making all of God's knowledge a function of his natural knowledge results in a form of fatalism because it restricts God's creative choices. Here Tiessen, who believes God does have libertarian freedom in at least some choices, parts company with Ware, Helm, and others. They argue that God freely created, but he was not free to not-create, and claim that this is not fatalism and does not lead to fatalism because some important distinctions remain. For example, under this scheme, the cause is not external to God as in the pagan myths (i.e., the Fates, sisters Clotho, Lachesis, and Atropos, who spin, measure, and cut the yarn of history and individual lives), but rather is the nature of God himself, so that there is no conflict. Similarly, Calvinists distance the necessity here (what they call "causal" necessity) from logical necessity as in Stoicism, and claim that fatalism only results when logical necessity controls all things. While there is still reason to doubt that defenses such as these are adequate to avoid the charge that the position mirrors historical fatalism, there is also reason to be wary of too quickly lumping all suggestions of necessity into fatalism, as Alan Rhoda has done in arguing that Molinism is fatalistic.[8] So if the Molinist wishes to defend his position against the open theist charges of fatalism and determinism by making finer distinctions than his opponent will allow, then he must also be prepared to allow for finer distinctions by Calvinists as well. To be sure, each distinction must be weighed for its relative strength and veracity, but it cannot be automatically dismissed or

---

8. Rhoda, "Dilemma"; Rhoda, "Five Roads to Fatalism."

lumped together with similar views. Still, further clarification seems justifiably requested.

Ware, Helm, (and possibly Frame) and others have argued that God has compatibilist freedom, partly because they see libertarian freedom as incoherent, and partly (and I think more importantly) because they think separating God's free knowledge from His natural knowledge improperly sets God's will in opposition to His nature. Obviously, I disagree, but this leads to a second misunderstanding I have observed between Molinists and Calvinists, and it has to do with the parsing of God's free knowledge.

Molinism and the Parsing of Free Knowledge

In my interactions with Bruce Ware on the differences between his proposal and Molinism as traditionally conceived, I have noticed that we were often talking past one another, where one or the other of us was simply unable to follow the other's point. I have long suspected that some of our confusion has to do with our equivocal use of terms, and it has been nowhere more evident than when we have attempted to come to terms over the prevolitional nature of God's middle knowledge. As noted, I assumed that Ware et al. would put middle knowledge as a part of God's free knowledge, and therefore could not understand how he could possibly claim that it was still prevolitional. Similarly, though, I was often puzzled by Ware's complaint against traditional middle knowledge with its commitment to libertarian freedom, because he seemed to allow for conditional excluded middle. Some of the confusion, I think, has to do with differences in conceiving of God's free knowledge.

Molinists have typically conceived of God's free knowledge as partitioned in a way very similar to how Calvinists have partitioned God's natural knowledge, though I do not know of any (Molinists) who have articulated it in a precise and careful way. However, when one considers Molinist claims for the system—that it can afford God the ability to bring about a world where everything that occurs may be said to be a part of his preordained plan, while also allowing the theologian to claim that some actions/events that occur are contrary to his will—it should become clear that there is more going on in the divine deliberative process than the mere three logical moments typically elucidated in Molinist texts. God is depicted as first knowing all logically and metaphysically necessary truths via his natural knowledge, and these truths (e.g., mathematical truths as well as possibilities) set the parameters for the type of world(s) he can actualize. He then knows all true counterfactuals of creaturely freedom via his middle knowledge, and these truths (about what all possible creatures would freely do in all possible circumstances) further delimit the type of world(s) he can actualize. Then God is depicted as weighing out these options over against his desire(s) and intention(s) for creating by first comparing the feasible worlds to those desires and intentions, and then choosing one of the feasible worlds that best meets those desires and intentions (and there is not necessarily only one!), and then actualizing that world (rather than another) by an act of will. All of the actions just described are seen to be a part of God's free knowledge. So the Molinist schematic could really be diagramed as follows:

Molinist schematic

1 **Natural Knowledge**	2 **Middle Knowledge**	3 **Free Knowledge**	4 **Free Knowledge**	5 **Free Knowledge**
Necessary	Contingent	Contingent	Contingent	Contingent
Independent of God's will	Independent of God's will	Dependent upon God's will	Dependent on God's will	Dependent on God's will
Logically and metaphysically necessary truths, as well as possibilities	Counterfactuals of (libertarian) creaturely freedom	God's intentions and desires	How feasible worlds match up with God's intentions and desires	God's decision to actualize a particular world
"All bachelors are unmarried"; "1+1=2"; "It is possible that grass is green"	"If John were in C, he would freely eat cheesecake"	"I (God) want to create a world where John freely eats cheesecake"	"I (God) can meet my goals by placing John in C"	"I will make a world where John is in C (and freely eats cheesecake)"

In fact, we might even want to divide up middle knowledge to include a second moment (in the above diagram, logical moment 3 or 2b, take your pick), in which we express God's knowledge of all feasible worlds, which would still be independent of God's will (he has no control by means of an act of will over which worlds are actualizable), and thus logically prior to his free knowledge.

Molinists have divided free knowledge this way so that they may speak of events/acts being part of God's plan and under his meticulous providential control by appeal to logical moment 5, while claiming those events may be contrary to his will (the particular event/act is not something he desired specifically) by means of appeal to logical moment 3. So, for example, a sin one commits may be a part of a world God chooses because it best meets his eschatological goals and does so with the least number of events that go against his desires, while the sin itself is not desired. Calvinists like Ware have not made such distinctions and I suspect they might see them as compromising God's simplicity, where God's desires may be contrary to his will.

The Molinist answer to these concerns is threefold. First, such division probably would compromise simplicity in the Calvinist scheme where free knowledge is part of natural knowledge, because it would set God's nature against himself. But in the Molinist scheme, God's decision is seen as a libertarianly free act, where he could choose to create or not-create, and presumably had multiple "best worlds" to choose from in actualizing (worlds that equally meet his goals/purposes in creating), and he does so in accordance with his will, but his greatest desire (e.g., a world where creatures are free and never sin) may have not been feasible, so his simplicity is not compromised. Second, this feature of Molinism mirrors the typical Calvinist distinction of "wills" in God (whether conceived as declarative/permissive, revealed/hidden, or some other set). If it compromises divine simplicity, then so also does such a distinction of wills; the Molinist placement of the distinction in logical moments of divine free knowledge seems to make more sense of the idea. Third, we have the example of Jesus' Gethsemane prayer, where the Son's immediate and specific desire seemingly conflicts with the will/plan of the Father but is submitted to it. I recognize that there are many ways of interpreting that pericope, and I am not prepared to defend this reading here, but I only refer to it to suggest that divine desires and divine plan do not have to perfectly align.

There has been much discussion in recent years of the possibility/impossibility of Calvinist middle knowledge and what such a proposal entails. It appears that, despite some efforts at dialogue, confusion still abounds regarding the exact areas of disagreement among Calvinists who wish to incorporate divine knowledge of counterfactuals of (compatibilist) creaturely freedom and Molinists, save their respective views of freedom. Bruce Ware agrees with Helm and Tiessen that counterfactuals of freedom are known by God's *natural knowledge*, but insists that it is still helpful to conceive of it as a separate logical moment from God's knowledge of logically and metaphysically necessary truths. Molinists have typically failed to make distinctions within God's natural knowledge and have thus accused such Calvinist positions of hard determinism or fatalism. By contrast, Molinists have traditionally parsed God's *free knowledge* into several logical moments, but have been criticized by Calvinists as compromising God's simplicity by distinguishing between God's desires and God's decisions. It is my hope that in this paper, I have been able to bring some clarity to the discussion of logical moments in a divine deliberative process, even if we cannot all agree that our differences have only been due to misunderstanding or semantic differences.

Conclusion

By way of conclusion, I wish to offer some suggestions for further study and discussion among those interested in these issues, and I wish to do so by means of questions for the different parties. While I have already suggested possible answers to the queries, further clarification would be beneficial. I will then comment briefly on the current state of research on Molinism and offer some suggestions for further study.

(1) Questions for Edwardsian Calvinists from Molinists: If God's actions logically and necessarily follow from his nature, how does "causal" necessity not devolve into "logical" necessity? If I were to have had different desires from those that I did have, would I have been a different person? If not, then why could God not have made me to have had different desires? If so, what is the locus of truths about me that constrain God's ability in creating?

It seems to me that, since the greater concern here has to do with this approach to Calvinism seeming to come to close to fatalism, further discussion about the historical nature of fatalism is in order, along with finer distinctions in terminology. More importantly, further discussion about the negative implications of fatalism are in order, with explanation of how Calvinism is guilty or innocent of these infractions.

(2) Questions for Calvinists who affirm libertarian freedom for God, but not for creatures, but still wish to place divine knowledge of counterfactuals of compatibilist creaturely freedom in his natural knowledge rather than his free knowledge (and thus, maintain the independence of their truth from God's will). Why does the logic governing counterfactuals of compatibilist creaturely freedom (beings of a certain sort, of necessity, must choose the way they do because of their fundamental nature(s)) not also dictate counterfactuals of divine freedom? If they hold for the one, it is hard to see how they must not hold for the other. Why not place divine knowledge of counterfactuals of compatibilist creaturely freedom in God's free knowledge?

(3) For Molinists, beyond questions about libertarian freedom and the grounding of counterfactual truth, questions remain about God's unity. How can God's desires be set in opposition to his will without compromising his omnipotence or simplicity? Do God's desires not emerge directly from his nature? Other questions regarding the nature of possibility and feasibility

arise: While Calvinists insist on an equation of would and could, so that God can do whatever he could do (all possibilities are feasible, though the limit is upon possibilities), in Molinism, the insistence on a distinction between what is possible and what is feasible suggests a weakness in God. If a world is possible, why is it not also feasible or actualizable? Isn't possibility, by definition, that in some world, an event occurs? How can Molinism then maintain that some possible worlds cannot be actualized without compromising God's omnipotence?

Last, I wanted to offer some thoughts on opportunities for further study on Molinism and Molina. The field is wide open, especially with regard to historical investigation. Kirk MacGregor has begun this work in his recent biography of Molina.[9] Brill recently published an edited volume that focused on Molina's contributions to metaphysics and the philosophy of law.[10] Molina's two most important and influential works, *Concordia* and *De iustitia et iure*, were the primary focus of the essays. While the volume contributed significantly to our understanding of Molina's work and thought, there is still more work to be done. While significant strides have been made in clarifying Molinism *vis-à-vis* Calvinism, greater understanding of Molinist soteriology is rightly desired. Some Molina scholars have argued that his views on efficacious grace are virtually semi-Pelagian, while others have vigorously denied these charges.[11] In-depth analysis of Molina's own words, including the context in which his comments on divine grace in salvation were made and any analogies drawn, is needed. Scholarship on Molinism would also benefit from the eyes of more historians; for example, analysis of the relationship of Molina's legal and political philosophy to his metaphysical commitments—especially regarding the nature and scope of human freedom and its implications for social philosophy—is greatly needed.[12] For example, Molina upheld the practice of indentured service and slavery in some circumstances, though he also critiqued the politics of slavery in sixteenth-century Portugal and Spain and was, in the eyes of some, more modern in his thought than his contemporaries. Further analysis and discussion is needed in order to synthesize his thought in these areas.

Another area that deserves more attention is the translation of Molina's works. Most of the *Concordia* (1588; 1595) remains untranslated (only Part IV has been published in English), as does Molina's *De iustitia et iure* (1593–1600) and his *Commentaria in Primam Divi Thomae Partem* (1592). It would

---

9. MacGregor, *Molina*.

10. Kaufmann and Aichele, ed., *Companion to Molina*.

11. Cessario, "Molina and Aquinas," 291–324.

12. See Laing, "Review."

seem that a market exists for translations of all of these works. In addition, an update of the critical edition of the *Concordia* would prove beneficial. So there is still much to be done. The discussion of Molinism has been taken to new heights by the application of analytical philosophy to its tenets, but the modern theological discussion of Molina and his thought needs to be an interdisciplinary project. It is my hope that others will be inspired to take up that work in order to elucidate the thought and to learn from this most influential and interesting theologian/philosopher of the Christian church.

Bibliography

Boyd, Gregory A. "Neo-Molinism and the Infinite Intelligence of God." *Philosophia Christi* 5.1 (2003) 187–204.

———. "The Open Theism View." In *Divine Foreknowledge: Four Views*, edited by James K. Beilby and Paul R. Eddy, 13–47. Downers Grove, IL: InterVarsity, 2001.

Cessario, Romanus. "Molina and Aquinas." In *A Companion to Luis de Molina*, edited by Matthias Kaufmann and Alexander Aichele, 289–323. Leiden: Brill, 2014.

Gaskin, Richard. "Conditionals of Freedom and Middle Knowledge." *Philosophical Quarterly* 43.173 (1993) 412–30.

Hasker, William. *God, Time and Knowledge*. Ithaca, NY: Cornell University Press, 1989.

———. "Middle Knowledge: A Refutation Revisited." *Faith and Philosophy* 12.2 (1995) 223–36.

———. "Must God Do His Best?" *International Journal for Philosophy of Religion* 16.3 (1984) 213–23.

———. "A New Anti-Molinist Argument." *Religious Studies* 35.3 (1999) 291–97.

Hess, Elijah. "Why the 'Neo-Molinist' Account of Open Theism Offers Free Will Theists the More Perspicuous Account of Divine Providence." Paper read at The Randomness and Foreknowledge Conference, Dallas, TX (October 24, 2014).

Kaufmann, Matthias, and Alexander Aichele, eds. *A Companion to Luis de Molina*. Leiden: Brill, 2014.

Laing, John D. Review of *A Companion to Luis de Molina*, edited by Matthias Kaufmann and Alexander Aichele. *Journal of the History of Philosophy* 53.1 (2015) 159–60.

MacGregor, Kirk R. *Luis de Molina: The Life and Theology of the Founder of Middle Knowledge*. Grand Rapids: Zondervan, 2015.

Rhoda, Alan. "A Dilemma for Molinism." Unpublished paper.

———. "Five Roads to Fatalism and the Openness of the Future." Unpublished paper.

van Inwagen, Peter. "Against Middle Knowledge." *Midwest Studies in Philosophy* 21.1 (1977) 225–36.

———. *An Essay on Free Will*. Oxford: Clarendon, 1983.

Werther, David. "Open Theism and Middle Knowledge: An Appraisal of Gregory Boyd's Neo-Molinism." *Philosophia Christi* 5.1 (2003) 205–15.

Ware, Bruce A. *God's Greater Glory: The Exalted God of Scripture and the Christian Faith*. Wheaton, IL: Crossway, 2004.

Wierenga, Edward. "Tilting at Molinism." In *Molinism: The Contemporary Debate*, 118–39. Oxford: Oxford University Press, 2011.

12

A Calvinist Perspective in the Conversation about Middle Knowledge

Terrance L. Tiessen

I AM HAPPY TO have been invited by John Laing to respond to his piece "On Parsing the Knowledge and Will of God, or Calvinism and Middle Knowledge in Conversation," because I am a Calvinist who believes that Molinism has made a significantly helpful contribution to our understanding of the role of God's knowledge in his decree. To make my interaction with Laing's essay easy to follow, I will use his subheadings as I interact with his work.

Middle Knowledge

What fundamentally differentiates my "hypothetical-knowledge Calvinism" from the Molinist model is the fact that, in keeping with the predominant Calvinist understanding of God's knowledge, I deny that God has, or needs, *middle* knowledge to gain all the advantages that Molina sought. Furthermore, I believe that a compatibilist understanding of God's meticulous sovereignty and morally responsible human freedom, such as Calvinism represents, is more coherent than Molinist incompatibilism, because it avoids the fatal grounding objection with regard to God's knowledge of counterfactuals concerning creaturely action. Since creatures are not libertarianly free, however, there is no reason to posit a third (or "middle") logical moment in God's knowledge. God knows counterfactuals as part of his natural or necessary knowledge, and that knowledge enables God to choose to actualize a world in which things turn out as God wills, even though many morally responsible decisions are made by his creatures, both human and angelic.

I commend Laing for his clear presentation of the "traditional Thomistic scheme" and Molina's "middle knowledge proposal." He has nicely demonstrated the manner in which Molina modified the traditional view, and he identifies Molina's intention for doing so.

Boyd's "Neo-Molinism"

I concur with Gregory Boyd that his "neo-Molinist" proposal is a helpful modification of the model of God's providence. I affirm that God's pursuit of the realization of his purposes, in a world where he had voluntarily limited his control in order to give moral creatures libertarian freedom, would be enhanced to some degree by his knowledge of "might counterfactuals." Although God is unable to know precisely what a free creature *would* do in any hypothetical circumstance, God can and does know the probability that they will act in a particular way. I disagree with Boyd significantly, however, in regard to just how large an advantage this grants to God. Given the immense number of decisions that humans around the world are making at any given moment, the accumulating effect of improbable decisions would ultimately make predictions, even by an omniscient God, very imprecise. If God could predict with 99% accuracy (for instance) what each person would do in a hypothetical situation, God would still be surprised and disappointed that things did not turn out as he had hoped, in a remarkably large number of cases. Nevertheless, God's disappointment will be considerably smaller than it would have been if his expectations had not taken account of his knowledge of probabilities. So, I concur with Boyd that his fellow open theists would be wise to appropriate his neo-Molinism. All forms of open theism give God a more active role in creation than models which attribute to God only simple foreknowledge, but Boyd's neo-Molinism is the most dynamic open theist perspective. As such, it testifies to the value of Molina's contribution to our consideration of God's providential work in the world, even though it rightly rejects the most distinctive aspect of the Molinist proposal, namely, the belief that God knows *with certainty* the counterfactuals of human action even though God has given moral creatures *libertarian* freedom.

Calvinist Middle Knowledge and the
Parsing of Natural Knowledge

I share Laing's puzzlement at the proposal Ware apparently made that God's free knowledge "is a subset, or subcategory, of natural knowledge." To make God's free knowledge part of God's necessary knowledge, and hence "independent of God's will," would make God's decree necessary, since God's free knowledge is essentially his knowledge of his own free decision in choosing to create this world, including every detail of its history. In the model depicted in Laing's chart of Ware's position, God has no free knowledge; all his knowledge is necessary. This would be so extreme a modification of classic Calvinism as to put it outside that position completely. Given my ignorance of Ware's own chapter, I can say nothing about agreement or disagreement with Ware himself, but I certainly do not agree with the model that Laing has laid out as representing Ware's position. As is evident in my conversation with Paul Helm, which appears earlier in this book, I am well satisfied with the classic Calvinist portrait of God's natural or necessary knowledge and of his free knowledge, the latter being logically (though not temporally) subsequent to God's decree, and the decree itself being a free decision.

Laing speaks of my contention that if God gives creatures soft compatibilist freedom (the freedom of spontaneity rather than of contrary choice), then the Achilles heel of Molinism, the grounding objection, is not a problem for Calvinism. I have proposed that God knows the counterfactuals of creaturely action necessarily, because his knowledge of those counterfactuals is made possible by God's knowing the principles of agent causation. Thus, God knows that "if John were in C, he would (compatibilistically) freely eat cheesecake." Within Molinism this simply won't work, because John is libertarianly free and, in a hypothetical world John is not making a decision while in C whether to eat or not to eat the cheesecake. Even if God were to observe that John, in numerous actual instances of C, chose freely to eat cheesecake, he could not say for certain that John would *always* do so when in C, precisely because, in the actual instances that God observed, *John could have done otherwise!* But within a soft compatibilist framework, this uncertainty does not obtain. What grounds God's knowledge of this counterfactual is his knowledge of the principles of agent causation. He knows that a moral creature with the qualities that John has, at the moment that he is making a decision in C, would act in a particular way because that sort of creature acts in that way in those particular circumstances. People exactly like John, when in C, either eat or refrain from eating cheesecake, and God knows which of these would be the case, because he knows the principles of causation that are in operation whenever moral creatures make decisions and act upon them.

Laing contends that I have "provided an answer to how God can know the true counterfactuals . . . not to how they can be true or what makes them true." But this is tacitly not the case. The grounding objection against the Molinist construct is that God cannot know true counterfactuals because, if creatures are libertarianly free, what makes those counterfactuals true is the decision made by the free creature. But, in a hypothetical situation, no decision exists, and so, at most, an omniscient being can know the probability that the creature would decide in a particular way but, by definition, the libertarianly free creature could always act unexpectedly or improbably. Not so in the case of soft compatibilistically free creatures. Their actions in hypothetical situations are completely knowable or predictable by an omniscient being who knows the nature, inclinations, affections, values, etc. of the hypothetical actor, and who knows the principles of causation by which creatures make decisions and act upon them. The omniscient being (God) knows, therefore, what small changes in "John," or in the hypothetical circumstances in which John's action is being contemplated, would bring about a different result.

Still more puzzling is Laing's statement that "Ware, Tiessen, Helm and others have not explained . . . what makes a particular person to develop the way he does, necessarily, such that even God could not will to make him develop differently." I, at least, have never suggested that God could not make a person develop differently. Because God knows the principles of soft compatibilist creaturely agency, he can occasion worlds in which people develop (through all the factors contributing to personal development, including God's own influences) in a particular way. This is *how* he can choose those who will be saved and direct the course of their lives so that they are the sort of people who, when they hear the gospel, and when the Spirit opens their spiritual eyes and ears, voluntarily believe the gospel and are saved thereby. This is how God's call of his elect is efficacious, always bringing them to saving faith, without coercing or forcing them. A different result would occur if God had given more grace, less grace, or a different kind of grace, or if God had providentially allowed different experiences, etc., to occur in an individual's life. Here lies the essence of soft compatibilism, and God's natural knowledge of counterfactuals is therefore immensely valuable to God's bringing about exactly the situation he desired, by means of the voluntary/uncoerced choices of moral creatures.

This framework could hardly be better described than it was in chapter III, article 1, of the *Westminster Confession of Faith*, concerning God's eternal decree: "God from all eternity, did, by the most wise and holy counsel

of His own will, freely, and unchangeably ordain whatsoever comes to pass
(Eph 1:1; Rom 11:33; Heb 6:17; Rom 9:15, 18) yet so, as thereby neither is
he the author of sin (Jas 1:13, 17; 1 John 1:5), nor is violence offered to the
will of the creatures; nor is the liberty or contingency of second causes taken
away, but established (Acts 2:23; Matt 17:12; Acts 4:27–28; John 19:11; Prov
16:33)." I'm not suggesting that the framers of the confession were hypothetical-knowledge Calvinists, but I'm reasonably hopeful that they would
see fairly readily how nicely this perspective undergirds the big picture that
they so carefully described.

Laing posits that I (and others) "want to argue that if it is true that in
circumstances C, [John] freely eat[s] cheesecake, then [John] is such that
[he] could not freely refrain from eating cheesecake in C, but more than
that, [we] claim that God could not create [him] so that in C, [he] freely
refrain[s] from eating cheesecake." This is correct, provided my description
above concerning the way in which persons develop is being taken into account. If that is so, then Laing has understood my perspective but, for some
reason, he has failed to understand its rationale. It is precisely because of
what I have just described above, that is, God's knowledge of the principles
of agent causation, that God could not arbitrarily make it the case that a
creature of the sort John is, when placed in circumstances C, would not
eat cheesecake. God could have occasioned the development of someone
very like John, but not exactly the same, who would hate cheesecake. What
God could not do is make it the case that someone exactly like John would
refrain from eating cheesecake in C.

I am sure that if Laing could grasp the import of the framework
that hypothetical-knowledge Calvinism puts forward, he would see that
a person who freely eats cheesecake in circumstances C is a person who
would always do so. And a God who knows the principles of agent causation knows that this is the case. So, if God wants John to refrain from
eating cheesecake, either something about John must be different when he
gets into circumstances C, or the same "John" must be in slightly different
circumstances (C_1) when the opportunity to eat or decline cheesecake occurs. All of this works because John is not libertarianly free. If he were, as
Molinists posit, then God could not know with certainty what this "John"
would do in circumstances C, or what a slightly different "John" would do
in circumstances C or C_1.

So why, I wondered, is an explanation that is so clear to me so fuzzy to
Laing? Happily, the reason emerges as Laing goes on. He writes: "I cannot
make sense of how [God's] nature so defines creaturely actions like cheesecake-eating. Why could it not be just as consistent with his nature that in C,
I freely refrain from eating cheesecake? The fact that both

In *C,* John eats cheesecake

and

In *C,* John refrains from eating cheesecake

seem to equally accord with God's nature."

Bingo! There, I think, is the problem that informs our talking past one another. Contrary to what Laing has just described, I do *not* propose that John's freely eating or not eating cheesecake derives from *God's* nature. Rather, it derives from *John's* nature. What is "natural" about it, is the principles of agent causation. So, in hypothetical-knowledge Calvinism, the situation is just as Laing thought it should be: this cheesecake eating situation is quite different from one in which *moral* issues are at stake. This is more like God's knowledge of mathematical truths or "laws" of logic than it is of God's moral law, which does derive from God's own moral nature. We must be truthful because God is truth. But we need not eat or refrain from eating cheesecake because of anything about God other than that which informs the absoluteness of mathematical truths (and here I get out of my depth very speedily).

So, God could have actualized a world in which John is not in *C,* but not one in which John (being who he is at the hypothetical time), if in *C,* could either eat or refrain. This is true, not because of who God is, but because that is simply the way it works in any possible world. If John is a creature who freely eats cheesecake in *C,* there were no worlds in which *that* "John" would freely refrain from eating cheesecake in *C.* But most likely there were worlds in which *John₁* freely eats cheesecake in *C,* and worlds in which John freely refrains from eating cheesecake because in those worlds C_1 or C_2 or C_3 pertains.

Laing proposes that my belief that God knows naturally whether Laing would or would not freely eat cheesecake in *C* equates "truth and necessity." There is a sense in which this is the case, but I am not sure it is the sense which is in Laing's mind when he makes this charge. I agree that God knows necessarily the truth concerning Laing's freely eating or refraining from eating cheesecake in any hypothetical set of circumstances. God knows these counterfactuals because he knows the principles of agent causation, but there is nothing *necessary* about this particular world having been a world in which John eats the cheesecake. God chose the world in which John (being the sort of person John is) would eat cheesecake in these particular circumstances, but nothing necessitated that God make that choice. God was free to choose a world in which this particular person never faced these particular circumstances. What God could not do is make a world in which exactly this sort of person in these particular circumstances acts differently, but this does not derive from a necessity of God's nature.

Laing hears some Calvinists to be saying that "the creation's necessity is tied to God's work; it couldn't not come to be," and he names me as one of them, but that is incorrect. In my view, God was under no necessity to create any world, nor to create this world if he did choose to create a world. By God's free will, he chose to actualize this particular world and its history. But if God wanted a world in which John freely eats cheesecake on some occasion, then, given soft compatibilism, John would need to become a particular sort of person and he would need to find himself in a particular set of circumstances. God need not do anything supernatural to bring that about, but he could deliberately permit secondary causes to act in certain ways so that this particular person would be in the circumstance where he would freely choose to eat cheesecake, and God could know that he would do so because he knows the principles of agent causation which cohere with soft compatibilist freedom.

I am puzzled by the statement that part of the reason why some Calvinist theologians posit that God has compatibilist freedom is that "they think separating God's free knowledge from his natural knowledge improperly sets God's will in opposition to his nature." This may not be pertinent to the debate between Molinists and Calvinists, but I don't understand why either would think that "opposition" between these wills is a potential problem. Certainly, God's moral perfection puts limits on what God can do, consistent with faithfulness to himself, but how could this entail collapsing free knowledge into natural knowledge? If God only had natural/necessary knowledge, then no room would be left for his decree, which determines the truths concerning the future, which God therefore knows freely. I can think of no Calvinist theologian who would go down that road, so either Laing needs to get rid of this particular thought or he needs to support it with citations.

Molinism and the Parsing of Free Knowledge

In a five-stage schematic, Laing has laid out a scenario which he deems to be a helpful way of unpacking the Molinist understanding of God's free knowledge, which he divides into three logical sub-moments. In the first of these, God enunciates his "desires and intentions," perhaps including a desire "to create a world where John freely eats cheesecake." Secondly, God assesses "how feasible worlds match up with those desires and intentions," such as the conclusion that God could meet his goals "by placing John in C." In the final stage of free knowledge, God is then portrayed as deciding "to actualize a particular world," which would be a world in which "John is in C and freely eats cheesecake."

In keeping with the Calvinist tradition, my own schematic has only two moments of knowledge, natural and free, with God's knowledge of counterfactuals of (soft compatibilist) creaturely freedom being a part of his natural knowledge. It does not give God a middle moment of knowledge because moral creatures are not libertarianly free and God's knowledge of what they would do is therefore not dependent upon creaturely choices; it follows from God's natural knowledge of the principles of agent causation. With regard to God's free knowledge, however, I do not conceptualize it as inclusive of God's decree (as per Laing's portrait of the Molinist scheme). I see things as Francis Turretin did when he asserted that God's free knowledge "depends upon his will and decree by which things pass from a state of possibility to a state of futurition."[1]

In my scheme, therefore, as in Turretin's, God's free knowledge "follows" his decree "because it beholds things future," and these are "not future except by the decree."[2] In this scheme, there is indeed something in the "middle," between God's natural and his free knowledge, but it is not another form of knowledge, dependent upon creaturely decisions; it is the logical moment of God's decree. There God utilizes his natural knowledge, particularly drawing upon his hypothetical knowledge, that is, his knowledge of counterfactuals. That, at least, is how my construct works, though the Reformed Orthodox (or Scholastic) theologians characteristically made little of God's hypothetical knowledge. This was because they were anxious to reject the Molinistic model, since it was developed in order to defend the libertarian notion of creaturely freedom. I share their antipathy to Molinistic synergism, and I concur completely with their monergistic understanding of divine providence, but I am convinced that Molina has laid out a proposal from which we can significantly benefit, without compromising God's independence of his creatures.

When I first saw merit in Molina's work, I adapted it to fit within what I then termed a "middle-knowledge Calvinist" model of providence.[3] It was never critical to me, however, that God's knowledge of counterfactuals

---

1. Turretin, *Institutes*, 1:213.

2. Ibid.

3. Tiessen, *Providence and Prayer*, 289–336.

of creaturely agency occur at a distinct or "middle" logical moment. Some years after laying out my understanding in *Providence and Prayer*, I wrote an article to defend it against the objections that had classically been made against divine middle knowledge. I titled it: "Why Calvinists Should Believe in Divine Middle Knowledge, Although They Reject Molinism."[4] At that time, I made this statement:

> It is more important to me to reach agreement among Calvinists that God makes significant use of his knowledge of counterfactuals (or true hypothetical events) than it is to reach agreement about *when*, logically, God has this knowledge. Nevertheless, I believe that this knowledge is sufficiently different in kind to be designated separately as *middle* knowledge.[5]

Some months after that article appeared in the *Westminster Theological Journal*, I received a letter from Paul Helm questioning my appropriation of middle knowledge. That was a very profitable interchange, and it resulted in the article that he and I co-authored, also published by *WTJ*, which appears earlier in this book. In the process of that conversation, Helm helped me to realize that the only reason God's knowledge of counterfactuals would need to be at a middle moment would be if creatures were libertarianly free. Since I deny that to be the case, I ought to stay with the traditional Reformed notion of God's natural knowledge. I was happy to have been convinced on this point, because I had always been concerned about the likelihood of my model of providence being confused with Molinism because we both spoke of divine "middle knowledge." This did not change my understanding of God's providence relative to his knowledge at all, but it does remove an unnecessary stumbling block to consideration of my proposal by other Calvinists. Accordingly, I now refer to my model as "hypothetical-knowledge Calvinism," which raises none of the fears which appropriation of "middle knowledge" legitimately arouses in the minds of Calvinists.

Apart from the important differences between my Calvinist position and that of Molinism which I have just enunciated, I have little concern about the Molinist scheme as Laing lays it out. But Laing thinks that some Calvinists would be concerned that God's simplicity would be compromised if "a sin one commits may be part of a world God chooses because it best meets his eschatological goals and does so with the least number of events that go against his desires, while the sin itself is not desired." I believe that a compatibilist model much better explains how this works, but the essence of the notion is precisely the sort of benefit I wish to appropriate from the Molinist

4. Tiessen, "Why Calvinists Should Believe," 345–66.

5. Ibid., 346.

model, while avoiding the incoherence that Molinism entails on account of the grounding objection. My position is not troubled by the concerns that Laing anticipates from other Calvinist perspectives, because I reject "the Calvinistic scheme where free knowledge is part of natural knowledge." In fact, as I have just demonstrated, that is a notion which departs very significantly from the Calvinist tradition. So I commend Laing for the way he addresses the difference between God's desire (which a Calvinist would call God's "moral will") and his decree (the will of God's eternal purpose or his "decretive will"). I see that distinction at work in God's decision to actualize this particular world rather than one of the many other possible worlds which God is able to know precisely because they are worlds in which God did *not* give creatures libertarian freedom (contra Molinism).

Concluding Suggestions for Further Study and Discussion

I am delighted that Laing and other Molinists wish the discussion between Molinists and Calvinists to continue. I expect this to be beneficial to both of us. Brief comment on Laing's sets of questions may be helpful to keep them alive in the conversation between Molinists and Calvinists, but I will not venture lengthy answers which would call for new chapters in this discussion.

Molinist questions for Calvinists

(1) In regard to the first questions for Edwardsian Calvinists, I concur that we need to elucidate the distinction between Calvinism and fatalism, since the latter is what Molinists (and other synergists) sometimes hear when they listen to Calvinists. That is why I included a chapter on the "fatalist model," in my book on models of divine providence.[6] Although I was not aware of any Christian theologians who assert fatalistic determinism, I included it among the models examined, for three reasons:[7] (a) Some positions are "clearly headed in this direction, although their proponents back away from the conclusion." As two examples of that danger, I looked briefly at single causality and at the embodiment of God. (b) The accusation is often heard from incompatibilists, and it is clear that Laing himself is one who suspects it. In my book, I cited William Lane Craig as an example of one who has

6. Tiessen, *Providence and Prayer*, 271–85.
7. Ibid., 273.

this impression, for he states that Paul Helm believes "theological fatalism."[8] Since Craig is himself a Molinist, this is obviously a matter needing to be aired in the conversation between our two groups. And (c) it seemed apparent to me that people who are taught compatibilist models, whether Thomist, Barthian, or Calvinist, may unwittingly lapse into fatalism. Proponents of incompatibilist models have been motivated to make some of their most controversial assertions particularly to avoid the fatalism that they assume compatibilism entails. I cited open theism's denial of comprehensive divine foreknowledge as a case in point. On the other hand, when synergists express their fears that monergists are headed in the direction of fatalism, their pushback sometimes sounds to the Calvinist like it is headed in the direction of arbitrariness and irrationality. So, I agree that conversation about this issue would be valuable.

(2) As a Calvinist who affirms "libertarian freedom for God, but not for creatures," I welcome conversation about the nature of God's freedom. The answers to Laing's two specific questions seems quite simple to me, but that does not remove the need for conversation, since we are not agreed that this is straightforward. To Laing's question why "the logic governing counterfactuals of compatibilist creaturely freedom" does "not also dictate counterfactuals of divine freedom," I answer that it does! God does not know counterfactuals of his *own* freedom, since the grounding objection is no respecter of persons.

As to why we should "not place divine knowledge of counterfactuals of compatibilist creaturely freedom in God's free knowledge," the answer is that they do not depend on the will of God. Apparently, however, it is not yet clear to Laing *why* this is so. I hope that comments I have made earlier in this essay have helped, but the question may still need to be discussed.

(3) The questions Laing raises about the unity between God's desires and his will, and concerning the nature of possibility and feasibility, are questions pertinent to both Molinists and Calvinists. So these will make for particularly animated discussion, in which the positions taken may occasionally find some Molinists and Calvinists agreeing with one another while disagreeing with their fellows.

I welcome the material that would be produced if/when the further study on Molinism and Molina for which Laing calls is accomplished. Having already profited significantly from the theological work of Molinists, I am a Calvinist who welcomes their further thinking in regard to matters of importance to both of us.

8. Craig, *Foreknowledge*, 26.

Calvinist questions for Molinists

To add to the agenda that Laing has put on the table from his Molinist perspective, I'm happy to identify now some questions which I as a Calvinist would like discussed by Molinists, in the company of my fellow Calvinists, particularly those who sympathize with hypothetical-knowledge Calvinism. These are questions that have arisen in my own mind as I have read both the work *of* Molinists and that of others writing *about* Molinism.

(1) Luis de Molina's goal in proposing that God had a middle moment of knowledge is undisputed. He wished to preserve the libertarian freedom of moral creatures, as Aquinas had previously attempted to do, but he doubted that this could be achieved compatibilistically, in the manner that Thomas had laid out. I call Thomism "hard compatibilism," because it deems *libertarian* creaturely freedom compatible with meticulous divine determination. Molina also wanted a model which attributes to God the maximum control possible in a manner compatible with creaturely freedom. It was Molina's conviction that moral responsibility requires libertarian freedom, in the sense of the power of contrary choice or the principle of alternative possibilities, so he attributes that sort of freedom to moral creatures *in* this world, while attributing to God the sovereign choice *of* this world, from among all the possible worlds. Molina wrote:

> *The third type is middle knowledge, by which, in virtue of the most profound and inscrutable comprehension of each faculty of free choice, He saw in His own essence what each such faculty would do with its innate freedom were it to be placed in this or in that or, indeed, in infinitely many orders of things—even though it would really be able, if it so willed, to do the opposite.*[9]

I owe my original introduction to Molinism to the work of William Lane Craig, who has been a leader of the Molinist cause within evangelicalism. In *Four Views on Divine Providence*, however, Craig took me by surprise. In his response to Gregory Boyd's open theist contribution, he affirmed Boyd's belief in libertarian creaturely freedom, but he denied that this entails the principle of alternative possibilities (PAP), which had been Boyd's own understanding. Craig proposed instead that a libertarian account of freedom requires only "the absence of causal constraints outside oneself that determines how one chooses," that is, "that we have genuine 'say-so' about our choices."[10]

---

9. Molina, *Foreknowledge*, 4.52.9.

10. Craig, "Response to Boyd," 225.

Initially, these brief comments from Craig led me to wonder if he had adopted a soft compatibilist understanding of freedom, perhaps in response to the grounding objection, which is one he has often encountered from Calvinists and open theists alike.[11] Until that time, the synergist theologians I met had usually defined libertarian freedom in terms of the PAP, as Molina had done. But Craig was denying this principle. Like many soft compatibilists in the Edwardsean mode, I consider non-coercion from external sources to be the essential requirement for moral freedom, so I could speak exactly as Craig has done here in the statements I just quoted from him. I deny the PAP, as Craig does, and I often speak of the importance of uncoerced agency. So I thought that perhaps Craig was now defining freedom in terms of spontaneity or non-coercion, which would make the grounding objection no longer applicable to his philosophical theology. Craig could then validly assert that it is possible for God to know how creatures would act in hypothetical situations, because they do not (at least, not always) have the power of contrary choice, so long as they act willingly. I wondered if Craig might have become a fellow "hypothetical-knowledge Calvinist."

I then learned that Craig had spelled out his understanding of freedom and revealed the influence of Frankfurt upon the development of his current view, in a Q&A on the web site of Reasonable Faith back in 2007. In response to the grounding objection, Craig wrote:

> If the compatibilist is right, then God could deduce the future free choices of men from present conditions which causally determine how they shall choose. But as you note, I'm a libertarian who thinks that causal determinism is incompatible with freedom. That doesn't imply that I hold to the Principle of Alternative Possibilities (PAP), which states that a free agent has in a set of circumstances the ability to choose A or not-A. I'm persuaded that so long as an agent's choice is not causally determined, it doesn't matter if he can actually make a choice contrary to how he does choose. Suppose that God has decided to create you in a set of circumstances because He knew that in those circumstances you would make an undetermined choice to do A. Suppose further that had God instead known that if you were in those circumstances you would have made an undetermined choice to do not-A, then God would not have created you in those circumstances (maybe it would have loused up His providential plan!). In that case you do not have the ability in those circumstances to make the choice of not-A, but nevertheless your choice of A is, I think, clearly free, for it is causally

11. See my "Craig's Understanding of Freedom: Molinism or Monergism?"

unconstrained—it [is] you who determines that A will be done. So the ability to do otherwise is not a necessary condition of free choice.[12]

Clearly, Craig had *not* come to share the position I hold, since he continued to self-identify as a Molinist, and what is uppermost in Craig's mind is a consistent rejection of "causal determinism." This comes up in his acceptance of the questioner's statement that, "prior to the exact moment of A, there were no specifiable set of circumstances by which to deduce that A would occur." Craig goes on to explicitly reject the compatibilist belief that "God could deduce the future free choices of men from present conditions which causally determine how they shall choose."

I now find myself confused. It appears to me that, in rejecting the PAP as necessary to freedom, Craig has removed the only thing that constituted his model indeterministic. Like Craig, Calvinist compatibilists regularly insist that moral responsibility requires that a person not have been coerced; they must have had "say so" in the action they committed. But if, as Craig now asserts, people do not (always) have the ability to do otherwise than they do when they choose in a morally responsible way, then the reasons for their choice lie within the person who makes the choice. A person of the quality *A* would do *x* in circumstances *y*. This is what makes it possible for God to know, as part of his natural or necessary knowledge, how creatures would act in all possible situations.

I wonder how content more traditional libertarians, for whom the PAP is fundamental to freedom, are going to be with Craig's current position. I'm sorry that Greg Boyd did not have the opportunity to respond to Craig's protest about Boyd's defining libertarian freedom as the PAP. Boyd looked to me like an "orthodox" libertarian at that point, and Craig looks revisionist. But his revisionism has obviously not gone to the extent of making him a determinist, as the title of my blog post suggested might be the case. It appears that Craig is a Source *Incompatibilist* but not one who affirms the PAP. I, on the other hand, am a Source *Compatibilist* who also rejects the PAP. As a form of incompatibilism, Craig's position is just as subject to the grounding objection as it would be if he affirmed the PAP. But I'm struggling to grasp what it is, in his view, that makes agent causation incompatible with meticulous divine providence, and what it is that constitutes the essential feature of human freedom that makes creatures morally responsible, *if creatures lack the power to have done otherwise than they do.* In further conversation with Molinists, I hope that this mystery will be elucidated for Calvinists like me.

12. Craig, "Q&A #23: Middle Knowledge."

What allows Craig to disavow the PAP while simultaneously disavow-ing determinism? He posits a situation in which "God knows that in a par-ticular set of circumstances you would undeterminedly choose to do A," although you had no power to choose otherwise. Does he think that God would only know, in his middle knowledge, what you would choose to do, but *not* know that you could not choose to do otherwise? It seems to me that Craig must think this, but that seems a strange idea, given Molinism's enthusiasm about God's middle knowledge. On the other hand, if God does know not only what you would undeterminedly choose but also that you could not undeterminedly choose otherwise, in what sense does the "free-dom" you possess qualify as libertarian? This does not strike me as the sort of freedom that Molinism has traditionally tried to preserve.

(2) Throughout the history of Arminianism, there have been Armin-ian theologians attracted to Molinism. But Roger Olson has argued that "once one believes that God *uses* middle knowledge to render certain that every creature does what they do by creating them and placing them in circumstances where he knows they will 'freely' do something, then deter-minism is at the door if not in the living room and that is inconsistent with Arminianism's basic impulses. *It makes God the author of sin and evil even if only inadvertently.*"[13] Olson's test case is Adam and Eve's first disobedience, where he sees the critical issue to be "whether God *rendered their act of disobedience certain.*"

Olson continues:

> Advocates of middle knowledge usually rely on a distinction between "certain" or "infallible" and "necessary," with only the latter making God the author of sin and evil. The argument is that God's use of middle knowledge to render the fall certain, even infallibly (it could not have not happened given God's fore-knowledge of what Adam and Eve would do and his creation of them and placing them in that situation) does not render the fall necessary. I tend to think that's a distinction without a dif-ference. That use of middle knowledge providentially to render the fall certain necessarily implies a plan in the mind of God that makes the fall not only part of God's consequent will but also part of his antecedent will. And, as everyone knows and agrees, the distinction between God's consequent will and God's antecedent will is crucial to Arminianism's argument that God is not the author of sin and evil. Why else would God use his

13. Olson, "Arminian Theology and Middle Knowledge."

middle knowledge providentially? And why would he use it at all if not for the purpose of meticulous providence?

Olson is aware of Calvinists who have used Molinism's concept of middle knowledge, "to 'explain' predestination and reprobation in order to get God 'off the hook,' so to speak, as not the author of sin and evil," and he cites Millard Erickson and Bruce Ware as "two evangelical Calvinists who use middle knowledge as the 'key' to reconciling God's sovereignty and human free will." But "*they* at least admit that their view of free will is compatibilism—that free will is compatible with determinism." So, if Olson's argument is correct, he thinks that these Calvinist theologians "'get it'—middle knowledge used by God for providential advantage requires a compatibilist view of free will."

Olson is not aware of any Arminian theologians who affirm compatibilism. They "all embrace libertarian free will," and, to Olson, "libertarian free will *means* 'ability to do otherwise than one does.'" So all Arminians "believe that creatures who sin do so with libertarian freedom. In other words, they could do otherwise. Well, at least Adam and Eve could have done otherwise than disobey God." But what does this entail for Arminians who appropriate the Molinist concept of middle knowledge? Olson sees that situation this way:

> If middle knowledge is true and God uses it for providential advantage, as Richard Muller says, offering inducements to creatures that God knows they will follow given their dispositions and inclinations, then God is not only "in control" but "actually controlling" everything including Adam's and Eve's disobedience. They could not have done otherwise even if they did it "freely." That is the very essence of compatibilism!
>
> Let's use an illustration. Suppose I know one of my students so well that I *know* (beyond any possibility of being wrong) that if I suggest he read a certain book he will misunderstand the subject of our course and go on to fail it. Without the book, he would pass the course. I suggest he read the book. Why? Well, perhaps because I need someone to fail the course. I don't grade on a curve and the dean is worried that I am not upholding academic standards. All my students pass with flying colors. My career is in jeopardy as is the academic credibility of the school. So I use my middle knowledge of the student's dispositions and inclinations to bring it about infallibly that he fails the course. Nothing I did took away his free will. He read the book voluntarily (no external coercion was used, only inducement). (Note: None of that would happen; it's purely hypothetical.)

Now, who is really responsible for, the "author of," the student failing the course?

And can it fairly be said that by rendering his failure certain, using my middle knowledge, I did not make it necessary?

Now, there's no point in appealing to God's freedom to do
whatever he wants to do. This is a debate among Arminians and
Arminians, following Arminius, are not nominalists. We all agree
that God is essentially good by nature and cannot simply do anything capable of being put into words. No informed Arminian
would say "Whatever God does is automatically good, just because God does it, period." So that objection to my scenario isn't
relevant to this context—a debate among Arminians.

I tend to agree with Eef Dekker, against several leading
Arminius scholars, that *if* Arminius used middle knowledge
to explain God's sovereignty, then he unwittingly contradicted
himself. He contradicted his own most basic principle which
is that God is by no means the author of sin and evil. He unwittingly fell into determinism *at that point* and should not
have relied on middle knowledge. Why he did, if he did, is a
separate question. I think reasonable answers can be imagined
(having to do with his desire to build bridges between himself
and his critics).

Olson is not prepared to say that "one cannot be an Arminian and a
Molinist." But he does think that "Molinism is a foreign body in Arminianism *even if Arminius himself used it!* If he did, it was a foreign body in his
own theology in the sense that it conflicted with his own basic belief commitments about God's goodness, God not being in any sense the author of
sin and evil, and creatures' free wills (especially in disobedience)."

Of course, I don't share Roger Olson's concern to preserve classic
Arminianism against revisionist proposals. From my monergist or soft-
compatibilist perspective, Molinism, Arminianism, and open theism are
three forms of synergism. Furthermore, I consider it historically misleading
to regard Molinism as a species of Arminianism. Rather, we should view
the relationship of Molinism to Thomism as analogous to that between
Arminianism and Calvinism.[14] Both Molinism and Arminianism were
synergistic proposals formulated with reference to the monergistic tradition within which they arose. The resulting dispute between Dominicans

14. According to Thomas Flint, a Roman Catholic philosopher who is also a Molinist, when picturing God's action in the world Roman Catholics pretty much have a
choice between the theological perspective of Thomas Aquinas (Thomism) or something akin to Molinism, and these correspond largely to the views of classic Calvinism
and Arminianism in the Protestant world ("Two Accounts," 148).

and Jesuits was as animated as the debate between Calvinists and Arminians. Unlike the Reformed Church, however, the Roman Catholic Church never took a position on the dispute. At one point, the Pope pronounced a moratorium on the discussion, and the Church has never made one or other position a matter of orthodoxy. On the other hand, the Synod of Dort clearly announced approval of Calvinism and rejection of Arminian (or Remonstrant) revisionism.

So I suggest that we do best to consider synergism the umbrella category for all three of these theologies, and not to subsume one to another. Within that broad category on one side of the great theological watershed between synergism and monergism, it is not surprising that many Arminians have appropriated Molinism's concept of middle knowledge, or that an open theist such as Clark Pinnock was a self-identified Arminian before he moved into open theism, which he saw as correcting the errors of classical theism that remained in Arminianism, such as divine atemporality.

Nonetheless, you may understand why this Arminian concern raises questions which I think Calvinists and Molinists can profitably discuss together. Olson has specified the PAP as essential to libertarian freedom, whereas Craig has affirmed the latter but rejected the former. It sounds as though Olson would be happy to listen in on the discussion ensuing from my previous questions regarding Craig's current position. What exactly does constitute creaturely freedom "libertarian"? Additionally, however, Olson has put on the table a very important skepticism about the authenticity of indeterminism in the Molinist construct.

Influenced strongly by Molinists' own intentions to reject determinism, I see Molinism's description of the way things happen in this world relative to God's action as a form of synergism, indeterminism, and incompatibilism. But Olson disagrees. As you can see from the material I cited from him above, he thinks that God's choosing this particular world with all of its particulars, including sin and evil, threatens our affirmation of God's goodness. He views Molinism as a form of determinism, and I think that his analysis cannot be lightly dismissed. Though we came to our perspectives from quite different directions, is there not some overlap between my suspicion (that Craig's rejection of the PAP might be heading him out of Molinism and into a compatibilist understanding of God's use of his knowledge of counterfactuals) and Olson's concern (that Molinism gives God too much control in his choice of this world to warrant our putting Molinism on the synergist side of the watershed)?

I have benefited from conversations with Molinists, as well as with other kinds of synergists, both Arminians and open theists. So I look forward to future interaction, addressing both the questions that John Laing has enunciated and the ones that I have raised here.

Bibliography

Craig, William Lane. *Divine Foreknowledge and Human Freedom: The Coherence of Theism: Omniscience.* Brill's Studies in Intellectual History 19. Leiden: Brill, 1991.
———. "Q&A 23: Middle Knowledge." Posted Sept. 24, 2007. Available at: https://www.reasonablefaith.org/question-answer/P20/middle knowledge.
———. "Response to Gregory A. Boyd." In *Four Views on Divine Providence*, edited by Dennis W. Jowers, 224–30. Grand Rapids: Zondervan, 2011.
Flint, Thomas P. "Two Accounts of Providence." In *Divine and Human Action: Essays in the Metaphysics of Theism*, edited by Thomas V. Morris, 147–81. Ithaca, NY: Cornell University Press, 1988.
Molina, Luis de. *On Divine Foreknowledge: Part IV of the Concordia.* Translated by and edited Alfred J. Freddoso. Ithaca, NY: Cornell University Press, 1988.
Olson, Roger. "Are Arminian Theology and Middle Knowledge Compatible?" Posted Sept. 4, 2013. Available at: http://www.patheos.com/blogs/rogereolson/2013/09/are-arminian-theology-and-middle knowledge-compatible/.
Tiessen, Terrance L. *Providence and Prayer: How Does God Work in the World?* Downers Grove, IL: InterVarsity, 2000.
———. "Why Calvinists Should Believe in Divine Middle Knowledge, Although They Reject Molinism." *Westminster Theological Journal* 69.2 (2007) 345–66.
———. "W. L. Craig's Understanding of Freedom: Molinism or Monergism?" Posted Jan. 31, 2013. Available at: http://thoughtstheological.com/w-l-craigs-understanding-of-freedom-molinism-or-monergism/.
Turretin, Francis. *Institutes of Elenctic Theology*, edited by James T. Dennison, Jr. Phillipsburg, NJ: Presbyterian & Reformed, 1992.

13

"Lord Willing and God Forbid"

Divine Permission, Asymmetry, and Counterfactuals[1]

GUILLAUME BIGNON

Introduction: "God permits evil"

CHRISTIAN THINKERS HAVEN'T BEEN afraid of the logical problem of evil in a long time. When atheists have asserted that God's existence is incompatible with evil, Christian theologians have long known to respond that it's perfectly possible for God to have morally sufficient reasons to permit evil. But while all Christians agree that it is so, not all Christians agree that *all* Christians can use that word: "permit." The coherence of a language of divine "permission" is one of the usual points of dispute between Arminians and Calvinists. On the one hand, Arminians hold to the so-called libertarian view of human free will, wherein God does not determine the outcome of free choices: given all that God does in the heart and mind of a human person at the moment of choice, the person still has the ability to choose one option or another, an ability which Arminians see as a necessary condition both for moral responsibility, and for one to speak of God merely "permitting" evil. On the opposite view, Calvinists assert that God's providence is such that he fully controls the outcome of human free choices: He determines that they shall do what they do, and given the totality of his providential work in their hearts and minds, they necessarily do so. Call this thesis "theological determinism." Now, some might disagree with my

---

1. An expanded version of this paper appears as chapter 10 of Guillaume Bignon, *Excusing Sinners and Blaming God: A Calvinist Assessment of Determinism, Moral Responsibility, and Divine Involvement in Evil*, Princeton Theological Monograph Series 230 (Eugene, OR: Pickwick, 2018).

claim that Calvinism entails determinism, but I take it as a matter of definition that determinism is the Calvinist view, since determinism is most likely required by at least some of the five points of Calvinism, and more or less explicitly affirmed by the *Westminster Confession of Faith*. The problem at hand for Calvinists, then, is to explain how God can be said to "permit" evil, if his providence is such that he determines everything that happens, the evil and the good.

The purpose of this paper is to explain how it is so: first, I want to alert libertarians that they have traditionally attached divine permission on the wrong foundation; and secondly, as I invite them to give up this deficient foundation, I want to offer in its place one that actually works for the job, and which should turn out to be of great interest to Molinists, as it will be available to them just as much as it will be to Calvinists. My hope with the present argument is then for these two teams to ultimately *agree* on this topic, sharing the same firm foundation to affirm the divine permission of evil.

The Argument as Pressed by Libertarians

Let us then begin with the objection at hand raised against Calvinist determinism. It is a very straightforward deductive argument that goes as follows:

> Premise 1—If determinism is true, then it cannot properly be said that God "permits" sin and evil.
>
> Premise 2—It must properly be said that God "permits" sin and evil.
>
> *Therefore*
>
> Determinism is false.

Some Calvinists might be inclined to protest about premise 2, but I for one think it is fine. There is a perfectly appropriate sense in which I want to say that God "permits" evil, and so the big question resides on premise 1, and whether that language is coherent given my Calvinist determinism.

Let us read the charge directly from the pen of some of its libertarian proponents. Thomas Flint writes:

> If God is perfectly good, then we cannot have him directly causing evil, especially the morally evil actions which his free beings all too often perform. Evil is *permitted* but not *intended* by God;

hence, we cannot have him predetermining it via intrinsically efficacious concurrent activity.[2]

Roger Olson writes:

> If it is logical for Calvinists to say God permits or allows evil, they can only mean that in a highly attenuated and unusual sense of "permits" and "allows"—one that falls outside the ordinary language of most people.[3]

Olson's formulation of the argument puts into focus the word "properly" I employed in premises 1 and 2 of the above syllogism. This controversy surrounds the meaning of the word "permission." It is a debate about semantics, but that does not mean it is a vain debate: if the concept of "permission" is indeed called for, then we'd rather not abuse language to make it fit in artificially with determinism. We would like to use the word properly.

The issue at hand is also one of *asymmetry* between good and evil. It is the question of whether determinists can maintain a difference in "kind" between God's providence over the good and his providence over evil. Can it properly be said that God "intends" the good (or something of the sort), but "permits" evil, *in distinction to* what he does in the case of the good? Anthony Kenny presses that charge as follows:

> An indeterminist can make a distinction between those states of affairs which God causes, and those which he merely permits: but in a deterministic created universe the distinction between causing and permitting would have no application to God.[4]

So the gauntlet is thrown: how can theologians maintain an asymmetry in God's providence over good and evil, and can determinists properly use "permission" language for God's control of human sin?

Libertarianism Is Not Sufficient

I will aim to show in a moment that libertarianism is not necessary for divine permission, but let me first argue that libertarianism is not *sufficient* for such, so that whether or not it is true, it is not the right anchor for the language of divine permission. The reason for this is that the sort of divine permission we're interested in must feature a divine *asymmetry* with respect to good and evil, which, if it is a problem, is a problem for both sides of

2. Flint, *Divine Providence*, 87–88.

3. Olson, *Against Calvinism*, 88.

4. Kenny, *God*, 87.

the debate—not uniquely for Calvinists. Why so? Because libertarianism, just like determinism, is affirmed by its proponents of *all* directly morally responsible free choices, *both* good *and* evil, *both* praiseworthy *and* blameworthy. So the libertarian who takes issue with the idea that God would determine evil will not solve the problem of asymmetry by merely making free will indeterminist; it will result in God no longer determining the good either, thereby failing to preserve any asymmetry. If indeterminism suffices for "permission" language, then libertarians will find themselves having to say in that sense that God merely "permits" the good as well. Like a bump in the carpet that reappears elsewhere when depressed, the issue of asymmetry will not be solved by simply bringing in libertarianism to avoid a divine authorship of evil: it will equally jettison the divine authorship of the good. In his critique of Calvinism, William Lane Craig argues that "if God foreordains and brings about evil thoughts and deeds, it seems impossible to give an adequate account of this biblical asymmetry."[5] But if libertarianism relieves God from "foreordaining and bringing about" human thoughts and deeds, then it does away with the *good* thoughts and deeds just as much as the *evil* thoughts and deeds. Similarly, when John Wesley says, "Whatsoever good is in man, or is done by man, God is the author and doer of it,"[6] or when Kenneth Keathley says, "God is the cause of whatever I do that is right; I am the cause of all my sins,"[7] they clearly owe us just as much an explanation of how *that* is possible given their libertarianism. So this issue of asymmetry is admittedly a difficult question, but it is one that all camps need to wrestle with, and a mere libertarianism cannot be the answer to our present question.

Now, pointing out that libertarians face the same problem doesn't solve the problem. So let me deal positively with the issue, and see how Christians in general and Calvinists in particular should in fact properly account for permission and asymmetry.

Asymmetry of Divine Will Is Not Sufficient

Some Calvinists have suggested that divine asymmetry may be found in the fact that God's "attitude" toward the good he brings about differs from that which he holds toward evil (all of which he equally brings about). They use the thesis of the so-called "two-wills" of God. While determinism entails that both good and evil in this world are "willed" by God in the decretive

---

5. Craig, *Only Wise God*, 47.

6. Wesley, "Free Grace," 545; quoted in Olson, *Arminian Theology*, 109.

7. Keathley, *Salvation and Sovereignty*, 91.

sense, an asymmetry remains in his "perceptive" will, in that the good is in agreement with God's precepts, while evil goes against them. There is in that sense an asymmetry in God's will with respect to good and evil, and John Frame describes a move in this direction by Reformed theologians:

> If God's permission is efficacious, how does it differ from other exercises of his will? Evidently, the Reformed use permit mainly as a more delicate term than cause, suggesting that God brings sin about with a kind of reluctance born of his holy hatred of it.[8]

I will concede that this "reluctance" of his when bringing about evil as opposed to his presumed endorsement of the good does amount to a certain asymmetry, but I think this cannot plausibly be the full answer. A language of "permission" of evil seems to demand more than this, because it doesn't merely describe an asymmetry in God's "feelings" or "attitude"; rather, it requires an asymmetry in God's *activity*, an asymmetry in God's providential *dealings*. It is plausibly an asymmetry in what God *does*, not merely in what he *thinks* about what he does. So let us press on, and unpack what "permission" calls for in terms of divine activity.

Definitions of Permission: Both Providential and Moral

Since the debate, at bottom, lies over the proper use of an English word, the dictionary is a good place to start. The *Oxford English Dictionary* defines permission as "The action of permitting, allowing, or giving consent; consent, leave, or liberty to do something," and "A licence or freedom to do something; the granting of such freedom."[9] Contemplating such dictionary entries, there are two definitions or common uses that need to be acknowledged, and rejected for our present purposes.

First, there is a *purely moral* understanding that says nothing about providence. It is the idea of permission as giving moral consent, or the legal right to do something, as in "it is permitted to run around the swimming pool," or "it is not permitted to sell alcohol to children." It is a fine use of the word, perhaps even its most common use, but in our case, we are talking about God's permission *of evil*, which by definition is *not* legally permitted in that way. Evil is a breach of God's moral law, and hence, whatever is meant by God's "permission" of evil, it isn't the giving of a moral license; it

8. Frame, *Doctrine of God*, 178.

9. "Permission," *OED Online*.

involves instead a sense of *providence*, wherein God is "making room for," or "refraining to prevent" a certain action, which, being evil, is still not legally, morally permitted.

And on the other hand, there is a use of "permission" that is *purely providential* and has no moral component whatsoever. It is also a perfectly acceptable sense of the word, whereby God is said to "permit" an outcome and "not permit" another, neither of which are morally good or evil. Acts 16:7 is probably one such instance, as we are told that the Spirit of Jesus *did not allow* Paul and Silas to go up to Bithynia. In the absence of divine command, there was presumably nothing moral or immoral about going into Bithynia or going down to Troas instead—the option God permitted. This type of permission, purely providential in nature, is still not the sense intended by our present objector, who very much presses Calvinists to justify divine permission *of evil*. So the sense of divine permission Calvinism is said to exclude is one that is both *providential* and *moral* (or rather *immoral*, really: a permission of evil).

Our use of the word should capture a certain kind of "passivity" in the one permitting. The action of "permitting" is supposed to feature a "hands-off" attitude, almost a passive disengagement on the part of God. It must be a "refraining" from some sort of intervention, thereby letting, allowing, or permitting the evil action to unfold without stepping in. These concepts are the reason why determinism is thought to be problematic here, because if God determines all things, how can he be "hands-off" of anything in the requisite sense?

Three Analogies with Active/Passive Counterfactual Pairs: The Burglar, the Sun, and the Sled

To answer that question and unpack these notions of passivity, permission and asymmetry, let me start with a simple, intuitive, and uncontroversial example, which captures well the sense of permission we are looking for. Suppose that a burglar is climbing up a ladder to break into the window of a third-floor apartment, when a passer-by approaches the foot of the ladder and sees him up there, halfway to the top, climbing to break in. At this point, the passer-by has a decision to make. Among the numerous possibilities open to him, two of them are of special interest for us: on the one hand, he could decide to prevent the burglary, say by pushing down the ladder and tripping the burglar. If he were to do so, the burglary would be prevented. Otherwise, if for whatever reason the passer-by thinks it preferable not to do so (he might find it wrong to send the burglar to a likely hospital bed, or he might be scared by the prospect of a future vengeance, or any good reason one could imagine), he then might decide to refrain from intervening, passively allowing the burglary to occur. This sort of situation captures very well the notions at play when we think of "permission" of evil in the sense relevant for our present purposes. The asymmetry in the passer-by's *action* is easy to appreciate here: whether or not the burglary occurs is at this point fully under his control; it is providentially up to him, *but* depending on which option he chooses, his *action* will vary in kind: if he decides against the burglary, he will need to actively, intently, perform the positive action of pushing the ladder, thereby preventing the evil at hand. But if he finds it preferable for the burglary to occur, then his control will be a purely passive refraining from any intervention, thereby *permitting* this evil, knowing that if he were to not intervene, the burglary would occur. This situation exhibits the sense of asymmetry we are looking for, and I suggest that if theologians are to properly apply permission language to God, it will involve something very much like that. But of course, some differences between the passer-by and God (especially on Calvinism) immediately come to mind. For one, the passer-by is not involved at all in the burglar's prior character formation, nor does he actively draw on the burglar's heart and mind to influence his decision at the moment of choice, whereas on Calvinism, God providentially determines the character and choice of the burglar in the first place, and when it comes to "intervening" or not, though external interventions of the same type as "kicking a ladder" are theoretically available to God, the type of intervention Christians typically have in view is an *internal* intervention, providentially influencing the hearts and minds of persons directly. These points are well taken and I shall discuss in a moment what can and cannot carry over when applying these concepts to God. Nevertheless, there is *something* that the ladder-kicking passer-by and the burglar tell us about permission and asymmetry in divine providence, and I suggest that it is this: they tell us that proper use of permission language to rescue asymmetry in one's providential activity rests upon the truth of two important conditional, counterfactual statements I casually stated in my above discussion of the passer-by. These two statements were as follows:

> 1-If the passer-by *were* to actively intervene (by kicking the ladder), the burglar *would not* commit the crime.

And,

> 2-If the passer-by *were* to passively refrain from intervening, the burglar *would* commit the crime.

Let us name the first one the "active counterfactual," and the second one the "passive counterfactual," giving us an "active/passive counterfactual pair." I contend that permission language and asymmetry in providential activity are premised upon exactly this kind of "active/passive counterfactual pairs." I will explain in a moment how these can be applied to divine providence, but interestingly enough, Jonathan Edwards himself offered an analogy that is not unlike mine to analyze the asymmetry at play in divine providence. He spoke of the relationship between the sun's presence and the production of light and warmth or darkness and coldness:

> There is a vast difference between the sun's being the cause of the lightsomeness and warmth of the atmosphere, and brightness of gold and diamonds, by its presence and positive influence; and its being the occasion of darkness and frost in the night, by its motion, whereby it descends below the horizon. The motion of the sun is the occasion of the latter kind of events; but it is not the proper cause efficient, or producer of them: though they are necessarily consequent on that motion, under such circumstances: no more is any action of the Divine Being the cause of the evil of men's wills.[10]

And then he unpacked the asymmetry in terms that come very close to my aforementioned "active/passive counterfactual pair":

> It would be strange arguing, indeed, because men never commit sin, but only when God leaves them to themselves, and necessarily sin when he does so, that therefore their sin is not from themselves, but from God; and so, that God must be a sinful being: as strange as it would be to argue, because it is always dark when the sun is gone, and never dark when the sun is present, that therefore all darkness is from the sun, and that his disc and beams must needs be black.[11]

Edwards rests the asymmetry upon the facts that if the sun *were* to approach and actively shine upon the location, there *would* be light, and if it *were* to passively withdraw from the location, there *would* be darkness instead. Such active/passive counterfactuals secure the asymmetry.

For good measure and before applying this material to divine providence, let me offer one final such illustration. Think of a bobsled, or a luge, sliding down the track under the control of its pilot, and consider the events of its acceleration and deceleration. For the pilot to bring about the one

---

10. Edwards, *Freedom*, 293.

11. Ibid., 294.

or the other, very different actions are required: to accelerate, all the pilot needs to do is let the sled slide, whereas a deceleration requires an active triggering of the brakes. This asymmetry of active and passive behaviors is secured by the fact that the sled is on a slippery downward track, guaranteeing that: 1) if the sled were left to its own device, it *would* accelerate; and 2) if the brakes were actively triggered, the sled *would* decelerate. This makes it very appropriate to describe the pilot's action as either actively stopping the sled, or passively "permitting" it to slide, albeit under his full control. Asymmetry and permission language are secured by the truth of active/passive counterfactuals.

Application to Providence: Active/Passive Counterfactuals of Freedom

Let us then seek to apply this material to God and his divine providence over good and evil. Can anything like that be affirmed of God's control of human choices if Calvinism is true? For this to be done, the two so-called "active/passive counterfactuals" would now have to be counterfactuals *of freedom*. They would have to be counterfactual statements about what humans *would* or *would not* freely do in various sets of circumstances, under various influences, divine and otherwise. This sort of language might begin to sound like Molinism, but it need not be: as long as determinism is affirmed and libertarian free will denied, there is nothing un-Calvinist about the truth of counterfactuals. The choices to which these counterfactuals pertain are free in the compatibilist sense, the notion of free will that is affirmed by Calvinists and denied by Molinists and all other libertarians.

Let us then examine these active/passive counterfactuals of determinist free will. For any given sinner and sin about which one wants to maintain a language of divine permission in the sense under discussion, Calvinists would have to affirm:

> 1-If God *were* to actively intervene, the sinner *would not* commit the sin

> And,

> 2-If God *were* to passively refrain from intervening, the sinner *would* commit the sin.

To establish the coherence of the model at hand, the question to address is this: how can Calvinists affirm those propositions, and more specifically, how could God be said to "passively refrain" from anything, if he is determining even the very choice to sin? To answer this question, let me begin by drawing an important distinction between two different sorts of causal factors that are at play in determining whether or not the sinner will sin. That human decision is influenced by two sorts of such factors: on the one hand are this person's nature, nurture, life events and character-formation history, all the way from his conception up *until the moment of choice*, and on the other hand are all the immediate influencers *at that moment of choice*: which circumstances is he placed in, and which forces—internal and external, natural and supernatural—are, on that moment, drawing him in different directions to make his choice one way or the other. Note that this conceptual distinction is uncontroversial: these two types of influences are affirmed by all libertarians as well. Only they maintain that all these influences do not collectively *determine* the choice one way or the other, but they do influence it. This uncontroversial distinction, then, allows Calvinists to affirm this: God is in full providential control of both sorts of influences, but his so-called "passivity" or "refraining from intervention" can be expressed legitimately with respect to his supernatural influence *on the moment of choice*. That is a point at which Calvinists can find a very legitimate asymmetry of divine action. If God were to refrain *from that active drawing on the moment of choice*, then the sinner *would* sin, because all that would be left within him to express itself in decision-making would be his nature and prior character, which of course Calvinists affirm are corrupted by original sin. Apart from God actively extending his grace to them, fallen sinners sin. "Man without grace can will nothing but evil," says Martin Luther.[12] The doctrine of original sin, understood very minimally as entailing that humans have a fallen nature that inclines them uniformly toward sin (no need here for anything stronger like total depravity, original guilt, or anything remotely controversial for Christians), explains the truth of one of our two counterfactuals: "If God were to refrain from divine intervention (namely an inner intervention in the form of a positive drawing of grace on the heart of the fallen sinner), the sinner *would* sin."

This conclusion is secured for every choice made by persons affected by original sin. Of course, one may raise the question of Adam's sin, but we will come back to it later. For now, let me turn to the second counterfactual in the pair, namely "If God were to actively intervene, the sinner would refrain from sinning." It is all the more easily affirmed by Calvinists in light of their doctrine of so-called "irresistible grace." There is, according to Calvinists, no amount of sinful inclination that divine grace cannot overcome. Philosophically, this comes from their upholding determinism,

---

12. Luther, *Bondage*, 318.

and it yields exactly the desired theological result: there always exists a type of supernatural drawing available to God, such that if he were to apply it, the sinner would refrain from sinning and would do the right thing instead. This secures the counterfactual at hand, and with it the truth of our active/passive counterfactual pair, thereby justifying the asymmetry at the moment of choice in this specific type of situation, and hence an appropriate language of divine permission in the face of determinism.

I have yet to discuss whether this rescues a true asymmetry in God's providence between *all* good and *all* evil, but before I do, let me address a possible objection to this specific situation. I suppose that one could object that focusing in this way on God's action at the moment of sin in relative disregard to his prior involvement in the person's character-building is inappropriate (maybe even disingenuous) for Calvinists as they must maintain that God determined *both*, but this would be missing the point of the maneuver. The point was not to relieve God from his control of evil, whether in creating sinners or in providentially controlling their sins. On Calvinism, he clearly determines all these things. Whether or not that involves him improperly in evil as the "author of sin" or something like it is another discussion for another day. Rather, the aim of the present model is to explain why *in determining human actions*, there can be an asymmetry of divine action in his actualizing the evil and the good. This much is secured by the present model. Coming back to the above illustration of the bobsled, one can similarly appreciate that the sled was initially placed on the track by the very same persons who subsequently piloted it down the track. They are thoroughly causally responsible for its present sliding down the track, but it remains that their controlling action during the race exhibits the proper asymmetry and justifies permission language: when they refrain from hitting the brakes, they properly "permit" the sled to slide. The same goes for God on Calvinism who as a result of the fall ordained that humans would have corrupted natures, but regulates their evil, particularly on the moment of choice, by a justifiably asymmetrical control. He actively extends grace to prevent sin, or passively refrains to do so, allowing naturally sinful people to sin when his good purposes require it.

Now someone else might complain that my model rescues asymmetry in this specific case, but fails to apply to *all* cases of good and evil. Couldn't we imagine a case where the situation is reversed, replacing our burglar on the ladder by a fire fighter, this time climbing to risk his life and rescue a baby from the flames? In that case, a passer-by who refrains from kicking the ladder would be "permitting the good." Is it not a failure of my model to rescue the proper asymmetry between good and evil?

Let me make two responses. First, I don't know that I necessarily need to refute the charge. Maybe my model applies here too, and *sometimes* justifies also a use of permission language for the good. Even so, it successfully refutes our initial Arminian objection, which was that divine permission of evil was *never* justified on determinism. I need not show that *all* evil is only permitted in that way and that this understanding of permission is *never* applicable to the good. All I need to do is show that *some* situations feature a providential control of evil justifying a language of permission in a way that would not apply to the good *in that situation*. This much I have done.

But secondly, I think we could fine-tune my model to actually satisfy the objection. We could say that a language of permission is excluded if God needs to actively intervene *on the moment of choice* to produce a righteous choice, *or at any point in his past life, to produce the righteous character that would naturally lead to his choosing the good*. Since original sin has humans beginning life with a disposition toward evil, any subsequent sin is just an expression of this original inclination that needs no divine intervention. But conversely, any righteous deed is the result of a character that has been actively improved by God's direct, active intervention, whether at the moment of choice, or at any point before it. This qualification nicely rescues a full asymmetry for every single good action and every single evil one after the fall. In that sense, all evil is permitted, and all good is actively extended. I think this conceptual analysis nicely unfolds a philosophically loaded statement by John Calvin: "simply to will is the part of man, to will ill the part of corrupt nature, to will well the part of grace."[13]

All that is left to explain, now, is the first sin of Adam. Since he had not yet fallen, one cannot use original sin to explain *his* first inclination toward evil. Does this reveal a failure of my model? I think not. Without original sin, what I fail to provide is an uncontroversial *explanation* for Adam's first inclination toward evil, but the *fact* that he had such an inclination should not be controversial: how could he have sinned if he lacked even an inclination? Phrasing it in terms of counterfactuals (supposing with Molinists that there are such truths), it is either the case that Adam *would* sin in the biblical circumstances, or he *wouldn't* sin in those. And since he *did* sin, then it's obviously the case that he *would* sin if God didn't actively extend additional grace to prevent the fall. So I may not have an uncontroversial explanation for *how* that counterfactual came to be true, but given the uncontroversial *truth* of this counterfactual, my model can just assume it, and with it, successfully explain the asymmetry in Adam's choice: he *would* sin

13. Calvin, *Institutes*, 2.3.5.

if left to his own device, and God passively permitted it—whether or not it was determined.

A Few More Libertarian Complaints

With these concepts in place, a couple of statements and objections by libertarians can now be assessed. In his critique of determinism, William Lane Craig equates God's causal determination of sin with his "moving" the will of the sinner to do evil: "By contrast, in the Thomist/Reformed view, God causes the agent to sin by *moving his will to choose evil*, which makes the allegation that God is the author of sin difficult to deny."[14] In the relevant sense, this description of divine providential activity is inappropriate given the model offered above. On that view God determines all that comes to pass, yet given the truth of the active/passive counterfactual pair, God could be said to "move" the will toward the *good* only, working against the tide of sinful nature, but on the moment of sin cannot in that sense be said to "move the will of the sinner to do evil." To *sin*, a fallen human will needs no "moving" by God; it is what it *would* do naturally apart from a particular divine intervention with special grace.

Another criticism is offered by John Sanders, contending that "permission" requires the leaving open of *multiple options*.

> The use of the word *permission* is problematic in the no-risk model. According to specific sovereignty, everything that occurs is precisely what God meticulously controls to occur. In this case, the term *permission* seems to mean the following. Suppose God had a rat that he wanted to run through a maze. Suppose further that every time the rat began to go down a path that God did not intend it to go, God placed a gate in its way that did not "permit" him to go that way. Eventually, the rat goes in the direction in which God "permits," since other paths were closed. This, however, would be a tendentious use of the word *permission*.[15]

Of course I am less than cheerful about comparing humans to rats, and we are not told what the relevantly shared property would be between the rat in the maze and the human being whose free will is determined, but more importantly, we are not told what is wrong with the use of the word "permission" in that sense. It seems perfectly appropriate to say that by

---

14. Craig, "Response to Helseth," 57.
15. Sanders, *God Who Risks*, 265.

blocking roads God is "not permitting" the rat to escape and by opening one he is "permitting" the rat to escape. Sanders thinks that for permission to be meaningful, God *must* leave several roads categorically open (which he presumably takes to entail indeterminism). But why think that? While the concept of leaving multiple options is certainly allowed by the word, it is not an essential part of the concept of permission, or in any case it is not shown to be so. Furthermore, as I have already pointed out a few times by now, if permission is thus rescued merely by asserting that God leaves the choice open between good and evil, then God thereby "permits" evil in the same sense as he "permits" the good, and providential asymmetry is unacceptably sacrificed.

A final difficulty is pressed by Jerry Walls, who takes permission to mean that the one permitting should "prefer" that an alternate choice be made. He explains:

> The problem is that permission language does not make much sense on compatibilist premises. Typically, to say an action is permitted is imply [sic] that one is not controlling that action. For instance, parents may permit their children to make bad decisions that they would prefer them not to make.[16]

And because determinism entails that God specifically chooses and providentially actualizes every contingent state of affairs in the world, it would seem that God wouldn't prefer things to be any different. But the sense of "preferring" that is relevant for permission language is in fact compatible with determinism. Logically, when God brings about a state of affairs that contains evil, on Calvinism, it is because in the grand scheme of things, this state of affairs will produce a compensating, greater good—whatever that good is, Christians are rarely told, though sometimes they are. God simply assessed that it was preferable to actualize this state of affairs containing evil, for the sake of the compensating greater good that it entails. In that sense, it is perfectly appropriate to say that God "would prefer" this evil not occur, *if only that greater good could be obtained without the necessary evil leading to it*. But on Calvinist premises, it cannot. Therefore, God, preferring the overall greater state of affairs, actualizes one he would "other things being the same" prefer not to obtain, but which "all things considered" he *permits* for good reasons.

In the end, William Hasker concedes that the concepts are coherent, and he only insists on the boundaries that determinists must keep in mind:

---

16. Walls, "Why No Classical Theist," 91–92.

No doubt, in this view, God "permits" evil actions without actively assisting them in the way that he assists good actions through his gracious influence. Nevertheless, *the evil actions are the necessary consequences of causes that were deliberately created by God with full knowledge of what their results would be.* God's involvement may be less direct than in the case of good actions, but it is no less decisive.[17]

That is exactly the correct distinction that Calvinists must maintain: permission of evil is less active, but no less decisive. Of course Hasker finds it too weak, but he grants that it is coherent, which concedes the present point: Calvinists can (and I shall) coherently maintain an asymmetry between God's control of the good and his control of evil; more than merely in his attitude, it is an asymmetry in his very providence, whereby he actively brings about the good, and more passively "permits" evil, both of which still occur under his meticulous control.

Is Permission Language Indeed Called For, and For What Purpose?

The argument against determinism under discussion contends that permission language is: 1) required for Christians, and 2) unavailable to determinists. The above analysis has established that permission language was in fact compatible with determinism, but the first question remains: is it in fact called for? Calvinists might be tempted to dismiss this language altogether and, for all they care, might not miss it much. Who says we should affirm divine permission? My above description justifies its coherent use, but is it something Calvinists *should* embrace? While not obviously so, I think it is, if for no other reason because the Bible at times seems to employ such permission language to describe divine providence,[18] and some of the most

---

17. Hasker, *Providence*, 130.

18. Bruce Ware (*God's Greater Glory*, 106–7) surveys the biblical language of divine permission and lists the following: "Your father [Laban] has cheated me [Jacob] and changed my wages ten times. But *God did not permit him to harm me*" (Gen 31:7); "Whoever strikes a man so that he dies shall be put to death. But if he did not lie in wait for him, but *God let him fall into his hand*, then I will appoint for you a place to which he may flee" (Exod 21:12–13); "and they [the demons in the Gerasene demoniac] begged him, saying, 'Send us to the pigs; let us enter them.' *So he gave them permission.* And the unclean spirits came out, and entered the pigs" (Mark 5:12–13); "In past generations *he allowed all the nations to walk in their own ways*" (Acts 14:16); "And when they [Paul and Silas] had come up to Mysia, they attempted to go into Bithynia, but *the Spirit of Jesus did not allow them*" (Acts 16:7); "For I do not want to see you now just in passing. I hope to spend some time with you, *if the Lord permits*" (1 Cor 16:7); "And this we will

important Reformed theologians and Reformed confessions of faith seem to do so as well.[19]

So if it is coherent and found in the Bible and the Reformed tradition, Calvinists should want to make good use of it, but let me say a word about the proper place of such language. It ought not be a strict, universal requirement in how one ought to speak of all divine providence over evil. The Bible sometimes uses permission language, but at other times, it also does not shy away from using very direct, active language in describing divine involvement in evil.[20] That means that the one isn't supposed to exclude the other; rather, both are meant to describe true aspects of God's control of evil, namely on the one hand that he is in full control of it, and yet on the other hand, that he does not endorse it for its own sake and that his mode of action in bringing it about differs from that of his bringing about the good. That is all. Permission language is not a device to diminish divine control of evil or excuse God for his involvement in it. John Sanders mentions "permission" as an attempted way out of making God the author of evil on Calvinism.[21] I agree it is not a good strategy, and should not be employed in that way. In that sense, I fully concur with Leigh Vicens as well, when she objects that "the appeal to divine permission will not help the divine determinist in absolving God of causal responsibility for sin."[22] It will not, because it cannot, and indeed need not, do that for Calvinists. Permission language is not necessary for maintaining divine sinlessness, as long as one maintains God neither does evil nor is evil. These misplaced concerns are the reason why John Calvin himself was critical of the language (as non-Calvinists are keen to point out[23]). But as John Frame explains, Calvin's concern was with the idea of "*mere* permission" as an attempt to reduce the scope of divine providence.[24] With a different intent, Calvin saw a proper place for permission

---

do *if God permits*" (Heb 6:3).

19. R. C. Sproul mentions Augustine, Aquinas, Luther, Calvin, Zanchius, Turretin, Edwards, Hodge, Warfield, Bavinck, and Berkouwer, and offers the samples of the following confessions exhibiting the asymmetry in view, which he calls "positive/negative": *The Reformed Confession* (1536), *French Confession of Faith* (1559), *The Belgic Confession of Faith* (1561), *The Second Helvetic Confession* (1566), *The Westminster Confession of Faith* (1643) ("Double Predestination").

20. In making that very same point, Daniel Johnson lists Gen 50:20, Exod 4:21, Deut 2:30, and Josh 11:19–20 ("Calvinism and the Problem of Evil," 27–31).

21. Sanders, *God Who Risks*, 264.

22. Vicens, "Divine Determinism," 179.

23. "The notion of permission loses all significant meaning in a Calvinist framework. Therefore, it's not surprising that Calvin himself was suspicious of the idea and warned against using it" (Walls and Dongell, *Not a Calvinist*, 132).

24. "Reformed theologians have also used the term, but they have insisted that

language, if used only presumably to describe the asymmetrical realities I explained above. He quotes Augustine approvingly: "For it [sin] would not be done if He did not permit it, and permission is given not without but by His will."[25] This is indeed probably how Calvinists should relate to divine permission language: warn against its possible misuse, but use it coherently to express the proper notions of divine disapproval of sin and asymmetry in divine action, while maintaining meticulous divine providence in light of their Calvinist determinism.

Calvinists and Middle Knowledge

Finally, I should note that a handful of Calvinists before me have sought to employ God's knowledge of counterfactuals of free will (as understood in a compatibilist, determinist fashion) to explain (among other things) this asymmetry in divine providence over good and evil. My present model is very much indebted to their endeavor. Most notable among them are Bruce Ware[26] and Terrence Tiessen[27] (Bruce Ware also lists John Frame as using the concept if not the same terminology[28]). This Calvinist endeavor has been occasioned by a recent renewal of Christian interest in *Molinism*, the view of providence put forward by the counter-Reformer Jesuit Luis de Molina. Put very briefly,[29] the Molinist view posited that human free will is libertarian, but sought to maintain a high view of divine providence by claiming that God has knowledge (and makes good use) of all counterfactuals of freedom (understood as libertarian freedom). He posited that this divine knowledge of counterfactuals, being both *contingent* and yet *prevolitional for God*, was logically "located" between God's so-called "natural knowledge" of all possibilities (truths that are necessary and prevolitional for God), and his so-called "free knowledge" of actualities (truths that are contingent and post-volitional for God), and hence would be appropriately named "middle knowledge." Accordingly, the Calvinists in question have labelled their view "Calvinist middle knowledge." Their proposal has been met with

---

God's permission of sin is no less efficacious than his ordination of good. Calvin denies that there is any 'mere permission' in God" (Frame, *Doctrine of God*, 177).

25. Augustine, *Enchiridion*, ch. 100, quoted in Calvin, *Predestination*, 68.

26. See Ware, *God's Greater Glory*.

27. See Tiessen, "Why Calvinists Should Believe," 345–66 and Tiessen, *Providence and Prayer*.

28. Ware, "Robots, Royalty and Relationships," 200.

29. For a full exposition of the view, see Flint, *Divine Providence*.

opposition from both Calvinists[30] and Molinists,[31] who have questioned the coherence of affirming "middle knowledge" while rejecting the libertarian nature of free will that was essential to Molinism. John Laing has argued that if free will is not libertarian, God's knowledge of counterfactuals is no longer prevolitional, and hence is not in the middle of anything,[32] and will collapse into either God's natural knowledge or his free knowledge. Both Ware and Tiessen have come to affirm it as a subset of natural knowledge,[33] Ware maintaining that the label "middle" knowledge remains useful and justified,[34] while Tiessen gave it up to avoid confusion with Molinism. In the end, John Laing invited these theologians (short of adopting his own Molinist view) to see these counterfactuals as part of God's free knowledge instead.

For our present purposes, it is not necessary to arbitrate these debates. None of what I have argued above commits me to any controversial view on these questions. Should my view be called "Calvinist middle knowledge"? Should the counterfactuals of compatibilist free will I focused on be seen as a subset of God's natural knowledge or his free knowledge?[35] None of these questions matters for the proposal at hand. All I care to affirm is that God has knowledge of such counterfactuals—however one wants to call this body of knowledge—the truths of which justify an asymmetry in divine providence over good and evil, affording a proper use of "divine permission" language in the way I explained above. However one ultimately resolves the interesting debates sparked by "middle-knowledge Calvinists," my proposal stands and justifies asymmetry and divine permission, thereby refuting the argument at hand against Calvinism based upon the necessity of affirming divine permission of sin.

30. See Helm, "Classical Calvinist Doctrine of God," 47.

31. Laing, "Compatibility," 455–67.

32. Ibid., 467.

33. Ware: "Although it is a subset of God's natural knowledge, it is a useful subset!" ("Responses to Paul Helm," 74); Tiessen: "God's knowledge of counterfactuals is not different from his knowledge of possibilities; it is therefore part of his necessary knowledge."

34. Ware, "Responses to Helm," 74.

35. On that matter, following Thomas Flint and Luke Van Horn, I am personally convinced that it is mainly a matter of whether or not one includes God's concurrent activity in the "circumstances" of a counterfactual's antecedent. If one does, such counterfactuals will count as natural knowledge, and if one does not, they will count as free knowledge. See Flint, "Two Accounts," 166–67 and Van Horn, "Incorporating," 818–19.

Conclusion: Divine Permission
for Molinists and Calvinists

In conclusion, let me summarize what I have argued.

First, I argued that a language of divine permission is *not* properly anchored on libertarianism, because mere indeterminism fails to account for asymmetry in divine providence over good and evil; and secondly, I have argued that a language of divine permission *is* properly anchored on the truth of those pairs of active and passive counterfactuals about what would or would not happen, if God were or were not to intervene by extending grace on the moment of choice (or before it).

Given this, divine permission is justified, not by libertarianism, but rather by the truth of those counterfactuals. My model is thus available to Calvinists who focus on the helpfulness of counterfactuals as I have just done (whether or not they decide to call this body of truth "Calvinist middle knowledge"), but it is also perfectly suited to Molinists, who, though they are libertarian, affirm divine middle knowledge of exactly those kinds of counterfactuals. *These* should be their foundation as well, for affirming divine permission and asymmetry in divine providence.

We can therefore see my present argument as having stolen from all libertarians the toy of divine permission language, only to return it to Molinists, as long as they can play nice and share it with their Calvinist friends.

Bibliography

Calvin, John. *Concerning the Eternal Predestination of God.* Louisville: Westminster John Knox, 1997.

———. *Institutes of the Christian Religion.* Translated by Henry Beveridge. Peabody, MA: Hendrickson, 2008.

Craig, William Lane. *The Only Wise God: The Compatibility of Divine Foreknowledge and Human Freedom.* Reprint, Eugene, OR: Wipf and Stock, 2000.

———. "Response to Paul Kjoss Helseth." In *Four Views on Divine Providence*, edited by Dennis W. Jowers, 53–62. Grand Rapids: Zondervan, 2011.

Edwards, Jonathan. *Freedom of the Will.* New York: Cosimo Classics, 2007.

Flint, Thomas P. *Divine Providence: The Molinist Account.* Ithaca, NY: Cornell University Press, 1998.

———. "Two Accounts of Providence." In *Divine and Human Action: Essays in the Metaphysics of Theism*, edited by Thomas V. Morris, 147–81. Ithaca, NY: Cornell University Press, 1988.

Frame, John M. *The Doctrine of God.* Phillipsburg, NJ: Presbyterian & Reformed, 2002.

Hasker, William. *Providence, Evil and the Openness of God.* New York: Routledge, 2004.

Helm, Paul. "Classical Calvinist Doctrine of God." In *Perspectives on the Doctrine of God*, edited by Bruce A. Ware, 5–52. Nashville: Broadman & Holman, 2008.

Johnson, Daniel M. "Calvinism and the Problem of Evil: A Map of the Territory." In *Calvinism and the Problem of Evil*, edited by David E. Alexander and Daniel M. Johnson, 19–55. Eugene, OR: Wipf & Stock, 2016.

Keathley, Kenneth. *Salvation and Sovereignty: A Molinist Approach*. Nashville: B & H Academic, 2010.

Kenny, Anthony. *The God of the Philosophers*. Oxford: Clarendon, 1979.

Laing, John D. "The Compatibility of Calvinism and Middle Knowledge." *Journal of the Evangelical Theological Society* 47.3 (2004) 455–67.

Luther, Martin. *The Bondage of the Will*. Translated by J. I. Packer and O. R. Johnston. Grand Rapids: Revell, 2009.

OED Online. Oxford: Oxford University Press, 2013. http://www.oed.com/view/Entry/141214/.

Olson, Roger E. *Against Calvinism*. Grand Rapids: Zondervan, 2011.

———. *Arminian Theology: Myths and Realities*. Downers Grove, IL: InterVarsity, 2006.

Sanders, John. *The God Who Risks: A Theology of Divine Providence*. 2nd ed. Downers Grove, IL: InterVarsity, 2007.

Sproul, R. C. "Double Predestination." Available at: http://www.ligonier.org/learn/articles/double-predestination.

Tiessen, Terrance L. *Providence and Prayer: How Does God Work in the World?* Downers Grove, IL: InterVarsity, 2000.

———. "Why Calvinists Should Believe in Divine Middle Knowledge, Although They Reject Molinism." *Westminster Theological Journal* 69.2 (2007) 345–66.

Walls, Jerry L. "Why No Classical Theist, Let Alone Orthodox Christian, Should Ever Be a Compatibilist." *Philosophia Christi* 13.1 (2011) 75–104.

Walls, Jerry L., and , Joseph R. Dongell. *Why I Am Not a Calvinist*. Downers Grove, IL: InterVarsity, 2004.

Van Horn, Luke. "On Incorporating Middle Knowledge into Calvinism: A Theological/Metaphysical Muddle?" *Journal of the Evangelical Theological Society* 55.4 (2012) 807–27.

Vicens, Leigh C. "Divine Determinism: A Critical Consideration." Ph.D. diss.: University of Wisconsin-Madison, 2012.

Ware, Bruce A. *God's Greater Glory: The Exalted God of Scripture and the Christian Faith*. Wheaton, IL: Crossway, 2004.

———. "Responses to Paul Helm." In *Perspectives on the Doctrine of God*, edited by Bruce A. Ware, 53–75. Nashville: Broadman & Holman, 2008.

———. "Robots, Royalty and Relationships? Toward a Clarified Understanding of Real Human Relations with the God Who Knows and Decrees All That Is." *Criswell Theological Review* 1.2 (2004) 191–203.

Wesley, John. *The Works of John Wesley*. 7 vols. Edited by Albert C. Outler. Nashville: Abingdon, 1986.

14

Calvinism vs. Molinism

Paul Helm and
William Lane Craig

Editors' Note: *This chapter is a transcript of a conversation hosted by "Unbelievable?" with Justin Brierley (Premier Christian Radio) on January 4, 2014. The transcript (which omits commercial announcements and edits contractions) was produced by Reasonable Faith and is used with permission. The original conversation is available at:* https://www.premierchristianradio.com/Shows/Saturday/Unbelievable/Episodes/Calvinism-vs-Molinism-William-Lane-Craig-Paul-Helm-Unbelievable.

JUSTIN BRIERLEY: Welcome along and today a fascinating discussion for you as we ask two views of divine sovereignty: Calvinism and Molinism are debated on the show today. Does God preordain the future including people's eternal salvation? Well, that's certainly a way of looking at Calvinism; if that's true it raises the question as to whether people have free will.

We're going to be exploring an alternative view today, as well, called Molinism. And two leaders in the field who join me on the program today. I'm so pleased to welcome into the studio William Lane Craig—well known as a Christian philosopher and theologian. He's an author and speaker [and] debated many leading atheists around the world. We recently had him on reviewing his debates with Lawrence Krauss in Australia, and Bill's the founder of Reasonable Faith.

Paul Helm is a leading Calvinist scholar and theologian. He's a teaching fellow at Regent College, Vancouver and he's defending the historic Calvinist view today. So, welcome gentlemen, both, to the program.

Well, let's introduce you in turn. Many listeners, Bill, are very familiar with your name. You've been on the show a number of times and of course well known in the world of apologetics. Perhaps, though, less well known is the fact that you are, effectively, a leading champion of what's called Molinism— a particular view of divine sovereignty, and many people may be unfamiliar with the concept altogether. We're going to have you explain that but just for the record we're recording this while you're over in the UK talking at a C. S. Lewis Symposium—around the fiftieth anniversary of Lewis' death. Has Lewis had a big impact on your life apologetically speaking?

WILLIAM LANE CRAIG: I would say that Lewis as a model for doing Christian apologetics has had a great impact on my life—less so as a thinker, however, I would say in all candor. For me, Lewis serves as a model of the Christian apologist in being willing to resist cultural currents that go contrary to Christianity, to have boldness to march to the beat of a different drummer. I think he's a model, as well, in the importance of producing a body of published work that can outlive oneself. The legacy of C. S. Lewis are these published works that have reached far, far more people for Christ since his death than he ever reached during his life. I think in that sense he's a real model for us today, and in his defense of what he called "mere Christianity" as opposed to the fine points of doctrine—I think that's a model. So, in one sense the discussion that we're having today goes beyond what Lewis' apologetics would have involved, which was just a mere Christianity.

JUSTIN BRIERLEY: [. . .] Let me introduce Paul. Paul, thank you for joining me on the program today. When did your interest in Calvin begin? Do you want to take us back to how it all started for you?

PAUL HELM: Well, it's inseparable from my childhood and my upbringing, really—an interest. But a scholarly interest, that's something that's developed more recently. I wrote a book in 1982, a small book on Calvin and the Calvinists, but more recently I've written fuller books on the way in which philosophical ideas have impacted on Calvin, and I'm more or less finished with that now. I think I've said everything I want to say in this area.

JUSTIN BRIERLEY: If you said everything you wanted to say, at the end of all those studies, how have you come to view the issue of God's sovereignty?

If you could put it in a nutshell, what is your view of the way God acts and predestines in the world today?

PAUL HELM: Well, it's a strong view of divine sovereignty. When the apostle Peter spoke of the death of Jesus he talked about it being by the determinate counsel and foreknowledge of God. Calvinists, or Augustinians, or a Pauline thinker will think not only of the death of Jesus being predestined but of all events being in the hand of God. That doesn't mean to say that God determines these acts in the way in which you and I are determined. Nonetheless, he's in control and in control, perhaps, in ways that we can't fully grasp or fully understand.

JUSTIN BRIERLEY: Calvin himself didn't just write on predestination; though that's often the thing people associate him with. How important would you say is his legacy, generally?

PAUL HELM: I think it's very important, but you are correct in saying that he is not a sort of one-theme theologian. He's a catholic (small "c") theologian and predestination is one of those elements as it is for Aquinas or for Anselm or for Augustine—the three A's. These are all predestinarians every bit as much, I believe, as Calvin was. So, in a sense, he inherited a tradition and he certainly lived with it and ran with it but he didn't invent predestination nor did he give it any particular twist of his own, in my view.

JUSTIN BRIERLEY: There is, these days, what's sometimes been termed a neo-Calvinist sort of stream—new Calvinist stream—within the churches where people are championing, even among young fashionable pastors—Calvin's doctrines and so on. Do you welcome that? Do you think that's a positive thing?

PAUL HELM: Yes, I think it is! I think that the term Calvinism can be used in a broader and narrower sense. It can be used, of course, to incorporate not simply his theology but also his ecclesiology. But you can narrow it to what he has to say about matters to do with Christian salvation and it's *that*, I think, that these people have taken an interest in recently.

JUSTIN BRIERLEY: Bill, coming back to you—Molinism. Now this may be a term that many people are not familiar with. Would you like to explain what it is and how you came to arrive at the decision that you are a Molinist?

WILLIAM LANE CRAIG: Yes! Molinism derives its name from Luis de Molina who was a sixteenth century Jesuit counter-Reformer. Unfortunately, Molina thought the central point of the Protestant Reformation was the denial of human libertarian freedom in favor of God's being the all-determining reality. And so what Molina was constrained to do was to offer an alternative to Luther and Calvin that would affirm the same sort of sovereign divine control that Paul spoke of a moment ago but without denying libertarian freedom. The view that Molina enunciated came to be called Molinism after his name. It eventually entered into Protestant theology through Jacob Arminius, and there is a kind of bastardized Molinism that goes under the name Arminianism today, though it usually is somewhat different from what Molina said.

JUSTIN BRIERLEY: So you wouldn't describe yourself as an Arminian in that sense?

WILLIAM LANE CRAIG: Well, I would in the proper sense but these names or labels can be very misleading and therefore it's very important that we define what we mean when we call ourselves a Calvinist or a Molinist or an Arminian.

JUSTIN BRIERLEY: Now, before you lay out the Molinist view, I'm sure you'd affirm lots of other aspects of what those Calvinists and Reformers were doing.

WILLIAM LANE CRAIG: Yes! In fact as Paul spoke a moment ago I thought, "I believe everything he just said!" which would make me a Calvinist. The Molinist has this very, very strong sense of divine sovereignty and meticulous providence. Molina said, "Not a leaf falls from the tree but that it does so either by God's will or permission." And if he were living today I think he'd say that the tiniest motion of a sub-atomic particle cannot occur but without God's direct will or permission. So, this is a very strong view of divine sovereignty and control.

JUSTIN BRIERLEY: You recently contributed to a book on four views of divine providence and divine sovereignty and there are other views out there—we're not representing everything that is in the public sphere at the moment. For instance, there's been a lot of debate over open theism—like Greg Boyd.

WILLIAM LANE CRAIG: Right, and I think Paul and I would be united in rejecting that sort of revisionist view.

JUSTIN BRIERLEY: Quite, but I think that's another debate perhaps for another time. But today we're looking at, specifically, the distinctives between Calvinism and Molinism. So, Bill, as simply as you can for the likes of me, as much as anyone else, can you explain how Molinism, as it were, reconciles human free will and God's foreknowledge?

WILLIAM LANE CRAIG: Yes. The key to understanding Molinism is Molina's doctrine of what he called middle knowledge. This is God's knowledge of everything that *would* happen under various circumstances, and he called it middle knowledge because it's in between, so to speak, God's natural knowledge, which is his knowledge of everything that *could* happen, and his free knowledge, which is his knowledge of everything that *will* happen. So, in between everything that could happen and everything that will happen is everything that would happen under different circumstances. The doctrine of middle knowledge says that God knows what you would have freely done if you had been in the apostle Peter's shoes. He knows whether you would have denied Christ three times or whether you would have been faithful or what. And so the key to Molina's doctrine of providence is that by means of his middle knowledge God knows what free agents would freely do in any set of freedom-permitting circumstances that God might put them in. So, by creating those circumstances and putting the agents in them, God then, so to speak, takes hands off and he lets the agent freely choose how he wants but he knows how that agent *would* choose if in those circumstances.

JUSTIN BRIERLEY: How they will use their free will . . .

WILLIAM LANE CRAIG: Well, more than how he *will* use it! Remember that's free knowledge. It's how he *would* use it if he *were* in those circumstances. And so then by creating the circumstances and putting the agent in it God's free knowledge falls out automatically. Then he knows how he will act and can control human history.

JUSTIN BRIERLEY: Okay. Now how does this then apply to, for instance, the issue of salvation? How does God then organize the world with this doctrine of middle knowledge in mind?

WILLIAM LANE CRAIG: For Molina, divine election to salvation is simply that aspect of divine providence that relates to salvation. And so what he would say is that the circumstances in which God puts a person include various gifts of divine grace, various solicitations of the Holy Spirit, and God knows how you would respond, for example, to the gospel if you were born and raised under such and such circumstances or you were to hear the gospel preached in such and such a way. And so by putting people in various circumstances God can elect certain persons to salvation without abridging their free will.

JUSTIN BRIERLEY: Okay, and so in that instance then do you believe that God has ordered the world in such a way that the maximum number of people who *would* believe and accept his salvation will do so?

WILLIAM LANE CRAIG: That's not part of Molina's doctrine, Justin. Molina said that God is free to choose whatever sort of world he wants with whomever he wants to be saved. Again, it's a very strong view of sovereignty. My *own* inclination is to think that God does want as many people to be saved as possible and therefore he would try to create people in circumstances which would be conducive to the greatest number being saved and the least number being lost, consistent with human freedom. But that's an idiosyncrasy of my own view. That's not Molina's view.

JUSTIN BRIERLEY: It's fascinating and it is a bit difficult to get your head around. It is a little bit more of having to think through those concepts. Perhaps explaining why it isn't, in a sense, as widely accessed by the general Christian population . . . Do you feel that it is becoming a more mainstream view that is gaining acceptance?

WILLIAM LANE CRAIG: I think that it's definitely got momentum on its side. When you look at the debate over divine providence it's very interesting that the Calvinists now, some of them I mean, are talking about a Molinistic-Calvinism. Some of the Arminians are talking about open theism that affirms God's middle knowledge of counterfactuals of freedom. So the extremes are being sucked, I think, towards the center of gravity in the middle, which is Molinism. Dean Zimmerman who is a prominent Christian philosopher recently said "that of the plethora of views available on divine providence Molinism probably has the largest percentage of Christian philosophers who would support it."

JUSTIN BRIERLEY: Paul, okay, you're very familiar with the Molinist view. Why has it not convinced you?

PAUL HELM: For a number of reasons, one is that I think that it's an unnecessary theory. What is done by God's natural knowledge and his free knowledge—what those terms cover—covers all that William Craig wants to apply to middle knowledge. So, it's unnecessarily complicated. But that's because for theological reasons. In Calvinism there's a stronger view of sin and the way in which it binds the will such that God's grace cannot only be offered to man, it has to be imparted to them for these men and women to become reborn and to become liberated from their sin. What Molinism does is to postulate, in common with the multitude of other views available, postulates a very strong sense of human freedom and God must respect that sense of human freedom in the way that Bill has been describing. One question is, do they have that freedom and, if they do have that freedom in the strong sense, how can God know it in advance? Bill seems to think that, "Well, God knows it in advance in the sense that he's got this sort of movie of it and reality will run in accordance exactly with the movie he's got, as it were, in his head." But if these people are free and free in the strong sense that Bill indicates, then how can God know that they will act in these circumstances?

JUSTIN BRIERLEY: Do you believe that in some sense Molinism collapses into a form of Calvinism?

PAUL HELM: Well, I think it collapses into a form of Arminianism. Arminianism is the view that God's foreknowledge is compatible with this strong sense of human freedom and Bill's view is that, with of course the Molinist's twists to it. It boils down to a kind of Arminianism.

JUSTIN BRIERLEY: Because if creatures are truly free, as far as you're concerned, that means God cannot know what they will choose.

PAUL HELM: Well, we've got different senses of freedom at work here, right? A Calvinist will affirm that human beings are frequently free.

JUSTIN BRIERLEY: So what kind of freedom do you affirm?

PAUL HELM: The sort of freedom that you've got as you're speaking to me now. Responding to remarks that I've made, responding to the situation that we're in, doing so in an uncoerced way. These are, as it were, cases of freedom for the Calvinist, typically. Of course, people can be coerced but the strange view of freedom that people have wills such that in exactly the same situation they're in now they could have, as it were, chosen differently in precisely that situation—this the Calvinist thinks is an unacceptably strong or an unbiblically strong sense of freedom, and one ought not, as it were, allow one's theology to orb around this view of freedom.

JUSTIN BRIERLEY: Does that cohere with the way you understand a Calvinist might view freedom, Bill?

WILLIAM LANE CRAIG: Yes, I think that Paul has correctly delineated the differences. One major difference would be with regard to your doctrine of grace. For the Calvinist grace is irresistible. For the Molinist grace is not irresistible, it becomes efficacious only when it meets with an affirmative response from the human agent. Another difference would be that the notion of freedom—I do think that a person in identical circumstances could choose one way or another. And I think that is biblical. You know the verse in Scripture when it says that in any situation in which we are tempted God will provide a way of escape so that we will be able to endure it. Now what that means is that in any situation in which a person succumbs to temptation and gives in, it was possible for him to take the way of escape and to endure it. So I think that teaches that in those circumstances, sin, temptation, or falling into temptation isn't inevitable. That person could have taken the way of escape. So I think that this doctrine of freedom is consistent biblically.

JUSTIN BRIERLEY: Now, Paul's criticism here, though, is that you described it as being like a movie playing out.

PAUL HELM: That's right. My worry at this point is that if God knows what would happen in these circumstances where Jones had the freedom we've just been talking about, why isn't Jones free to actually exercise that freedom when it comes to pass?

WILLIAM LANE CRAIG: Well, isn't it just what I said a moment ago? In identical circumstances a person has the ability to choose A or not-A. It seems to me that is what Scripture affirms, and I don't see any reason to think that that's not true. That makes us responsible for sin because we freely choose sin. So, given that it doesn't seem to me that Molinism is deterministic. It's at the heart of this view that by his middle knowledge God knows how people *would* freely choose in these circumstances and he doesn't make them choose that way and the circumstances are not deterministic. They're freedom permitting. He just *knows* how they would choose.

PAUL HELM: But how can he know them if in the actual circumstances the people have this very strong view of freedom to choose alternatively in a given set of circumstances? Why can't they go off in the other direction?

JUSTIN BRIERLEY: Why couldn't they go off script in that sense?

WILLIAM LANE CRAIG: Well, they *could.*

PAUL HELM: So, there's a world in which they do! And you have a problem, I think; Bill has a problem at this point just as Arminians have a problem with divine foreknowledge and human freedom. He can say, "Well, God just does" and we'd have to accept his word for it. God just does. But there's a mystery there.

WILLIAM LANE CRAIG: Well, if I might address that issue—how does God know how free agents would act in any circumstances? I think it's because there are these subjunctive hypothetical propositions which are true or false. These are *if-then* statements in the subjunctive mood—grammatically. Like, "If I were rich, I would buy a Mercedes." Now, I may not be rich and so I don't buy one but that's a subjunctive conditional, and I think we use these *all the time* in planning.

If I were to ask the boss for a raise he'd tear my head off! If I were to pull out into traffic now I would make it. If we were to send the army around the left flank we would prevail. These kinds of subjunctive conditionals are inherent to rational planning and activity and more importantly, I think, Justin, just for our purposes today, the Scripture is full of these kinds of subjunctive conditional statements. So, anybody who believes in verbal plenary inspiration has to affirm that these are true or false. Now, let me just give one example. In 2 Corinthians 2:8: Paul says, "If the rulers of this world had understood this they *would not* have crucified the Lord of glory." Now that is a subjunctive conditional that I think, as Christians, we want to say is true. And if that's true then God must know it because God is omniscient and he knows all true propositions.

JUSTIN BRIERLEY: Let's come back to that because obviously Paul gave another verse, which he believes suggested the opposite. You started off with that verse about Jesus' crucifixion being foreordained, foreknowledge, and so on. So, we've obviously got verses that could be applied in both directions here, haven't we?

PAUL HELM: I'm not denying, no one would deny, that there are such things as subjunctive conditionals. As Bill said, the world is filled with subjunctive conditionals—things we might have done, things we would have done, . . . , and so on. The question, however, is how is it to be interpreted and what gives them their truth value? Is that truth value dependent upon this very strong sense of freedom that Bill espouses? That's what makes the difficulty for a Calvinist. If they're *so free* how does God know that what they're going to do, or what he thinks they're going to do, at some time in eternity or some time in the past, will actually take place? Why doesn't he have the power to choose the alternative and indeed exercise that power on occasions?

JUSTIN BRIERLEY: For you, [Bill], as I've said, this reconciles the issue of human freedom and God's foreknowledge . . .

WILLIAM LANE CRAIG: And foreordination! I want to make it clear, Justin, lest I be misunderstood. I think God does preordain everything. Molinism has a strong sense of sovereignty. You can't deny, biblically, preordination. It's in the New Testament—προορίζω (*proorizo*). God has foreordained, but the Molinist perspective is that his foreordaining things takes account of human freedom and what he ordains and therefore his foreordination doesn't annihilate human freedom. I wouldn't want folks to think I don't believe in foreordination.

JUSTIN BRIERLEY: Sure. And for you that presents a problem because the issue concerns whether God is the author of evil, for instance, whether human sin is something that is chosen by us or we're not actually ultimately responsible. These are the big problems that Calvinism, for you, throws up. Is that correct, Bill?

WILLIAM LANE CRAIG: Yes, I think that's right. And, particularly for me, an anguishing difficulty would be that I take, at face value, the passages in the New Testament about the universal salvific will of God. That is to say, that God *really does* want all persons to be saved and come to a knowledge of the truth, as Paul [the Apostle] says (cf. Acts 17:26–8). I think that if we take these passages at face value it either leads to universalism, which we know isn't true, or it means there is something that impedes God's perfect will being done because all persons aren't saved—and that seems to me to be human freedom. God will not coerce or overpower someone in order to save them. He will respect their freedom of choice as an individual and some persons freely choose to separate themselves from God forever despite his will that they be saved and his every effort to save them.

JUSTIN BRIERLEY: Feel free to chip in at this point, Paul. What's your response to the way that Bill sees salvation and people's free choice?

PAUL HELM: One thing, a multitude of people don't have the opportunity to hear the gospel. It isn't as if the gospel sounds to everybody and each person has an opportunity, in a kind of clear headed and deliberate way, to say yea or nay. That isn't our world. Our world is one in which there are millions of people who have never heard of Christ. So I don't see that description, as it were, to begin with. And the other is, of course, the Calvinist (equally with Bill) wants to affirm the wickedness of people under certain circumstances. It is by wicked men that Jesus was crucified, as Peter says. He didn't say, "Oh, well! Because God has foreordained this, these people were not wicked." He holds together both the foreordination of God and the wickedness of people.

JUSTIN BRIERLEY: Can it be wicked if the person, as it were, didn't ultimately choose? It was actually something that they were always going to do because God had foreordained it.

PAUL HELM: Well, *they were the choosers.* It was not God who chose that in the sense in which the wicked men chose it. Bill uses the phrase, you use the phrase, I think, that God's the author of sin and I've never really been able to understand what that phrase means. Does it mean that God is a sinner? Does it mean that God has somehow the malevolent wishes of a sinner? That he's somehow selfish in some way which is despicable? I don't understand what the phrase means to begin with. So I don't see there's a charge, as it were, to be resisted at that particular point.

WILLIAM LANE CRAIG: Let me respond, first, to the problem of the geographical expanse of the gospel over the twenty centuries of Christian movement. It seems to me that here middle knowledge and Molinism provides a very attractive understanding of this. Namely that God has so providentially ordered the world that persons who would respond to the gospel if they heard it are born at times and place at which they do hear it. So that those who fail to hear it are only persons who wouldn't have responded to it even if they had heard it. And thus no one is lost because of historical or geographical accident. And I find that this view is very biblical because in chapter seventeen of the book of Acts, Paul says that from one man God made every nation of men, that they should inhabit the face of the whole earth, and he determined the exact times and places that they should live. He did this that men might seek after God and reach out for him and find him because he is not far from every one of us. For in him, we live and move and have our being (cf. Acts 17:26–28).

That, to me, is consonant with a Molinist perspective. By contrast, on the Calvinist view, you have to say that God has just elected—for most of Christian history—so far people living in Western Europe or the United States and just overlooked the rest of these folks. So I find Molinism, again, to provide an answer to this question that is difficult for all of us as Christians.

JUSTIN BRIERLEY: And now, the second point that was raised there . . . about God being the author of evil or sin or whatever.

WILLIAM LANE CRAIG: That, I think, depends on how the Calvinist explains divine providence. Many Calvinists that I have spoken with understand divine providence and sovereignty to mean that God *causally* determines everything that happens. And that's why it all unfolds the way he wants to because *he is* the one who causally moves the will this way or that. If that's the case that means that God moves some people to sin and that would make him the author of sin both in the sense that the reason the person wills to sin is because God is the one who moved his will to do that. He's like the puppeteer who pulls the strings on the puppet's arms to make him do what he wants. But it would also impugn or make God the author of sin in a more profound sense in that it would seem terribly, morally wrong to do that. To move another person to sin and then to hold that person morally responsible for that—that seems to impugn the goodness of God.

PAUL HELM: Well, to start with what Bill began starting with I think is bread and butter for the Calvinist—that God has determined the nations and the ways in which the nations develop, and the culture of those nations, and so on. That's a very strong statement to divine sovereignty, it seems to me in Acts there.

JUSTIN BRIERLEY: Bill, though, just to stay on that issue, is saying that the problem is that it seems terribly unfair on a Calvinist view of that inasmuch as these people had no . . .

PAUL HELM: Yes, but you see I personally reject any kind of human analogy between the divine relationship to his creation, and that of a puppeteer or a programmer. These are all, as it were, creature to creature relationships. But I presume that the infinite God has resources at his disposal that are, as it were, beyond the resources that human beings have at their disposal at this particular point. And, of course, Calvinists have always made a distinction between God's relationship to evil and his relationship to good. He permits evil. It's under his control but he permits it.

JUSTIN BRIERLEY: But if, as Bill suggests, God is literally causing people to do wrong things—evil things—does God then not become, as it were, the author of evil in that sense? In what sense is it just permitting if God is the one who has caused it?

PAUL HELM: Because he's nonetheless respecting the wills of people who act their agency so that when I tie my shoelace it isn't God who's tying my shoelace, it's me tying my shoelace. I have sets of beliefs and situations in life which is not that of God but is my own set of circumstances. No doubt given to me by God but not his—mine nonetheless.

WILLIAM LANE CRAIG: I want to affirm what Paul says about "God has resources for providentially ordering the world that go beyond puppetry and causal determinism." But what I want to know is why couldn't that resource be middle knowledge? Middle knowledge will do the trick. And so I find that when I read the *Westminster Confession* I resonate with virtually everything that's in it except for one clause. There's one clause that says God's providence is not based upon how he knew people *would* respond and so it's clearly an anti-Molinist . . .

PAUL HELM: Bill couldn't subscribe to the very strong statements of the *Westminster Confession* on the bondage of the will to sin. There's a stronger doctrine of grace in that *Confession*. . . . I don't have it committed to memory but it's there.

JUSTIN BRIERLEY: You've raised this already—this strong bondage to sin that the Bible speaks of that is confirmed in the *Confession*. Is that a problem for you, Bill?

WILLIAM LANE CRAIG: Well, I don't think it is because I, with I think virtually all Christians who aren't Pelagians, will affirm the need for prevenient grace. Natural man does not seek the things that are of the Spirit of God, they're foolishness to him. So, no one apart from God's initiative would ever come to God and I think that is the bondage of the will of which Paul speaks. We're lost in sin and therefore it needs to be God's prevenient grace that reaches out and begins to draw people through the convicting power of the Holy Spirit to himself. But the difference would be, again, that whereas the Calvinist sees that calling and drawing as irresistible, I would want to say that at some point along the line that it is resistible. As Stephen said to the Jewish persecutors of his day, "You hard-necked people! You always resist the Holy Spirit!" (cf. Acts 7:51)

JUSTIN BRIERLEY: Now, in that sense, those hard-necked people doing the resisting, that is in some sense ordained by God that they would resist.

PAUL HELM: Yes. He leaves them to their own sinful devices or their own sinful desires. That's the way I understand it. But you see, there is more to grace than the prevenience of it. It's rather like a kiss of life. The grace of God coming to us all is like a kiss of life or it's like the dragging of a person who can't help themselves out of an icy pond that they've gotten into trouble. In other words, it's a monergistic, unilateral activity on the part of God.

JUSTIN BRIERLEY: And does Bill's view, the Molinistic view, undermine that in some way, inasmuch as it takes away something of the all-pervasiveness of God's grace if humans have a hand in their own salvation, inasmuch as they freely choose?

PAUL HELM: Yes, for me it does. It goes some way, of course, but it doesn't go, for the Calvinist, all the way that they think the Scriptures require of us. Many are called. That is, there is, of course, a universal call of the gospel but few are chosen. This choice is this irresistibility that Bill has mentioned but that he does not want to go so far as simply talking in terms of God's encouragement of people, and of his prompting of people. But there's more to it, I think, than that.

WILLIAM LANE CRAIG: Well, I would strongly reject the charge that Molinism or Arminianism leads to some kind of synergism where we are partly to credit for our salvation. When Paul says, in Ephesians 2.8, that by grace you have been saved through faith and this is not your own doing; it is the gift of God, lest anyone should boast. The word *this* is in the neuter gender in Greek. Faith is feminine. So he's not referring to faith as the gift of God; rather, commentators will say that it is the whole process of salvation by grace through faith, which is the gift of God. And nowhere does Scripture speak of faith as a work which we perform which merits salvation. Over and over again Paul opposes faith to works. Faith and works are opposite to each other. I think that one of the mistakes Calvinists make is thinking that if we exercise faith in God we have somehow performed a work. That's a very non-Pauline point of view.

PAUL HELM: I haven't said anything about a work but you're causally contributing, nonetheless, to your salvation. It may not be something that is praiseworthy or meritorious in some kind of medieval sense, but nonetheless without the contribution of this strong sense of freedom you will not receive the grace of God effectively.

WILLIAM LANE CRAIG: Right, and I would affirm that.

JUSTIN BRIERLEY: But for you that doesn't undermine the idea that it's all God's initiative?

WILLIAM LANE CRAIG: Right, because it's not meritorious.

JUSTIN BRIERLEY: In the same way that you can receive a gift from someone, you don't, as it were, do anything to receive that gift; you just open yourself up to having it.

WILLIAM LANE CRAIG: Yes, it's the passive acceptance of what someone else has done on your behalf.

PAUL HELM: Another question is, what energizes that passive acceptance? What energizes the response of faith? Is it the person himself with Bill's very strong sense of libertarian freedom doing something of which he can give and then withdraw, give and then withdraw, as it were, that there can be no irresistibility about it? It can be an in-out, in-out business. Tuesday and Wednesday I could be a Christian. Thursday and Friday not—then Tuesday and Wednesday he can be a Christian again. Open to his faith to do that. That, I think . . .

JUSTIN BRIERLEY: Yes, does it present a problem with this sort of "once saved, always saved?"

WILLIAM LANE CRAIG: Now that's an additional issue to talk about and here I think that persons who affirm freedom would probably differ on whether or not a regenerate person can apostatize and lose salvation. There is the doctrine that when we are regenerated by God we're indwelt with the Holy Spirit and sealed by the Holy Spirit for salvation. So I think that there's a diversity of perspectives.

JUSTIN BRIERLEY: Well, let's perhaps not chase that rabbit trail. That perhaps is beyond the realm of this program. Let's go to a typical [Calvinist] passage . . . Romans 8 is often used by Calvinists as a typical example of predestination, election of a certain people to salvation and so on. Paul, do you want to just explain?

PAUL HELM: I think you're thinking about what's sometimes called the golden chain in Romans 8: whom he did foreknow then he did predestinate, whom he predestinated then he also called, whom he called then he also justified. What should we say to these things? If God is for us who shall be against us? (cf. Rom 8:29–31) And so on in that chapter. . . . That chain, of course, is a staple for the Calvinist, certainly.

JUSTIN BRIERLEY: So, we do have here a tricky text for the Molinist, Bill. It appears that God fully . . .

WILLIAM LANE CRAIG: Well, the first link in the chain is foreknowledge, right? Προγινώσκω (*Proginosko*), whom he foreknew. And if that encompasses middle knowledge then there's just no problem and I would say the same about the text from Acts 4 that Paul quoted at the beginning of the program where the church at prayer says to God, "Truly in this city there were gathered together against thy holy servant Jesus, Herod and Pilate and all the people, to do exactly as thy will and thy plan had foreordained" (cf. Acts 4:27–8). This is according to God's foreknowledge. He knew what Herod would do if king. He knew what Pilate would do if prefect in first century Palestine. He knew that the people would call for the release of Barabbas rather than Jesus. So all of this unfolds according to God's plan, according to his foreknowledge.

JUSTIN BRIERLEY: But they are free within that plan?

WILLIAM LANE CRAIG: Right, because it's based upon how he knew they *would* freely act if placed in those circumstances.

JUSTIN BRIERLEY: Now, I suppose a question that occurs to me is, "Well, is that not just Calvinism at one removed?" Because it's still going to happen.

WILLIAM LANE CRAIG: This is what open theists will say because it has such a strong affirmation of divine sovereignty, but I take that to be a good thing, a biblical thing. But the huge difference is, as I've said before, on this view grace isn't irresistible, the person really can do differently in those circumstances if he wants to, it's just that he can't escape God knowing how he would freely choose. But God takes hands off and says, "All right, it's up to you. Do what you want."

JUSTIN BRIERLEY: [Addressing Paul Helm] You are shaking your head.

PAUL HELM: I am, because I don't see that the foreknowledge of God is spectator-like. I think the foreknowledge of God is simply what he knows with respect to his own mind. It's what he himself knows what he wants to happen. In accordance with that foreknowledge, he predestinates, which is simply the means to the end of the predestinating. You have, as it were, this continuous sequence of connected events of the golden chain leading to the glorification of the people of God.

JUSTIN BRIERLEY: In that sense, when that talks about the election of people to salvation, that's God very specifically choosing some people for salvation and, by the same token, other people are evidently bypassed and hence will be lost. I think for a lot of people that seems morally wrong.

PAUL HELM: Let me say a word about that. We think of God's goodness as his omnibenevolence, right? Though the facts don't look that way, do they? The facts of the world don't look like the world of an omnibenevolent God in quite that way. That's how I would come at it, really.

JUSTIN BRIERLEY: So we don't experience the world so we need to somehow understand that God's benevolence is not necessarily the same as [we'd understand].

PAUL HELM: . . . The whole fabric of the Bible has to do with his choice—his choice of a people. Does he bypass the other people when choosing the Jews and choosing Abraham? Yes, of course he does. In choosing Abraham he not chooses these others. In choosing Jesus to be, as it were, the elect Redeemer, other ways of salvation are bypassed.

WILLIAM LANE CRAIG: Well, as I said earlier, I take at face value the passages in the Scripture teaching the universal salvific will of God—that he wants all people to be saved. Even in the Old Testament, being a part of the corporate nation of Israel was no guarantee of salvation. If a person were an evil, wicked person, just being a Jew was no guarantee. And there are non-Jews in the Old Testament who clearly have a relationship with God. Job would be a perfect example. Job wasn't even a Jew. He was from Uz. He was a non-Jewish person yet clearly Job knew God.

JUSTIN BRIERLEY: So, in that sense then when Romans 8 speaks of people being elected to salvation (when you also believe that God wants all people to be saved) in what sense is God electing individual people then in that passage?

WILLIAM LANE CRAIG: I would say in a secondary sense. The primary sense of election is corporate. God has called out a people to himself and then if you want to be a member of that elect body of chosen people it's up to you. . . . So you have all these corporate images in Scripture: the olive tree with branches grafted in or broken off (cf. Rom 11:17–32), the building of living stones and the priesthood of believers (cf. 1 Pet 2:5), the body with its different members and parts (cf. 1 Cor 12:12–3; Rom 12:4–5), the nation of Israel, the commonwealth, all these corporate images.

PAUL HELM: I was making a very simple point, really. Bill is going on about it, but I was making a very simple point that the fabric of our faith depends upon God's choice and his not-choice. That's fundamental to the Bible as a document. It's fundamental to its character, to what it contains, that he chose a people and that through them the Messiah came; and that in choosing them, effectively choosing them, not choosing them in a kind of watery sense, but choosing them because he works all things out of the counsel of his own will. This included. In choosing A, he doesn't choose B.

JUSTIN BRIERLEY: I know that one thing you wanted to bring up before we finished up today, Paul, is that you think Molinism has other aspects to it that get rather confusing and messy. Did you just want to explain one concern?

PAUL HELM: If I can very briefly. It concerns, really, where it leaves God's sovereignty. The situation as I understand it is somewhat messier than we've discussed so far in our program. That is to say, that the conditions that God chooses to actualize—there are certain worlds that he chooses which are feasible worlds and there are certain other worlds which he can't possibly choose because they're not feasible. So, the worlds that he does choose may contain exercises of human freedom, which inhibit other exercises of human freedom. So, it's very messy.

JUSTIN BRIERLEY: When we're talking about possible worlds in which God can see that in this particular world people would choose to do this under these conditions and in another do this under another set of conditions. Not all of those possible worlds are open to God's choosing. I'm sure you understand the origin of this.

WILLIAM LANE CRAIG: Right, and I think this is a very significant distinction and I think has great theological fruitfulness. So, the Molinist will want to affirm that there are some worlds which are infeasible for God to actualize. And I suggested that perhaps one of these would be a world of universal salvation. Perhaps in any world of free creatures that God might create *some* would freely reject his grace and separate themselves from him forever. So that even though it's *logically possible* for there to be a world of universal salvation, perhaps it's infeasible for God given these subjunctive conditionals that we talked about.

JUSTIN BRIERLEY: Yes, because there may not be a world in which everyone would choose freely to be saved.

WILLIAM LANE CRAIG: Exactly. I do say that, or I do affirm that, and I think that you can get great theological mileage out of that distinction.

JUSTIN BRIERLEY: As far as you're concerned, God is more concerned with the human freedom than having a world in which everyone gets saved. That would be the choice, as it were, that God's making.

WILLIAM LANE CRAIG: Yes, yes, I suppose that's right—that he would not exercise a sort of divine coercion in order to save people, that he will respect people's wills and say, "I'm not going to make you go to heaven. If you choose to reject me and my grace and my love for you then I will allow you to do so."

JUSTIN BRIERLEY: Okay. I think Paul's concern is that, by there being worlds which are not feasible for God to choose, that somehow undermines God's sovereignty because then it is suggesting . . .

PAUL HELM: It weakens it. You see the emphasis now is not on God's choosing me because he wanted me to be his child eternally and unconditionally and by his grace, but he's chosen a *world* and I happen to be a part of that world.

JUSTIN BRIERLEY: So you're sort of a byproduct of a world where he's trying to maximize, say, the most number of people saved.

PAUL HELM: Whatever his conditions of feasibility are, there are certain worlds that are ruled out—that's clear. But coming, as it were, closer to the center, what the conditions of feasibility are seems to be what we couldn't possibly be clear on. That would have to remain a mystery. Nonetheless, his love for me is not, as it were, direct and personal. It's because I'm part of a world which is the world overall that he wanted.

WILLIAM LANE CRAIG: I don't see that at all! I wouldn't agree with that at all! God loves each individual and wants that person to be saved, and he will choose to create a world *of individuals.* So the world isn't primary; the individuals are primary and they build together a kind of world as you accumulate individuals. But what the Molinist does say that I think the Calvinist finds objectionable is that God is not in control of which subjunctive conditionals are true. He doesn't determine the truth value of these subjunctive conditionals; that's outside his control and the Calvinist finds that objectionable.

PAUL HELM: That's right. The whole notion of middle knowledge as portrayed by Bill is objectionable to the Calvinist. As I said in the beginning, he can shunt all of this stuff into one of God's other two sources of knowledge.

JUSTIN BRIERLEY: I think that's been a very helpful distinction to have at the end actually—a point at which this actually breaks in terms of the view of God for a Molinist and a Calvinist because in the end, in that sense, God . . . would you say God is in some sense limited by the fact that he has chosen a world in which human freedoms will . . .

WILLIAM LANE CRAIG: No, not quite just yet. Actually, it's consistent with middle knowledge that this world is totally determined. It's possible that God looked at all of the indeterministic worlds that have freedom in them and said, "Oh, those are lousy worlds! I don't want any of them! I'm going to choose one in which I determine everything!" So, middle knowledge is actually consistent with causal determinism but . . .

PAUL HELM: Molina would turn in his grave if he heard that!

WILLIAM LANE CRAIG: But where it does presuppose libertarian freedom is, again, that these subjunctive conditionals are not within God's control. That's correct.

JUSTIN BRIERLEY: But that doesn't undermine God's sovereignty?

PAUL HELM: Well it does and it doesn't really, that's the problem.

WILLIAM LANE CRAIG: There are worlds that are *infeasible* for God in virtue of these subjunctive conditionals.

PAUL HELM: Maybe it may be a condition of him choosing the world he's chosen that people don't get as much freedom in that world as they would in other worlds, for example. I might trample on their toes. I am chosen—I may be chosen as someone who freely tramples on their toes, as it were.

JUSTIN BRIERLEY: So your freedom may be at the expense of another person's freedom.

PAUL HELM: Yes indeed, and there's nothing he can do about it except choose a different world. That's why *worlds* are preeminent in this, not individuals. He doesn't *love* . . . Paul says, "He loved me and gave himself for me." I don't know if he could say that in quite the unqualified way that I think he does say it.

JUSTIN BRIERLEY: Okay, we're going to draw that to a close. Bill, thank you for being on the program; Paul as well. In conclusion then, you would encourage people who perhaps have struggled with this whole issue of human free will and God's foreordination to embrace Molinism, presumably. You think that is a biblical and an intellectually satisfying way of reconciling this.

WILLIAM LANE CRAIG: I think it is *a* biblical and intellectually satisfying view. I'm not claiming that it is *the* one view but I'm saying it provides a model that integrates human freedom with divine sovereignty in a way that is biblically consistent and intellectually satisfying. And therefore this model is one that shows that these doctrines are coherent and credible.

PAUL HELM: And I think that it's intellectually mystifying to introduce this very strong sense of human freedom in the way discussed earlier and it's not a price that's worth paying and it's not biblical.

CLOSING STATEMENTS BY JUSTIN BRIERLEY

Conclusion

Prospects for Further Discussion

JOHN LAING, KIRK R. MACGREGOR,
AND GREG WELTY

THE PRESENT VOLUME HAS provoked, both implicitly and explicitly, a host of questions that merit further discussion between Calvinists and Molinists. Several of these questions have already been raised in the preceding chapters. This conclusion aims to delineate the central questions that remain outstanding and seem to hold the greatest promise for fruitful Calvinist-Molinist dialogue. These questions will be presented in roughly the order in which they first emerge in the text.

Outstanding Questions

The conversation over Molinism, evolution, and intelligent design immediately prompts the question: what is the content of middle knowledge? Does middle knowledge only properly refer to God's prevolitional knowledge of counterfactuals *of creaturely freedom*? Or are there *further* kinds of contingent, counterfactual, prevolitional truth—truths not specifically about creaturely freedom—that can comprise middle knowledge? Should it be said that Molinists who take the object of middle knowledge to be all counterfactuals—those regarding creaturely freedom, those regarding (at least) indeterministic natural processes, and any other proposition of the form "In the following circumstances, such-and-such *would* happen"—have evolved Molinism beyond the intent of Luis de Molina? To answer this question, historical investigation into the scope of Molina's project in the *Concordia* is warranted. While Molina's project surely focused on counterfactuals of creaturely freedom, it may not be limited to such counterfactuals. In addition, there is room for further logical and conceptual investigation into the nature of "counterfactuals of genetic mutation." At issue is whether (or not) they are relevantly analogous to counterfactuals of creaturely freedom, such that their truth requires them to be classified as middle knowledge rather than as natural knowledge or free knowledge.

Related to this question is the definition of randomness, particularly in the case of mutations occurring in the development of life. Does randomness simply mean, as Plantinga, Mayr, and Sober suggest, that there is no correlation between a mutation and its utility for the organism? Or does randomness also mean that, at a given developmental step, any of a range of mutations are equally likely and that the ensuing mutation occurs indeterministically? If the former ("random" = no correlation), then God does not need middle knowledge in order to create through random mutations, for he can directly will whatever sequence of steps that he wants. If the latter ("random" = indeterminism), then Molinists can argue God may well need prevolitional knowledge of all counterfactuals in order to create through random mutations, for such knowledge seems to afford God the means of apprehending how any indeterministic process he wishes to create would unfold. Alternatively, in this case Calvinists can argue along Plantinga's lines that God can easily determine the outcome of a physically indeterministic process, through a "divine collapse causation" interpretation of quantum mechanics. If there can be a nonphysical cause of a physically indeterministic process, then there wouldn't be a dichotomy between physical indeterminism and divine determinism. In any event, the voices of Christians working in the mathematical and biological sciences would prove very helpful in pinning down the nature of randomness.

A third question concerns whether, on Molinism, counterfactuals do or do not depend on God. On the popular level, a firestorm of controversy erupted among Reformed voices following William Lane Craig's 2011 online statement, "The counterfactuals of creaturely freedom which confront Him are outside His control. He has to play with the hand He has been dealt."[1] The immediate Reformed rejoinders were: Who dealt God the cards? Shouldn't we worship the "dealer" instead of God? The Molinist would surely reply that there is no dealer. But does this imply that God is constrained by luck? It seems that many, though certainly not all, Calvinists and Molinists maintain that, according to Molinism, at least counterfactuals of creaturely freedom do not depend on God in any sense. Should Calvinists

---

1. Craig, "Q&A #239."

and Molinists believe this? If so, then the grounding objection emerges as prominent. Calvinists will argue that the grounding objection needs to be answered for Molinism to be tenable, while Molinists will argue that the grounding objection is based on the theory of truth-maker maximalism (i.e., in order to be true, every true proposition requires a truth-maker) and attempt to dispute truth-maker maximalism. Perhaps even worse, counter-factuals of creaturely freedom would seem to undermine God's aseity, as they somehow exist outside of God and confront God with their reality. This is an ironic implication, as Craig himself has worked to stem the threat to divine aseity from abstract objects, conceived à la Platonism. In other words, wouldn't counterfactuals of creaturely freedom, despite Craig's own antirealism and best efforts to the contrary, be Platonic abstract objects on his card-dealer analogy?

But perhaps Calvinists and Molinists should not believe Molinism entails that counterfactuals of creaturely freedom are independent of God. For Molina appears to have thought otherwise: "God does not get His knowledge from things, but knows all things *in* Himself and *from* Himself . . . God has within Himself the means whereby He knows all things fully and perfectly; and this is why the existence of created things contributes no perfection to the cognition He has of them and does not cause any change in that cognition."[2] This suggests that middle knowledge is self-contained in God, such that counterfactuals of creaturely freedom (and all other counterfactuals) are ontologically dependent on God. It is undisputed in Reformation scholarship that Molina was a conceptualist, regarding what the Platonist took to be abstract objects as ideas in the mind of God. So now the issue arises: can counterfactuals of creaturely freedom (and counter-factuals in general) be ideas in the mind of God? If so, then the grounding objection, so to speak, may well fall to the ground. However, it might be protested that if *A* is an idea in the mind of God, then *A* cannot be logically contingent; *A* must be logically necessary. In that case, creaturely freedom would be eviscerated. Is this protest a legitimate concern, or does it commit the fallacy of division (i.e., since God is logically necessary, all God's innate ideas must be logically necessary)? Does it or does it not make sense to say that a necessary being eternally possesses contingent ideas? John Laing has begun work on this topic in his 2000 dissertation on Molina's doctrine of supercomprehension,[3] and surely further work here needs to be carried out by metaphysicians.

---

2. Molina, *Foreknowledge*, 120.

3. Laing, "Supercomprehension"; cf. Laing, *Middle Knowledge*, 100.

If such work can be successfully undertaken, then Craig's card-dealer analogy is highly misleading. Counterfactuals of creaturely freedom would be independent of the will of God, but not independent of the being of God. This is exactly the case with the laws of logic. But no one would say that God is "confronted" by the law of non-contradiction or the law of excluded middle and has to play the hand he's dealt. For such laws are ideas of God. Is the same true of counterfactuals of creaturely freedom?

Some Calvinists might not be convinced by the above line of response to Craig's claim that the counterfactuals "are outside his control," for while Molina's conceptualism about propositions might very well reconcile the *existence* of counterfactuals with God's aseity, it might do little if anything to reconcile their *truth-value* with God's aseity. Arguing that counterfactuals *ontologically* depend on God doesn't help us see how they *alethically* depend on God—that is, how their truth-value is grounded in aspects of God's nature. These Calvinists would say that putting propositions in the mind of God neither helps nor hinders Molinism, since the former only addresses the matter of propositional existence (which is necessary), whereas the grounding objection is about the matter of propositional truth-value (which is contingent). The *truth* of the counterfactuals seems to have ontological significance for God on the Molinist scheme, as their truth renders certain possible worlds unactualizable by God, even weakly unactualizable. That *seems* to have unwelcome consequences for God's creative options, such that conceptualism isn't of help here. *Prima facie*, the necessity of God's being or nature seems suitable to serve as a truth-maker for necessary truths like the law of non-contradiction or the law of excluded middle, which is why these necessary truths don't "confront" God in any way; they are made true by God. It is harder to see how the necessity of God's being could be the truth-maker for contingent truths like the counterfactuals of creaturely freedom.

At the very least, Molinists should clarify why claims about propositional existence help to account for their truth-value as well, as these two issues seem distinct. And Calvinists should take seriously the charge of "truth-maker maximalism" when they raise the grounding objection. What is so wrong with at least *some* truths not having a truth-maker? Doesn't that just mean Molinism might strike some as metaphysically odd, rather than constitute a proof that Molinism is undoubtably incoherent or theologically suspect? Perhaps the grounding objection is overrated by many Calvinists.

Assuming for argument's sake that the grounding objection, for whatever reason, does not go through and that Molinism is at least logically consistent, does Molinism make God the author of evil to the same extent (which may be no extent at all) that Calvinism makes God the author of evil? A crucial disconnect between Calvinists and Molinists surrounds whether divine intent plays a decisive role in answering this question. It may seem that Calvinists and Molinists would be on level pegging in saying that God never intends evil for evil's sake; God always intends good but realizes that sometimes goods are predicated on various collateral evils, which he therefore permits. But here it seems the Molinist could complain against the deterministic Calvinist (as opposed to the mysterian Calvinist). For on Molinism, it may simply be the case that there is no way to accomplish some good without the collateral evil. But on deterministic Calvinism, is there any such thing as a good that cannot be accomplished without some collateral evil? If God determines everything, then why doesn't God just determine everything to be good? Can't God determine anything he wants? Here the crux of the dilemma looks to emerge. Saying that God needs evil to get various goods on determinism appears to suggest there is something logically possible—God getting such goods on determinism—that God cannot do, hence robbing God of his omnipotence. The Molinist therefore assumes the Calvinist won't go this route. But saying that God doesn't need evil to get the greater good but selects the evil anyway looks, to the Molinist at least, as though God intends the evil *per se*, thus making God the author of evil in a morally objectionable sense that could not be predicated of Molinism. It would be quite profitable for deterministic Calvinist thinkers to assess whether or not the Molinist's logic is correct and, if incorrect, to show where the Molinist goes wrong.

One route which deterministic Calvinistic thinkers might take is to stress that, for all we know, there *are* goods that cannot be accomplished without some collateral evil. One cannot get the good of bravery in the midst of battle, unless there is the danger of battle. One cannot get the good of enduring magnificently in the face of cancer, unless there is cancer. This has little to do with Calvinism, and everything to do with the fact that some goods are *defined* as goods precisely because they are a response to, indeed an overcoming of, various evils. So they can't exist without the evils. (It would be no part of Calvinism to say that *all* goods are like this, of course.) While God can certainly 'determine everything to be good' (consider a toy world containing only cats, dogs, rivers, and trees), it might be that many *deep* goods aren't to be had without the evils to which they are a response. So with respect to some goods it *isn't* possible to get them without permitting various evils. If what Calvinists are talking about here are *universe*-size goods, both spatially and temporally, then can Molinists both (i) specify the full range of divine purposes at work in the actual world, and (ii) make the case that God *can* secure all of those purposes without permitting evil? Perhaps *no one* can accomplish the first step, and if so, then prospects for accomplishing the second step look dim.[4] Once again, Molinists and Calvinists should recognize what they very likely have in common in this difficult area of theodicy and God's relation to evil, while not sacrificing what is distinctive to their approaches as they pursue better answers to these enduring questions.

A question for those Calvinists who wish to appropriate middle/hypothetical knowledge into their schema is whether or not middle/hypothetical knowledge is in fact a subset of natural knowledge. Interestingly, Molina himself believed that middle knowledge was "a sort of natural knowledge":[5]

> Through His natural knowledge God comprehends Himself, and in Himself He comprehends all the things that exist eminently in Him and thus the free choice of any creature whom He is able to make through His omnipotence. Therefore, before any free determination of His will, by virtue of the depth of His natural knowledge, by which He infinitely surpasses each of the things He contains eminently in Himself, He discerns what the free choice of any creature would do by its own innate freedom, given the hypothesis that He should create it in this or that order of things with these or those circumstances or aids—even though the creature could, if it so willed, refrain from acting or do the opposite.[6]

Molina claimed that middle knowledge is a type of natural knowledge in the sense that possessing middle knowledge is essential to God, owing to his omniscience. Where Molina first raised the conceptual distinction between natural and middle knowledge was in saying that natural knowledge consists of only metaphysically necessary truths, while middle knowledge includes metaphysically contingent truths. (As previously indicated, it is an open question whether middle knowledge, on Molina's view, also includes various counterfactuals that are metaphysically necessary.) Would the middle/hypothetical-knowledge Calvinist perhaps grant that some of the counterfactuals God knows are factually necessary but not metaphysically necessary? Or is the middle/hypothetical-knowledge Calvinist committed to the view that all counterfactuals are metaphysically necessary? Further engagement with Molina's work by middle/hypothetical-knowledge Calvinists is here warranted.

What seems to motivate the middle/hypothetical-knowledge Calvinist are the joint convictions that God's prevolitional counterfactual knowledge

4. Cowan and Welty, "Pharaoh's Magicians Redivivus," 169–72.

5. Molina, *Foreknowledge*, 122.

6. Molina, *Foreknowledge*, 119.

is at least implied in Scripture and that a particular construal of the grounding objection is undefeatable. That construal of the grounding objection asks how God could know counterfactuals of libertarian freedom, finds no way God could know such things, and therefore concludes that God cannot know these counterfactuals. Most Molinists would take issue with this form of the grounding objection by claiming that even if we cannot explain *how* God knows counterfactuals of libertarian freedom, this constitutes no argument *that* God cannot know them. For God is omniscient, and the only limits on God's omniscience are logical limits. So long as it is logically possible for God to prevolitionally know counterfactuals of libertarian freedom, God, as an omniscient being, must know them. To give an analogy, a panentheist might use a parallel construal of the grounding objection to ask how God could create *ex nihilo*, find no way God could create *ex nihilo*, and therefore conclude that God cannot create *ex nihilo*. And any orthodox Christian would retort, "I may not know *how* God can create *ex nihilo*. But that's irrelevant. God is omnipotent, and the only limits on God's omnipotence are logical limits. So long as it is logically possible for God to create *ex nihilo*, God, as an omnipotent being, must be able to create *ex nihilo*. Absent any proof that *creatio ex nihilo* is logically impossible, your objection holds no water." So the question for the middle/hypothetical-knowledge Calvinist is this: what is the proof that it is logically impossible for God to prevolitionally know counterfactuals of libertarian freedom? If there is a proof, then it seems Molinists should become middle/hypothetical-knowledge Calvinists. If there is no proof, then it seems middle/hypothetical-knowledge Calvinists should become Molinists.

Middle/hypothetical-knowledge Calvinists might reply that the proof is easy to give. For God to prevolitionally know counterfactuals of libertarian freedom, there must be something there for God to know. These truths must be true independent of the will of God (since they're known by him prevolitionally). And if God's necessary nature doesn't make them true (thus converting them into natural knowledge), then either (i) something distinct from God makes them true, or (ii) nothing makes them true. Either answer sets up a contradiction: if (i), then divine aseity is challenged, for then God's creative options are constrained by a reality distinct from him; and if (ii), then divine aseity is again challenged, for God's creative options are hampered by nothingness. Since God's knowledge of these counterfactuals would contradict his aseity either way, it follows that it is logically impossible for God to have such knowledge. No such parallel proof is available with respect to God's ability to create *ex nihilo*, and so the cases aren't relevantly parallel. (None of this would show that traditional Calvinists or Molinists should be *middle/hypothetical-knowledge Calvinists*, of course.)

An important question for Calvinists in general to wrestle with is whether or not God possesses libertarian freedom. In particular, did God's nature require that God voluntarily create the actual world, or could God have chosen to create a different world or even no world at all? To put it another way, does God get to decide between alternatives as to what his providential plan will be? It seems that Calvinists who wish to understand God's free knowledge as a subset of his natural knowledge would have to say that, indeed, God's freedom is compatibilist in nature, such that God voluntarily settles on a providential plan and voluntarily creates the actual world even though he could not do otherwise. By contrast, it appears that those Calvinists who maintain the distinctiveness of God's free knowledge and God's natural knowledge would maintain that God—and God alone—possesses libertarian freedom; only God functions as an unmoved mover. Intriguingly, such Calvinists frequently turn the tables on Molinists by commenting that if God possessed middle knowledge, then God knew which feasible world was the best world. As an all-good being, wouldn't God be obligated by his very nature to create the best feasible world? If so, it could be asserted that Molinism blasphemously grants humans libertarian freedom at the expense of God's own libertarian freedom! So the issue is whether or not the Molinist can successfully meet this challenge.

Several lines of response have presently been offered. One line holds that there is no such thing as the best feasible world, for perhaps there is an infinite series of feasible worlds increasing in value. Another line holds that God's possession of middle knowledge does not entail the existence of just one best world; rather, there is an infinite spectrum of worlds all tied for the status of being the best feasible world. Perhaps there are multiple unsurpassable feasible worlds. While God's being all-good indeed entails that he choose from among this spectrum or choose to create no world at all (since the divine life of inter-Trinitarian relationships already exhibited complete perfection, to which no world could ever add), God still has the libertarian freedom to choose between (infinitely many) alternatives. Yet another line of response is that perhaps God is not under obligation to create the best, *even if* there were a single best option, since that would preclude the category of divine grace. Hence it remains open for discussion between Calvinists and Molinists whether or not any of these lines of response succeed in meeting the Calvinist challenge.

Indeed, the argument that God's knowledge of 'the best world' precludes God's being free in his creative act doesn't seem to be a distinctive *Calvinist* challenge in the first place. It is an *atheist* challenge to theism more generally (cf. William Rowe's *Can God Be Free?*). If the argument works, it works against the Calvinist too; adding the category of middle knowledge to one's perspective on omniscience or providence doesn't make the problem *worse* for the Molinist. It is a *non sequitur* to infer from the fact of middle knowledge, or from omniscience more generally, that *there is* a best feasible world, or that if there is one God is obligated to create it. Perhaps Molinists and Calvinists can unite in deflecting this objection together!

Turning to free knowledge, a question for the Molinist is whether or not free knowledge can be legitimately parsed. In other words, some Calvinists and Molinists alike may wonder whether what Molina called "an absolutely complete and unlimited deliberation"[7] is a moment (or series of moments) of knowledge at all or if it is an intervening act of will logically coming between God's middle knowledge and God's divine creative decree. To be sure, God's absolutely complete and unlimited deliberation is helpfully parsed into God's evaluation of his intentions/desires and how feasible worlds match up with God's intentions/desires, and the Molinist may wish to include the divine creative decree in this deliberation or place it as a succeeding act of will. But is all of this part of free knowledge or a decision-making process that logically precedes free knowledge? This question merits further investigation among Molinists.

Another question meriting further Molinist discussion—and a question of interest to Calvinists and Arminians—is whether or not Arminianism is, in fact, a form of Molinism. Molinists themselves sharply disagree over this question. Some have argued that Arminius faithfully appropriated Molina's thought, rendering Molina's doctrine of middle knowledge an Arminian staple and Arminianism nothing more than "Protestant Molinism."[8] Others have argued that Arminius, while aware of the term "middle knowledge," misunderstood its original intention and hence posited a distinct version of "middle knowledge" that Molina explicitly rejected in the *Concordia*.[9] Voices outside the Molinist camp have chimed in on this question as well. Equating Arminianism and Molinism is the prominent Calvinist historical theologian Richard Muller,[10] while asserting the distinctiveness of Arminianism and Molinism is the prominent Arminian historical theologian Roger Olson.[11]

Tied to the question of the relationship between Arminianism and Molinism is the issue of whether, on Molinism, election is corporate or individual. Some Calvinists seem to assume that Molinist election, like

---

7. Molina, *Foreknowledge*, 173.

8. Dekker, "Was Arminius a Molinist?" 337–52.

9. MacGregor, *Molina*, 18–24.

10. Muller, *God, Creation, and Providence*, 161.

11. Olson, *Arminian Theology*, 196.

Arminian election, is corporate, such that God does not predestine individuals to salvation but predestines a group or a world. Such Calvinists are concerned that, on Molinism, God's love for the individual is not direct and personal; rather, God loves individuals to the extent that they contribute to the feasible world he wanted. Molinists retort that God's love for the individual is direct and personal; the individual is primary, and God wants every individual to be saved. It is simply that these individuals accumulate into a world. Surprisingly to many, Molina thought that Romans 9 taught individual predestination, asserting that Jacob, Esau, and Pharaoh refer strictly to the persons in question. In addition to Romans 9, Molina took Exodus 33:19, Malachi 1:2–3, 2 Timothy 2:20, Ephesians 1:4–5, Ephesians 1:11, Ezekiel 11:19–20, Ezekiel 36:26–27, Romans 8:29–30, and 1 Peter 1:1–2 as indicating that, for each individual, God has freely chosen from before the foundation of the world whether that individual would be saved (elect), damned (reprobate), or nonexistent.[12] The question facing contemporary Molinists is whether Molina's own teachings on predestination (found in the untranslated book seven of the *Concordia*) is too Calvinistic for their liking. The question facing some contemporary Calvinists is whether Molina's doctrine of predestination indeed, as Molina thought, entails sovereign individual predestination or whether his doctrine turns out, despite his intentions, to be a form of corporate election.

A related question, raised by some Calvinists against Molinism, is whether a strong Molinist doctrine of individual predestination generates ethical conundrums almost exactly parallel to those raised by some Molinists against Calvinists. On Molinism, why does God create people whom he knows will end up in hell? A possible answer suggested by Craig: maybe they are transworldly damned—their counterfactuals are such that they would never freely accept God's grace no matter what. So God is off the hook for not saving them. But then why is he off the hook for *creating* them? Again, a possible answer: like Roger Dorn in the movie *Major League II*, they take a hit for the team, the "best feasible world" team. If God *didn't* create them, fewer people overall would be saved, and so the world would be worse than it would otherwise be. Doesn't that strike Molinists as just as ethically dubious as the compatibilist Calvinism they are rejecting? God creates these transworldly damned individuals because he needs them in order to ensure the salvation of other people. Their sinking in hell is the price God pays to rise others to heaven. Some Calvinists would say this parallels their standard view on reprobation, rather than being an improvement upon it. In either case, God creates people whom he knows will go to hell,

---

12. MacGregor, *Molina*, 133–57.

and he does so to advance his own purposes: either to display his grace (to others, on the Molinist view) or his justice (to them, on the Reformed view). In either case, bad things happen to people as a means to further God's more ultimate ends.[13] On this, both sides can agree, but what they cannot seem to agree on—and thus may require more dialogue—is whether the outcome is relatively the same on both models of providence, or if one model provides a stronger view of divine goodness, holiness, grace, justice, or love.

Should this line of question-and-answer speculation bother the Molinist? One thing Calvinists should get clearer about is the *status* of these *tu quoque* ("you too") arguments in the Molinist/Calvinist dialogue. They have been instanced in this volume on occasion, but what do they really show? Perhaps they are a distraction from providing more principled, positive arguments for one's doctrine, and are thereby to be avoided. Or perhaps they provide a twofold service: (i) revealing certain questions to be so deep and so enduring that their resolution transcends what *either* Molinism or Calvinism brings to the table, and (ii) helping participants to the discussion refocus their attention on the *real* differences between the two views. After all, it isn't a given that any approach can answer just *any* question thrown at it, and it might be the better part of wisdom for both sides to frankly acknowledge this up front.

A question facing not just Molinists but libertarians of all stripes is whether libertarian free will requires the principle of alternate possibilities (PAP). Most Molinists (including John Laing and Kirk MacGregor, two editors of this volume) and libertarians in general argue that libertarianism indeed requires the PAP; without the PAP, libertarianism collapses into compatibilism. Craig seems to be of two minds on this issue. On the one hand, he has stated, on the basis of the Frankfurt examples, that libertarianism does not require the PAP but only requires not being caused to do something by causes other than oneself. On the other hand, he admits that the Frankfurt examples fail in the cases of human examples of prevention or intervention and insists, in his dialogue with Helm, that "a person in identical circumstances could choose one way or the other" and that creatures could, but will not, act contrary to God's providential plan. But that simply is the PAP. So the confusion surrounding the PAP needs to be sorted out by Molinists.

Other Molinists, and many Calvinists, would agree that if libertarianism does require the PAP, then libertarianism and compatibilism are truly distinct, and the differences expressed in this volume between middle/hypothetical-knowledge Calvinism and Molinism stand. But they would also

13. Welty and Cowan, "Won't Get Foiled Again," 439–42.

hold that even if libertarianism does not require the PAP, libertarianism and compatibilism would not be different in name only, such that the middle/hypothetical-knowledge Calvinist and Molinist are really saying the same thing. For "Frankfurt libertarians" (who accept that Frankfurt examples have some force against PAP) will still insist on "ultimate responsibility," a sourcehood condition on free will that insists that as long as you are the *ultimate* cause of your intentions and your tryings, then you are responsible, otherwise not. If so, then the substantive difference between Frankfurt libertarianism and compatibilism would remain.

Craig's motivation for at least occasionally denying the PAP is his desire to preserve Christ's impeccability, namely, to affirm that Christ freely resisted temptation but at the same time could not have succumbed to it. Here several intriguing queries arise of clear interest to Calvinists and Molinists. First, can Christ have freely resisted temptation while remaining impeccable (as classically understood) only if compatibilism is true and libertarianism is false? If the answer is yes, then the Molinist will have to say either that Christ did not freely resist temptation or that the doctrine of impeccability needs revision. Various follow-up questions hold import for all Christians. What would be the cost of affirming that Christ successfully resisted temptation but did not do so libertarianly freely? Does this mean we can no longer regard Christ as the model after whom we should pattern our lives regarding our own struggles with temptation? Does it mean that libertarian freedom is a concept which applies only to non-divine humans like us but not to the only divine human, viz., Christ? And what would be the cost of revising the doctrine of impeccability? Prominent evangelical theologian Millard Erickson has suggested precisely this move, arguing that Christ must have been able to sin in order to freely withstand temptation.[14] In this case, impeccability would simply mean that it is certain, but not necessary, that Christ never sins, past, present, or future. Such certainty, it seems, would only be able to stem from a Molinist conception of God's middle knowledge. But, we may ask, what would have been involved in the hypothetical case that Christ had sinned? Does the answer require revisions—potentially radical revisions—to theology proper? Or is this an unnecessary worry, such that what might be called necessary impeccability may safely be given up in favor of certain impeccability? To put it another way: does a correct understanding of Christ's impeccability necessitate that God has middle knowledge in the way the Molinist imagines (which could potentially be argued on "certain impeccability"), or does a correct understanding of Christ's impeccability necessitate that compatibilism is

---

14. Erickson, *Word Became Flesh*, 563.

true (which could potentially be argued on "necessary impeccability")? This could prove a topic for lively Calvinist-Molinist interaction!

Final Reflections

This book has suggested multiple avenues of future research by and dialogue between Calvinists and Molinists. Whether they agree or disagree, Calvinists and Molinists surely have much to learn from each other. Surveying the book's chapters, it seems that middle/hypothetical-knowledge Calvinists and mysterian Calvinists potentially share the most common ground with Molinists. For middle/hypothetical-knowledge Calvinists appear, like Molinists, to take issue with the final clause of the following statement from the *Westminster Confession of Faith*: "Although God knows whatsoever may or can come to pass upon all supposed conditions; yet has He not decreed anything because He foresaw it as future, *or as that which would come to pass upon such conditions*" (III.2; emphasis added). Calvinists and Molinists would agree with the two preceding clauses: God possesses knowledge of all *possibilia* (part of his natural knowledge); and God's decree is not based on his looking ahead down the corridors of time and seeing what creatures will do (prior to the decree, there is no such thing as time or future creatures, since God has not yet decreed to bring time or creatures into existence). Indeed, God's natural and middle/hypothetical knowledge are conceptualist in nature, not perceptualist. But is the final clause—affirming God has not decreed anything as that which would come to pass under various conditions—warranted, or is it a purely reactionary move by the framers of the *Westminster Confession* against the feared Catholicism and Arminianism of middle knowledge? If the final clause is warranted, then middle/hypothetical-knowledge Calvinism and Molinism alike go out the window, since God does not make creative use of his knowledge of that which would come to pass under various conditions. Notice that the final clause does not assert that God lacks this knowledge (it does not say one way or the other); it simply asserts that God does not use such knowledge in his decrees. Could the middle/hypothetical-knowledge Calvinist and Molinist, based on their agreement that God possesses some prevolitional counterfactual knowledge, concur that Westminster's assertion here is unwarranted on the grounds that refusing to act on knowledge runs contrary to God's nature as all-wise? For isn't the essence of wisdom the sound application of knowledge?

The mysterian Calvinist and Molinist could stake out common ground based on their agreement with the *Westminster Confession* that God ordains everything that comes to pass without doing violence to the will of creatures or taking away the liberty or contingency of secondary causes (III.1). Here several interesting questions arise. If the divine decree doesn't remove the contingency of secondary causes, then is it the case that humans possess libertarian freedom? And if the mysterian Calvinist also judges as purely reactionary Westminster's denial that God doesn't use prevolitional counterfactual knowledge, then could the mysterian Calvinist affirm that employment of middle knowledge is the means by which God decrees everything without doing violence to or removing the contingency of creatures' wills?

Like other Calvinists, middle/hypothetical-knowledge Calvinists and mysterian Calvinists would probably part company with Molinists on matters of soteriology, particularly irresistible grace and limited atonement. But not necessarily, for the middle/hypothetical-knowledge Calvinist and mysterian Calvinist could appropriate the Congruist version of Molinism, formulated by the early seventeenth-century Catholic reformer Francisco Suárez. According to Congruism, God gives all persons in the world he creates a completely sufficient grace for salvation, such that the lost have no one to blame but themselves. However, God knows that everyone would freely reject this default level of grace. Thus God elects certain individuals out of the *massa perditionis* for salvation, giving the elect a congruent grace. This is a special quality of grace that is so perfectly adapted to the unique characters, temperaments, and situations of the elect that they infallibly yet freely respond affirmatively to its influence. Such at least comes very close to the doctrine of irresistible grace. Since God only intends to save through Christ's cross those whom he gives congruent grace, the atonement likewise seems to be limited in scope. (In response, Calvinists—whether of the middle knowledge or mysterian variety—would suggest there needs to be a disambiguation of the term "sufficient" in the context of this discussion, for Calvinists may mean something different by this term than Catholic Congruists. Since the terminology of "necessary" and "sufficient" is teleological in character [necessary *for what?* sufficient *for what?*], its context of usage must always be specified to avoid confusion. For many Calvinists, a "sufficient" grace for salvation given to all, that doesn't *result* in salvation for the recipients, at best only satisfied a necessary but not sufficient condition for salvation.[15])

The collaborative work on this volume, both in the conference papers presented at the national meeting of the Evangelical Theological Society and in the special papers produced for the volume, has been an effort grounded in Christian love for God and for one another. It is our hope that the avenues of potential Calvinist-Molinist interaction suggested in this conclusion and

15. Welty, "Election and Calling," 234–35 fn. 31, 236.

elsewhere throughout the book will be pursued, as the desire of all participants has been to grow in the knowledge and grace of our Lord and Savior, Jesus Christ (2 Pet. 3:18) and to serve the church, Christ's body.

Bibliography

Cowan, Steve and Greg Welty. "Pharaoh's Magicians Redivivus: A Response to Jerry Walls on Christian Compatibilism." *Philosophia Christi* 17.1 (2015) 151–73.

Craig, William Lane. "Q&A #239: Molinism and the Soteriological Problem of Evil Once More." Available at: https://www.reasonablefaith.org/writings/question-answer/molinism-and-the-soteriological-problem-of-evil-once-more/.

Dekker, Eef. "Was Arminius a Molinist?" *The Sixteenth Century Journal* 27.2 (1996) 337–52.

Erickson, Millard J. *The Word Became Flesh: A Contemporary Incarnational Christology.* Grand Rapids: Baker, 1991.

Laing, John D. *Middle Knowledge: Human Freedom in Divine Sovereignty.* Grand Rapids: Kregel, 2018.

Laing, John D. "Molinism and Supercomprehension: Grounding Counterfactual Truth." Ph.D. diss.: Southern Baptist Theological Seminary, 2000.

MacGregor, Kirk R. *Luis de Molina: The Life and Theology of the Founder of Middle Knowledge.* Grand Rapids: Zondervan, 2015.

Molina, Luis de. *On Divine Foreknowledge: Part IV of the Concordia.* Translated by Alfred J. Freddoso. Ithaca, NY: Cornell University Press, 1988.

Muller, Richard A. *God, Creation, and Providence in the Thought of Jacob Arminius.* Grand Rapids: Baker, 1991.

Olson, Roger E. *Arminian Theology: Myths and Realities.* Downers Grove, IL: IVP Academic, 2006.

Welty, Greg. "Election and Calling: A Biblical Theological Study." In *Calvinism: A Southern Baptist Dialogue,* edited by Brad Waggoner and E. Ray Clendenen, 216–46. Nashville: B & H Academic, 2008.

Welty, Greg, and Steven Cowan. "Won't Get Foiled Again: A Rejoinder to Jerry Walls." *Philosophia Christi* 17.2 (2015) 427–42.

Made in the USA
Coppell, TX
27 February 2021

50911694R00174